Cases on Research and Knowledge Discovery:

Homeland Security Centers of Excellence

Cecelia Wright Brown
University of Baltimore, USA

Kevin A. Peters
Morgan State University, USA

Kofi Adofo Nyarko
Morgan State University, USA

A volume in the Advances in Information Security, Privacy, and Ethics (AISPE) Book Series

Information Science REFERENCE

An Imprint of IGI Global

Managing Director:	Lindsay Johnston
Production Editor:	Jennifer Yoder
Development Editor:	Austin DeMarco
Acquisitions Editor:	Kayla Wolfe
Typesetter:	Michael Brehm
Cover Design:	Jason Mull

Published in the United States of America by
Information Science Reference (an imprint of IGI Global)
701 E. Chocolate Avenue
Hershey PA 17033
Tel: 717-533-8845
Fax: 717-533-8661
E-mail: cust@igi-global.com
Web site: http://www.igi-global.com

Library of Congress Cataloging-in-Publication Data

Cases on research and knowledge discovery : homeland security centers of excellence / Cecelia Wright Brown, Kevin A. Peters, and Kofi Adofo Nyarko, editors.
    p. cm.
  Includes bibliographical references and index.
  ISBN 978-1-4666-5946-9 (hardcover) -- ISBN 978-1-4666-5947-6 (ebook) -- ISBN 978-1-4666-5949-0 (print & perpetual access) 1. United States. Department of Homeland Security. 2. Terrorism--United States--Prevention. 3. National security--United States. I. Wright Brown, Cecelia. II. Peters, Kevin A., 1955- III. Nyarko, Kofi Adofo, 1977-
  HV6432.4.C37 2014
  353.3'2740973--dc23
                              2014001635

This book is published in the IGI Global book series Advances in Information Security, Privacy, and Ethics (AISPE) (ISSN: 1948-9730; eISSN: 1948-9749)

British Cataloguing in Publication Data
A Cataloguing in Publication record for this book is available from the British Library.

All work contributed to this book is new, previously-unpublished material. The views expressed in this book are those of the authors, but not necessarily of the publisher.

Advances in Information Security, Privacy, and Ethics (AISPE) Book Series

ISSN: 1948-9730
EISSN: 1948-9749

MISSION

As digital technologies become more pervasive in everyday life and the Internet is utilized in ever increasing ways by both private and public entities, concern over digital threats becomes more prevalent.

The **Advances in Information Security, Privacy, & Ethics (AISPE) Book Series** provides cutting-edge research on the protection and misuse of information and technology across various industries and settings. Comprised of scholarly research on topics such as identity management, cryptography, system security, authentication, and data protection, this book series is ideal for reference by IT professionals, academicians, and upper-level students.

COVERAGE

- Access Control
- Device Fingerprinting
- Global Privacy Concerns
- Information Security Standards
- Network Security Services
- Privacy-Enhancing Technologies
- Risk Management
- Security Information Management
- Technoethics
- Tracking Cookies

IGI Global is currently accepting manuscripts for publication within this series. To submit a proposal for a volume in this series, please contact our Acquisition Editors at Acquisitions@igi-global.com or visit: http://www.igi-global.com/publish/.

The Advances in Information Security, Privacy, and Ethics (AISPE) Book Series (ISSN 1948-9730) is published by IGI Global, 701 E. Chocolate Avenue, Hershey, PA 17033-1240, USA, www.igi-global.com. This series is composed of titles available for purchase individually; each title is edited to be contextually exclusive from any other title within the series. For pricing and ordering information please visit http://www.igi-global.com/book-series/advances-information-security-privacy-ethics/37157. Postmaster: Send all address changes to above address. Copyright © 2014 IGI Global. All rights, including translation in other languages reserved by the publisher. No part of this series may be reproduced or used in any form or by any means – graphics, electronic, or mechanical, including photocopying, recording, taping, or information and retrieval systems – without written permission from the publisher, except for non commercial, educational use, including classroom teaching purposes. The views expressed in this series are those of the authors, but not necessarily of IGI Global.

Titles in this Series

For a list of additional titles in this series, please visit: www.igi-global.com

Cases on Research and Knowledge Discovery Homeland Security Centers of Excellence
Cecelia Wright Brown (University of Baltimore, USA) Kevin A. Peters (Morgan State University, USA) and Kofi Adofo Nyarko (Morgan State University, USA)
Information Science Reference • copyright 2014 • 334pp • H/C (ISBN: 9781466659469)
• US $215.00 (our price)

Multidisciplinary Perspectives in Cryptology and Information Security
Sattar B. Sadkhan Al Maliky (University of Babylon, Iraq) and Nidaa A. Abbas (University of Babylon, Iraq)
Information Science Reference • copyright 2014 • 334pp • H/C (ISBN: 9781466658080)
• US $245.00 (our price)

Analyzing Security, Trust, and Crime in the Digital World
Hamid R. Nemati (The University of North Carolina at Greensboro, USA)
Information Science Reference • copyright 2014 • 281pp • H/C (ISBN: 9781466648562)
• US $195.00 (our price)

Research Developments in Biometrics and Video Processing Techniques
Rajeev Srivastava (Indian Institute of Technology (BHU), India) S.K. Singh (Indian Institute of Technology (BHU), India) and K.K. Shukla (Indian Institute of Technology (BHU), India)
Information Science Reference • copyright 2014 • 279pp • H/C (ISBN: 9781466648685)
• US $195.00 (our price)

Advances in Secure Computing, Internet Services, and Applications
B.K. Tripathy (VIT University, India) and D.P. Acharjya (VIT University, India)
Information Science Reference • copyright 2014 • 405pp • H/C (ISBN: 9781466649408)
• US $195.00 (our price)

www.igi-global.com

701 E. Chocolate Ave., Hershey, PA 17033
Order online at www.igi-global.com or call 717-533-8845 x100
To place a standing order for titles released in this series,
contact: cust@igi-global.com
Mon-Fri 8:00 am - 5:00 pm (est) or fax 24 hours a day 717-533-8661

Table of Contents

Section 1
Homeland Security Centers of Excellence

Chapter 1
The Challenges of Obtaining Credible Data for Transportation Security
Matt Campo, Rutgers University, USA
Michael Greenberg, Rutgers University, USA
Henry Mayer, Rutgers University, USA
Karen Lowrie, Rutgers University, USA

Chapter 2
The Center for Secure and Resilient Maritime Commerce: A DHS National
Julie Pullen, Stevens Institute of Technology, USA
Michael Bruno, Stevens Institute of Technology, USA

Chapter 3
Command, Control, and Interoperability Center for Advanced Data Analysis:
Asamoah Nkwanta, Morgan State University, USA
Janet E. Barber, Central Michigan University, USA & Prince George's
Community College, USA

Section 2
Research and Knowledge Discovery

Detailed Table of Contents

Section 1
Homeland Security Centers of Excellence

Chapter 1
The Challenges of Obtaining Credible Data for Transportation Security
Modeling 1
Matt Campo, Rutgers University, USA
Michael Greenberg, Rutgers University, USA
Henry Mayer, Rutgers University, USA
Karen Lowrie, Rutgers University, USA

This chapter focuses on the National Transportation Security Center of Excellence
(NTSCOE) established in August 2007 to develop new approaches to defend, protect,
and increase the resilience of the nation's multi-modal transportation infrastructure,
and to create education and training programs for transportation security. The Center for Transportation Safety, Security, and Risk (CTSSR) at Rutgers University,
an NTSCOE institution, developed models that address multi-modal resilience
of freight and transit transportation networks. Data collection processes for each
project presented significant hurdles for the research team in developing credible
and accurate modeling tools. For any given data need, the potential exists for data
gaps, collection, and processing errors, publication and use restrictions, and the
need to obtain the most timely information. These challenges must be foreseen by
researchers and practitioners in order to better accommodate potential restrictions
on both data collection and dissemination while still providing users with a tool
that improves decision making.

    Julie Pullen, Stevens Institute of Technology, USA
    Michael Bruno, Stevens Institute of Technology, USA

This chapter describes efforts from the DHS National Center of Excellence in Maritime Security's (CSR) Maritime Domain Awareness (MDA) technologies in support of layered surveillance. The layers include satellite-based wide area views, HF Radar systems providing over-the horizon situational awareness, and near-shore and harbor sensing utilizing underwater acoustic technologies. Integration of these systems accomplishes vessel detection, classification, identification, and tracking. Applications for end-users including U.S. Coast Guard (USCG) and Customs and Border Protection (CBP) have demonstrated the delivery of actionable information in operationally relevant settings. The Center won the DHS S&T impact award two years in a row for its role in providing vital data during the US Airways plane landing on the Hudson River and during the Deepwater Horizon oil spill. Furthermore, research in port resiliency has yielded a port disruption planning tool, the Port Mapper, that assisted government leadership during the closure of the Port of NY/NJ by Hurricane Sandy. Work at the Center is focused on delivering MDA data streams from emerging and advanced technologies into the hands of the operators in ways that are compatible with command decision support systems.

    Asamoah Nkwanta, Morgan State University, USA
    Janet E. Barber, Central Michigan University, USA & Prince George's
        Community College, USA

This chapter presents an overview of the educational and research programs of the Command, Control, and Interoperability Center for Advanced Data Analysis (CCICADA) in an integral way. CCICADA is based at Rutgers University and is one of the components of the Department of Homeland Security (DHS) Center of Excellence (COE) Center for Visualization and Data Analytics (CVADA). CVADA is co-led by Rutgers University and Purdue University. Purdue's Visual Analytics for Command, Control, and Interoperability Environments (VACCINE) Center and Rutgers University's CCICADA Center were established as a DHS Homeland Security Center of Excellence in 2009. Although Purdue's focus is on visualization sciences, and Rutgers' focus is on data sciences, these two CVADA components are working closely on a number of activities, projects, and programs.

The following case study discusses methods for detecting and locating two different types of radio receivers. Functional stimulated emissions detectors are constructed, and their performance is analyzed. Stimulated emissions are capable of detecting super-regenerative receivers at distances of at least one hundred meters and accurately locating superheterodyne receivers at distances of at least fifty meters. These results demonstrate a novel technique for detecting potential explosive threats at stand-off detection distances.

In its efforts to respond to national workforce imperatives, the Center for Secure and Resilient Maritime Commerce (CSR), led by Stevens Institute of Technology, created an intensive summer research program tailored to undergraduate and graduate-level students. The Summer Research Institute is designed to engage multidisciplinary student teams in rigorous, hands-on research in collaboration with the Center's researchers and industry and government partners. The research fields include maritime security, remote sensing technologies, emergency response and management, and Marine Transportation System (MTS) resilience. The program aims to enhance the professional development of students, while increasing their interest in advanced academic study and careers in the maritime/homeland security domain.

The working relationships between Native American tribes, the states, and the federal government have been strained for centuries. These intergovernmental interactions have led to a fragmented system whose attempt to deliver public service is consistently met with opposition. One area where this has become increasingly evident is within homeland security and emergency management policy. This study used a cross sectional survey to gather information about the beliefs tribes held about the various aspects of their working relationships with states and the federal government within the context of homeland security and emergency management.

Chapter 7

This chapter discusses a model for the teaching and learning of STEM by under-graduate students, teachers, and faculty at Morgan State University that focuses on visual analytics. This project represents an interdisciplinary approach to the teaching and learning of STEM at a Minority Serving Institution funded by the Department of Homeland Security. The chapter also outlines salient strategies associated with challenges at the University. In addition, the chapter discusses partnerships developed with VACCINE, a DHS Center of Excellence at Purdue University, that supports DHS priority research in the areas of visual analytics.

Chapter 8

As an essential element of homeland security, critical infrastructure protection requires a professional, highly educated workforce and community of leaders at all levels of government and in the private sector. Yet there are few structured and comprehensive higher education programs in critical infrastructure protection. This case study reviews an education initiative that partners the U.S. Department of Homeland Security with the Center for Infrastructure Protection and Homeland Security at the George Mason University School of Law in an effort to develop and distribute critical infrastructure protection courses and materials that will become part of a comprehensive, unified approach to homeland security education.

Chapter 9

This project examined the issues of role conflict and resilience among first responders who have participated in major disaster events. This case also seeks to advance the mission of the Science and Technology Directorate of the Department of Homeland Security (DHS) by providing information needed for advancing the development of simulation models and effective training curricula to assist first responders in their quest for preparing and responding to future disaster events.

Chapter 10

Kevin A. Peters, Morgan State University, USA

Nira C. Taru, Morgan State University, USA

This chapter highlights seven (7) DHS programs/research that involved faculty and students at Morgan State University, a Minority Serving Institution (MSI) that was linked to a DHS Center for Excellence. The programs were developed in part from partnerships and collaborative efforts from researchers and principal investigators at Morgan State University and several DHS Centers of Excellence. Researchers from Morgan State University submitted summaries of their DHS-funded programs and activities. In addition, information was gathered from DHS Websites pertaining to their collaborative work with a DHS Center of Excellence (COE). This chapter emphasizes the importance of collaborative research and programs that support the overall mission of DHS in providing opportunities for MSIs to work with COEs in DHS priority research areas.

Chapter 11

Cecelia Wright Brown, University of Baltimore, USA

This chapter presents an Information Technology and Engineering (ITE) professional development training project designed to increase the number of teachers in an urban school district with proficient skills, tools, and content knowledge in computer/information technology, engineering technology, and technical certifications that will support students in Science, Technology, Engineering, and Mathematics (STEM) fields. Through this process, high school teachers will use tools, resources, and training to understand homeland security issues and career opportunities for students in their schools. The overall goal of the ITE profession development training was designed to increase the technical proficiency of STEM teachers in urban high schools serving historically underserved students to support students in Information Technology (IT), engineering. and homeland security careers, thus nurturing a homeland security science and engineering workforce.

Chapter 12

Kevin Peters, Morgan State University, USA

Cecelia Wright Brown, University of Baltimore, USA

Kofi Nyarko, Morgan State University, USA

The previous chapters in this book demonstrate how collaborative research linked to DHS Centers for Excellence support the overall mission of DHS, while at the same time support research by faculty and students at institutions of higher education. The added value and success of these programs highlight the importance of developing effective partnerships that can lead to quality research experiences for faculty, students, and teachers. In addition, the highlighted research stresses the importance of developing a strong workforce that begins long before students make the transition to institutions of higher learning. It is important that early career faculty researchers and experienced researchers, as well as undergraduate and graduate students, understand DHS research priority areas that can effectively support the overall mission of DHS. The collaborative research that is linked to other federal and state agencies is important in addressing complex security issues that have an impact on the general public.

Foreword

The challenges of homeland security demand the timely application of scientific insight and technological solutions that must robustly keep pace with a changing threat and hazard environment. Our ability to harness the most advanced technical and scientific understanding through disciplined research and problem solving is critical to the success of our collective capability to prevent, protect, mitigate, respond to, and recover from the worst events we can imagine. Well over a decade ago, during the early phase of the formation of the U.S. Department of Homeland Security, key investments were made in developing consortia of universities and other research institutions to focus on the grand challenges envisaged in securing our nation.

With this book, Dr. Cecelia Wright Brown and her colleagues take us on a journey through the research and applications that have shaped and impacted the constellation of DHS Centers of Excellence. The book's contributors make an effort to link research to practical applications that reminds us of the important investments that have been made in research and education. The book tracks those results through operational implementation while characterizing their influence on concepts of operation, the overall body of knowledge, and on strategic redirection of future research objectives, operational requirements, and acquisition decisions.

Dr. Wright Brown brings decades of experience as an engineer, physicist, and educator. Together with her colleagues, Drs. Kevin Peters and Kofi Nyarko, as well as the other contributors, the authors capture the importance of the Science and Technology (S&T) Center of Excellence (COE) enterprise on the readiness of our nation to meet evolving threats, and how vital this S&T investment is to enabling knowledge discovery. The book will serve to energize interdisciplinary problem solving, evidence-based research, and stimulate cost-effective practical applications for our security and safety. The authors offer the first independent, comprehensive look at the body of work accomplished by the COEs and organize this in a manner meaningful to practitioners, public safety leadership, basic and applied researchers, and private sector industrial partners who design, develop, test, evaluate, and support systems and technologies. A wide spectrum of professionals from security managers to laboratory technicians, from computer scientists to mathematicians and engineers will benefit from this treatment of the COE enterprise.

Dr. Wright Brown uniquely understands the research and applications nexus at which government, academia, and industry must partner to optimize outcomes. Beyond her long commitment to higher education, she has been a remarkable force for collaboration among private and public entities, and she serves in key roles to develop training and education opportunities beyond the university setting, as demonstrated in her service on the American Board for Certification in Infrastructure Protection (ABCIP), which is finalizing a new certification program from practitioners in infrastructure protection and resilience. She is committed to developing the competent workforce of tomorrow that is capable of leading our homeland security programs for decades to come. It is with this dedication to education and training, to knowledge discovery and transfer, that the authors have created a timely resource to help us understand, enhance, and sustain the most beneficial outcomes of our nation's investment in the COE enterprise.

As a colleague of Dr. Wright Brown for many years, I know she has dedicated her professional career to collaboration, team building, and institutional partnerships that strengthen our readiness and thus our public safety. Drs. Wright Brown, Peters, and Nyarko are uniquely positioned to provide this independent, unbiased analysis of the COEs, which should be welcomed by all who share their commitment to the safety and security of future generations. Given my nearly 40 years of service to emergency management, security, and infrastructure protection, I have seen thousands of programs, initiatives, and transformational technologies emerge, grow, and in many cases, perish as institutional commitments or inspirational leadership falters. It is imperative that from time to time we stop, reflect on what we have done, and learn what worked, what had a positive impact, and why it made a difference. This book will make a major contribution to that assessment, the prioritization of research ahead, and to the enhancement of educational opportunities for the homeland security workforce of our future.

Robert J. Coullahan
Readiness Resource Group Incorporated, USA

Robert J. Coullahan *is a leader in national preparedness; critical infrastructure protection; Command, Control, Communications, Intelligence, Surveillance, and Reconnaissance (C4ISR) systems; and advanced technology development and integration. After completing active US Army duty in the 1970s, he relocated to Washington, DC area and for over 35 years has supported government and commercial operations. He served in management roles for over 20 years with Science Applications International Corporation (SAIC), where he was Senior Vice President. For five years, he served as Vice President for Government and International Programs, leading an award-winning university consortium that created the World Data Center-A for Human Interactions in the Environment for the US Global Change Research Program. He is the President and Founder of Readiness Resource Group Incorporated (RRG), a veteran-owned business supporting professional services for homeland security, infrastructure resilience, and energy and transport systems. He is board certified in emergency management, security management, and continuity management. He attended Rutgers University and earned his bachelor's degree from the University of California and both an M.S. in Telecommunications and an M.A. in Security Management (Forensic Sciences) from The George Washington University.*

Preface

This book offers a wide scientific scope, which invites the reader to become a learner and an involved participant. The reader observes and reads about science cases and research in knowledge discovery and the creation of constructive statistical models from big data about complex and intertwining relationships among people and behavior, places and location, things and purpose, and events and situational factors. It is about safety, security, and survival in a sometimes chaotic virtual and real world.

It is no question that incidents of computer crime, natural disasters, terrorism, air traffic crime, cruise ship piracy, mass shootings, bombings, cyber attacks, information technology-enabled frauds, information security problems, and human trafficking have been on the rise. Confronting these problems requires a good understanding of the challenges that exist in the new millennium, such as control of organizational operations, developing management skill and practices, use of appropriate information processing, accurate information technologies, and establishing exceptional disaster recovery plans. According to some of the present literature, the challenge of extracting and mining data draws upon research in Web discovery and statistics as well.

Additionally, the chapters in this book present an extensive array of interesting challenges and thought-provoking ideas that promote maverick thinking and innovative solutions to problems, as well as motivate positive state-of-the art and state-of-the-science change. Research is good; however, the works and writings of the authors herein advance information in understanding the actual stories culled out of big and small data to make certain that some of the above challenges are met with success.

These endeavors are important as our world goes aggressively and progressively into the realm of constant alertness for safety, and higher education for understanding what must be done to ensure safety and security. These pioneering authors share with the readers information about diligent Science, Technology, Engineering, and Mathematics (STEM) students and their mentors who are taking brave steps in the sciences. These sciences include the arts and behavioral sciences. Through their various disciplines and research, their workshops, seminars, and learning techniques, these scientists forge ahead on a crucial mission. The author contributors include leading educators, practitioners, and researchers from institutions of higher learning, public and private industries, corporate companies, as well as government laboratories. They are all leaders in their fields.

The reader as participant, observer, and scientist must be prepared to think deeply, for there are continuous research, studies, theories, and writings needed in order to give support in these scientific fields of study to determine what is best for our country's safety and security. Your creativity and ingenuity in whatever field could be needed today and tomorrow, as industries and companies are beginning to work hand-in-hand with higher education institutions to curb and ultimately eliminate security problems and teach best behavioral practices in the face of crises.

What do we need to know in order to smooth out the glitches? We work; we learn; we study; we research. We are evolving in our discovery of knowledge and methods of data extraction. This evolution is a scientific and academic revolution. Therefore, as mentioned, teamwork among institutions and industries is a must. Hence, the numerous chapters written share with readers information about partnerships and the data the authors have gathered dealing with environmental protection and security.

Topics include essential security issues, such as homeland and environmental security, including infrastructure, transportation and maritime security, data and electronic security, and the application of research from case studies. Data collected and analyzed offer answers to ensure present and future safety and security.

The chapters also show that there has been a great deal of growth in the initiation, generation, collection, extraction, and analyses of data. Advances in methodology and data collection have inundated the society with data of all types and have ignited an urgent need for discovery and original and innovative tools and techniques that can aid in changing data into a practical and applicable knowledge base. In essence, the science is in the chapters; the story is behind and within the data.

ORGANIZATION OF THE BOOK

Chapter 1 introduces the reader to the challenge of ensuring credible data, a thorn for many a scientist. This chapter presents this need through information on the need for secure travel within our society. The authors share with us that the National Transportation Security Center of Excellence (NTSCOE) was established to create new ways to increase the resilience of the nation's multi-modal transportation infrastructure. In doing this, they also study defense, as well as protection. The NTSCOE also has training programs including research opportunities in the study and education of transportation security. These latter efforts can ultimately foster ways to foresee challenges in security as well as data gaps. Solutions and efforts are, of course, underway to develop credible and more efficient data collections for evaluation and analyses.

Chapter 2 presents to the reader a look at travel from a different venue, as the authors of this chapter share the importance of satellite surveillance in maritime security. The Department of Homeland Security National Center of Excellence in Maritime Security's (CSR) Maritime Domain Awareness (MDA) applies emerging technologies not only in surveillance tools, but in port resiliency with the aid of a Port Mapper, which was instrumental in aiding with Hurricane Sandy safety and security efforts. Another very useful tool is a "state-of-the-science" weather model that has the capability to forecast weather conditions down to a ~300 m resolution. Securing our seaports has always been important; however, since 9/11, DHS has been even more vigilant in this area of safety. Staying alert will necessitate tapping into the knowledge base of academia and research. As the authors implore, the science and technological work and developments of experts in the maritime and other scientific fields will be utilized.

Chapter 3 provides an integrated overview of workshops, lectures, projects, and other educational and research programs supported by the Command, Control, and Interoperability Center for Advanced Data Analysis (CCICADA). They are a component of DHS, Center of Excellence. The authors report that the COE is well underway in ensuring intense research and study, professional and scientific writings and academic literature, and meaningful internships, workshops, teaching technologies, and seminars in various areas of work, interdisciplinary and transdisciplinary disciplines, and partnerships. These partnership endeavors include state-of-the-art and state-of-the-science lessons in data science, fusion center assessment (which can work in tandem with travel and maritime studies), social media and security, studies in homeland security strategies for safety, data collection, organization studies, human trafficking eradication, nuclear detection, and modeling and stimulation research. Students as well as professionals are afforded many opportunities to sustain and support scientific undertakings in many areas of study. As mentioned in this chapter and some others, there are continuous research efforts and work in port resilience, bio-surveillance, natural disaster preparedness, stadium security, evacuation planning, epidemiology, behavioral response, social media analysis, resource planning and allocation, cybersecurity, emergency alerting, and information privacy. In essence, CCICADA as a Center of Excellence is continuously organizing academic and intellectual meetings of the minds among recognized researchers and other experts in the data sciences. Their purpose is to conduct research from many venues and disciplines initiated by experts interested in the study of complex DHS Homeland Security challenges, problems, concerns, but also solutions.

Chapter 4 makes the point that in the face of conflict-prone situations and environments, improvised explosive devices with remote detection capabilities can play an instrumental and positive role in ensuring safety. This would entail working closely with the ALERT center (Awareness and Localization of Explosives-Related Threats) to apply these unique techniques. The authors share that remote detection-radio receivers can aid in the uncovering of radio-controlled explosives. Sneaky is a positive word in this brilliant science, as the weak stimulation of a low-powered radio signal can transmit through containers and walls virtually undetected, unlike chemical traces, which can be more easily detected. This project has developed many radio-receiver detectors. However, the research partnership continues to grow as they seek answers to a few technical questions. Solutions and answers will likely transfer into working hand-in-hand with industry partners. This is a goal.

Chapter 5 communicates that workforce development is imperative if we want our citizenry to compete successfully and globally. It is one of the missions of the DHS Center of Excellence in Port and Maritime Security, the Center for Secure and Resilient Maritime Commerce (CSR) to ensure this success in the discipline of the maritime sciences, also discussed in chapters 2 and 3. The authors impart that our students must be exposed to a larger scope of scientific work as future scientists, professionals, and practitioners. They should be afforded opportunities to learn and intern in experiential learning activities that improve academic and professional development, as well as promote creativity. The DHS COE, CSR Maritime Commerce research fields include remote sensing technologies, emergency response, management, security, and Marine Transportation System (MTS) resilience.

Chapter 6 is titled "Frienemies: Assessing the Interactions between Native American Tribes and the U.S. Government in Homeland Security and Emergency Management Policy." The authors write by way of sharing an assessment of the communication (or the lack thereof) between the Native American community and the U.S. Government homeland security and their emergency management policy. One important thing about security and safety in any situation and discussion is to understand and know who your friends are and especially who your enemies are in order to ensure safety. A play on both words friends and enemies, is the fun word "frienemies." As the authors note, the word is not so much fun, however, when it comes to serious safety and security matters in one's environment. The authors explain the strained relationship between the U.S. Government and Native Americans as they both try to come to a fair sense of balance concerning the issues. To get to some semblance of agreement, a cross-sectional survey was distributed with the aim of collecting data and information about native tribal beliefs and their relationship with the USA and the U.S. Government as these beliefs relate to U.S. Homeland Security and Emergency Management. The study will aid in providing stability in communications in order to build upon future research in the area of homeland security and public policy with a focus on Native American community and issues.

Chapter 7 focuses on the importance of teaching and training undergraduate students, faculty, and teachers in the field of visual analytics. The model for the teaching and learning is STEM-based. This academic project denotes an interdisciplinary approach at a Minority Serving Institution funded by the Department of Homeland Security. This effort has broadened the participants' academic and educational horizons, enhancing their knowledge in the area and introducing them to empowering and innovative methodologies, workable theories, and creative lectures, workshops, and projects.

Chapter 8 explains the importance of infrastructure protection. However, there are only a small number of comprehensive higher education programs in the critical infrastructure protection area of study. The authors state that this could be a crucial component of homeland security. Critical infrastructure protection is the utilization and services of a high-quality, educated, expert workforce ready to assist with the security and safety of citizens. This would entail and include a community of highly educated leaders at all levels and sectors of government, public and private. These constituents are also needed to promote the effort to develop educational programs in this area of need.

Chapter 9 offers important information about faculty and student research opportunities. The author of this chapter shares that it was 2005 when DHS started offering Summer Research Fellowship opportunities to faculty members at Minority Serving Institutions (MSI). These faculty members in turn are able to offer research opportunities for their students. Howard University was one of the fortunate and participating MSI institutions. The author's research progresses the efforts of DHS. For example, natural and manmade threats and disasters are inescapable, and therefore, our American public has an intense dependency on our first responders as protectors and defenders in the face of crime and natural disasters. However, our first responders are human and sometimes may need physical preparation and mental strategies in order to be grounded and ready to protect and defend. The social sciences play an integral role in assisting with this endeavor, and therefore, the author of this chapter offers information, research, and a better understanding of the human dynamics and concerns of the first responders who must act in response to danger in order to protect our citizens. This research advances the development of necessary training and simulation models to aid first responders, which subsequently helps directly or indirectly with the safety, security, and survival of American citizens.

Chapter 10 focuses on seven DHS research programs linked to the COE. These research programs are housed at Morgan State University, Baltimore, Maryland, and were developed to some extent from collaboration and partnership efforts due to the hard work of researchers and principal investigators at MSU. This chapter also brings to light the innovative, creative, inclusive, distinctive, and high-quality educational experiences of MSU students, faculty, staff, and teachers from surrounding areas. Many of the DHS-connected programs and projects build on the other and are intended toward working directly with STEM students with an interdisciplinary approach. The ultimate goal is the transference of knowledge, as well as applicable scientific research in the safety and security fields. This effort has been proven with numerous success stories of students and teachers who have had the opportunity to participate in excellent programs through DHS, COE. The authors report that MSU students have learned from their educational experiences how to apply their knowledge and training to progress and improve technologies that could perhaps benefit major DHS research initiatives.

Chapter 11 imparts significant information about the importance of professional development and education in general. Particularly, the author relates information about a University of Baltimore (Maryland) project geared toward increasing the knowledge base of STEM teachers in a particular urban school district. The research derived from collaborative homeland security-STEM contact. The subsequent professional development project in Information Technology and Engineering (ITE) is specifically designed to ensure the computer and technology proficiency of more teachers through professional training. The hope is that more students will become interested in the sciences as these teachers nurture them academically in the direction of homeland security science and engineering workforces. Education, higher or lower, is the imparting of information in an instructive way. Teachers must understand how to be instructive as they teach technology in the classroom. The participating teachers reported a high success and satisfaction rate. This project for professional development is a good start in the direction for more competency and comfort in teaching with technology. Constant professional development is a necessity, as what students need technically and the way they learn electronically continue to evolve.

Chapter 12 is a wrap up and summary of the intertwining chapters on safety, security, and survival. The authors also share closing remarks about the chapters. In conclusion, the book shows how partnerships through collaborative research with the Department of Homeland Security, Centers of Excellence is two-fold and sustain and support the overall mission of DHS as well as faculty, students, researchers, and teachers. This concluding chapter leads with a statement from the Department of Homeland Security (DHS) that they will make every effort to secure America from terrorism, threats, and natural disasters. The reader will learn from perusing each chapter that DHS has support from leaders of many disciplines and fields to assist with the study and research for the society's ever-increasing needs. Educational leaders, scientists, and students help with data collecting, data organization, data extraction, data analyses, data evaluation, social media, technological projects, and progressively, more professional development in their efforts to apply best strategy and tools for safety, security, and survival in the face of crises.

SEQUENCE FOR EDUCATIONAL AND ORGANIZATIONAL COLLABORATIONS

This book posits a theme for innovative and creative research, lectures, work, and discussions presented by an array of education teams, authors, and partnerships. They identify challenges as well as solutions in the collection, organization, management, and extraction of big and small data in security information and research in the new millennium. The Centers of Excellence (COE) have paved a way for many of these endeavors. Below is a list of COEs across America (Website information follows):

Centers of Excellence

- The Command, Control, and Interoperability Center for Advanced Data Analysis (CCICADA): A Department of Homeland Security Data Sciences Center of Excellence (COE) is based at Rutgers University and is one of the components of the Department of Homeland Security (DHS) Center of Excellence (COE).
- The Visual Analytics for Command, Control, and Interoperability Environments (VACCINE) Center is based at Purdue University and is one of the components of DHS Homeland Security Center of Excellence.
- The Center for Visualization and Data Analytics (CVADA) is led by VACCINE of Purdue University (visualization sciences co-lead) and CCICADA of Rutgers University (data sciences co-lead) and will create the scientific basis and enduring technologies needed to analyze massive amounts of information to detect security threats.
- The Studies of Terrorism and Responses to Terrorism (START), a COE of DHS based at the University of Maryland. This is a major group in the study of terrorism. They are also a consortium that brings together the leading experts and researchers in the study of terrorism. START has developed meticulous analyses and methodologies that will significantly benefit policy and operations within the homeland security enterprise.
- The Center for Risk and Economic Analysis of Terrorism Events (CREATE), led by the University of Southern California, develops advanced tools to evaluate the risks, costs and consequences of terrorism.
- The Center for Advancing Microbial Risk Assessment (CAMRA), led by Michigan State University and Drexel University established jointly with the U.S. Environmental Protection Agency, fills critical gaps in risk assessments for mitigating microbial hazards.

- The Center of Excellence for Zoonotic and Animal Disease Defense (ZADD), led by Texas A&M University and Kansas State University, protects the nation's agricultural and public health sectors against high-consequence foreign animal, emerging, and zoonotic disease threats.
- The National Center for Food Protection and Defense (NCFPD), led by the University of Minnesota, defends the safety and security of the food system by conducting research to protect vulnerabilities in the nation's food supply chain.
- The National Consortium for the Study of Terrorism and Responses to Terrorism (START), led by the University of Maryland, informs decisions on how to disrupt terrorists and terrorist groups through empirically grounded findings on the human element of the terrorist threat. START has provided major advances in research and findings in the area of terrorism and response to terrorist situations. START's expertise in the multi-faceted nature of terrorism continues to benefit the nation's defense against terrorist acts through meticulous security measures and better understanding of preparedness (see chapter 9).
- The National Center for the Study of Preparedness and Catastrophic Event Response (PACER), led by Johns Hopkins University, optimizes our nation's preparedness in the event of a high-consequence natural or man-made disaster.
- The Center of Excellence for Awareness and Location of Explosives-Related Threats (ALERT), led by Northeastern University and the University of Rhode Island, will develop new means and methods to protect the nation from explosives-related threats.
- The National Center for Border Security and Immigration (NCBSI), led by the University of Arizona in Tucson (research co-lead) and the University of Texas at El Paso (education co-lead), are developing technologies, tools, and advanced methods to balance immigration and commerce with effective border security.
- The Center for Maritime, Island, and Remote and Extreme Environment Security (MIREES), led by the University of Hawaii and Stevens Institute of Technology, focuses on developing robust research and education programs addressing maritime domain awareness to safeguard populations and properties in geographical areas that present significant security challenges.
- The Coastal Hazards Center of Excellence (CHC), led by the University of North Carolina at Chapel Hill and Jackson State University in Jackson, Miss., performs research and develops education programs to enhance the nation's ability to safeguard populations, properties, and economies from catastrophic natural disaster.

- The National Transportation Security Center of Excellence (NTSCOE) comprises seven institutions and was established in accordance with HR1, implementing the recommendations of the 9/11 Commission Act of 2007. The NTSCOE will develop new technologies, tools and advanced methods to defend, protect, and increase the resilience of the nation's multimodal transportation.

See:

- http://ccicada.rutgers.edu/about.html
- https://www.dhs.gov/st-centers-excellence
- http://www.start.umd.edu/start/publications/START_Brochure_WEB.pdf

The Knowledge Discovery Laboratory

As shared, there is cutting-edge research and literature within these pages providing a number of learning and research approaches in collaboration between and among universities, companies, independent laboratories, and businesses. These approaches hone studies for better comprehension of theories, methodologies, and application of information gauged from data and for forging these research partnerships. Their works focus on what is needed, the methodology and strategies for solutions, the research and data collection, the discovery, and then the explanation of information extracted from data.

Knowledge Discovery Laboratory is another center of research geared toward the teaching of scientific knowledge for understanding. KDL is a research group housed in the School of Computer Science at the University of Massachusetts Amherst. KDL researches and develops innovative techniques for knowledge discovery, studies the fundamental principles of data analyses, and applies these techniques to appropriate tasks in various research areas including relational knowledge discovery, Web mining, fraud detection, scientific data analysis, and other relevant issues. Other areas of knowledge discovery referenced in this text are data visualization, pattern recognition, machine learning, optimization, and high-performance computing, which aids in the delivery of highly developed business intelligence and Web mining.

The rapid and continuous growth of Internet research, the vast utilization of electronic databases, and online data collection from surveys and other research tools and databases have caused an enormous and immediate need for KDL's assistance with new theories, methodologies, and science models.

See: https://kdl.cs.umass.edu/display/public/Knowledge+Discovery+Laboratory

CONCLUDING REMARKS: LOOKING FORWARD

There is cutting-edge research within these pages. The authors demonstrate how to meticulously insert the story behind the data for readability and layperson understanding. Their works focus on what is needed, the approach towards solutions, the research and work, then the discovery, that is, the story behind the data and science.

This book is about science, but is also about education. Education entails learning and teaching. Specific skills and certain knowledge should be obtained. Education at its utmost is lifelong, as everyday life over and over again proves to be instructive. In the American struggle for safety, security, and survival, we have been instructed to ensure security and safety in whatever common sense way possible. The studies and research conducted by the experts must be swift. As we experience ever more tragedy and grief in our mist, we are going to need strategy.

This collaborative book endeavor demonstrates that communities must find ways to decrease risk in emergency situations. They must also become partners within and outside their immediate environments. Citizens must communicate and interact with each other in order to increase social support systems, as well as relational and organizational linkages for safety, security, and survival. With the numerous types of social media and the number of people connecting with each other electronically, positive behavioral modifications are less difficult to put into practice.

These chapters illustrate that it is also important to implement and work on adequate and efficient technological controls in order to cultivate behavioral and learning practices successfully. It is imperative that people communicate effectively in cases of natural disasters, terrorism, air traffic crime, cruise ship piracy, mass shootings, bombings, or cyber attacks.

This is a timely book, as our present-day intellectuals and a new cohort of Generation Me's, X's, Y's, and Z's are acquiring computerized and computer-type skills that could ultimately bring about a comprehensive knowledge base of information. As these chapters indicate, this newfound knowledge and research could be groundbreaking in the discovery of even greater techniques and tools for safety, security, conduct modifications, and behavioral enhancements if there is continuous study.

The authors of this book, as mentioned, contend through their writings and research that by investing in the education of STEM and social sciences students, the development of safety strategies, research, security policy, business, and organizational partnerships guarantees practical and intellectual protection that ensures ongoing work and research toward best practices for the safety and security of Americans.

Chock full of novel research, methodologies, theories, and actionable ideas, *Cases on Research and Knowledge Discovery: Homeland Security Centers of Excellence* and its interconnected chapters from contributing authors offer a new roadmap for leading educators and scientists. From here, they are able to go forward with even more innovative and cutting-edge research in the area of Homeland Security.

Cecelia Wright Brown
University of Baltimore, USA

Kevin A. Peters
Morgan State University, USA

Kofi A. Nyarko
Morgan State University, USA

Janet E. Barber
Central Michigan University, USA & Prince George's Community College, USA

Acknowledgment

The premise for this book was born out of the tragedy that struck us all on September 11, 2001. Since that terrible day, countless numbers of individuals have contributed to make this country safer. Some of those efforts have been made possible by the Department of Homeland Security Centers of Excellence, and we would like to take a moment to acknowledge the importance of their work and the progress we have made as a nation, in part, thanks to these contributions. We thank the chapter contributors, who took time out of often very packed schedules to share the wonderful work being done in these Centers of Excellence.

We thank the contributors from Rutgers University for discussing the challenges of obtaining credible data for Transportation Security Modeling as well as possible mitigation strategies. We thank the contributors from Stevens Institute of Technology for promoting the layered surveillance efforts from the DHS National Center of Excellence in Maritime Security's Maritime Domain Awareness technologies. In addition, we acknowledge their efforts with the following: a summer research institute designed to engage multidisciplinary student teams in rigorous hands-on maritime security; remote sensing; emergency response and management research; and their discussion on Intergovernmental Relationships between Native American tribes, the states, and the Federal Government regarding Homeland Security and Emergency Management Policy.

We thank the contributors from Morgan State University and Central Michigan University for providing insight into the educational and research programs of the Command, Control, and Interoperability Center for Advanced Data Analysis as well as Morgan's efforts to strengthen STEM teaching and learning in addition to DHS-related research. We thank contributors from the Missouri University of Science and Technology for shedding light on methods for detecting and locating two different types of radio receivers, which improves the nation's capability to detect potential explosive threats at greater distances. We thank contributors from George Mason University School of Law for discussing their infrastructure protection higher education initiative. Lastly, we thank the contributor from University of Baltimore for reviewing training efforts designed to increase the number of teachers with proficient STEM skills in an urban school district.

We would also like to thank the members of the Editorial Advisory Board, who provided critical guidance in the early stages of the development process. The board was instrumental in preparing and distributing the call for cases as well as evaluating the proposals that were submitted. They also provided invaluable support in coordinating the review process and conducting the reviews for all the cases.

We would further like to thank Robert J. Coullahan for taking the time to succinctly capture the significance for the contribution of this book. Finally, special thanks to the DHS Science and Technology Directorate, Office of University Programs directors and managers for their support and technical assistance across the research projects that have been developed. The authors take responsibility for the content associated with this publication.

Cecelia Wright Brown
University of Baltimore, USA

Kevin A. Peters
Morgan State University, USA

Kofi Adofo Nyarko
Morgan State University, USA

Section 1
Homeland Security Centers of Excellence

Chapter 1

The Challenges of Obtaining Credible Data for Transportation Security Modeling

Matt Campo
Rutgers University, USA

Henry Mayer
Rutgers University, USA

Michael Greenberg
Rutgers University, USA

Karen Lowrie
Rutgers University, USA

EXECUTIVE SUMMARY

The National Transportation Security Center of Excellence (NTSCOE) was established in August 2007 to develop new approaches to defend, protect, and increase the resilience of the nation's multi-modal transportation infrastructure, and to create education and training programs for transportation security. The Center for Transportation Safety, Security, and Risk (CTSSR) at Rutgers University, an NTSCOE institution, developed models that address multi-modal resilience of freight and transit transportation networks. Data collection processes for each project presented significant hurdles for the research team in developing credible and accurate modeling tools. For any given data need, the potential exists for data gaps, collection, and processing errors, publication and use restrictions, and the need to obtain the most timely information. These challenges must be foreseen by researchers and practitioners in order to better accommodate potential restrictions on both data collection and dissemination while still providing users with a tool that improves decision making.

DOI: 10.4018/978-1-4666-5946-9.ch001

INTRODUCTION

The United States Department of Homeland Security (2007b) defines the NTSCOE as a consortium of seven different universities with goals that include the development of new technologies, tools and advanced methods to defend, protect and increase the resilience of the multimodal transportation infrastructure in the United States. University members included:

1. Connecticut Transportation Institute at the University of Connecticut,
2. Tougaloo College,
3. Texas Southern University,
4. Center for Transportation Safety, Security and Risk (CTSSR) at Rutgers, the State University of New Jersey,
5. Homeland Security Management Institute at Long Island University,
6. Mack Blackwell National Rural Transportation Study Center at the University of Arkansas,
7. Mineta Transportation Institute at San José State University.

As part of this Center of Excellence, CTSSR undertook the development of resilience modeling tools for use by transportation related agencies and stakeholders, in addition to the development of front-line employee training videos and associated training products. Two of these tools, each of which contains several simulation models, will be discussed herein, Supporting Secure and Resilient Inland Waterways and the Rail Security Model.

The Supporting Secure and Resilient Inland Waterways (SSRIW) project sought to develop a Web-based prototype decision support system that could integrate geographic information systems and optimization models to assist in planning support for offloading barge cargo during a sudden catastrophic closure of an inland waterway. A project goal is to assist the United States Coast Guard (USCG), United States Army Corps of Engineers (USACE), and other waterway security stakeholders in understanding the resiliency of inland waterway transportation system components and to create a planning tool that will allow public and private parties to plan and collaborate on emergency freight movement decisions.

The Rail Security Model developed by CTSSR brought together three complementary simulation models to offer insights into events that can cause cascading impacts in rail and connected transportation systems, explore the consequences of those events, and identify investments that could increase system resilience after accidents and attacks. The models work together to examine how a terrorist event would affect passenger flows and train movements, visualize and quantify contaminant exposure, and estimate regional economic impacts of these events. To obtain data and validate assumptions, the CTSSR team worked with planning and security personnel from NJ Transit, Amtrak, the New Jersey Office of Homeland Security and Preparedness, and the U.S. Department of Defense (DOD).

In this chapter, the authors will illustrate several data challenges through the discussion of model development for the aforementioned projects. First, the authors will discuss the constituent stakeholder groups for each research product, illustrating the difficulty in developing a good understanding of the complicated relationships required to develop and analyze system resilience. Next, the authors present a discussion of the stated needs for these modeling tools and the potential value derived from the development of such tools from both the public and private sector. Following that discussion, the cases and development of both tools will be presented, with a particular focus on data collection and the relationships and methods needed to identify and use the appropriate data sets. The cases are followed by a consolidated discussion of the issues and challenges faced in the modeling research, seeking to draw comparisons and illustrate common barriers and leading practices in working on detailed modeling projects. The chapter will end with solutions and recommendations for those involved in or considering embarking on research or modeling projects related to transportation security.

Overview of Inland Waterway Security and Resilience

The DHS has developed a series of sector-specific plans for specific components of built infrastructure defined as critical infrastructure and key resources. The Transportation Systems sector includes the inland waterways system, in particular the locks and dams that support the navigation of the system. In addition, the system also has critical interdependencies with other systems, including the provision of coal to the power systems along the Ohio River, providing cooling water for large industrial and power plants, exports of agricultural products, and other sector impacts (United States Department of Homeland Security, 2007). The system also handles unique shipments, such as rocket parts carried to shuttle launch sites (Associated Press, 2012).

The USCG is responsible for securing maritime commerce and traffic along the waterways (United States Department of Homeland Security, 2012). The USACE is responsible for the operations of the infrastructure (locks, dams, etc.) along the waterways in addition to the management of the navigation drafts that support commercial tug and barge shipping (United States Army Corps of Engineers, 2012). Security entities at the state level will differ depending on the particular organization of state and local government; however, entities that can be expected to be involved with security at this level can include state departments of emergency management, transportation, commerce and other agencies. Municipal or county police forces, emergency response agencies, and other local or regional organizations are also accountable in the security of the waterway. In addition to the public sector, there are several private stakeholders that must participate in the security of the waterway system. These stakeholders can include shippers, carriers, terminal operators and other concerned industries.

These entities are often brought together for disaster planning through a variety of means at the state and federal level. The Department of Homeland Security, as an example, is responsible for the National Exercise Program, which seeks to improve the exchange of information, identify threats and hazards, and create and improve upon operational strategies and structures during catastrophic disasters (Federal Emergency Management Agency, 2013). The National Level Exercise in 2011 examined an earthquake along the New Madrid seismic zone affecting waterways in the transportation system. On a more regular basis, these entities are organized into Area Maritime Security Committees (AMSC). An AMSC is a USCG forum that involves federal and nonfederal officials who identify and address risks in a port and assist the Coast Guard in developing the Area Maritime Security Plan for communication and coordination among stakeholder groups and enforcement agencies. The Coast Guard and the Area Maritime Security Committee are required to conduct or participate in exercises to test the effectiveness of AMSPs at least once each calendar year, with no more than 18 months between exercises (United States Government Accountability Office, 2012). The broad variety of stakeholders involved, and the need to share data among stakeholders during both exercises and real-time events, was part of the impetus for the research performed by CTSSR and the Mack Blackwell National Rural Transportation Study Center at the University of Arkansas.

CASE DESCRIPTION

Overview of Rail Transit System Security

Amtrak's Northeast Corridor (NEC) runs from Washington to Boston, sharing its right-of-way in New Jersey with both an active transit system (NJ Transit) and freight operations in a few locations. According to Greenberg et al. (2011b) the NEC is one of the most heavily traveled passenger rail segments in the United States, which could make it a potential target for terrorists. In addition, recent events, including Hurricane Sandy, have demonstrated the capability of natural disasters to cause significant disruptions in transit and transportation systems in the Northeast Corridor (Levin, 2012).

The Transportation Security Administration (TSA) is the federal agency involved in enhancing the security of mass transportation systems through enhancing the protection, response and recovery from man-made and naturally occurring hazards (Transportation Security Administration, 2012). Large transit systems may also employ their own police forces, as is the case with New Jersey Transit and Amtrak. These agencies are supported at the state level with offices of homeland security, emergency management, and departments of transportations. In addition, municipal or county police forces, emergency response agencies, and others work together to help secure the rail system. While joint training exercises are conducted that include federal, state and local agencies working together to respond to an emergency, there is a need for planning tools that can help to provide realistic estimates of consequences and impacts of various hazard scenarios. Integrated models can help decision-makers and planners to understand how to build more resilience into systems by allowing them to run numerous iterations of possible scenarios to see how their systems respond.

Demonstrated Need for a Planning Support Tool for Inland Waterway Disruption

Major disruptions to the waterways can be caused by terrorist events, natural disasters and degraded infrastructure. Recent examples include low-water conditions from a drought in late 2012 and flooding in the spring of 2013, both of which can cause significant impacts to commercial shipping operations along the waterway (Davey, 2013; Schwartz, 2012). As discussed in Campo et al. (2013), the responses to river closures have varied based on the preferences of shippers, carriers, and commodities shipped. Response strategies have included rerouting cargo, mooring barges in areas of refuge, and other strategies that could potentially create risks of barge groundings or break away barges.

In order to address system recovery and help manage waterway traffic after significant disruptive events, the USCG calls upon the Marine Transportation System Recovery Unit (MTSRU). The MTSRU is charged with responding to and subsequently resuming traffic along a waterway in order to minimize disruptions for commercial shipping, utilizing a system that is based on cooperation and co-ordination of multiple stakeholders within an area of responsibility (United States Coast Guard, 2008). Under this process, cargo prioritization and decisions are based on a series of predetermined priorities focused on cargoes critical to disaster response and basic services (United States Coast Guard, 2008). For example, priority movements can range from road salt in the winter to the provision of oil and gas products.

The decision support tool being developed seeks to further inform the process of prioritization by:

- understanding the value of the cargo at risk of being stranded,
- understanding critical national needs,
- considering the potential economic loss to shippers.

Looking at all of these factors together allows decision makers to maximize the value of the cargo recovered from the water, or minimize the risk presented by potential stranded hazardous cargo along the waterway.

Demonstrated Need for a Model for Predicting Risk and Economic Impacts of a Terrorist Attack or Accident on the Northeast Rail Corridor

The importance of the rail system, and in particular the heavily used Northeast Corridor, is discussed in detail in Greenberg et al. (2013), Greenberg et al. (2011a), and Greenberg et al. (2011b). The primary purpose for the development of the model was to generate a prototype tool that could allow stakeholders to simulate impacts of a terrorist or other disruptive event and run scenarios for those events in a coordinated fashion using operational, environmental, and economic models. The potential to model cascading impacts is an important feature, for example immediate lost sales in neighboring businesses or potential wages lost. More severe events could pose longer-term impacts, disabling the region's transportation system for months. Such an event could also lead to prolonged economic consequences cascading down the rail corridor and spreading out into the surrounding communities and larger region. (Greenberg et al., 2011a; Greenberg et al., 2011b; Greenberg et al., 2013)

The security of the transit system is largely dependent on a broad group of stakeholders. As a result, the model developed for this project seeks to inform a broad group of decision-makers with a risk-based perspective of economic, environmental and operations impacts. These impacts will be of different value for each agency, and as a result, these models require close cooperation with the user community to determine the data needs, the capabilities and processes for collecting the data and the format and use of the outputs of the model.

The cases described below were undertaken between 2010 and 2012. We will discuss each case separately in order to illustrate the unique characteristics of each transportations system. We will then draw comparisons between the two in order to illustrate more general findings for transportation security modeling.

Challenges in Collecting Inland Waterway Transport Data

The Supporting Secure and Resilient Inland Waterways (SSRIW) project seeks to develop a Web-based prototype tool to provide timely knowledge and awareness of alternatives available to offload critical barge cargo in the event of a catastrophic disaster. (see Table 1)

Some data and limitations are discussed in Campo et al. (2013) where a detailed discussion of data collection regarding terminal and waterway infrastructure attributes is presented. The decision support system is designed to include the waterway, rail and terminal resources for the transport system. This is a purposefully limited view of the system for prototype development, as it does not include the highway, labor or other supporting resources and infrastructure that would be required to fully operate the system in the event of an emergency.

Waterway Statistics Data Availability and Challenges

As discussed in Campo et al. (2013), waterway traffic statistics are kept by the USACE, as they are obtained by monitoring the throughput at lock locations and docks. Waterway traffic statistics are usually aggregated; detailed statistics for dock-to-dock flows are available for research and other uses within the Army Corps under the auspices of other federal agencies because of the sensitive business nature of the data. The research team was only able to view a small portion of the available data for validating assumptions for cargo flows and commodities through a region. Therefore, it was imperative for the team to develop scenarios that could account for potential variability in the traffic on the waterway, and allow users to edit such traffic based on their access to sensitive information.

Table 1. Data needs and availability for the supporting secure and resilient inland waterways model

Supporting Secure and Resilient Inland Waterways		
Data Group	**Publicly Available**	**Not Publicly Available**
Waterways	• Commodity Tonnage • Lock locations • Aggregate traffic statistics	• Barge speed and travel distances • Dock-to-dock travel statistics
Terminals	• Physical characteristics and locations • Material handling equipment available	• Response planning and contract agreements for business continuity purposes • Potential to use material handling equipment for other non-specified purposes
Rail	• Physical characteristics and locations	• Private routing and operations planning • Response planning and contract agreements for business continuity purposes

Source: Authors

Terminal Capability Data Availability and Challenges

As discussed in Campo et al. (2013), the primary source of data used to ascertain terminal characteristics was the "Port and Waterway Facilities" data published by the USACE Navigation Data Center. This data was subsequently reconciled against several other federal data sets and aerial imagery to validate the attributes captured in the disparate sources. Indeed, many data sets were gathered to administer programs in response to federal programs. For example, the USCG, USACE, Internal Revenue Service, Customs and Border Patrol, and other agencies each collect different types of data on terminal facilities (McDonald, 2012). The team also reviewed the description of infrastructure, material handling equipment, and storage equipment by cross-referencing terminal data and aerial imagery. This analysis resulted in the researchers having the capability to determine the commodities handled at each facility; however it was also time consuming.

While the data collected for this exercise was a good start for developing a prototype, the researchers recognize that the only true way to determine the capacity of the terminal is to work on estimates with the owners who have the operational knowledge to determine the capabilities of their facilities (Campo et al., 2013). This data collection process would be tremendously time consuming to undertake, unless done gradually as a part of the research.

Freight Rail Data Availability and Challenges

The team leveraged data from Oak Ridge National Laboratory (ORNL) to determine the capacity of the rail network that receives offloaded freight from the waterways, and to determine potential alternative routes (Southworth et al., 2007). However, many data sets were gathered from both public and private programs also, which had to be reconciled against the network. This reconciliation required the CTSSR team to update the network capabilities based upon transportation improvements, facility closures, and other changes in the physical environment that had occurred in the study region, in conjunction with the reconciliation of the port terminal capabilities. The scope of this project did not allow the researchers to develop a full intermodal network for the entire country, which would have required the aforementioned reconciliation and data collection processes on a much larger scale. Proving enough value to undertake the investment in such a task can be a significant hurdle in a constrained fiscal environment.

Even if such reconciliation were to take place, the rail infrastructure is privately funded and operated by railroads. Those organizations would need to be deeply involved with any routing of trains or other necessary measures required in responding to the demand to remove cargo from the waterway. In addition, Campo et al.

(2013) detailed a series of other constraints including the availability of personnel, equipment, insurance coverage, and other considerations for waterway stakeholders to consider.

Discussion

The decision support tool developed by CTSSR was created to assist waterway stakeholders in planning for catastrophic failures of the waterways due to manmade or natural events. Data needs included:

1. Detailed operating characteristics of rail and port terminal infrastructure
2. Estimates of cargo movement along the waterway

The primary difficulty in collecting the data required for the decision support system was the assimilation of data from multiple data sources to create a more cohesive data set representing the physical infrastructure along the waterway system. The process was time consuming, and even after reconciling several different data sets, the researchers realized the system user would ultimately need to be able to define the capability of the system. Similarly, the cargo movements along the inland waterway can vary based on geography, season, market conditions, navigation conditions, and other variables identified by the researchers. Therefore, while the researchers have developed test scenarios based on their understanding of the infrastructure and typical operating conditions, the tool was also designed to allow the user the capability to input and model their preferred characteristics.

Other data simply cannot be accounted for without undertaking a detailed interview and stakeholder engagement process. Private corporations must consider the competitive nature of their information, and therefore must be careful when sharing such information. The development of the Area Maritime Security Committees and other groups allow for the secure discussion that information during the planning process, in addition to any model outputs that have not otherwise considered arrangements regarding labor agreements, pre-existing business continuity planning, or other competitive strategies that could affect decision making.

Challenges in Collecting Rail Transit System Security Data

The Rail Security Model is discussed in detail in other articles prepared by the authors, referenced herein for the benefit of the reader who wishes to understand the technical aspects in more detail (Greenberg et al., 2011a; Greenberg et al., 2011b; Greenberg et al., 2013). In summation, the Rail Security Model is a compilation of three different prototype models that, together, estimate the operational, public health, and economic impacts of an industrial accident along a railway corridor in Northern New Jersey. The operational model, funded by DHS through NTSCOE, is an industrial systems model built with ARENA software that simulates transit operations along a rail corridor in the vicinity of a critical hub station. The CTSSR team examined how a perturbation of the operations affected passenger flows and train movements along the rail lines and in the station, including congestion. The second model, funded by the U.S. Department of Defense (DOD), examined the potential health impacts of a contaminant plume released from a leaking freight train car on a hub station and the surrounding area. Combining the plume model with the industrial systems model yielded estimates of deaths, injuries, service disruptions, physical damage to assets, and environmental effects concentrated on the rail system. The third model, also supported by DOD, estimated the economic impacts from a failure of the transportation system to deliver people and products to their destinations; including the monetary costs of deaths, injuries, and ecological impacts. The econometric model simulated the impact on the New Jersey economy. (Greenberg et al., 2011a; Greenberg et al., 2011b; Greenberg et al., 2013) (see Table 2)

In developing and assembling the aforementioned models, the research team faced a daunting challenge in collecting a variety of different data from multiple sources. The industrial systems model was built by obtaining data from NJ Transit, Amtrak, and local and state experts. The plume scenario models require making assumptions about amounts of hazardous materials and meteorological conditions, and merging them with data collected to build the first model. The economic model also relies on certain publicly available data based on the United States Census and other federal sources.

Table 2. Data needs and availability for the rail security model

Rail Security Model Data		
Group	**Available**	**Not Available**
Rail Operations	• Schedule • Passengers per train • Number of trains and cars available at usual times	• Attributes of passengers • On-time performance and cause characteristics • Ability to use other assets for response (e.g. light rail, freight rail) • Location of other responding rail assets inventory
Plume	• Model capacity • Concentration • Terrain • Prevailing winds	• Capacity to monitor status and toxins at stations • Capacity to shelter or evacuate • Capacity to bring emergency vehicles to station and evacuate injured
Economic	• Model capacity • Regional employment	• Counts of individuals in vicinity at specific times • Damage function for exposure • Cost of prevention and resilience solutions • Behavior of reasonable businesses over the short and long term

Source: Authors

Rail Data Availability and Challenges

While there is publicly available data about major disruptions along rail lines, there may be limitations to the amount of information that can be made available based on the timing, financial resources and regulations regarding the dissemination of data to various entities. For example, the transit agency was not able to provide the research team with certain on-time performance metrics for the system (Greenberg et al., 2013). Therefore, the researchers made a set of assumptions about waiting time, boarding, and other operations based on actual data and conversations with operators.

Data limitations can also result from limited resources available for modeling. Given the limited financial resources for this project, it was not feasible to build the entire transit system in the study area. Therefore, the model cannot include impacts to the entire rail, light rail, bus and road infrastructure. This limited the research team's capability to fully identify the cascading effects (e.g., road congestion) likely to occur in both primary and tertiary transport networks being studied (Greenberg et al., 2013)

The team also did not have access to recent data about the attributes of passengers on the NEC, and therefore impacts to those individuals are not accounted for in the model, which is an issue because they are relatively affluent and limited work schedule flexibility could result in significant lost wages. Additionally, the team was unable to ascertain the capacity of other rail rights of way or other rail assets to assume operations during or after an incident to mitigate any potential delays caused by damaged infrastructure. These items are critical to developing a fuller picture for this analysis in the future.

Plume Model Data Availability and Challenges

Data for air quality is available through climatic data sources. However, there are a number of detailed attributes that could be used to further refine the flow of toxins given a release into an open environment. Several dozen air dispersion models are available. SCIPUFF (Second-Order Closure Integrated Puff) was used in this model, and it can describe time-varying three-dimensional concentration profiles of plumes, and predict both the average concentration and the concentration variance out to regional scales. (Greenberg et al., 2013)

In order to determine the impacts of such an event, the team utilized information from the United States Census Bureau to define the populations that could be affected by the modeling scenarios. However, knowing the number of people residing in the affected area does not fully capture the impact of the event. For example, it is also important to understand the number of people on platforms and in surrounding areas that are not permanent residents of the area. In addition, understanding their behaviors during an event could play a critical role in understanding their susceptibility for exposure to an industrial accident. These are factors for which the researchers had to make assumptions.

In addition to estimating the response and behavior of passengers or residents directly affected by an incident, analyzing the adjacent uses and human activities is also critically important for planning. For example, there is a hospital and there are several schools within ½ mile of the station in the model. In order to avoid double-counting children and school employees, they are not counted in the impacts of the event, nor are the people passing through the area using other modes of transport, or potential attendees at entertainment venues in the area. This likely resulted in a very conservative estimate during our modeling. Another piece of data concerned the availability and capability of individuals to shelter in place, and the capacity of those shelters, which was not defined by any of our clients or interviewees. Such information could play a critical role in both planning and response to a hazardous event.

Economic Data Availability and Challenges

The economic model is built from publically available data. However, many assumptions were required from the project team, including a scope of the costs to be considered for the model. Data and resources were not available to fully analyze the complete economic impact of such a major catastrophic event, which include costs associated with the loss of key employees or a stigma effect that could cause relocation out of the area. These effects have been previously observed after the July 2005 London underground bombing (Prager et al., 2011).

Discussion

The researchers developed a prototype model that consisted of three separate but coordinated modeling approaches to determine the operational, public health, and economic impacts of an industrial accident along a heavily populated and traveled rail corridor. Data needs included:

1. Detailed characteristics of transit stations and rail operations,
2. Chemical, environmental, and built environment constraints for plume modeling,
3. Economic estimates to determine impacts of disruptions.

Several difficulties were encountered by the researchers, including the data requirements in terms of specificity and timeliness. The researchers were able to overcome these challenges by utilizing simulation software that allowed for assumption testing, ultimately demonstrating the ability to reproduce undisturbed rail operations (Greenberg et al., 2011a). However, the choice of this modeling approach could also represent a challenge for implementation and continued maintenance by users or clients. While ARENA is a standard industrial systems model, these simulations cannot be done by a novice. A similar challenge was experienced in the selection of the air pollution model, which is a widely applied simulation method that also requires a skilled user. The number of potential chemical agents, environmental variables, and other inputs for the plume model require its users and analysts to define the problem with realistic boundary conditions. The econometric model has similar challenges with regard to the volume of data needed and requisite user skills. In the absence of data for costs, population impacts, human behaviors, and other variables, the research team and the accuracy of the economic model becomes reliant upon the experience and technical expertise of the users.

In the absence of some key data, the model developed for rail security must balance the desire to base results on the best theory and data with the goal of maximizing usefulness to the defender community that will use them for pre-emptive security and transportation resilience planning. It becomes a challenge to avoid making the results and the models themselves too complex to be useful (Greenberg et al., 2011b). While the three models do not present a complete portrait of the impacts, they can be used as a template for others, and help provide better decision making for users. The model template can also allow the user group to focus on the collection of more and better data in the future to refine analyses and enhance capabilities for risk based decision making.

Technological Concerns: User Limitations and Model Integration

Concerns related to technologies were related to user capabilities and the volume of data required to implement certain technologies. User capabilities play a critical role in the development of both models. The model developers and users must be able to conceptualize and understand the data needs and volume of data required when proposing certain methods for model development. These methods can determine how much time is required. In both cases, after realizing the amount of data required to develop specific constraints, researchers focused on creating cases that reasonably estimated real-life situations and allowed the models to be flexible enough to allow users to enter their own data, and test their own assumptions. While allowing users to test their own assumptions through scenario analyses provides a critical capability for mitigating the cost of definitive data, it assumes that the users have the requisite skill sets and capabilities to generate reasonable assumptions. In the case of the rail security model, Greenberg et al. (2013) suggest that models could require masters-level experts in systems engineering and atmospheric chemistry, among other disciplines.

The volume of data needed to properly utilize certain methods can ultimately constrain the efficacy of a modeling or decision tool. It is important to understand the speed at which decisions must be made in order to appropriately develop data needs and requirements that will be calculable within the time frame for decision making. For the inland waterways planning support tool, the team is developing a Web-based platform that is intended to provide on-site support for planning and decision making during response exercises and meetings. As a result, the amount of calculations is limited to those that can be performed in a relatively short period of time. In comparison, the rail security model is intended as a planning model that can be run at any time, i.e. not tied to particular operations or projects. The time it takes to run of the model is therefore less critical. The model could be built on three different platforms and require the time of experts needed to update and apply the model to given circumstances.

Management and Organizational Concerns: Data Sharing and Program Support

Many of the federal sources of data are produced by specific agencies for specific programs; however, they may all be recording data on a common asset. This results in a manual collection, reconciliation, and aggregation of data, in some cases, to obtain a representative set of characteristics for a particular entity such as a port terminal or segment of rail line. In addition, it can cause confusion among stakeholders as to who holds the authoritative representation of a data set. There are currently initiatives underway to improve these situations, such as the Federal Industry Logistics Standard initiative; these additional efforts could yield increased productivity for security stakeholders along with value delivered to public and private sector participants utilizing the data for business or operational purposes (McDonald, 2012).

The organizational capabilities of security organizations are a management concern in addition to a technological concern. As modeling technologies advance, or as threats changes, different skill sets may be required within an organization to accurately assess threats and work with stakeholders to develop credible analyses and assumptions. For example, further development of the Web-based decision support system for the inland waterways project could potentially require in-house Web development and geographic information systems specialists. The high-level expertise needs for the rail security model have also been discussed. Agencies and other stakeholders must continue to analyze the skill sets available within their organizations to ensure that they are capable of assessing security threats and analyzing those threats as they arise.

The construction of detailed decision making models and simulation tools can be highly informative and helpful to the security stakeholder group that is the intended audience. However, building these models using currently disconnected public data files could result in a form that creates a security concern or could be of value to a potential actor.

CURRENT CHALLENGES FACING THE ORGANIZATION

The DHS, along with other federal, state and local agencies, is consistently faced with changing terrorist threats and events. One of the more complex situations is cyber security, a point of vulnerability for any computer-based model that is used on a system with Internet connectivity. These threats should be incorporated into risk models. Another challenge for the security community is not necessarily the threat of terrorism but the threats that natural hazards and climate change may pose to the surface and maritime transportation systems in the United States. These "all hazard" approaches require sophisticated and through modeling tools to be able to both estimate and provide defensible approaches for funding the homeland security enterprise.

The sharing of data within and between federal, state and local entities is currently undergoing significant changes. Each level of government has realized that in order to better serve their constituents, data sharing will become more necessary. This is also occurring between public and private sector entities. The use of data "exchanges" is an emerging practice between the public and private domain. For example, the maritime exchanges in some domestic ports are independent parties that offer data for system management to be utilized by all parties. The entities publish their data to the exchange domain, where it is shared among all stakeholders.

Resources and funding are also an issue for federal, state and local agencies charged with planning for and responding to catastrophic events. Valuable, detailed modeling approaches can be expensive and time consuming. The models described in this chapter seek to respond to specific national needs, yet can remain unused until a specific programmatic process is followed to officially implement any of the proposed solutions through a program or legislation. Several agencies that supported the development of the rail security model indicated that the onerous data requirements could be cost prohibitive for their agency alone to bear (Greenberg et al., 2013). It is imperative to share these options with clients up front in order to assure that the end result of any modeling approach truly meets the needs and critical decision points for the agency stakeholders.

SOLUTIONS AND RECOMMENDATIONS

Given the challenges above, we offer several recommendations to allow the homeland security community to develop credible data for analyses in a more efficient and effective matter. We have discussed specific data sets to illustrate data challenges and offer recommendations for responding to data challenges, including:

1. Set data standards across agencies and invest in their continued collection and analysis to enhance value and communication with other stakeholder groups. In particular, the development of authoritative data sources and indices to be utilized by other agencies for common identification could be helpful in expediting communication between agencies, in addition to allowing users to easily cross-reference data sets.
2. Data sharing and communication is critical to the success of modeling. An example of such collaboration occurs in Area Maritime Security Committees, where private business information can be understood through exercises and user meetings with other port stakeholders. In other cases, users have developed exchanges between public and private sector entities that allow an independent third party to receive and hold data, mitigating some concerns of competitive advantage or confidentiality. While it is not imperative that all security stakeholder entities for a given system share data on an ongoing basis, there is potential to better collaborate and plan or manage emergency events.
3. In the presence of uncertain data, it is helpful to provide tools that allow users to develop reasonable sets of scenarios and assumptions to inform decision-making. However, the methods used can sometimes require a significant amount of data and technical expertise to execute. Researchers and practitioners should carefully consider the appropriateness of modeling choices based on data requirements and the potential restrictions on security data in particular because of its inherently sensitive nature.
4. Under certain circumstances, it may be risky or detrimental to use detailed and accurate data, as the results of such analyses could be used to inform potential adversarial actors. Researchers and practitioners must carefully consider how the results of their analyses might be used to defeat security measures before undertaking detailed analyses.

Developing relationships with agencies, users, and data stewards will be necessary in considering and addressing the recommendations. Engagement by these stakeholders during the design of any research or analysis can help to mitigate concerns about data confidentiality, the potential to provide intelligence to adversaries, the capabilities of the client to operate and maintain resulting products or methods, and the need to develop relationships with other agencies or stakeholders responsible for critical portions of data. A more considered approach to data standardization, sharing, and dissemination could be critical to the development of analyses that have increased credibility among the broad stakeholder groups responsible for securing the nation's infrastructure.

DISCLAIMER

This research was supported by the United States Department of Homeland Security, Science and Technology Directorate, University Programs, under Grant Award Number 2008-ST-061-TS007 and by the Construction Engineering Research Laboratory of the U.S. Department of Defense, under Project #10 01 F; Grant # W91232T-10-1-001 P00002. The opinions, findings, conclusion and recommendations expressed herein are those of the authors and do not necessarily represent the views of the Department of Homeland Security or U.S. Department of Defense.

REFERENCES

Associated Press. (2012, January). *Ship carrying rocket parts hits Kentucky bridge.* Retrieved May 10, 2013, from, http://usatoday30.usatoday.com/news/nation/story/2012-01-27/kentucky-bridge-collapse/52813592/1

Campo, M., Mayer, H., & Rovito, J. (2012). Supporting secure and resilient inland waterways: Decision framework for evaluating offloading capabilities at terminals during catastrophic waterway closures. *Transportation Research Record: Journal of the Transportation Research Board, 2273*(1), 10–17. doi:10.3141/2273-02

Davey, M. (2013, April). In Midwest, drought gives way to flood. *New York Times.* Retrieved May 10, 2013, from http://www.nytimes.com/2013/04/26/us/in-midwest-drought-abruptly-gives-way-to-flood.html?_r=0

Federal Emergency Management Agency. (2013). *National exercise program.* Retrieved May 10, 2013 from, http://www.fema.gov/national-exercise-program

Federal Railroad Administration. (2013). *FRA office of safety analysis web site.* Retrieved May 10, 2013, from http://safetydata.fra.dot.gov/OfficeofSafety/default.aspx

Greenberg, M. R., Altiok, T., Fefferman, N., Georgopoulos, P., Lacy, C., & Lahr, M. ... Roberts, F. S. (2011b). A set of blended risk-based decision support tools for protecting passenger rail-centered transit corridors against cascading impacts of terrorist attacks. In *Proceedings of the US Department of Homeland Security Science Conference–Fifth Annual University Network Summit*. Washington, DC: US Government.

Greenberg, M. R., Lioy, P., Ozbas, B., Mantell, N., Isukapalli, S., & Lahr, M. et al. (2013, June). Passenger rail security, planning, and resilience: Application of network, plume, and economic simulation models as decision support tools. *Risk Analysis*. doi:10.1111/risa.12073 PMID:23718133

Greenberg, M. R., Lowrie, K., Mayer, H., & Altiok, T. (2011a). Risk-based decision support tools: Protecting rail-centered transit corridors from cascading effects. *Risk Analysis, 31*(12), 1849–1858. doi:10.1111/j.1539-6924.2011.01627.x PMID:21564145

Levin, A. (2012, December). *NJ transit had $400 million in Hurricane Sandy damage*. Retrieved May 10, 2013, from,http://www.bloomberg.com/news/2012-12-06/nj-transit-had-400-million-in-hurricane-sandy-damage.html

McDonald, D. (2012, June). *Federal industry logistics standardization: Supporting a federal navigation information framework and integration*. Paper presented at Diagnosing the Marine Transportation System: Measuring Performance and Targeting Improvement. Washington, DC.

Prager, F., Beeler, Asay G., Lee, B., & von Winterfeldt, D. (2011). Exploring reductions in London underground passenger journeys following the July 2005 bombings. *Risk Analysis, 31*(5), 773–786. doi:10.1111/j.1539-6924.2010.01555.x PMID:21231940

Schwartz, J. (2012, November). After drought, reducing water flow could hurt Mississippi River transport. *New York Times*. Retrieved May 10, 2013, from http://www.nytimes.com/2012/11/27/us/hit-by-drought-mississippi-river-may-face-more-challenges.html

Southworth, F., Peterson, B., & Lambert, B. (2007). Development of a regional routing model for strategic waterway analysis. *Transportation Research Record: Journal of the Transportation Research Board, 1993*, 109–116. doi:10.3141/1993-15

Transportation Security Administration. (2012). *Mass transit*. Retrieved May 10, 2013 from, http://www.tsa.gov/stakeholders/mass-transit

United States Army Corps of Engineers. (2012). *Civil works navigation.* Retrieved May 10, 2013, from, http://www.usace.army.mil/Missions/CivilWorks/Navigation.aspx

United States Coast Guard. (2008). *Commandant instruction 16000.28.2008.* Retrieved May 10, 2013, from http://www.uscg.mil/directives/ci/16000-16999/CI_16000_28.pdf

United States Department of Homeland Security. (2007a). *Transportation systems: Critical infrastructure and key resources sector-specific plan as input to the national infrastructure protection plan.* Retrieved May 10, 2013 from http://www.dhs.gov/xlibrary/assets/nipp_snapshot_transportation.pdf

United States Department of Homeland Security. (2007b). *Science & technology directorate centers of excellence.* Retrieved May 10, 2013, from http://www.dhs.gov/st-centers-excellence

United States Department of Homeland Security. (2012). *USCG missions: Maritime security.* Retrieved May 10, 2013, from http://www.uscg.mil/top/missions/MaritimeSecurity.asp

United States Government Accountability Office. (2012, September 11). *Maritime security: Progress and challenges 10 years after the maritime transportation security act, statement of Stephen L. Caldwell, director homeland security and justice* (Report GAO-12-1009T). Retrieved May 10, 2013 from, http://www.gao.gov/assets/650/647999.pdf

KEY TERMS AND DEFINITIONS

AMSC: Area Maritime Security Committee.
ARENA: Specialized software that simulates transit operations.
CTTSSR: Center for Transportation Safety, Security, and Risk.
DHS: Department of Homeland Security.
DOD: Department of Defense.
MTSRU: Marine Transportation System Recovery Unit.
NTSCOE: National Transportation Security Center of Excellence.
ORNL: Oak Ridge National Laboratory.
SCIPUFF: Second-Oder Closure Integrated Puff.
SSRIW: Supporting Secure and resilient Inland Waterways.
TSA: Transportation Security Administration.
USACE: United States Army Corp of Engineers.
USCG: United States Coast Guard.

Chapter 2
The Center for Secure and Resilient Maritime Commerce:
A DHS National Center of Excellence in Maritime Security

Julie Pullen
Stevens Institute of Technology, USA

Michael Bruno
Stevens Institute of Technology, USA

EXECUTIVE SUMMARY

The DHS National Center of Excellence in Maritime Security's (CSR) Maritime Domain Awareness (MDA) work develops and applies emerging technologies in support of layered surveillance. The layers include satellite-based wide area views, HF Radar systems providing over-the horizon situational awareness, and near-shore and harbor sensing utilizing underwater acoustic technologies. Integration of these systems accomplishes vessel detection, classification, identification, and tracking. Applications for end-users including U.S. Coast Guard (USCG) and Customs and Border Protection (CBP) have demonstrated the delivery of actionable information in operationally relevant settings. The Center won the DHS S&T impact award two years in a row for its role in providing vital data during the US Airways plane landing on the Hudson River and during the Deepwater Horizon oil spill. Furthermore, research in port resiliency has yielded a port disruption planning tool, the Port Mapper, that assisted government leadership during the closure of the Port of NY/NJ by Hurricane Sandy. Work at the Center is focused on delivering MDA data streams from emerging and advanced technologies into the hands of the operators in ways that are compatible with command decision support systems.

DOI: 10.4018/978-1-4666-5946-9.ch002

INTRODUCTION

Post-9/11, securing our seaports while at the same time maintaining a flow of commerce has been a top priority for the Department of Homeland Security. For example, the Maritime Transportation Security Act implemented in 2004 stipulates risk-based port security measures and establishes Area Maritime Security Committees as coordinating bodies.

The Centers of Excellence provide DHS with the mechanism and capability to reach into the knowledge base of academia in specific areas of urgent need for science and technology development. The maritime domain is an area where advanced technologies can positively impact core DHS mission areas including maritime safety and security, search and rescue, contraband and migrant smuggling, terrorist activity, and illegal fishing interdiction. The Center for Secure and Resilient Maritime Commerce (CSR) was designed to rapidly develop, prototype and transfer new technologies so they can more quickly add value in assuring a safe, secure, and resilient Marine Transportation System (MTS).

The CSR brings together a unique group of academic institutions and public and private partners that is led by Stevens Institute of Technology, Hoboken, New Jersey. Besides Stevens Institute, the partnership includes the following academic institutions: Rutgers University, University of Miami, University of Puerto Rico, Massachusetts Institute of Technology, and Monmouth University. The non-university partners in the CSR include the Port Authority of New York and New Jersey, the Mattingley Group, the Pacific Basin Development Council, and Nansen Environmental Remote Sensing Center.

The CSR strategy to achieve its mission centers on the creation and sustainment of a truly collaborative research and education enterprise that draws on the strengths of each partner, as well as their leveraged relevant DHS and non-DHS research activities. We believe that these unique attributes – collaborative; integrated research & education; and leveraged relationships with Federal, State, local government, and industry stakeholders – position the CSR for continued long-term success and impact.

The CSR research activities are built around two primary realms:

1. Maritime Domain Awareness (MDA): the development of sensor technologies, analysis tools, and decision aides that can enable an effective understanding of anything associated with the Maritime Domain that could impact the security, safety, economy, or environment of the United States.
2. MTS Resiliency: the development of models, tools, and decision aides that can assist policy makers and decision-makers responsible for making organizational changes and resource allocations to enhance resiliency in our nation's MTS.

Figure 1. Spiral development process for CSR research and development

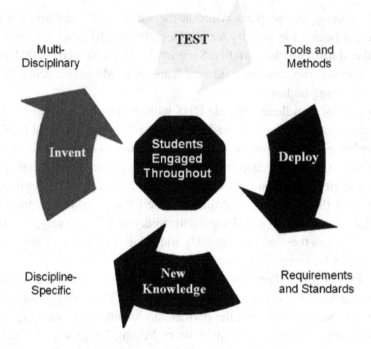

Through the first five years of operation, the CSR efforts have been guided by a Spiral Development approach to solving the complex issues facing the MTS. This approach, illustrated in Figure 1, has required that the individual research projects – in satellite, radar, and underwater acoustics sensors - achieve the necessary fidelity to provide improved understanding and capabilities, as well as technology products that can be examined via field experiments in the real-world environment. These activities have led to the transitioning of new technologies to beneficial use in the field by the US Coast Guard, US Navy, NOAA, National Geospatial-Intelligence Agency (NGA), and the City of New York, among others. They have resulted in the CSR being awarded the DHS S&T Impact Award in two of its first three years of existence.

The CSR researchers and educators are committed to ensuring that our new knowledge, technology products, tools, and educational programs are responsive to the wide range of stakeholders that we serve. Success in this endeavor requires that we:

- Partner with the end users to understand their needs;
- Partner with industry, as well as government and university laboratories, to understand technology gaps and to work toward filling those gaps.

Successful transitioning of Intellectual Property begins with reaching out to the end user, understanding their needs, and building the trust necessary to enable the "productization" of a prototype device, model, tool, or algorithm. It was this sort of outreach in fact that led to the adoption of CSR-developed technologies and algorithms by end users that include the US Coast Guard (Search and Rescue, oil spill response); Customs and Border Protection (illicit vessel detection and tracking); the US Navy (Naval Undersea Warfare Center, Swimmer Detection System); and the NGA (oil spill response).

In this chapter, we give examples that highlight the spiral development process and how partnering with the end-user and other entities have led to new technologies in the field.

BACKGROUND

The Center for Secure and Resilient Maritime Commerce (CSR), along with the University of Hawaii's National Center for Islands, Maritime, and Extreme Environments Security (CIMES), are the U.S. Department of Homeland Security's (DHS) National Center of Excellence for Maritime, Island and Extreme/Remote Environment Security (MIREES). Established in 2008, the Center supports DHS efforts to provide for the safe and secure use of our nation's maritime domain (including island and extreme environments and inland waterways), and a resilient MTS, through advancement of the relevant sciences and development of the new workforce.

Maritime Domain Awareness

The Maritime Domain is defined by the International Maritime Organization as "all areas and things of, on, under, relating to, adjacent to, or bordering on a sea, ocean, or other navigable waterway, including all maritime-related activities, infrastructure, people, cargo, and vessels and other conveyances." The MDA projects examine the basic science issues and emerging technologies to support the use of a layered approach to the problem. The layers include satellite-based wide area surveillance; HF Radar systems providing over-the horizon surveillance; and nearshore and harbor surveillance systems centered on underwater acoustic technologies. Integration of these systems is aimed at achieving vessel detection, classification, identification, and tracking. The new knowledge and new and improved technologies and algorithms developed under this research area are projected to achieve real-time, all-weather, day/night, multi-layer maritime surveillance from the open ocean to estuaries, harbors and inland waterways, all at high-resolution. We have conducted targeted projects with DHS stakeholders (including USCG and CBP) and demonstrated the ways our technologies could be used singly and in conjunction with each other to enhance MDA in operational settings.

The University of Miami's Center for Southeastern Tropical Advanced Remote Sensing (CSTARS) leads the space-base applications and is developing new understanding and new processes for receiving and analyzing large maritime area data from multi-satellite and multi-frequency sensors such as Synthetic Aperture Radar (SAR) and electro-optical (EO) sensors. Algorithms continue to be developed to employ the data to detect vessels and wakes, including small ships, in harbors, inland waterways, the coastal ocean and the high seas. Algorithms are also being developed to integrate this vessel detection information with ground-based systems such as Automatic Identification System (AIS), and the other MDA layers (Bruno et al., 2011).

Rutgers University's High-Frequency Surface Wave Radar (HF Radar) team is developing robust detection algorithms that recognize ship-associated HF Radar signals above the background noise (e.g., surface waves). Algorithms continue to be developed to support vessel detection and tracking capabilities using compact HF Radars, demonstrating that ships, including small ships, can be detected and tracked by multi-static HF Radar in a multi-ship environment, while simultaneously mapping ocean currents. This has been demonstrated for Puerto Rico (in collaboration with UPRM) (Corredor et al., 2011), and NY/NJ harbor—with real-time detection attained (Roarty et al., 2011).

Stevens Institute of Technology leads the near-shore and harbor surveillance system portion of the MDA project. Much of the Stevens effort has been devoted to the development of a passive acoustic array that can provide low-cost, highly portable acoustic surveillance capability. The signal processing is based on the cross-correlation of signals received by several hydrophones (Chung et al., 2011). Originally designed for scuba diver detection, the system has been applied to measuring the acoustic signature characteristics of vessels in the heavy traffic of NY Harbor for longer deployment (Zucker et al., 2009) and for shorter experiments in San Diego, Den Helder, Netherlands, Newport, Rhode Island and Miami and Panama City, FL, among others.

MTS Resiliency

Port authorities and terminal operators are concerned with absolute throughput, but also increasingly with the flow of the cargo. Just-in-time inventory management policy by the shippers has made them focus on the reliability of the cargo delivery. Security is of utmost importance for the Department of Homeland Security, as a primary aim of the agency is to protect the homeland against any avoidable disruption. After Katrina, numerous companies began using advance sourcing technology to plan their reactions to unexpected supply chain disruptions, increased the number of their suppliers, and analyzed the cost impacts of mode capacity on different routes. Individual shippers have developed their own contingency plans. The multiple disasters that recently struck Japan illustrate how vital contingency and resiliency planning are to supply chain continuity. Moreover, Hurricane Sandy and the resulting weeklong closure of the port of NY/NJ further demonstrated the importance of resiliency in the face of disruptions caused by natural hazards. Moving from private to public stakeholders, the risk analyses and consequence management approaches become far more complex than those faced by an individual shipper (Mansouri et al., 2010). The tools developed by MIT's Center for Transportation and logistics are aimed at addressing key needs in MTS resiliency.

TOOLS AND TECHNOLOGIES FOR MDA AND RESILIENCY OF THE MTS

Issues, Controversies, Problems

"A primary challenge in the years ahead is the integrated use of these [sensors] and perhaps other sensors, as components in an operational maritime security decision-support system that can be implemented across our nation's ports, waterways and coastal regions" (Bruno, 2012). And this is not just a domestic concern. International issues such as smuggling and piracy create a series of geographical intersections in the Caribbean, western Pacific and African regions. Maritime security professionals are coming together internationally to share approaches and brainstorm solutions (Pullen, 2011). Above all, the safe and secure flow of commerce cannot be emphasized enough. And hence MTS resiliency must never be far from the focus.

The Defense Department (DOD) shares overlapping concerns in securing its naval assets overseas. And some of the technologies developed in the defense sector are candidates for use on the domestic front. However, maritime security technologies originating in DOD can be costly. Acoustic detection solutions developed for the Navy typically cost many millions of dollars and are meant to secure extensive areas of the offshore region. Also, the law enforcement culture in which DHS components function is vastly different from the military culture. This factor alone puts different constraints on the technology solutions that will find traction within the homeland security and first responder community.

Solutions and Recommendations

Our resiliency work, led by MIT's Center for Transportation and Logistics, aims to provide the modeling framework, visualization tools, and data that will enable an assessment of the present state of the U.S. MTS in terms of vulnerability, capacity, and ultimately, resilience, as well as the tools necessary for an eventual capability to design for resilience to disruptions.

A novel web-based application called the Port Mapper addresses key questions such as:

- Where could cargo move to if there were a disruption at a major US port?
- What other ports handle the same cargo types as the disrupted port?
- How far away are those ports?
- Does the US system of ports have enough capacity to handle a disruption to a major US port?
- How much additional port capacity is necessary for the US ports to handle a disruption and avoid significant delays and costs to the US economy?

Port Mapper provides end-users with the capability to visualize port locations and also to conduct real-time and scenario based disruption analysis. Port Mapper consists of two formats, a web-based visualization application and a spreadsheet database tool. Developed by CSR researchers Jim Rice and Kai Trepte of MIT Center for Transportation & Logistics (CTL), Port Mapper allows end-users to look up every U.S. port or cargo type by Standard Industrial Classification (SIC) code and locate options for rerouting of cargo in the event of port closure. Port Mapper is a decision support tool designed to assist maritime stakeholders as they develop response and resilience plans in the event of U.S. port disruptions. Utilized by U.S. Coast Guard senior leadership during Hurricane Sandy and the resultant week-long closure of the Port of NY/NJ, Port Mapper enabled the USCG to visualize options for the redirection of cargo to alternative port locations. Port Mapper is being further enhanced in direct response to the needs of end-users such as USCG, and others (e.g., Department of Transportation).

In Year 5, CSR developed a vision for the End-2-End (E2E) centerpiece project focused on Maritime Domain Awareness. CSR is developing and transitioning emerging technologies to support the use of an *integrated, layered* approach to MDA. No one technology is going to be able to meet all the demands of the end-user. Technologies will have limitations in different operating conditions or perhaps different times of day. The layers that we have evaluated and we are implementing include satellite-based wide area surveillance; High-Frequency (HF) Radar systems providing over-the-horizon surveillance of the approaches; and near-shore and harbor surveillance systems centered on underwater acoustic technologies. The key to our work is integrating the data streams from these systems together to develop more robust situational awareness – leading to surface and underwater vessel detection, classification, identification, and tracking.

CSR experiments in Miami and New York/New Jersey harbors have demonstrated the value of this layered approach. In fall 2010 we brought our three technology layers to the Port of Miami, where we detected and tracked a range of different target sizes, from jet skis to cruise ships. First by satellite, then by radar and acoustics, we were able to localize the targets through the different sensing modalities, and provide additional information about characteristics of the vessel. In NY/NJ harbor we have done this type of experiment every year and engaged our Summer Research Institute students in the design and analysis of the work (DeFares et al., 2014).

Our E2E efforts focus on the development of a fully integrated MDA system linked to decision-support systems that can be operated by the USCG, CBP and Navy. We are implementing our layered technology in two sites, NY/NJ harbor and the Caribbean/Puerto Rico, by conducting sustained real-time operations – going beyond the short-term experiments that were achieved in our earlier years. Our students do summer internships embedded with the operators at Coast Guard in their command centers and contribute to the evolution of the technologies and their adoption by the end-user community. And we demonstrate the portability of our approach by participating in relevant exercises and deploying in multiple ports throughout the country.

Based on the successful transitioning of several MDA-related CSR technologies during the first 5 years, including satellite sensor algorithms, HF Radar systems, and a passive acoustic sensor system, we are continuing our aggressive strategy to conduct field evaluations of the MDA systems, perform required systems integration, and facilitate their adoption by relevant organizations. This requires close partnership with stakeholders, including USCG, CBP Air and Marine, domestic port authorities, and industry representatives, including the MTS industry and sensor developers.

Partners

- **Satellite:** Intelligence and Defense Agencies. For example, together with the Navy and Joint Interagency Task Force – South (JIATF-S) and other groups, CSTARS is developing an automated vessel tracking system for open-ocean transit and harbor-side including AIS and satellite data as gap fillers.
- **HF Radar:** CODAR Ocean Sensors, Ocean Power Technologies, Center for Innovative Technologies, Applied Mathematics, Inc., University of Puerto Rico, and the U.S. Integrated Ocean Observing System (IOOS). For example, IOOS support has funded the acquisition, installation and maintenance of the New York/New Jersey HF Radar sensor network.

- **Underwater Acoustics:** DHS S&T Borders & Maritime Security Division and Navy Undersea Warfare Center (NUWC). For instance, through support from DHS Borders and Maritime, advanced algorithms for localization and classification of Targets of Interest are under development.

Expected Outcomes

Applications for this technology include vessel tracking and illicit vessel and underwater threat detection, classification and tracking. The range of targets includes underwater threats like scuba divers, submarines and UUVs (Unmanned Underwater Vehicles), to jet skis and small vessels that can be perceived by acoustics. USCG and CBP will have increased information and localization of vessel traffic so that they can enhance MDA and optimize the deployment of airborne assets. The impact of these technologies is already becoming manifest. Real-time multi-static vessel detections are now being generated in the segment of the HF Radar network surrounding New York Harbor and are now being delivered to the Navy's Open Mongoose data fusion engine for MDA. Current satellite work has demonstrated skill in detecting go-fast and other small vessels in the Caribbean Basin. In the Caribbean it is anticipated that illicit vessel detection will be improved by the flow of acoustic data.

Detailed Description

For the NY/NJ harbor, surveillance data from satellite, radar and acoustics will be combined to provide a basic integrated view of the approaches to the harbor and near-shore (Hudson River). We will mirror our integrated MDA capability at the Coast Guard Sector New York and national fusion centers (e.g., National Maritime Intelligence-Integration Office, NMIO). Our Caribbean test-bed is being established in Puerto Rico in the vicinity of Mona Island, between Puerto Rico and the Dominican Republic. We will build out this test-bed to provide basic actionable information to USCG, CBP and the Navy on possible illicit vessel activity. In addition, we will participate in agency exercises to demonstrate the portability of our technologies. In the out years, we will establish a fully integrated linkage to decision-support systems used by USCG, CBP and the Navy.

E2E MDA effectiveness will be established based on end-user usage statistics for applications including Search and Rescue (SAROPS) and vessel detection and tracking partially based on Coast Guard visual analytics. Our work complements the E2E efforts of our sister center, CIMES, which is focused on the Arctic environment and where the CSR radar work is also a key component. Others that we will engage include S&T Borders and Maritime for feedback and support in developing the radar and acoustics portion, and the Coast Guard Research and Development

Center who will function as a transition agent for our work. Our DHS Career Development Grant Fellowship masters' students and Summer Research Institute students will participate by working on aspects of algorithm development and data displays (DeFares et al., 2014). Through their work with CSR researchers, their knowledge of maritime technologies will contribute significantly to their employability in the maritime domain.

Transition and Intellectual Property (IP)

Our underwater acoustics demonstration last year on the border is expected to be a key input to establishing performance requirements for systems to detect small vessels. We are also in discussions with Coast Guard about requirements for acoustic detection systems. We will work with commercial partners to produce a capability for acquisition by CBP and USCG. The radar work will have a strong emphasis on tracking algorithms to make the data feeds maximally useful to decision support systems downstream who can subscribe to the data flow via Open Mongoose and the Environmental Data Server (EDS). Satellite data will be layered with the other MDA feeds to provide enhanced situational awareness.

We are continuously looking for transition opportunities using all vehicles available (e.g., CRADAs, Memoranda of Understanding, Licensing Agreements, patent disclosures, copyrights, etc.). As an example, the passive acoustic work resulted in a patent granted and licensing agreement executed. We have been working with our related university offices to obtain support needed toward transitioning existing IP. In addition, we are continuously building relationships with industry partners that have the capability to help in transitioning our research capabilities into an operational product (this includes the participation in joint solicitations, SBIRs, and STTRs).

MDA Technologies

The MDA projects examine the basic science issues and emerging technologies to support the use of a layered approach to the problem in operationally relevant settings. One of the fundamental questions we seek to answer is the limit of resolution of each of the component sensor technologies (e.g., space-based, HF Radar, and underwater acoustic); or in other words: "how small is too small?" or "how far is too far?" This issue of resolution is driven by the concern for threats associated with small surface vessels, UUVs, and divers. Ultimately, this layered surveillance capability should provide the means to enable adequate surveillance-based understanding of our waterways so that we can accurately define "the normal," with all of its variability. Only then can we accurately define and detect the "departures

Figure 2. Layered MDA for the NY/NJ Harbor showing Hudson River vessels from AIS (blue), radar (red) and acoustic-sensed bearings to targets (green lines). Video and acoustic feeds are shown in other panels. The correspondence of the green lines and red icons builds confirms that multiple modalities are seeing the targets (and they are not on AIS)

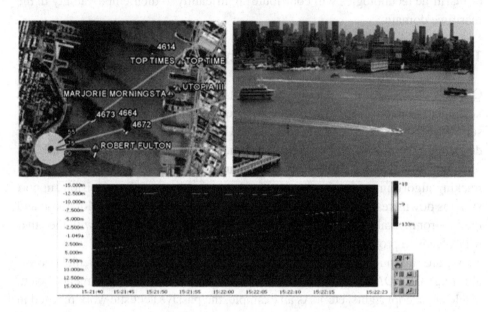

from the normal," or anomalies that can in concert with decision-support systems trigger a response. (see Figure 2)

The University of Miami's Center for Southeastern Tropical Advanced Remote Sensing (CSTARS) utilizes Synthetic Aperture Radar (SAR) images that have been collected and applied to a range of operational settings. In DeepWater Horizon, the persistent imaging provided critical information about the extent of oil coverage of the Gulf waters based on the sheen, or change in surface water properties and their reflectance due to the oil spill. Besides being awarded the DHS S&T Impact award for this work and its value to a host of government agencies involved in the spill response, CSR's satellite imagery has provided actionable information for the Coast Guard in other settings. Images of oil drilling rigs in the Caribbean are being used to monitor potential spills. And experiments with Go-Fast boat targets sponsored by CBP have demonstrated the ability to detect these vessels from space based on their wake effects, and even produce an accurate assessment of their speed.

The Rutgers shore-based HF Radar systems originally were designed to measure ocean surface currents in the coastal ocean. The first significant transition of the CSR radar work was the delivery of the real-time ocean current data to the

Environmental Data Server (EDS) so that decision support tools at the command centers could subscribe to the data feed. The primary beneficiary was the Coast Guard's Search and Rescue Optimal Planning System (SAROPS). SAROPS on the east coast preferentially uses the radar surface currents because they were found to significantly reduce the projected search area and therefore more efficiently utilize Coast Guard assets in order to save more lives more quickly.

Rutgers University's HF Radar team is developing robust detection algorithms that recognize ship-associated HF Radar signals above the background noise (e.g., surface waves). These signals were previously discarded in the ocean current measurements, but now they form the signal that is retained and processed. In collaboration with commercial partner CODAR, algorithms continue to be developed to support vessel detection and tracking capabilities so that ship trajectories can be formed. HF Radar installations are compact and can detect and track multiple ships while also mapping ocean currents. Further, Rutgers has been developing novel algorithms for improved ship position detection based on the use of multiple radar detection images. This allows the range of the coverage to be extended.

Hardware systems and software developed and tested in the CSR New York Harbor test-bed and at the Port of Miami are being transferred to the University of Puerto Rico for testing in Caribbean waters. The University of Puerto Rico at Mayagüez (UPRM) is focused on the installation and operation of HF Radar in remote areas such as the Mona Passage for the multi-use applications of ship detection and tracking, and surface current mapping. In the summer of 2012 this capability was demonstrated for the Mona Island passage, using Coast Guard assets as targets, along with other targets of opportunity. This is an important milestone as it proves that real-time detection of vessels by radar can be achieved in relatively remote environments. In a comparable installation along the Alaskan coast in the Arctic, real-time vessel detection was also demonstrated. Both of these accomplishments extend the radar vessel detection capability to diverse settings and show its versatility and robustness.

The radar vessel detection data to date reveals that every place CSR coastal radars have been deployed the systems find about 30% of vessels in the approaches to port are not transmitting on AIS. This could be because they have turned off their signal, or are not required to participate (e.g., because they are below 300 gross tons). But it represents a non-negligible portion of the traffic transiting the coastal area. As the radar vessel detection data becomes sustained (real-time) and delivered into the command centers, it is poised to contribute to the situational awareness in the maritime domain.

In the case of our ongoing effort to enable HF Radar over-the-horizon vessel detection and tracking, we recently initiated a significant partnership that can both inform the technology development (by better understanding existing Government

Off-the-Shelf capabilities) and accelerate the speed at which the technology can be fielded in an operational environment. This partnership was facilitated by DHS S&T and involves the multi-agency data sharing and information fusion effort known as Open Mongoose. Bi-static systems will also be employed, with the aim of enabling high-resolution, real-time vessel detection. Significant leveraging of existing and planned research programs and radar hardware will occur throughout, including ongoing programs with NOAA and with the State of New Jersey. We have demonstrated the use of a multi-static HF Radar system distributed along a coastal ocean region for the purpose of vessel detection - initially in a realistic environment along the approaches to NY Harbor, then to a more remote locations (Puerto Rico and Alaska), and eventually in an operational environment as a component of Open Mongoose.

Stevens Institute of Technology leads the near-shore and harbor surveillance system portion of the MDA project. Much of the Stevens effort in Years 1 through 5 was devoted to the development of a passive acoustic array that can provide low-cost, highly portable acoustic surveillance capability. The signal processing is based on the cross-correlation of signals received by several hydrophones. The system was applied to measuring the travel direction and acoustic signature characteristics of vessels in the heavy traffic of NY Harbor as well as in the Port of Miami and San Diego, where many types of vessels (from jet skis to cruise ships) are typically present.

Systems Integration and Field Test and Evaluation

Since CSR began its work, we have been demonstrating how individual MDA technologies work well by themselves (e.g., acoustics, HF Radar, and satellite surveillance) as well as combined in a layered approach (Bruno et al., 2011). However, in order to facilitate the development and implementation of a complete surveillance system, we need to examine real-world, real-time detection, classification, and tracking of maritime threats including small vessels, while also addressing the question of identifying anomalous behavior through pattern recognition and machine learning. The experiment that was performed at the Port of Miami in April, 2011 will be used as the first step toward this goal. During the Miami experiment, we tested hand-offs between the various sensor technologies, and collected a large amount of small vessel data. Similar experiments have been conducted in NY/NJ harbor during the CSR Summer Research Institutes. In our sixth year, in the context of our E2E efforts, these integration efforts are being pursued even further. Visualization of the layered feeds (radar, acoustic, satellite) occurs in Stevens' Maritime Security Laboratory and is being shown to key stakeholder Command Centers. (see Figure 3)

Feedback from these end-users will guide the development of visualization interfaces that can work alone and also feed into existing decision-support tools. Based on our experience transitioning prior data streams, end-users are reluctant to acquire

Figure 3. The Stevens Institute of Technology Maritime Security Laboratory for visualization

yet another stand-alone decision support system that does not connect with their other systems. The demands on operators' attention in the Command Centers can be extreme and the fewer systems they have to monitor, the better. At Stevens, we have a skilled and insightful team, led by Jeff Nickerson, that works on how groups make decisions and what kind of decision aides and visualizations facilitate decision-making. Stevens decision support research is investigating the impact of information visualization in facilitating the CSR's E2E objectives, which aim to use the information from the CSR's other subprojects (acoustic signals, satellite imagery, radar) as well as the past findings of our decision support research projects. Building on the cumulative findings of the previous information visualization and decision support studies, this team is conducting experiments to examine ways of displaying information, inclusive of vessel and weather and environmental data sets, as layers to better serve Coast Guard mission areas. Their investigations cover enterprise systems like the Coast Guard's WatchKeeper program, a vessel monitoring and MDA decision support tool which is a target for our data transition.

FUTURE RESEARCH DIRECTIONS

An emerging concept in sensor integration is "tipping and cueing" – or the notion that sensors can turn each other on and off, or cue each other to look in certain directions based on external input. For instance environmental conditions may be such that passive acoustics performance produces a lower range on a given day due to snapping shrimp or ice floes. In these cases the radar data might be weighted more highly or elevated in value. This type of "smart integration" that takes account of environmental conditions requires not just surveillance sensors, but weather and ocean real-time measurements and forecasts. At Stevens Institute and partner institute Rutgers University we have a long history of ocean observation. The Center for Maritime Systems at Stevens has been forecasting ocean and river conditions in the NY/NJ harbor region using a sophisticated high-resolution 3D hydrodynamic model (Bruno et al., 2006; Bruno & Blumberg, 2004; Georgas & Blumberg, 2009) for over 10 years. The New York Harbor Observing and Prediction System (NYHOPS) forecasts two days in advance key ocean parameters including water level, waves, temperature, salinity, storm surge, and currents. NYHOPS predictions were utilized by emergency responders immediately after the US Airways plane landing on the Hudson River. This particular application of operational river forecasting and observing in a crisis received a DHS S&T Impact award for CSR. It also made a huge impact before and during Hurricane Sandy.

CSR partners, Stevens Institute and Rutgers University, along with several private and government collaborators and their collective suite of 200 sensors in the NY and NJ coastal regions, provided critical water level data along with state-of-the- science storm surge forecasting to emergency responders and urban and coastal communities during Sandy. Prior to and after Hurricane Sandy made landfall, CSR and Stevens received numerous requests for data and served as a key resource for groups including U.S. Coast Guard Sector NY, New York State and New York City Office of Emergency Management, Con Edison, New York City Department of Environmental Protection, Long Beach Island, NJ, the City of Hoboken, NJ, and divisions within NOAA (National Weather Service, National Center for Environmental Prediction, National Hurricane Center, etc.). The unprecedented nature of the event was verified by in situ observations. Coastal flood elevations in New York Harbor were the highest in all ~350 years of New York City history (Orton et al., 2011). The Rutgers University team conducted real-time ocean data collection from a glider during the storm, and monitored the accuracy of various storm prediction models, all with the aim of improving our scientific understanding of this historic and destructive event.

Additionally we have been forecasting weather conditions in the NY/NJ area down to ~300 m resolution using a state-of-the-science weather model designed to account for the way that buildings modify the air circulation (Pullen et al., 2007; Holt and Pullen, 2007). The model produces highly accurate forecasts of local winds and temperatures that surpass the skill of current National Weather Service products (Meir et al., 2013). There are a variety of different security applications for ultra-high resolution coastal air-sea models (Pullen et al., 2008; Pullen et al., 2013). During the Fukushima crisis, maritime traffic was disrupted at many Japanese ports due to the concern of radiological contamination to vessels and containers. The utilization of air-sea dispersion modeling played a vital role (Pullen et al., 2013).

Figure 4. 1.33 km resolution weather prediction for the NY/NJ region. 2-m air temperature every 3 hours is shown over half a day. The heating up of the urban area, or urban heat island, is shown.

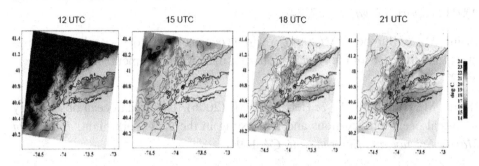

The linkage of sensors with information on the evolving conditions in the ocean and atmosphere that impact security, is a vital connection that will improve the hand-off of sensor data and facilitate tipping and cueing. This linkage will maximize the utility of multi-modal sensor arrays for MDA.

In addition, the Coast Guard is interested in linking our port resiliency tools with environmental information of ocean and weather conditions, to create a seamless planning tool. These types of synergies between data streams and capabilities are expected to proliferate as decision-makers seek more sophisticated and flexible tools.

CONCLUSION

The Center for Secure and Resilient Maritime Commerce is a DHS Center of Excellence in Maritime Security. It was competitively designated in 2008 and is led by Stevens Institute of Technology. The Center's work involves MDA tools and technologies as well as port and MTS resiliency research. Examples of transitions of technology are covered in the chapter and have been achieved with a spiral development approach that places training and education as a central component. Our continuing efforts focus on our E2E centerpiece project of getting actionable MDA data from our layered technologies into the decision support tools of end-users. The technology layers include satellite, HF radar and passive acoustics. The deployment of the technologies in operationally relevant settings in collaboration with various DHS components have allowed us to refine the data streams on the path to transition.

Future work will integrate our resiliency tools on port disruption with models predicting the environmental conditions in the ocean and atmosphere. Sensor operations will also benefit from a more explicit linkage with air/sea environmental data and forecasts to facilitate tipping and cueing between the different sensing modalities.

REFERENCES

Bruno, M. (2012). Maritime domain awareness – A call for enhanced capability. *AAPA Seaports Magazine, 27*, 34.

Bruno, M., & Blumberg, A. (2004). An urban ocean observatory – Real-time assessments and forecasts of the New York harbor marine environment. *Sea Technology, 45*, 27–32.

Bruno, M., Blumberg, A., & Herrington, T. (2006). The urban ocean observatory - Coastal ocean observations and forecasting in the New York bight. *Journal of Marine Science and Environment, C4*, 1–9.

Bruno, M., Sutin, A., Chung, K., Sedunov, A., Sedunov, N., & Salloum, H. et al. (2011). Satelli.te imaging and passive acoustics in layered approach for small boat detection and classification M*arine. Technology Society Journal, 45*(3), 77–87. doi:10.4031/MTSJ.45.3.10

Chung, K., Sutin, A., & Bruno, M. (2011). Cross-correlation method for measuring ship acoustic signatures. *Proceedings, 160th Meeting Acoustical Society of America, 11*, 1-12.

Corredor, J., Amador, A., Canals, M., Rivera, S., Capella, J., & Morell, J. et al. (2011). Optimizing and validating high-frequency radar surface current measurements in the Mona passage. *Marine Technology Society Journal, 45*(3), 49–58. doi:10.4031/MTSJ.45.3.6

Georgas, N., & Blumberg, A. (2009). *Establishing confidence in marine forecast systems: The design and skill assessment of the New York harbor observation and prediction system, version 3 (NYHOPS v3).* Paper presented at the Eleventh International Conference in Estuarine and Coastal Modeling (ECM11). Seattle, WA.

Holt, T., & Pullen, J. (2007). Urban canopy modeling of the New York City metropolitan area: A comparison and validation of single-layer and multi-layer parameterizations. *Monthly Weather Review, 135*, 1906–1930. doi:10.1175/MWR3372.1

Kessel, R., & Pullen, J. (2011). Summary of the 2nd international waterside security conference. *Marine Technology Society Journal, 45*(3), 12–13. doi:10.4031/MTSJ.45.3.14

Mansouri, M., Nilchiani, R., & Mostashari, A. (2010). A decision analysis framework for resilience strategies in maritime systems. *IEEE Systems Journal,* 484 - 489.

Meir, T., Orton, P., Pullen, J., Holt, T., Thompson, W., & Arend, M. (2013). Forecasting the New York City urban heat island and sea breeze during extreme heat events. *Weather and Forecasting, 28*(6), 1460–1477. doi:10.1175/WAF-D-13-00012.1

Orton, P., Georgas, N., Blumberg, A., & Pullen, J. (2012). Detailed modeling of recent severe storm tides in estuaries of the New York City region. *Journal of Geophysical Research-Oceans, 117*, C09030. doi:10.1029/2012JC008220

Pullen, J., Chang, J., & Hanna, S. (2013). Air/sea transport, dispersion and fate modeling for the Fukushima nuclear power plant crisis. *Bulletin of the American Meteorological Society, 93*(13), 31–39. doi:10.1175/BAMS-D-11-00158.1

Pullen, J., Ching, J., Sailor, D., Thompson, W., Bornstein, R., & Koracin, D. (2008). Progress toward meeting the challenges of our coastal urban future. *Bulletin of the American Meteorological Society, 89*(11), 1727–1731. doi:10.1175/2008BAMS2560.1

Pullen, J., Holt, T., Blumberg, A., & Bornstein, R. (2007). Atmospheric response to local upwelling in the vicinity of New York/New Jersey harbor. *Journal of Applied Meteorology and Climatology, 46*, 1031–1052. doi:10.1175/JAM2511.1

Roarty, H., Lemus, E., Handel, E., Glenn, S., Barrick, D., & Isaacson, J. (2011). Performance evaluation of SeaSonde high-frequency radar for vessel detection. *Marine Technology Society Journal, 45*(3), 14–24. doi:10.4031/MTSJ.45.3.2

Zucker, M., Sedunov, A., Zhdanov, V., & Sutin, A. (2009). Passive acoustic classification of vessels in the Hudson River. *The Journal of the Acoustical Society of America*. doi:10.1121/1.3249261

KEY TERMS AND DEFINITIONS

CBP: Customs and Border Protection.

Marine Transportation System (MTS): As defined by the Department of Transportation Maritime Administration, "consists of waterways, ports, and intermodal landside connections that allow the various modes of transportation to move people and goods to, from, and on the water."

Maritime Domain Awareness (MDA): Defined by the International Maritime Organization as "the effective understanding of anything associated with the maritime domain that could impact the security, safety, economy, or environment."

NMIO: National Maritime Intelligence-Integration Office.

NOAA: National Oceanic and Atmospheric Administration.

NYHOPS: New York Harbor Observing and Prediction System.

SAROPS: Search and Rescue Optimal Planning System used by the Coast Guard.
USCG: United States Coast Guard.
UUVs: Unmanned Underwater Vehicles AIS: Automatic Identification System.

Chapter 3
Command, Control, and Interoperability Center for Advanced Data Analysis:
A Department of Homeland Security Data Sciences Center of Excellence

Asamoah Nkwanta
Morgan State University, USA

Janet E. Barber
*Central Michigan University, USA &
Prince George's Community College,
USA*

EXECUTIVE SUMMARY

The purpose of this chapter is to summarize and give an overview of the educational and research programs of the Command, Control, and Interoperability Center for Advanced Data Analysis (CCICADA) in an integral way. CCICADA is based at Rutgers University and is one of the components of the Department of Homeland Security (DHS) Center of Excellence (COE) Center for Visualization and Data Analytics (CVADA). CVADA is co-led by Rutgers University and Purdue University. Purdue's Visual Analytics for Command, Control, and Interoperability Environments (VACCINE) Center and Rutgers University's CCICADA Center were established as a DHS Homeland Security Center of Excellence in 2009. Although Purdue's focus is on visualization sciences, and Rutgers' focus is on data sciences, these two CVADA components are working closely on a number of activities, projects, and programs (Command, Control, and Interoperability Center for Advanced Data Analysis, 2013).

DOI: 10.4018/978-1-4666-5946-9.ch003

ORGANIZATIONAL BACKGROUND

The Department of Homeland Security Centers of Excellence perform critical research and development activities to provide the necessary homeland security tools, technologies, and training to help safeguard the United States against terrorist threats and attacks, and natural disasters. Congress mandated the creation of a center or centers of excellence in the Homeland Security Act of 2002. The following quote comes from the 2013 amended Homeland Security Act of 2002:

The Secretary, acting through the Under Secretary for Science and Technology, shall designate a university-based center or several university-based centers for homeland security. The purpose of the center or these centers shall be to establish a coordinated, university-based system to enhance the Nation's homeland security (Department of Homeland Security, 2002).

The Department of Homeland Security Centers of Excellence are sponsored by the DHS Office of University Programs and supported by the Oak Ridge Institute for Science Education (ORISE). Since 2003, ORISE has provided assistance to the DHS Office of University Programs to establish a system of university-based homeland security centers of excellence in accordance with the Homeland Security Act of 2002 (Oak Ridge Institute for Science Education, 2013). In 2004, a homeland security workshop was convened, and the aim and main focus were to create a summary report that DHS could use in order to more strategically select relevant and specific university-based, homeland security centers of excellence (Shaw, 2004). In this same year, the first COE was funded and established.

The Center of Excellence network is a consortium of universities that are developing new ideas, technologies and critical knowledge for homeland security. All COEs work closely with academia, industry, DHS components and first-responders as well as provide essential training for future homeland security experts. The research portfolios of the COEs consist of basic and applied research that addresses both short and long-term needs of DHS. The COE network of university centers currently includes twelve Centers of Excellence one of which involves CCICADA of the CVADA Center.

The origins of CCICADA, formerly known as Command, Control, and Interoperability (CCI), are rooted in three previously DHS-funded Centers: the Center for Knowledge Integration and Discovery (CKID) at the University of Southern California, the Center for Multimodal Information Access and Synthesis (MIAS) based at the University of Illinois at Urbana Champaign, and the Center for Dynamic Data Analysis (DyDAn) of Rutgers University. We will give a brief overview of DyDAn whose focus was on discrete sciences.

Table 1. DyDAn research projects

Analysis of Large, Dynamic Multigraphs	Continuous, Distributed Monitoring of Dynamic, Heterogeneous Data	Applied Research
Analysis of Large, Dynamic Multigraphs Arising from Blogs	Continuous Distributed Data Stream Monitoring	Potential Uses of Entropy in Bio-surveillance
Universal Information Graphs	Message Filtering and Entity Resolution/Author Identification (machine learning)	Enabling and Enhancing Crime Prevention and Analysis at NY/NJ Port Authority
Statistical and Graph-Theoretical Approaches to Time-Varying Multigraphs	Dynamic Similarity Search in Multi-Modal Data	Sensor Management for Nuclear Detection
Adding Semantics to Interconnecting Semantic Graphs Algorithms for Identifying Hidden Social Structures in Virtual Communities	Optimization and Learning Privacy-Preserving Data Analysis	

The DyDAn Center was established in 2006 as a DHS Center of Excellence and was based in Rutgers University's Center for Discrete Mathematics and Theoretical Computer Science (DIMACS). It was one of four University Affiliate Centers of the Institute for Discrete Sciences (IDS). The IDS center was a joint project between the DHS and several national laboratories, based at Lawrence Livermore National Laboratory. DyDAn researchers were tasked with developing new techniques for drawing inferences from massive flows of data that arrives continuously over time. DyDAn's research consisted of two primary areas of theoretical research: Analysis of Large, Dynamic Multigraphs, and Continuous, Distributed Monitoring of Dynamic, Heterogeneous Data (Homeland Security Center for Dynamic Data Analysis, 2009). In addition to the theoretical research, applied research was performed. See Table 1 for some of the DyDAn research projects.

The DyDAn researchers studied novel technologies to find patterns and relationships in dynamic and sometimes large datasets. The DyDAn research programs covered topics in Knowledge Discovery, Information Management and Discrete Mathematics (Homeland Security Center for Dynamic Data Analysis, 2009). Additionally, DyDAn created educational programs for all levels and constituents of academia and incorporated these programs for future and ongoing research. For example, according to Roberts (2004), bio-terrorism sensor-location problems are researchable projects for homeland security based student activities.

The establishment of CVADA, the new 2009 Department of Homeland Security Center of Excellence, continued the research, training and education programs begun under DyDAn, as well as continued under other Rutgers University homeland security funded projects, centers and partnerships.

CASE DESCRIPTION

Mission and Goals of CCICADA

CCICADA's goal is to introduce existing research to not only professional analysts and researchers of various disciplines, but also to students that are being groomed to replicate studies in order to gain more insight, find new solutions and to validate and explain studies in order to further and add to STEM literature. This mission is shared through CCICADA's Official Website statement that:

[Our] mission is based on the philosophy that it is not enough simply to develop new theory and the technologies that embody it. We must train a new cadre of technically knowledgeable people to use and perpetuate this technology.

CCICADA's educational goals are grounded by education and research. The Center addresses these goals through partnerships which aid in ensuring that CCICADA fulfills their goals and missions by providing research and educational activities, conferences, and workshops to scientific constituents. CCICADA's Fact Sheet states that their "research involves the full range of activities involved in improving access to multimodal information through transforming information to new forms to allow efficient and productive display and supporting synthesis through collaborations between humans and automated methods" (CCICADA Official Website, 2013).

CCICADA shows STEM diversity by the use of the following list of applications and research topics. This diversity supports CCICADA's purpose and mission.

- Critical infrastructure protection.
- Syndromic surveillance for natural and man-caused diseases.
- Inspection of containers at ports.
- Identification of authors from text.
- Protection against invasive species.
- Customs and border protection operations.
- Defense against threats to cyber infrastructure and data.
- Data management in emergency situations.
- Risk analysis.
- Non-intrusive data gathering techniques.

Carafano and Weitz (2009) emphasize in their article that scientifically-based university centers arrange and organize intellectual meetings between and among recognized researchers and other experts in the field to conduct research from various disciplines geared toward the study of complex homeland security issues and challenges. These research efforts are geared toward solutions concerning border securities as well as toward finding ways to lessen the impact of emergencies due to natural disasters. In essence, CCICADA's goal and work are to focus on multifaceted and challenging problems in data sciences that address present and emerging homeland security threats.

Data science is the focus of CCICADA research. The field of data science is a science of analyzing, preparing, collecting, visualizing, and managing large data sets by incorporating information and study from various STEM and social science disciplines (Stanton, 2012). Many DHS homeland security activities require that quick conclusions be reached as a result of analyzing large streams of data. Some characteristics of the data are that it arrives continuously over time, it comes from many different sources, it comes in many different forms, and that it is subject to some errors and uncertainties. The field of data sciences is one that is suited for addressing massive flows of data. This field will help speed up the analysis of large data streams, assist with identifying homeland security threats, help mitigate the effects of natural or man-made disasters, and allow DHS to work more effectively.

CCICADA Partners

CCICADA consists of a community of partner institutions. These partners are universities, industries, corporations, as well as minority-serving institution partners. The CCICADA teams boost world-class leaders in the field of data sciences. These leaders have proven track records of working with the homeland security community. CCICADA teams are multidisciplinary and work directly with experts from various STEM and social sciences fields. The current CCIADA partners are:

- Alcatel-Lucent Bell Labs*
- Applied Communication Sciences—Formerly Telcordia ATS
- AT & T Labs- Research*
- Carnegie Mellon*
- The City College of New York
- Geosemble Technologies*
- Howard University*
- Morgan State University*
- Princeton University*
- Regal Decision Systems
- Rensselaer Polytechnic Institute*
- Rutgers University-Lead Institution*
- Texas Southern University*
- Tuskegee University*

- University of Illinois at Urbana-Champaign*
- University of Massachusetts-Lowell*
- University of Medicine and Dentistry of New Jersey (UMDNJ)
- University of Southern California*

(* Denotes an initial CCICADA partner)

CCICADA Education Initiatives

CCICADA's education initiatives, plans, and goals support and exemplify their mission. They are developing another and a new generation of homeland security researchers, scientists, and social science and STEM educators who are trained and innovative enough to implement, connect and apply novel solutions to previous ones. This is accomplished by providing education and training to professionals in research and science, as well as to students. Again this success is surrounded by the incredibly broad areas and disciplines positioned around and supported by institutional connections, technological information and access. CCICADA's purpose is to quickly make current research accessible to classrooms and professionals in the field in order to further research and study in a meaningful and purposeful way. New classroom modules for use at the K-12 level are included in these initiatives. This way programs are fully integrated, as students and professionals are working congenially in CICADA laboratories at various levels of work and education. Consequently, the educational initiatives involve students in all research projects and connect a vast number of education programs with relevant project themes. CCICADA professionals (researchers) are tasked with presenting lectures, tutoring, and organizing and conducting workshops. These educational initiatives have fostered education programs that have marked new courses which promoted certificate programs, homeland security workshops, summer programs in data sciences, and tutorials for precollege and college teachers, as well as for homeland security and law enforcement professionals.

Data Sciences Summer Institute (DSSI)

This institute started at partner institution, the University of Illinois – Urbana Champaign, one of CCICADA's successful and main educational programs, and is their Data Sciences Summer Institute. CCICADA states that it is one of their keystone programs and provides extensive training for a new generation of up-and-coming scientists. This educational program includes an invitation to computer science students into a residential summer research programs which consist of an eight-week scientific and research opportunity. The purpose is to assist science students from universities that might have limited research resources and exposes them to a diversity of educational, learning, and research opportunities. Additionally, Data Sciences Summer Institute (DSSI)/CCICADA science leaders state that:

It is our intention that the curriculum developed in the DSSI will be a first stop for anyone whose career—whether practical or research oriented—is based in knowledge discovery and visual analytics. DSSI's six-week residential summer program consists of a four-week training session, during which undergraduates, graduate and participating faculty are in residence at UIUC, coinciding with a four-week research session, the first half of which coincides with a training session. For broader and more rapid impact, we will invite partner institutions and national labs to rely on these course materials as they establish research or training groups of their own (CCICADA Official Website, 2013).

Students in DSSI programs have gained opportunities to work and intern in large scientific laboratories and are mentored to get an intellectually better understanding of future graduate studies and careers. The students gain opportunities to interact, research, collaborate and publish with experts in the field. The purpose is to also train and teach new and future scientists to become experts in disciplines of interest to homeland security. However, because of the high cost to maintain DSSI, CCICADA's DSSI was suspended for 2012-2013. New models for DSSI funding are being investigated.

Reconnect Workshop

The CCICADA Reconnect workshops give higher education faculty from teaching institutions the opportunity to gain experience in understanding mathematics and computer sciences in homeland security. They are introduced to progressive and contemporary research issues relevant for classroom lectures and activities. Research subjects and topics from these workshops are presented by experts from various disciplines in a week-long series of activities, lectures, and presentations.

Reconnect subjects on mathematical methodology, natural language processing, bio-surveillance, and data analysis in law enforcement have fostered new courses in universities and colleges across America. The Reconnect program is equally important in government and industry businesses. In these areas of work, higher education faculty is offered opportunities to gain valuable knowledge in various areas of emerging research and techniques.

Research Experiences for Undergraduates (REUs)

One of the main goals of the REU program is to offer undergraduate students meaningful and exciting research experiences that whet academic appetites. CCICADA literature on REUs shares that "students get a taste of the international scientific enterprise through partnership with an international research center" (CCICADA Official Website, Fact Sheet, 2013, para. 1). Having a positive research experience can go a long way with helping direct participants in the right personal directions for future educational and career goals, as student participants are mentored one-on-one in various areas of research and study. Educators and others support the importance of introducing STEM subjects into different disciplines, and data from various educational sources can be applied toward understanding mentorship advice to aid in determining strategies that can help college students to develop good plans for life success and college completion (Barber, 2012).

The CCICADA collaborations and mentorships start at the orientation level. Following orientation(s), there is a weekly Seminar Series where students gain opportunities to listen to and learn from local and national speakers. The Seminar Series also gives the students the opportunity to take two educational trips to recognized partner companies or research institutions, such as AT&T and IBM, which offers the students a chance to become acquainted with industry, corporate and institutional research. REU student research and other projects have led to some important CCICADA advances in cybersecurity and other scientific research (CCICADA Official Website, 2013).

The students are required to create, organize and share two presentations about their science projects. Initially, each student creates a presentation describing his or her research problem and what he or she hopes to achieve from this research project. In the end, the students present the final results from their work, successfully concluding the program (CCICADA Official Website, 2013 – REU Program).

Graduate Fellowship Research Program

CCICADA offers fellowships to students to assist them in pursuing graduate studies at Rutgers University and are funded through the U.S. Department of Homeland Security. These fellowships support students up to three years and aid in their pursuit of research interests that are applicable to data analysis and decision making for homeland security. Academic and research areas of special importance are: mathematics, computer science, industrial engineering, computer engineering, statistics, biological sciences, and the decision sciences. Additionally, applicants from other STEM disciplines are allowed to apply as long as their research interests are relevant to homeland security research endeavors. Fellowship participants are invited to the full range of activities offered by CCICADA. The fellows are exposed to many interdisciplinary research and education programs. Ongoing research include: biosurveillance, epidemiology, port resilience, stadium security, evacuation planning, natural disaster preparedness and response, resource planning and allocation, cybersecurity, information privacy, emergency alerting, social media analysis, and nuclear threat detection (CCICADA Official Website, 2013).

Postdoctoral Program

CCICADA offers post-doctoral research positions. Applicants are selected based on their academic achievement. If selected, renewals of positions are contingent on funding and performance. In 2013, there were two associate positions offered. The first position was for an associate in nuclear detection. The applicants had to be a recent Ph.D. in computer science, statistics, industrial engineering, operations research, or a closely related field. In addition, they had to have a background in nuclear physics or nuclear engineering. The selected applicant will create and apply models assessing the effectiveness of testing protocols for devices that detect nuclear terrorist threats. The selected applicant will also be required to write proposals and publish research from being a participant in CCICADA projects. Travel is required for both positions. The second position was for a general associate working in various areas and working with internationally recognized faculty in the field of data science. The applicants for this position had to be a recent Ph.D. with interest in STEM fields such as operations research, industrial engineering, computer science, statistics and discrete mathematics. The position is project oriented and will focus on methods such as mathematical modeling, combinatorial optimization, data analysis, and event simulations. (CCICADA Official Website, 2013).

National Association of Mathematicians (NAMs) MathFest

CCICADA is associated with the National Association of Mathematicians in that they work together to ensure that students have opportunities to grow educationally in scientific endeavors. NAM is a non-profit professional organization. It tasks all constituents to actively participate in workshops, conferences, and to achieve excellence in the mathematical sciences. NAM also encourages mathematical development of underrepresented Americans and addresses the unfortunate under-representation of minorities in the mathematics field and mathematical sciences workforce.

Every fall, NAM organizes and holds a very successful MathFest that features a series of programs aimed at undergraduate and graduate students and faculty nationwide. Participants have an opportunity to listen to speakers, have a Q & A with expert panels, and become actively involved in educational and research sessions. This MathFest has a focus on Minority Serving Institutions. The participating students are tasked with giving presentations pertaining to their research. They also get mentorship and guidance on careers in the mathematical sciences, information on how to apply to graduate school, as well as advice and suggestions on how to be a successful graduate student. MathFest provides exposure to many students, educators and scientists to research that relates and applies homeland security issues to the mathematical and computer sciences field. See the National Association of Mathematicians 2013 Website for more information about NAM's MathFest.

Modules and New Courses

CCICADA provides undergraduate college and high school classes an in-depth introduction as to how the mathematical and computer sciences might apply to homeland security matters. These students' learning materials and modules have been researched and prepared by experts in the field and are based on current research. The modules cover a diversity of topics, such as bio-surveillance, cryptography, food safety, and emergency evaluation strategies. These efforts promote more CCICADA-led curricula and courses in others areas of study as well. Some new areas of study are: the behavioral sciences, optimal learning, privacy, and cryptography (CCICADA Official Website, Fact Sheet, 2013). These efforts advance CCICADA as a worldwide model for institutional research and learning. We note that some of the teaching modules and new courses are developed as a result of the efforts of CCICADA's Reconnect Workshop.

CCICADA RESEARCH, STUDIES, AND EXPERIMENTS

Research and the Three Key Concepts of Homeland Security

Information obtained from CCICADA's 2013 unpublished brochure notes that national homeland security's strategy is designed to achieve three key concepts of DHS. These concepts are: security, resilience, and customs and exchange. The strategies and concepts are incorporated in DHS and CCICADA missions as noted in this chapter, and according to literature and information obtained from CCICADA's most recent Website and literature provided to the authors of this chapter from Margaret "Midge" Cozzens, CCICADA's Education Director, CCICADA's research is coordinated across various projects and many partner institutions as seen in Tables 2-5 of this chapter. The research activities are involved with improving access to multimodal information through transforming this information to new forms to allow efficient and productive displays of research. The director notes that the Science and Technology division of the Department of Homeland Security directs, supervises and controls science and innovative technology that ensures the welfare and well-being of Americans. For example, terrorism is one of our most serious threats, and as a response to this dilemma, experts from partner institutions have converged to alleviate this problem. "CCICADA focuses on data sciences (data analytics)" where "teams of researchers use the fundamental methods of data science to" create avenues to store information, organize it, then retrieve the information in any way that it might present itself to the teams. These teams of researchers are responsible for securing solutions to security problems (CCICADA, Unpublished Brochure, 2013, pp. 1-2).

CCICADA researchers strive to eliminate or at least alleviate security risks. They determine quicker ways to detect disease, analyze crime for prevention, develop secure sport stadiums, analyze ways to prevent nuclear and bio-terrorism, human trafficking, and they work on different research projects that could be security risks to the safety and well-being of Americans. This is accomplished by having the ability to think critically and come to logical conclusions from massive amounts of data (CCICADA, Unpublished Brochure, 2013, p. 2). Data tell a story, and data-driven decision making for safety could encourage behavior modifications, stimulate mental resilience (Barber, 2012) and may also be a lifesaver if used accurately. One key CCICADA workshop addressing human behavior was the Mathematical Models for Behavioral Epidemiology where participants broached the question as to "whether or not local behavioral interventions can scale up to affect nationwide disease risks." Such questions "necessitate the creation of new types of investigative models" and the expertise of medical sociologists, mathematicians, health officials, and others (CCICADA Official Website, 2013, see Educational Opportunities, Project #5, para. 3).

In the process of seeking health, security, and safety of citizens, collections of big data are becoming a necessity and a norm as research scientists and law enforcement seek solutions. The challenge could be the accuracy of collecting and analyzing this big data (Jacobs, 2009) in order to get to the story and on to safety. See more information about data, security, safety and social media in the following sections.

A Call for Safety: Nuclear Detection Strategies

The psychological impact and devastation of a possible nuclear attack in the United States give pause and make us realize the importance of cultivating and progressing strategies of detection of radiation-emitting materials. Law enforcement, scientists and citizens must be concerned before such a serious incident occurs. CCICADA researchers and Homeland Security have been working in this area of concern.

Statistical and Machine Learning Methods for Manifest Data Analysis

Customs information is collected at overseas points of embarkation using a variety of customs forms, including a ship's manifest and bill of lading. Prior to arrival at US ports, Customs and Border Protection does screening based on such data to determine whether the shipment poses a potential risk. Identifying mislabeled or anomalous shipments through scrutiny of manifest data is one step in a multi-layer inspection process for containers arriving at ports. Before shipments are released from foreign ports, high risk cargo can be more thoroughly inspected for nuclear or radiological materials. Sophisticated methods of statistical analysis, "machine learning," and data visualization enter into unique risk scoring methods developed at CCICADA and allow for the identification of departures from "normal patterns" that raise suspicions about shipments (CCICADA Official Website, Fact Sheet, 2013, para. 2).

Introduction: Research, Collecting, Organizing and Analyzing the Data

Acquiring scientific knowledge is an ongoing and cumulative process that depends on a researcher's continuing ability to gather, collect, manage, analyze, and share data. Though these might seem like simple tasks for a researcher, there are numerous challenges related to each task. Collecting and gathering data involve both generating new data and accessing existing information often buried in large quantities of data (secondary analysis). These data may be in texts, in large databases, in various media formats contained in the vast array of social media sites, or even in literature. Extracting these data and the information it provides can prove a daunting task; however, CCICADA has found innovative ways to apply their research. One of CCICADA's application areas is the prevention of the illegal use of people, i.e., human trafficking for the profit of others. The victims are more often than not, women and children. CCICADA is assisting FBI, police, and other law enforcement by gathering, compiling and correlating data from open sources about the abuse and illegal use of humans for profit "and integrating this information with data from law enforcement sources to build an enhanced law enforcement system that describes and ranks likely groups of people who will become targets," mostly children and women. Devices developed to prevent human trafficking have applications to the FBI, analysis of escort services, and the Microsoft Digital Crimes Unit (CCICADA Official Website, 2013; Unpublished Brochure, 2013, p. 4). How could a more magnifying and strategic look at social media help?

Social Media, Safety and Homeland Security

Some social media outlets are: Twitter, Facebook, Flickr, eBuddy, LinkedIn, StumpleUpon, Pinterest, Instagram, and email just to name a few. Various social media outlets play a major part, albeit electronically, in human-to-human communication in today's society. For example, on a daily basis, one-half of all teenagers send about fifty text messages, and ninety percent of high school seniors visit a social media site at least once a day (Lenhart, 2010; Myers, 2010). According to the International Telecommunication Union (2010), approximately seven billion human beings communicate by using their cell phones by voice or texting when they are not face-to-face. Subsequently electronic-communicative interactions between and among humans have been proven to exist in a large way.

Human-to-human contact by way of social media are becoming more and more involved as a potential safety measure in today's society. Norris, Stevens, Pfefferbaum, Wyche, and Pfefferbaum (2008) contend that, communities must find ways to reduce risk during and after emergencies. When there are limited resources, people must engage with each other and increase social support systems to create community organizational linkages for safety. With the various types of social media and the number of people electronically connecting, behavioral changes are easier to implement, and there are positive implications here as well for teaching citizens best practice and ways to communicate in case of emergency, and to connect in cases of mass shootings, terrorism, cyber attacks, or to inform law enforcement about information on human trafficking.

Human Trafficking and Social Media

According to CCICADA, research partners and scientists from the Center for Human Trafficking at the Annenberg School for Communication and the University of Southern California's Information Science Institute "have developed methods for reviewing and analyzing large social media communications and Web posts to help identify potential cases of human trafficking" (Official Website, Fact Sheet, 2013, p. 1). This is a positive attacking a negative, as according to Mark Latonero, Research Director of the Annenberg Center on Communication, Leadership, and Policy, and professor at the University of Southern California, "many human traffickers used Craigslist, Facebook, and other social media sites to recruit sex workers and solicit clients" (Koebler, 2012, para. 3). However, this particular social media outlet has shifted to the use of cell phones. "[H]uman sex traffickers have started largely relying on prepaid mobile phones to conduct business, according to a new report by the University of Southern California." Now, however, according to Latonero, mobile or cell phones are "the new frontline battleground in the fight *against* [authors' emphasis]" human trafficking (Koebler, 2012, para. 2). Looking at data extraction in the area of human trafficking, CCICADA scientists, partners, and researchers also work in the area of dissecting and analyzing social media and Internet-based communicative methods in hopes of alleviating this problem. "Techniques have and are being developed to take massive and diverse data sources to find patterns and anomalies. The recent advances use content and photo recognition methods to enhance information" (CCICADA Official Website, Fact Sheet, 2013, para. 2) about human trafficking and other crimes.

The following information is extracted from CCICADA's Human Trafficking Fact Sheet:

The project at USC to combat Human Trafficking focuses on finding underage prostitutes and working with law enforcement to eradicate the criminal entities. The researchers gather and combine a variety of Twitter and Website posts (e.g., escort service Websites or posted advertisements on venues such as CraigsList and Backpage). They identify patterns in posted advertisements, most consisting of non-trustworthy information such as false addresses or false ages, in order to identify what information can be trusted and suggest ways to trace those posting the information. With the help of expert elicitations from leading law enforcement experts, the CCICADA researchers determine the specific data areas that give indication across sites that an individual who is being promoted as age-appropriate is indeed young and perhaps enslaved unwillingly. Methods are used to help determine the likely ages of those identified and the team further investigates whether the photos obtained from the Websites and Twitter or advertisement profiles are good enough to provide accurate age reconciliation information.

The CCICADA researchers have worked in partnership with several law enforcement entities and other stakeholders on this project: State of California Office of the Attorney General; Los Angeles Police Department; Los Angeles Task Force on Human Trafficking (City of LA); the US Department of Justice; the Federal Bureau of Investigation; US Department of State; United Nations (CCICADA Official Website, Fact Sheet, 2013).

Homeland Security and the First Responder Group have requested that CCICADA analyze and investigate the use of social media and how it can effectively be utilized to massively inform citizens about security threats. Social media is beginning to be used to identify, by way of innovative and creative techniques, criminals not only in the area of human trafficking, but also in terrorism and other homeland threats. These creative social media techniques could be used to solve or potentially solve different problems in emergency situations and could be of great assistance to homeland security. Extracted from CCICADA's Fact Sheet, some examples follow:

Alerts and Warnings in Social Media (AWSM)

Example: According to CCICADA research, the primary idea of AWSM is that human beings observe their environments and oftentimes (or mostly) utilize social media activity, such as, Twitter, Facebook, text messages, Instagram and other media, to share and provide basic information or to discuss and describe their perspectives on various matters (CCICADA Official Website, Fact Sheet, 2013). The AWSM information from the CCICADA Fact Sheet explains:

This form of observational sharing can be thought of as an interconnected and intelligent distributed 'sensor' network. The information flow on the non-private part of the networks can be tracked to determine what may be occurring in real or near-real time. Using this information, analysts and managers can perhaps recognize catastrophes through monitoring and thus plan responses as appropriate. Another potential benefit: Anomaly Detection-recognizing problems before they occur or as they are occurring. Recent examples of "flash mob" attacks and natural disasters give perfect examples of this concept (CCICADA Official Website, Fact Sheet, 2013).

AWSM Hat Chase Experiments

Example: Assessing the risks in conducting an experiment that would essentially send an alarm about a particular emergency, CCICADA researchers, partners, and scientists developed an experiment that would mimic and act as a "surrogate" for such an emergency. This experiment would in turn allow CCICADA scientists to study the behaviors as to how that emergency information might be sent out and spread most expeditiously and effectively through social media (CCICADA Official Website, Fact Sheet, 2013). Note the "Hat Chase" experiment by use of "crowd-sourcing" technique:

The project researchers designed and conducted two 'hat chase' experiments to gain such insights. On Hat Chase day, a small group of individuals donned one of seven eye-catching hats and spread out across all four Rutgers University campuses in New Brunswick, NJ. Dozens of student teams organized and coordinated to spot the hats, identify their locations, and get the word out to as many people as possible. The competing Hat Chase teams provided anonymous records of their conversations with each other, thus providing CCICADA researchers with a rich set of data that can be used to investigate issues related to "crowdsourcing" and strategies the teams used for searching for hats and then reporting sightings to team members (CCICADA Official Website, Fact Sheet, 2013).

Crowdsourcing is the observance of the behavior of large networks of people in the online or physical (offline) community in an effort to solve problems. The participants are usually volunteers, depending on the study (Howe, 2006).

The Microwork in crowdsourcing takes skill; the research can be conducted independently (Yang, Adamic, & Ackerman, 2008) and with large institutions. This type of work can engage dialogue and solutions to societal securities; however, there are limitations. For example, there are limits to the use of crowdsource research as the definitions can sometimes become "blurred." Authors tend to give different definitions of crowdsourcing according to their academic disciplines or specialties, which can cause a consistent global picture of the term to be lost (Estelles-Arolas & Gonzalez-Ladron-de-Guevara, 2012).

According to Yang, Adamic, and Ackerman (2008), crowdsourcing is a good tool to use when there are limited funds, computer inadequacies, and the task at hand or the problem to be solved is small; this is microwork. Macrowork on the other hand calls for more sophisticated uses of crowdsource research (Yang, Adamic, & Ackerman, 2008) like the CCICADA "Hat Chase" project.

"Many homeland security agencies have partnered in this [The "Hat Chase"] project: NJ Office of Homeland Security and Preparedness, the New Jersey College and University Public Safety Association (CUPSA), and the campus police at Rutgers University and Rensselaer Polytechnic Institute" (CCICADA Official Website, Fact Sheet, 2013). Further research and finding new and innovative ways to get the word out about emergencies or other security threats through digital or electronic media to large crowds of people are imperative.

Gathering, Extracting and Managing Research Data

According to CCICADA, statistics are used and computed to direct enforcement actions. Tools developed to solve security problems have applications to the Microsoft Digital Crimes Unit, analysis of escort services, the FBI, and other law enforcement at crowded events, such as mentioned earlier, a concert arena or stadium. Large sports venues are also where terrorists or cyber attacks are more likely to occur. "Early identification that someone is preparing a cyber attack by examining and extracting data from online forums is another example of CCICADA's work designed to protect the homeland" (CCICADA, Unpublished Brochure, 2013, p. 4). Below, CCICADA explains the project:

The goal of this project is to detect indications in the electronic media of possible cyber attacks before they happen by developing techniques for semantic analysis of messages sent in forums. This analysis of different meanings contained in messages seeks to identify network entities trying to obtain sensitive data that they will put to malicious use. Research is conducted to determine what subjects and potential threat topics an adversary would be interested in using vast quantities of existing data from a variety of sources. With this list of subjects and possible threat topics, and newly developed text extraction tools these forum texts are analyzed, entities are recognized, and information is extracted, creating an early warning system. This work has been facilitated through collaboration with NISA – the National Information Security Authority—in Israel. These text extraction tools have a variety of uses beyond identification of potential cyber attacks, including the identification of possible human traffickers through their posts on various Websites, and identification of potential terrorists as they prepare their attacks. One of these extraction analysis tools is a software prototype called traffic cop, which "scrapes" ads and posts on various Websites to count the frequency of certain kinds of activities to better identify "hotspots" (CCICADA, Unpublished Brochure, 2013, p. 4).

The CCICADA Official Website (2013) information notes that since the September 11, 2001 (9/11) attacks, large areas and crowd situations across America have been locations of concern for homeland security. They feared more terrorist attacks on American citizens. With the 2013 Boston, Massachusetts bombings, a new urgency to protect citizens attending functions at sports and entertainment arenas has arisen. The new director of the National Counterterrorism Center asserted the importance of law enforcement remaining alert to the threat from homegrown extremists, as this problem is a persistent one in America (Annual Aspen Security Forum, 2013). A homegrown extremist could also be a mentally ill individual with extremely violent tendencies. The end result of the danger to citizens is the same as if a mass shooting or bombing were carried out by a religious fanatic or political zealot. It is time for initiatives and ideas to go into the realm of applications towards safety. Perhaps this conversation could start with dialogue and meetings between homeland security not just with law enforcement agents, but along with psychiatrists, psychologists and other mental health officials and behavioral experts. Big data to determine the story or stories behind the media influence of violence due to watching violent television and playing violent video games is also imperative (Myers, 2010, pp. 25, 379).

CCICADA collects data at many places using research and participant observation, as well as video analysis. One important project that CCICADA has been working on for a while is called the *Stadium Project*. For example, observation data was collected at soccer games: the International Soccer game between Mexico and

Wales, and also the soccer game between Argentina and Brazil. Other venues of observation have been at the Advance Auto Parts Monster Jam in June 2012, and the Hot 97 Summer Jam. Video analysis was conducted for a national football league (NFL) event in January 2012. The collected data was analyzed by using a Java application; it was then applied to inspection times at MetLife Stadium (CCICADA, Unpublished Brochure, 2013, p. 5).

"Patrons in the initial wave at the gate opening were observed, and a second group of patrons entering 30 minutes before event time were observed. The effect of several factors important to inspection times were evaluated from the data": pat downs; bag check, the location of the inspection such as at the gate, in a lane where an inspector was present, the time before the event such as early vs. late, and the kind of event such as soccer match, monster truck, etc. "Statistical methods were applied once these factors were recognized." Interestingly, this statistical analysis shows that the variation in methods, inspection times, researchers and inspectors are a lot greater than could be explained by chance alone (CCICADA, Unpublished Brochure, 2013, p. 5).

The organization and management of crime information are big challenges facing police, FBI, CIA, law enforcement in general, and homeland security entities. Accurately analyzing data is a critical component of predicting future crimes. As such, it is not the gathering, collecting and/or extracting data that is the most difficult entity; it is the storage and management of the data so that research analysis is possible, then logically usable in order to predict future crimes (CCICADA, Unpublished Brochure, 2013, p. 5).

"*Crime Maps* is a visualization tool developed by CCICADA, which is designed to extract information to understand the nature of the event, support field decisions, and prioritize activities and resources." This tool includes crime activity, activity in general, crime information, spatio-temporal analysis and content. The information is ultimately presented on maps which in turn allows law enforcement, research analysts, and the general public to access critical real-time information, assisting in lowered risk for victimization. CCICADA has partnered with police enforcement in Champaign, Illinois, the New Jersey State Police, the Maryland State Police, the Los Angeles California Police Department, the Port of Authority of New York Police Department and at the University of Illinois in order to realistically create integrated real-time crime information management systems (CCICADA, Unpublished Brochure, 2013, p. 5). This is practical and innovative research at its best.

Fusion Center Assessment (CCICADA Fact Sheet Information)

Fusion centers have also been established as a result of 9/11 Commission requests and recommendations. They work in tandem with state and local jurisdictions as well as with the cooperation from the federal government (CCICADA Official Website, Fact Sheet, 2013). The following excerpts share more information about fusion center competencies:

They [fusion centers] serve as focal points for the receipt, analysis, gathering, and sharing of information and situational awareness between the federal government and state, local and private sector partners on emergencies such as blizzards, hurricanes, floods, or other major natural occurrences as well as in the event or threat of an aggressive terrorist attack. Fusion centers are uniquely situated to enable front-line law enforcement, public safety, fire service, emergency response, public health and private sector security personnel to understand local intelligence and implications of national intelligence, thus enabling local officials to better protect their communities. Fusion centers provide interdisciplinary expertise and situational awareness to inform decision-making at all levels of government. They conduct analysis and facilitate information sharing while assisting law enforcement and homeland security partners in preventing, protecting against, and responding to large scale weather/natural events or terrorism (CCICADA Official Website, Fact Sheet, 2013).

A mature, fully functioning national network of fusion centers is critical to share homeland security information and intelligence among and between federal, state, and local governments and with private sector partners as part of a national Information Sharing Environment. The US DHS Office of Intelligence and Analysis has asked CCICADA to assist in an evaluation/assessment of the fusion center process. The CCICADA project supports the development of a performance management framework, primarily how to measure and track the progress and overall maturity of fusion center capabilities. CCICADA researchers are providing input on the development of a Web-based fusion center self-assessment tool; developing a scoring methodology; and assisting in the development and iterative refinement of a model for the national network of fusion centers (CCICADA Official Website, Fact Sheet, 2013).

Fusion Center Partners of CCICADA have worked with fusion centers in Maryland, New Jersey, and New York City. They give advice on social media software and outlets, situational awareness tools, as well as safety and security. Some of CCICADA's work and data research on fusion centers have also been with the New Jersey State Police, Maryland State Police, the New York City Office of Emergency Management, and FEMA (CCICADA Official Website, 2013).

Projects with the Federal Emergency Management Agency

FEMA Overview

From the CCICADA Official Website Fact Sheet (2013): CCICADA is in partnership with FEMA Region II which covers NJ, NY, Puerto Rico, and the Virgin Islands. CCICADA and FEMA's mission is to examine risks and attempt to alleviate unsafe event impact and to analyze large datasets that arise from the research of natural disaster planning, response, recovery. Data: The partners have collaborated and discussed different ways to help in analyzing and managing large pre-response, response, and recovery datasets, and to visualize these data. The plan is to also develop hand-held applications for first responders. This partnership involves two important projects: Flood mitigation and Climate change.

Flood Mitigation

Given the magnitude of the impact of flooding events on local and regional econo-mies, personal property and government resources, FEMA is in need of planning tools to identify event risk and impact of related flood mitigation strategies. This is not an easy task. Flood risk prediction and mitigation strategy success likeli-hood are complex. And, prior work in this area has not taken full advantage of modern data analysis and modeling/simulation tools. Working in partnership with the DHS National Transportation Center of Excellence at the Bloustein School of Public Policy at Rutgers University, the Flood Mitigation project has three primary components: (1) Community Assessment: profiles of communities most affected by flooding on the Raritan; interviews with community leaders and other stakeholders; (2) Economic Modeling: costs/benefits of flood mitigation projects/strategies and (3) Risk Analysis: estimating event risk and the risk reduction possibilities of different mitigation strategies. The goal is development and application of new methods of analysis (CCICADA Official Website, Fact Sheet, 2013, para. 2).

Climate Change

FEMA has invited CCICADA to discussions about climate change issues, in particu-lar to meet with and consult with the NYC Climate Change Initiative. The goal is to assist in the risk assessment and planning process in the event of increasing extreme weather/climate events and potentially rising sea levels. Relevant CCICADA work on climate and health in coordination with the Centers for Disease Control involv-ing mathematical modeling, simulation, and algorithmic tools of risk assessment, should be helpful in examining the impact on major infrastructure (power plants, roadways) and to plan for large scale evacuations and shelter resource requirements (CCICADA Official Website, Fact Sheet, 2013, para. 3).

Modeling and Simulation Research

CCICADA is making strides at attempting to solve the large amount of data that is acquired and that requires researchers, analysts and others to develop tools to simplify big data and create models of their parts. "Modeling tools assist analysts in arriving at possible options or decisions that they must make so that they might better understand the consequences of these actions" (CCICADA, Unpublished Brochure, 2013, p. 6).

Once models are developed to represent the main characteristics or behaviors of the system process, simulations that imitate the operation of this process or system overtime can be performed. Simulation can be used to illustrate the future real effects of alternative conditions, behaviors, and/or courses of action. "Simulation is also used when the real system cannot be engaged, because it may not be accessible, or it may be dangerous or unacceptable to engage, or it is being designed but not yet built, or it may simply not exist" (CCICADA, Unpublished Brochure, 2013, p. 6).

The U.S. Government places a high priority on protecting American citizens in public venues, such as entertainment auditoriums or sports arenas. For example, let's consider the problem of evacuating a sports event at a stadium. How can a big sports stadium be evacuated quickly in the event of a bomb threat, terrorist attack or natural disaster like Hurricanes Katrina or Sandy? "CCICADA, with its partner Regal Decision Systems Inc. and stadium management and security, has developed sophisticated tools for simulating evacuation of stadiums." The purpose of the simulation tools is to calculate the time needed to shelter people or to move them to safety. "Evacuation routes from different stadium sections, location of security personnel during an evacuation, physical obstacles, and likely crowd dispersions are all part of the model developed before the simulations are run." CCICADA has also developed training materials for pertinent personnel. "The results of this work were found useful and important during a lightning storm emergency at the new MetLife Stadium in New Jersey" (CCICADA Official Website, 2013; CCICADA, Unpublished Brochure, 2013, p. 6).

Information from the CCICADA Official Website as well as the unpublished CCICADA brochure (2013) shares that the evacuation model and subsequent simulations provided research teams with information well beyond such simple logistics as how long will it take to evacuate a full sports or concert stadium. The behavioral aspect and their potential impact was one thing not included in the first models and the subsequent planning processes. Now psychological and behavioral factors such as the possibility of getting lost, deliberate motion in a different direction than intended, the chaos of the time and the need to wait for family and friends, must be added. Assessing the latter and as discussed early on in this chapter, "[o]ur need to belong motivates our investment in being continuously connected" (Myers, 2010, p. 394), which can play a major role in safety as the "need to belong" relates to social media and communication within large and small settings.

Concert attendees or fans at a game have unique characteristics that impact timely evacuations, such as amount of alcohol consumption, their affiliates, the emotion of the music or game, and other natural or unique factors. According to CCICADA's (2013) updated brochure, CCICADA is developing new models that take these factors into account. "Once these models are created, new simulations will be conducted, processes will be adjusted and new training materials will follow" (p. 6).

Eliminating the Limitations of Big and Small Data

There is a natural tendency for high anxiety when experiencing or even discussing emergencies or emergency situations; therefore data during or about emergencies can be potentially conflicting and/or inconsistent. As mentioned above, these data could include collected data on crimes such as the prevention of human trafficking, detection of disease, cyber attacks or terrorism. The inconsistencies in the data could be due to bias, extraneous variables, or many other reasons. A major and current welcomed challenge of CCICADA in data gathering and analysis is to create and develop innovative computational tools to address the problem of trustworthiness or human intent to deceive. "We are searching for an appropriate degree of trust in claims that are made by everyone relative to the data. Once definitions are made precise, we will develop metrics to measure the accuracy, possible biases, and especially the completeness of the extracted data" (CCICADA, Unpublished Brochure, 2013, p. 5).

Table 2. Research Theme 1: Information gathering and distillation

Project	Government Partner	Non-Government Partner	Status
Human Trafficking	FBI, Coast Guard	Law enforcement	Non-exploratory
FEMA Data Analysis Needs	FEMA	N/A	Exploratory
TSA Data Integration	TSA	N/A	Exploratory
Search for Unstructured and Networked Data	FEMA, TSA, Coast Guard	Law enforcement	Exploratory

Table 3. Research Theme 2: Information network analysis

Project	Government Partner	Non-Government Partner	Status
Social Media and Emergency Response	DHS, Coast Guard, FEMA	Law enforcement, Port Authority of NY/NJ, NJ Office of Homeland Security	Non-exploratory
Hidden Knowledge Discovery, Analysis, and Summarization	N/A	Law enforcement	Exploratory
Trustworthiness Framework and Technologies	FEMA	Law enforcement	Non-exploratory
Disease Events	CDC	NJ Department of Health	Non-exploratory
Social Media and Emergency Response	DHS, Coast Guard, FEMA	Law enforcement, Port Authority of NY/NJ, NJ Office of Homeland Security	Non-exploratory
Hidden Knowledge Discovery, Analysis, and Summarization	N/A	Law enforcement	Exploratory
Trustworthiness Framework and Technologies	FEMA	Law enforcement	Non-exploratory

Table 4. Research Theme 3: Information-driven modeling and simulation

Project	Government Partner	Non-Government Partner	Status
Interaction with Coast Guard on COAST Modules and Beyond	Coast Guard	N/A	Non-exploratory
Information-based Container Inspection	CBP	N/A	Non-exploratory
Economics and Security: UCASS	Coast Guard	Port Authority of NY/NJ, NYC OEM, NJ OHSP, Mall Security, Indianapolis Dept. of Public Safety	Non-exploratory
Interaction with Coast Guard on COAST Modules and Beyond	Coast Guard	N/A	Non-exploratory
Information-based Container Inspection	CBP	N/A	Non-exploratory

Table 5. Research Theme 4: Information-driven decision making

Project	Government Partner	Non-Government Partner	Status
Data Methods for Risk Assessment	Coast Guard, FEMA, TSA	N/A	Non-exploratory
Information-based Inspection Procedures at Sports Stadiums	CBP, TSA, DNDO	N/A	Non-exploratory

Research Ideas and Initiatives

As noted above, it is emphasized that CCICADA's research and its data can be transitioned to practical applications. This is part of CCICADA's technology transfer. Some past CCICADA research projects are on building and broadening knowledge from collected data, extracting information from various media, analyzing and extracting relations, events, ideas, and opinions from texts and academic literature, and projects on enriching knowledge by using inference (2009). More recent projects stem from the past ones, such as understanding human trafficking, gathering information and distillation, an exploratory look at FEMA's data analysis needs, social media and emergency response, and Interoperability: Next generation communication (2012). The following Tables list and detail some of the 2012-13 projects.

CONCLUSION

The objective of this chapter has been to share the significance and importance of the educational activities and research of the Command, Control, and Interoperability Center for Advanced Data Analysis (CCICADA). Its corporate sphere, housed at Rutgers University, is a component of the Department of Homeland Security and is also partners with various science centers, universities, and businesses. CCICADA's theory and mission is based on the philosophy of best practices in educating and training upcoming homeland scientists who will be able to create new and innovative strategies in, for example, homeland safety, bio-surveillance, high technologies, multimodal information and the behavioral sciences. In essence, CCICADA's educational goals are grounded in education and research, as their educational initiatives, plans, and goals support and illustrate their mission. Their many programs and projects have honed the research skills of many, and have taken CCICADA's work in new and innovative directions in big data research, social media techniques, safety and security.

Preceding CCICADA, the Dynamic Data Analysis Center was one of the University Affiliate Centers of the Institute for Discrete Sciences (IDS). DyDAn researchers were assigned to develop new techniques for drawing inferences from huge flows of data that arrive continuously over time. DyDAn's research consisted of two main areas of theoretical research: Analysis of Large, Dynamic Multigraphs, and Continuous, Distributed Monitoring of Dynamic, Heterogeneous Data (Homeland Security Center for Dynamic Data Analysis, 2009). In addition to the theoretical research, applied research was performed. The IDS center was a project between the DHS and many national laboratories that were based at Lawrence Livermore National Laboratory.

Obtained from chapter information discussing the new significance of social media's association to Homeland Security safety endeavors, social media outlets could be looked upon as security conduits. Social media outlets such as the Internet, Twitter, Facebook, Instagram, eBuddy, and even cell phones could be and have been lifesavers in the face of threat. All of these social media outlets could play a major role in communication. One big threat to American citizenry is that of human trafficking which shows a large statistic for the victimization of our youth. On a daily basis one-half of all teenagers transmit approximately fifty text messages. Ninety percent of high school seniors visit a social media site at least once a day (Lenhart, 2010; Myers, 2010). The International Telecommunication Union (2010), reports that about seven billion human beings communicate by using their cell phones for texting or voice. Herein lies a segue for communication in the face of threat, not just for the youth, but for anyone.

Norris, Stevens, Pfefferbaum, Wyche, and Pfefferbaum (2008), assert that it is imperative that communities adopt behaviors that reduce risk during and after emergencies. When there are inequities in resources and when communities of people are threatened, communities must connect with each other and increase social support systems to create community and organization safety nets. Human-to-human contact and social media are becoming more involved as a potential safety measure to lessen threat. With these types of social media and the number of people electronically connecting, there are positive implications for teaching citizens the best behaviors and actions to take in order to communicate in case of emergency, and to unite in cases of terrorism, cyber attacks, or to inform law enforcement about information on human trafficking and other crimes (CCICADA Official Website, Fact Sheet, 2013). CCICADA and homeland security educate students in various areas in order that they become future leaders in the training of others to better understand these types of threats and how to avoid them.

CCICADA's educational and research initiatives have promoted education programs, conferences, and science projects that have encouraged new courses which in turn produced certificate programs, homeland security workshops, summer programs in data sciences, and tutorials for precollege and college teachers, as well as homeland security and law enforcement professionals, university faculty, and STEM students. The information shared here can be viewed as a channel to encourage even more ideas for science and educational programs to ensure an even wider opportunity of learning and training among science analysts, behavioral scientists, researchers, students of varying disciplines of study and corporate administrators concerned with the safety and well-being of citizens in a fast growing and rapidly-changing homeland society. Norris, Stevens, Pfefferbaum, Wyche, and Pfefferbaum (2008) state that, "[c]ommunities have the potential to function effectively and adapt successfully in the aftermath of disasters" (p. 127). We, as scientists, understand human strength and resilience; however, CCICADA is interested in ensuring that citizens are secure before disaster as well. As suggested by Carafano and Weitz (2009), CCICADA as a Center of Excellence is arranging and organizing intellectual meetings between and among recognized researchers and other experts in the fields of data science to conduct research from various disciplines, geared towards the study of complex DHS Homeland Security issues, challenges, and problems.

REFERENCES

Annual Aspen Security Forum. (2013, July 18). *Intelligence and counterterrorism – Panel discussion*. National Counterterrorism Center. Retrieval information: CSPAN2 and http://www.aspeninstitute.org/policy-work/homeland-security

Barber, J. E. (2012). Envision success: Exploring data on personal well-being could help. *Instructional Forum-The Academic Affairs Area Journal*, *27*(2), 5–6.

Carafano, J. J., & Weitz, R. E. (2009). Complex systems analysis: A necessary tool for home security. *Backgrounder. Heritage Foundation*, *2261*, 1–7.

Command, C., & the Interoperability Center for Advanced Data Analysis (CCICADA). (2013). *About CCICADA*. Retrieved from http://ccicada.rutgers.edu/about.html

Command, C.Interoperability Center for Advanced Data Analysis (CCICADA). (2013). *CCICADA* [Unpublished Brochure]. Piscataway, NJ: Rutgers University.

Department of Homeland Security. (2002). *Homeland Security Act of 2002, title I*. Retrieved from http://www.dhs.gov/homeland-security-act-2002

Department of Homeland Security. (2008). *Reading by numbers*. Retrieved from http://www.dhs.gov/reading-numbers

Department of Homeland Security. (n.d.). *Centers of excellence.* Retrieved from http://www.dhs.gov/st-centers-excellence

Estellés-Arolas, E., & González-Ladrón-de-Guevara, F. (2012). Towards an integrated crowdsourcing definition. *Journal of Information Science, 38*(2), 189–200. doi:10.1177/0165551512437638

Homeland Security Center for Dynamic Data Analysis. (2009). *DyDAn research projects.* Retrieved from http://www.dydan.rutgers.edu

Howe, J. (2006). Crowdsourcing: A definition. Crowdsourcing Blog. Retrieved from http://crowdsourcing.typepad.com/cs/2006/06/crowdsourcing_a.html

International Telecommunication Union (ITU). (2010). *ICT facts and figures.* Retrieved from www.itu.int/ict.

Jacobs, A. (2009, July 1). The pathologies of big data. *ACMQueue.* Retrieved from http://queue.acm.org/detail.cfm?id=1563874

Koebler, J. (2012, November 16). *Phones become the 'frontline' of human sex-trafficking.* U.S. News and World Report. Retrieved from http://www.usnews.com/news/articles/2012/11/16/report-phones-become-the-frontline-of-human-sex-trafficking

Lenhart, A. (2010, April 20). *Teens, cell phones, and texting.* Pew Internet and American Life Project. Retrieved from www.pewresearch.org

Myers, D. G. (2010). *Social psychology* (11th ed.). New York: McGraw-Hill Publishers.

National Association of Mathematicians. (2013). *NAM.* Retrieved from www.nam-math.org

Norris, F. H., Stevens, S. P., Pfefferbaum, B., Wyche, K. F., & Pfefferbaum, R. L. (2008). Community resilience as a metaphor, theory, set of capacities, and strategy for disaster readiness. *American Journal of Community Psychology, 41*(1-2), 127–150. doi:10.1007/s10464-007-9156-6 PMID:18157631

Oak Ridge Institute for Science Education (ORISE). (2003). *ORISE supports research for solutions to homeland security needs.* Retrieved from http://orise.orau.gov/scientific-peer-review/difference/homeland-security.aspx

Roberts, F. S. (2004). Why bioMath? Why now? In F. Roberts, & M. Cozzens (Eds.), *BioMath in the schools* (pp. 3–34). Providence, RI: DIMACS – American Mathematical Society.

Shaw, A. (2004). *University research centers of excellence for homeland security: A summary of a workshop*. Washington, DC: National Research Council, National Academies Press.

Stanton, J.M. (2012, May 20). *Introduction to data science*. Syracuse, NY: Syracuse University School of Information Studies.

Yang, J., Adamic, L., & Ackerman, M. (2008). Crowdsourcing and knowledge sharing: Strategic user behavior on taskcn. In *Proceedings of the 9th ACM Conference on Electronic Commerce*. ACM.

KEY TERMS AND DEFINITIONS

Command, Control, and Interoperability Center for Advanced Data Analysis (CCICADA): A constituent of the Department of Homeland Security (DHS) Center of Excellence (COE) Center for Visualization and Data Analytics (CVADA).

Crowdsourcing: The observance of the behavior of large networks of people in the online or offline community as a way to solve problems. The participants are generally volunteers.

Data Science: A science of analyzing, preparing, collecting, visualizing, and managing large data sets by incorporating information and study from various STEM and social science disciplines.

Data Sciences Summer Institute (DSSI): A keystone of CCICADA's education program. DSSI was initially developed at partner institution the University of Illinois – Urbana Champaign to encourage computer science students in universities with small research programs to pursue graduate studies and to expose students to the national research laboratories.

Department of Homeland Security Center of Excellence: An association of many universities and businesses whose work and research is to create and produce innovative and groundbreaking high technologies and critical knowledge in homeland securities. COE is sponsored by the DHS Office of University Programs and supported by the Oak Ridge Institute for Science Education (ORISE).

Discrete Science: Examines, studies, and analyzes patterns and assignments of large data sets, including schedules and arrangement. The purpose is to utilize this science to establish connections between individuals or groups and to provide better ways to identify changes in data patterns.

Homeland Security: No definitive definition exists for this special and important entity. Its purpose is multifaceted, as one of its main purposes is to "secure" the safety and well being of all citizens of America.

Modeling and Simulation: Modeling tools can be used by researchers to better understand consequences of actions or behaviors, and simulations are used to show the ultimate real effects of different conditions and courses of action or behavior. Simulation is also used when the actual system cannot be engaged, or because it may not be accessible. It may not yet be built, or it simply may not exist.

Reconnect: Workshops that expose undergraduate teaching faculty to the interchange between the mathematical and computer sciences and the department of homeland securities by introducing the faculty to relevant research topics that can be implemented in classroom lectures, activities, and presentations.

Research Experiences for Undergraduates (REUs): REU programs provide undergraduate students with an interesting and important research experiences that will positively enhance their academic decisions and future educational and career goals.

Social Media: Internet, Website, and electronic means of communicating socially. Operationally defined here, social media is described in a more complex way than the term is generally expressed. It is looked at as more than being useful for socializing, but also as an Internet, networking tool for security, where humans are able to electronically and quickly communicate with each other in case of emergency or homeland threat.

Section 2
Research and Knowledge Discovery

Chapter 4
Detecting Electronic Initiators Using Electromagnetic Emissions

Colin Stagner
Missouri S&T, USA

Steve Grant
Missouri S&T, USA

Sarah Seguin
University of Kansas, USA

Daryl Beetner
Missouri S&T, USA

EXECUTIVE SUMMARY

The accurate and timely discovery of radio receivers can assist in the detection of radio-controlled explosives. By detecting radio receivers, it is possible to indirectly infer the presence of an explosive device. Radio receivers unintentionally emit low-power radio signals during normal operation. By using a weak stimulation signal, it is possible to inject a known signal into these unintended emissions. This process is known as stimulated emissions. Unlike chemical traces, these stimulated emissions can propagate through walls and air-tight containers. The following case study discusses methods for detecting and locating two different types of radio receivers. Functional stimulated emissions detectors are constructed, and their performance is analyzed. Stimulated emissions are capable of detecting super-regenerative receivers at distances of at least one hundred meters and accurately locating superheterodyne receivers at distances of at least fifty meters. These results demonstrate a novel technique for detecting potential explosive threats at stand-off detection distances.

DOI: 10.4018/978-1-4666-5946-9.ch004

ORGANIZATION BACKGROUND

Remote detection of improvised explosive devices is essential to guaranteeing safety in conflict-prone environments. The Missouri University of Science and Technology (Missouri S&T) works closely with the Awareness and Localization of Explosive-Related Threats (ALERT) center in order to develop practical, cutting-edge technology for countering explosive-related threats. Missouri S&T is a state university located in Rolla, Missouri and is formerly known as the University of Missouri—Rolla.

In recent years, the university has experienced steady, aggressive growth. Since 2003, according to institutional research reports, undergraduate and graduate enrollment have each increased by over 40%, and operating revenue has grown by 134%. University research is funded principally by grants and contracts from participating institutions. In 2012, the university accrued over $31.2 million U.S. Dollars in such funding, which is a 17% increase since 2003 (Kumar et al., 2012). A portion of this funding is used to finance emerging research for detecting improvised explosive devices (IEDs).

Missouri S&T's counter-IED research takes place in concert with government agencies, such as the Department of Homeland Security, and military organizations like the Leonard Wood Institute. The executive director of the Leonard Wood Institute has praised the university's accomplishments, asserting that Missouri S&T is "the number one place to do something about detecting IEDs" (Bruns, 2009). As of early 2013, the university maintained at least fifteen different counter-IED projects in areas such as detection, neutralization, and blast mitigation. The research conducted for the ALERT Center of Excellence focuses on the detection of explosive devices and blast mitigation.

The following case study presents the key findings from the ALERT Center project for the detection of electronically-initiated explosive devices.

CASE DESCRIPTION

Explosive devices typically contain at least three components: propellant, a payload, and an initiator. Each of these components provides a different opportunity to detect the device. Although the first two components are the most specific indication that explosives are present, another way to detect potential explosive devices is to detect the initiator. Explosive devices are commonly initiated using proximity sensors or remote triggers (Wilson, 2006; Griffith, 2007). Such initiators generate electrical signals which can radiate into the environment as electromagnetic emissions. By detecting potential initiators, it is possible to indirectly infer the presence of an explosive device.

The purpose of this work is to improve techniques for detecting specific types of electronic initiators. Radio receivers of every variety, such as doorbells, automobile key fobs, two-way radios, and cellular telephones, have been used by insurgents as remote initiators (Smith & Coderre, 2008). For example, the devices used in the 2013 Boston Marathon bombings contained parts from a remote-control car (Chuchmach, 2013). These radio receivers unintentionally radiate low-power radio signals during normal operation. By using a weak stimulation signal, it is possible to inject a known signal into these unintended emissions. This technique has proven to be effective at detecting super-regenerative (Seguin, 2009a) and superheterodyne (Stagner, Conrad, Osterwise, Beetner, & Grant, 2011) radio receivers. The following sections detail the research and development process of an improved radio-receiver detector.

Technology Concerns

At present, there are three main techniques for detecting explosive devices: manual search, portal screening, and chemical trace detection. Manual search techniques utilize explosives ordinance disposal (EOD) technicians to find and neutralize explosives. Clearing an area is a time-consuming, dangerous task which can expose personnel and resources, such as robots, to risk. In portal screening techniques, a secure area is defined, and persons entering the area are subject to a thorough search. This technique results in large delays and great expense: the United States spends $4.8 billion dollars per year on security checkpoints for its airports (*Department of Homeland Security Appropriations Bill, 2009*, 2008).

Both of these search methods are often augmented with some type of explosives-detection sensor. The 2001 shoe bombing plot and the Christmas Day bombing attempt in 2009 illustrate the need for such sensors. Chemical traces are the most specific indication that explosives are present, and the ALERT Center has developed a number of different techniques for detecting them. By characterizing the chemical composition and behavior of high-explosives, such as ammonium nitrate (Davidson, Chellappa, Raja, Dattelbaum, & Yoo, 2011), it is possible to build more reliable sensors. Terahertz imaging techniques offer improved portal screening with an inherent explosives-detection capability (Dai et al., 2011).

Standoff detection—the ability to detect explosives from outside of their effective range—is an important, emerging area of research. Raman spectroscopy has the potential to detect chemical traces on surfaces, using lasers, at great distances (Pacheco-Londoño, Ortiz-Rivera, Primera-Pedrozo, & Hernández-Rivera, 2009). These techniques have inherent disadvantages, however. All chemical trace systems, including canines, have difficulty detecting explosives which are housed in air-tight containers (Nambayah & Quickenden, 2004). Scanning a large area can be extremely time consuming. Obstacles like hills, trees, and buildings can prevent detection. Indirect methods, which detect the non-explosive components, can be useful in these situations.

Many types of electronic devices generate and process high-frequency signals. These signals can radiate from resonant features in the device's printed circuit board (PCB) and packaging, escaping into the environment as *unintended electromagnetic emissions*. Others have demonstrated that these emissions can reveal information about a device's purpose and internal state (Sekiguchi & Seto, 2008). Unlike chemical traces, these unintended emissions can propagate freely through closed containers and vehicles. This approach makes rapid, non-line-of-sight device detection feasible at relatively long range.

In order to provide a substantial advantage over the direct methods, an electronic initiator detector must offer high sensitivity and selectivity. A high-sensitivity detector should be capable of detecting weak, unintended electromagnetic emissions—the power of which is strictly limited by regulation. A highly selective detector should be capable of separating devices which pose an explosive-related threat from the extraordinary variety of electronic devices which do not. Selectivity and sensitivity can be improved by using specific knowledge of the emissions' characteristics.

Stimulated Emissions: The Core Technique

Radio receivers are, by design, highly responsive to weak electromagnetic signals. It is trivial to inject a known signal into a radio receiver: all that is necessary is to transmit a radio signal within the radio's receive band and receiving range. This can

Figure 1. In stimulated emissions detection, a probe signal (the "stimulation") is used to change the internal state of an electronic device. The change in state alters the device's unintended electromagnetic emissions, which radiate back out into the environment

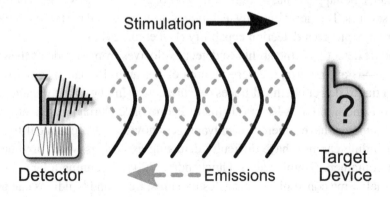

be accomplished by using relatively low power so as not to interfere with licensed radio users. This weak stimulation signal can alter the radio receiver's unintended emissions in a predictable manner—it can change their spectral content, duty cycle, and/or power. Often the emissions are separated in frequency from the stimulation, making them easy to detect. This technique, which is depicted in Figure 1, is called *stimulated emissions* detection, and it has been patented by Missouri S&T (Beetner, Seguin, & Hubing, 2008).

The idea of using electromagnetic interactions to detect a device is not new. A common method of detecting the presence of an electronic device is to use a "bug scanner," which stimulates an emission to detect non-linear junctions. These bug scanners work by illuminating a desired target with a known electromagnetic stimulation that is then modulated by non-linear junctions in the device, causing it to re-radiate harmonics of the original stimulation signal (Dourbal, 1998).

These "bug" detectors are often difficult to use in practice. A large number of non-linear junctions respond to this type of stimulation. For example, the non-linear response from a rusty nail is similar to the response from an electronic device such as a radio receiver. The reflected power is typically about 90 dB below the incident power, requiring these detectors to either be used at very high power or at close range to be effective. Hand-held devices that operate at "low" power levels of 1 – 3 W typically have a range of only a few meters. Others have shown that the power required to induce non-linear effects in a digital device is, at stand-off detection distances, prohibitive (Flintoft, Marvin, Robinson, Fischer, & Rowell, 2003).

In contrast, the stimulated emissions detectors can operate at transmitter power levels less than 200 mW and can achieve useful detection ranges which exceed fifty meters. Stimulated emissions are known to function with both super-regenerative and superheterodyne receivers. These receivers, and their unintended emissions, are discussed in the following sections.

Super-Regenerative Receivers

Super-regenerative receivers are low-cost radio receivers which are used in a wide variety of consumer electronics. They are popular in doorbells, garage door openers, key-less entry systems, remote sensing, remote control toys, and many other applications where low-rate data is required. The super-regenerative receiver (SRR) costs less than $3 U.S. Dollars in components but is limited to linear modulation formats, such as amplitude modulation (AM) (Zimmerman, 1999). This limitation is a result of the cost-saving regenerative circuit that these devices include.

An SRR functions by allowing the incoming radio signal, received from the antenna, to oscillate in an under-damped feedback loop. Over time, the oscillations increase in magnitude, much like feedback from an acoustic amplifier which is too close to its microphone. When the oscillations reach a certain critical threshold, they are quenched (i.e., reduced to zero) by a separate circuit, and the process begins again.

As detailed in Giacoletto and Landee (1977), the time between quenches is logarithmically proportional to the magnitude of the incoming radio signal. By measuring this inter-quench time, a super-regenerative receiver can estimate the magnitude—but not the phase—of the received signal. This makes the SRR a discrete-time system. Most super-regenerative receivers quench and sample at ultrasonic rates of a few hundred kHz, which is sufficient for low-rate data.

Super-regenerative receivers tend to have high-power electromagnetic emissions. Others have shown that SRRs have impulsive emissions which are readily detectable, without processing, at close range. These emissions are centered (in frequency) around the carrier frequency to which the device is tuned (Shaik, Weng, Dong, Hubing, & Beetner, 2006). These pulses originate from the quenching circuit. A sample of these emissions is given in Figure 2.

One tool for detecting periodic impulse signals, such as the quenching emissions, is the Fast Folding Algorithm (FFA). The FFA, which was developed in Staelin (1969) for radio astronomy, searches over many candidate periods by overlapping the signal with time-delayed versions of itself. A time-memory trade-off reduces the computational complexity. SRR emissions are not ideal impulses, however, but they can be modeled as square pulses. This simplification enables a filter-bank approach, which is known as cascading correlation.

Figure 2. Pulses from a super-regenerative receiver in the time-frequency domain. These unintended emissions are nearly periodic

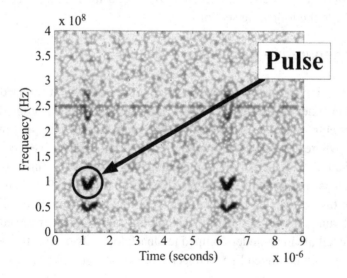

Figure 3. As the power of the stimulation is increased (top), the inter-pulse time (bottom) decreases. This behavior is caused by the super-regenerative receiver's quenching circuit

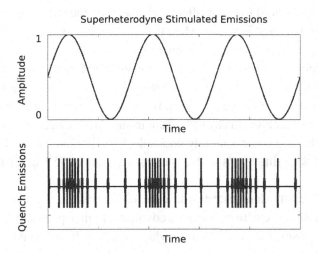

In the cascading correlation technique, the electromagnetic emissions are digitally filtered with a large number of candidate pulse trains of various periods. The output energy of each filter is averaged over many consecutive periods. A device is detected if the energy output of one of the filters exceeds some threshold; this indicates that a signal with the filter's periodicity is present. This passive technique, which does not require a stimulation, is capable of detecting typical SRRs at ranges of about forty meters.

The quenching emissions are, by design, stimulated emissions. Since the quench rate—and thus the quenching emissions—depends on the magnitude of the stimulation, super-regenerative receivers have stimulated emissions. By varying the stimulation power, as depicted in Figure 3, it is possible to alter the inter-quench time. This behavior is confirmed by Seguin (2009a) with measurements of actual super-regenerative receivers. Stimulated emissions enables the use of several novel detection algorithms.

One difficulty with the cascading correlation technique, as with most detection methods, is setting the detector's threshold. The RF noise present in a given environment can vary over time and with space, and this noise contributes to the observed energy at the filter's output. Other devices, which are not radio receivers, may also have unintended electromagnetic emissions which corrupt the measurement. Another disadvantage is that the filter bank is most effective only when the device's quench rate is known. Stimulated emissions helps solve both of these problems.

If the stimulation signal is the dominant (i.e., strongest) signal being received by an SRR, altering the stimulation's power will change the period of the emissions. This, in turn, changes the filter output which contains the SRR's electromagnetic emissions. The threshold for each filter can be set with the stimulation signal off. If a filter's output increases in power when the stimulation signal is transmitted, then the change is likely due to a super-regenerative receiver.

This technique was tested using a narrow-band 50 MHz continuous wave (CW) stimulation. Since the stimulation is narrow-band, it is simple to remove from the wideband emissions with a narrow notch filter. This technique was tested on a real super-regenerative receiver in an outdoor environment. At extreme distances, where the passive technique was essentially unusable, the stimulated emissions approach was capable of detecting SRRs with a true positive rate of 95% and a false positive rate of 11%.

The above results demonstrate the ease of adapting a passive algorithm to stimulated emissions detection, but more advanced, higher-performing methods are available. By transmitting a stimulation which is a pseudo-random (PN) code, it is possible to detect the presence of the code—in a robust manner—with a correlator. PN codes are used to great effect in the Global Positioning System (GPS), where they enable data transmission under extremely poor noise conditions (Gleason & Gebre-Egziabher, 2009).

The most effective technique, given the constraints imposed by the super-regenerative receiver, is to use a PN code with an on-off keying (OOK) modulation. An OOK-modulated PN code is transmitted into the environment, and the magnitude of the received emissions is calculated. If the emissions' magnitude correlates strongly with the PN stimulation, then a super-regenerative receiver is present. This architecture is similar in nature to a spread-spectrum communications system.

A similar version of this approach, which used amplitude-shift keying (ASK) signals, was tested in Seguin. The algorithm does away with the processor-intensive filter bank and uses a square-law detector instead. This eliminates the need to know (or guess) the device's quench rate, greatly improving the potential for detecting unfamiliar, uncharacterized SRRs. The algorithm, as the receiver operating characteristic (ROC) curve in Figure 4 indicates, outperformed the cascading correlation approach and achieved reliable detection at distances of up to one hundred meters (Seguin, 2009b). This stimulated emissions approach has proven to offer reliable, long-range detection of super-regenerative receivers.

Superheterodyne Receivers

While modern devices use a variety of radio receiver designs, the superheterodyne receiver remains one of the most common. Broadcast radio receivers, cellular

Figure 4. Modulating the stimulated emissions results in a more reliable detector. The reliability—i.e., the ability of the detector to separate true positives from true negatives—is quantified by the area under the curves

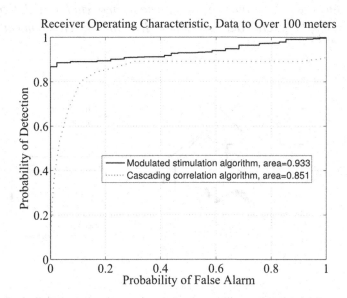

phones, and two-way radios frequently incorporate superheterodyne receivers. They are more expensive, but more flexible, than super-regenerative receivers. Superheterodyne receivers make a nearly-perfect copy of the incoming radio signal at a lower frequency. Such an accurate copy allows advanced modulation formats, such as frequency modulation (FM) or frequency-shift keying (FSK), to be used. This makes superheterodyne receivers ideal for reproducing high-quality voice and high-rate data signals.

Radio communication systems use high-frequency signals to transmit information. Radio carrier frequencies can exceed several gigahertz in frequency, but the bandwidth of the message signal—i.e., the information being transmitted—is much, much less. For example, commercial FM uses a carrier frequency near 100 MHz to transmit a 150 kHz-wide message signal, and Wi-Fi (IEEE 802.11g) uses a 2.4 GHz carrier frequency to send a digital signal which is only 20 MHz wide. It is advantageous to discard the high-frequency carrier signal, which does not contain any information, and retain only the message signal. This substantially reduces the difficulty of processing (i.e., demodulating) the radio signal.

Superheterodyne receivers eliminate the carrier by performing a process known as *frequency translation*. Frequency translation reduces the frequency of the incoming radio signal, lowering it to a fixed intermediate frequency (IF). The IF has a much lower frequency than the original radio signal, but it has a sufficiently high

Figure 5. In a superheterodyne receiver, the mixer shifts the RF input both down in frequency (IF component) and up in frequency (up-mixing component). These signals are plotted conceptually below. The receiver itself keeps only the IF component; the other signals are filtered out. The up-mixing component has a high frequency, and—before it can be filtered out—tends to radiate into the environment

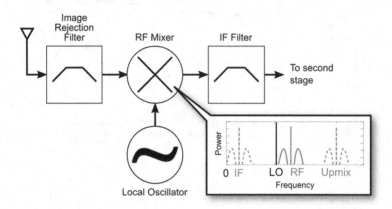

frequency to preserve the message signal. Frequency translation is an application of the modulation theorem of the Fourier Transform, which states that it is possible to change the frequency of a signal by multiplying it with a cosine.

This cosine multiplication has an unintended consequence, however. From the modulation theorem, as given in Bracewell (1999), lowering the frequency by f produces a second component which is shifted up in frequency by f. This unwanted component is referred to herein as the *up-mixing component*, as it is an up-mixed (rather than down-mixed) copy of the received signal. This signal is mathematically required to exist whenever strictly real (i.e., non-complex) signals are used. This behavior is depicted in Figure 5.

The radio receiver uses a filter to discard the up-mixing component. Before it is filtered out, however, the up-mixing component can radiate from the device as unintended electromagnetic emissions. The up-mixing component has a frequency that is much higher than the original radio frequency; in some cases, it is almost double. For General Mobile Radio Service (GMRS) receivers, which have been the subject of extensive study, the up-mixing frequency exceeds 900 MHz. At such high frequencies, very small structures can act as resonant antennas, making the up-mixing emissions likely to radiate.

This finding has enabled the development of stimulated emissions techniques for detecting superheterodyne receivers. The up-mixing emissions are an exact copy, subject to certain constraints, of the signal that the device is receiving. These emissions are mathematically required to exist and, since they have a high frequency, are likely to radiate. Prior research indicates that real-world consumer radio receivers have detectable stimulated emissions (Stagner et al., 2011).

If a weak stimulation signal is broadcast into the environment, a superheterodyne receiver will re-radiate that signal, on a different frequency, as a stimulated emission. Using this information, the ALERT Center of Excellence has produced novel techniques for detecting the presence and physical location of superheterodyne receivers.

Detecting Superheterodyne Receivers

Stimulated emissions detection outperforms existing, passive methods for detecting superheterodyne receivers. Passive techniques focus on detecting the cosine mixing signal, which is referred to as the local oscillator (LO). The LO emissions can be relatively strong, and others have demonstrated that they can be detected using periodograms (Wild & Ramchandran, 2005). Existing research focuses on broadcast receivers such as television sets, however, and does not include communications receivers.

Communications receivers, such as walkie-talkies, are designed for intermittent use. In order to conserve power, most devices have a power-saving function which inhibits—among other things—the radio receiver. Measurements indicate that, if a communications receiver does not detect a signal of interest, it will periodically deactivate its local oscillator to save power. This greatly decreases the effectiveness of periodogram techniques.

In order to determine the effectiveness of stimulated emissions with communications receivers, representative devices were selected for emissions testing. These tests were conducted using General Mobile Radio Service (GMRS) receivers. GMRS is a low-power radio service which uses analog frequency modulation (FM) in the 460 MHz band. Such services have not changed much since their inception (Noble, 1962), and neither have radio receivers. The superheterodyne receiver pre-dates the transistor (Swinyard, 1962), and most receivers on the market today use similar designs.

A stimulation signal was selected for maximum compatibility with GMRS receivers. GMRS receivers are designed to receive FM signals and, as such, may incorporate non-linear amplifiers which distort AM signals. In addition, the up-mixing emissions frequency varies with respect to the intermediate frequency and the local oscillator frequency. Because of this, the emissions can exhibit considerable frequency ambiguity, and it is necessary to select a signal which correlates well even when frequency-shifted.

One appropriate stimulation signal is linear, frequency-modulated (LFM) chirp. LFM chirps are sinusoidal signals with a frequency that varies linearly with respect to time. Linear chirps match-filter effectively even when shifted in frequency (Levanon

Figure 6. The stimulation signal (top) and the corresponding stimulated emissions from the GMRS receiver (bottom). The stimulation and the emissions appear almost identical. The "holes" (i.e., missing signal) in the emissions are due to the radio receiver toggling its local oscillator on and off to conserve power. The stimulation signal partially inhibits this power-saving behavior, making the device easier to detect

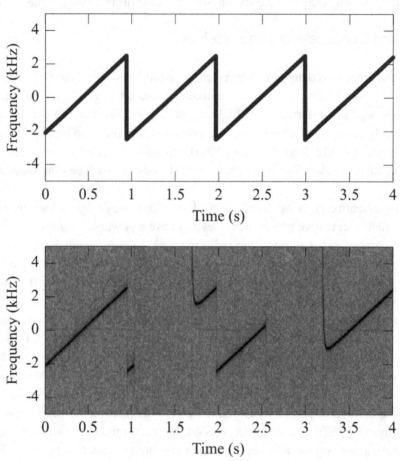

& Mozeson, 2004a). Others have shown that the performance of a matched filter depends on the signal's time-bandwidth product (Jankiraman, 2007). Chirps which are 1024 ms long and have a bandwidth equal to the maximum allowable frequency deviation for GMRS (5 kHz) have a sufficient time-bandwidth product for detection.

Testing indicates that GMRS receivers have identifiable up-mixing emissions. Close-range measurements of a GMRS receiver's emissions, which are shown in

Figure 7. Matched filter detection, combined with a threshold detector, can be used to detect known signals such as stimulated emissions. If the emissions closely match the stimulation signal, the matched filter will output more energy. A threshold test can be used to determine if a superheterodyne receiver is present

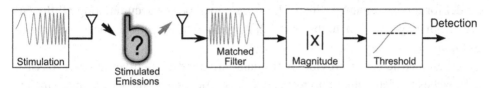

Figure 8. Stimulated emissions (top) is a more accurate detector, at equivalent SNRs, than the passive periodogram approach (bottom) described in Wild and Ramchandran (2005). Adapted from (Stagner et al., 2011), © 2011 IEEE. Used with permission

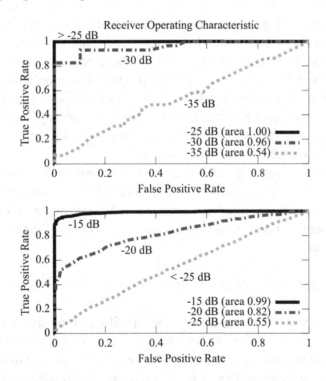

Figure 6, clearly indicate the presence of the original stimulation signal. These measurements demonstrate that GMRS receivers can pass arbitrary signals through their superheterodyne front-end, up-mix, and retransmit them. This makes matched-filter detection possible.

Since superheterodyne receivers have emissions which are nearly identical to the stimulation signal, it is possible to use matched filters to detect these receivers. A matched filter is the optimal linear filter for detecting a *known* signal which is corrupted with additive white Gaussian noise (Turin, 1960), which is a typical model for a noisy channel. Such filters are a method for accumulating all the energy from long-duration, high-bandwidth signals. The detection process is outlined in Figure 7.

Stimulated detection provides both quantitative and qualitative gains over passive approaches for detecting radio receivers. Theoretical performance testing, which is detailed in Stagner et al. (2011), indicates that the matched filter detector has a 5–10 dB performance increase over a passive detector. The ROC curves for the detector, which was tested in a simulated environment, are given in Figure 8. In addition, matched filter detection provides high certainty that the detected device is actually a radio receiver.

One challenge with detecting LO emissions is that it is difficult to differentiate the narrow-band LO signal from other narrow-band signals, which are commonly radiated unintentionally from a wide variety of other electronic devices. Stimulated emissions can significantly enhance detection selectivity. In order for a device to re-radiate a weak stimulation signal, it must be sensitive to such signals by design. For the re-radiated signal to occur within a specific frequency range, the device must have a mixer and an oscillator operating within a specific frequency range. In other words, the device must be a radio receiver.

Stimulated emissions offers an improved method for detecting electronic initiators. As a side-effect of this active detection process, it is also possible to calculate the round-trip time of the stimulated emissions. This property, which is discussed in the subsequent section, enables the accurate, indoor radio-location of potential explosive threats.

Locating Superheterodyne Receivers

Radio receivers have many uses; they're not specific to explosive devices. When a receiver is detected, a follow-up search is necessary to confirm the presence of an explosive threat. Knowing the position of the receiver, referred to herein as the target device, as well as whether or not it is moving, would substantially expedite this search. Determining the position of radio emitters—intentional or not—is a well-studied problem, and many solutions exist. Position-finding methods can vary in complexity from simple directional antennas to the complicated mathematics of global navigation satellite systems.

A radio position-finding system estimates either the power, the angle of arrival, or the time of arrival of the incoming radio signal. Power estimates are minimally useful for finding radio receivers, however, as they require that the source radiate isotropically—i.e., equally in all directions (Patwari, Hero III, Perkins, Correal, & O'Dea, 2003). Stimulated emissions radiate opportunistically, from structures which are not purposely-built isotropic antennas. Since the emissions' power depends on the device's orientation, and the orientation cannot be known, power measurements are not a reliable estimator of position.

Angle-of-arrival (AoA) techniques are well-developed and are capable of locating unintended electromagnetic emissions. Angle of arrival can be estimated using directional antennas. These antennas can be physically directional, as in (Moseley, 1955), or virtually directional using antenna arrays and beam-forming techniques (Orfanidis, 1988). Antenna arrays have been proven to enhance the channel capacity of communication systems (Zheng & Tse, 2003), and in recent years they have become a standard part of such systems. It is unsurprising, then, that others have developed antenna array techniques for locating super-regenerative receivers (Thotla, Ghasr, Zawodniok, Jagannathan, & Agarwal, 2012).

Multipath propagation poses a problem for AoA and position-finding techniques in general. In multipath propagation, a radio signal reflects from smooth, conductive objects. This results in multiple waves arriving at the receiver. Studies have shown that, in indoor propagation environments, it can be difficult to distinguish multipath from direct-path signals (Spencer, Rice, Jeffs, & Jensen, 1997). In this case, the estimated angle to the target device will be incorrect—often, wildly so. This makes it worthwhile to investigate other methods for position-finding.

Figure 9. Time of arrival measures the round-trip time of a signal. In this case, the signal in question is the stimulated emissions, which propagate at the speed of light from the detector to the target—and back again. The stimulation signal must interact with the circuitry inside the target device, which imposes an additional delay

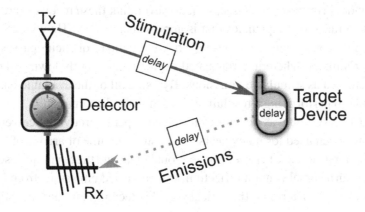

Time of arrival (ToA) measures the round-trip time of a signal and, assuming that it propagates at a known velocity, determines the distance to the source. This technique is used in radar and radio-navigation systems. ToA is inherently compatible with stimulated emissions: both techniques require the transmission and reception of a known signal. This behavior is illustrated in Figure 9. Lee & Scholtz (2002) demonstrated a ToA technique which is resistant to multipath, and similar systems may outperform AoA in indoor environments. Time of arrival can either complement or serve as a lower-cost, single-antenna alternative to angle of arrival.

In order to be of practical use, a radio-location system must make highly accurate ToA measurements. The main factor impacting this accuracy is the available bandwidth. In Skolnik (1960), it was proven that the accuracy of commonly-used radar signals is proportional to the bandwidth of the signal. Under practical conditions, high-bandwidth signals are necessary to make meaningful measurements. This limitation arises chiefly from the uncertainty principle of the Fourier Transform.

In order to clearly demarcate the time of arrival, it is necessary to use a stimulation signal with rapid transitions. Faster transitions result in less error because the detector can find the transition point with greater accuracy. This is particularly true when the signal-to-noise ratio (SNR) is poor. By the uncertainty principle, these rapid transitions result in a signal which is less concentrated in the frequency domain (Pinsky, 2002). In other words, faster transitions require more bandwidth. The 5 kHz linear chirps used in the previous section do not have enough bandwidth to offer adequate performance.

The bandwidth available for stimulated emissions is limited by the target device. In Stagner et al. (2013), it is demonstrated that the bandwidth limitation is due primarily to the device's *image rejection filter*. The image rejection filter (see Figure 5) is designed to limit the overall bandwidth which can enter a superheterodyne receiver. Since this filter operates at radio frequencies, it is typically a low-order device which passes much more bandwidth than the receiver requires.

For example, GMRS receivers are designed to tune to and receive a band that is 175 kHz wide. Prior research has shown, however, that these receivers are actually sensitive to a range of frequencies that is approximately 23 MHz wide (Stagner et al., 2013). This contiguous, 23 MHz-wide band of radio frequencies passes through the receiver's mixer, where it is translated in frequency—both down and up—and is also re-emitted as stimulated emissions. By using all of the available bandwidth, it is possible to perform high-resolution time-of-arrival estimation.

A radar-like system was developed to locate superheterodyne receivers. Radar systems have been used for many years to measure the time of arrival of weak signals. The major difference between conventional radar and the technique used herein is that the return signal is not a reflection; it is modified emissions from the target device. In order to determine the efficacy of this technique under realistic conditions, the radar system was implemented in hardware and tested, using consumer radio receivers as targets.

The system, which is documented in more detail in the following section, used linear FM chirps which were 16 MHz wide. Extensive testing, conducted in Stagner et al. (2013), indicates that the system could determine the range to two different receivers. These target devices were "off the shelf" walkie-talkies which had no inherent radio-location capabilities. The radar system could, nonetheless, determine the position of the target with less than five meters of root mean square error, under real-world noise and multipath conditions. The accuracy of the system, plotted in Figure 10, matches Skolnik's accuracy model (Stagner et al., 2013).

Time of arrival-based location has one major hurdle, however, which must be addressed prior to its inclusion in commercial, national-security products. As shown in Figure 9, the target device imposes its own delay on the stimulated emissions as the stimulation signal is received and then re-radiated. This delay can be large compared to the distance-dependent speed of light delay and, more importantly, may differ substantially from device to device. This makes it difficult to determine the absolute range to the target device.

Even if the absolute range is unavailable, ToA can still determine the *relative* range to the device. Relative range can be used to observe changes in the device's

Figure 10. The noise performance of the radar-like system. The experimental performance (data points) fits the theoretical model of accuracy (dashed line). A higher SNR results in a more precise position fix. These tests and their results are described in detail in Stagner et al. (2013). © 2013, IEEE. Used with permission

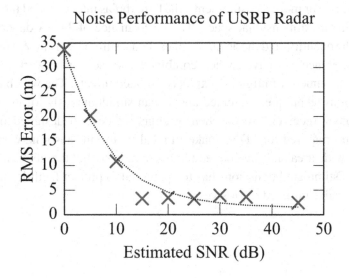

Figure 11. Time-of-arrival measurements taken at three different points. The difference in arrival time between each pair of points defines a hyperbola in between them. The intersection of two such hyperbola can locate the target device in 2D space

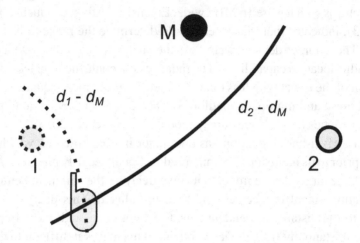

range over time and—with multiple antenna sites—space. The former technique can be used to determine how the target is moving relative to the transmitter, and the latter is a powerful position-finding technique known as time difference of arrival (TDoA). TDoA techniques are used to great effect in global navigation satellite systems (Gleason & Gebre-Egziabher, 2009).

In TDoA, relative range estimates from multiple, known positions are combined to determine the position of the target. As shown in Figure 11, the difference between arrival times, taken at two different positions, locates the target on a hyperbola between them. With three or more measurements, the hyperbolas intersect, and the target can be located in two-dimensional space. The performance of TDoA depends on the geometry, the quantity, and the accuracy of each measurement (Bard & Ham, 1999).

Time difference of arrival, when combined with sensor network technology, offers a new avenue for mitigating explosive-related threats. The wideband stimulated emissions technique, presented above, can simultaneously locate and detect superheterodyne receivers—even when the target device is not designed to be found. The geometry required for TDoA makes it ideal for use in sensor networks, which can cover a wide area and can cooperatively locate potential threats. When used in this manner, stimulated emissions has the potential to protect facilities and checkpoints from radio-initiated explosives.

Technology Components

Measuring stimulated emissions requires two vital radio frequency (RF) components: a transmitter and a receiver. In the initial investigations reported in Seguin, these measurements were conducted using traditional lab equipment: signal generators, spectrum analyzers, and oscilloscopes (2009a). This approach has a number of important drawbacks, however. Most signal generators are strictly-analog systems which can only perform analog modulations, such as AM and FM. This necessitates the use of additional hardware, such as waveform generators, to produce the desired stimulation signal.

The receiver side, depending on the exact configuration, was similarly complicated. A variety of analog mixers and filters were used to lower the frequency of the unintended emissions, allowing them to be sampled at lower rates. Digital sampling was performed using oscilloscopes, which posed their own set of difficulties. Oscilloscopes have a finite memory space for digital samples, and the oscilloscopes used in Seguin could only capture several consecutive milliseconds of data before exhausting this space.

Once the samples were obtained, they were transferred to a personal computer (PC) for further processing. This step required the use of slow, low-throughput IEEE-488 (GPIB) interfaces. As a result, the stimulated emissions system developed in Seguin could only sample intermittently, and the data transfer itself introduced over one second of latency. The complete measurement setup consisted of numerous pieces of bulky, fragile equipment, and it was not particularly portable. This system was built as part of the preliminary investigation of the stimulated emissions approach, which was successful, however more convenient solutions exist.

Figure 12. A software-defined radio system. The hardware components, including the real-time digital system, are designed to be as minimalist as possible. This grants the host computer more flexible access to the radio signal and spectrum

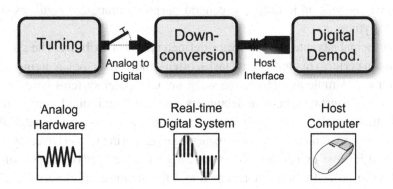

Software-defined radio (SDR) platforms replace purpose-built analog communications circuitry with high-speed digital signal processing (DSP). As its name implies, most of the radio signal processing takes place in software: typically on a standard PC. An SDR digitizes radio signals in much the same way that a sound card digitizes audio, except that the process takes place at a much higher speed. The components of an SDR system are illustrated in Figure 12.

The hardware component of an SDR system, often referred to as the "front-end," is designed to be minimalist and flexible. An analog radio receiver—either super-heterodyne or direct-conversion—is used to select the desired frequency and bandwidth. The signal is then sampled using high-speed analog to digital converters (ADCs). A comprehensive overview of the digitization process can be found in Oppenheim and Schafer (1999). Some ADCs operate fast enough that the analog front-end can be omitted entirely.

The limiting factor in an SDR system is, typically, the interconnect between the front-end and the host computer. This interconnect, such as Universal Serial Bus (USB) or PCI Express, has limited throughput—i.e., USB 2.0 has a maximum transfer rate of about 32 MiB/s. In order to meet real-time deadlines, it is necessary to limit the data rate to that of the interconnect. This is accomplished by discarding the unnecessary portions of the radio signal: a process known as digital down-conversion.

Digital down-conversion is the digital equivalent of analog frequency translation. The signal is shifted in frequency until the band of interest is centered at baseband. (Quadrature sampling is used to preserve the magnitude and phase of the signal.) The signal is then band-limited, using digital filters, to the frequency range of interest. Once it has been filtered, the sampling rate can be reduced without distorting the signal. The reduction in sampling rate greatly decreases the amount of data that must be transferred and processed.

Once the data is transferred to the host computer, application-specific signal processing is performed. Typically, these tasks include demodulation and, for data signals, framing. In stimulated emissions, the goal is to search the down-converted radio signal for the presence of some known stimulation signal. The algorithms to do so can be written in ordinary, general-purpose computer languages such as C++ and Python.

The principal advantage of software-defined radio is flexibility. The same SDR platform can perform many different tasks, often simultaneously. Changing the DSP algorithm is as simple as altering the software. Computer systems have access to advanced user interfaces, built-in debuggers, and nearly-unlimited storage, making them an attractive alternative to dedicated hardware. It is no surprise that SDRs are popular with research and other non-recurring engineering tasks (Ulversoy, 2010).

The ALERT research group at Missouri S&T has developed two major software-defined radio projects, both for research and for demonstration purposes. These projects, which are detailed in Stagner et al. (2011), Stagner et al. (2013), and in the next two sections, are intended to validate the effectiveness of stimulated emissions. They also, by extension, demonstrate the usefulness of SDR to research and academia.

Matched-Filter Detector

Many different SDR platforms are available, ranging from hobbyist kits ($20 U.S. Dollars) to purpose-built computer systems for maximum sensitivity and throughput ($7000 U.S. Dollars or more). The matched filter detector used by Missouri S&T was built using the Ettus Research Universal Software Radio Peripheral (USRP), which was selected due to its proven performance and wide range of available transceiver modules. The USRP's companion software, GNU Radio, is designed to support real-time designs. The DSP operations (i.e., functions) are described using the Python scripting language. When the system is started, these operations are executed continuously on the incoming data from the SDR (Ferrari, Flammini, & Sisinni, 2009).

The matched filter detector is designed to detect superheterodyne receivers using the method outlined earlier in this chapter. As per Figure 7, the system detects radio receivers by transmitting a 5 kHz linear FM chirp and searching for the chirp on another, defined frequency using a matched filter. When the program is started, it generates a baseband, complex-sampled chirp of a user-specified length. The chirp's matched filter, which is a finite impulse response (FIR) digital filter, is then derived and stored. This detector is implemented entirely using the USRP's companion software, GNU Radio.

The program then instructs the USRP to transmit this chirp repetitively and sample the radio spectrum at the up-mixing emissions frequency. The received signal is then filtered through the matched filter. If a radio receiver is present, the matched filter

Figure 13. The assembled USRP test setup fits neatly on a table top. It can be disassembled and stored in a small box for transport

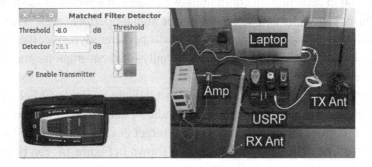

will output an impulse-like spike every chirp period. A Neyman–Pearson detector, as described in Van Trees (2001), is used to decide if a radio receiver has been detected: The power output of the matched filter is compared with a fixed, user-specified threshold, and a detection is declared if the power exceeds the threshold.

The matched filter detector includes a simple GUI for setting and viewing the detector's threshold. A visual and audible alarm are activated if a radio receiver is detected. The detector operates in real-time, updating its display continuously as new data is received. The complete hardware setup, as shown in Figure 13, fits neatly on a tabletop and is easy to transport.

This real-time implementation offers substantial advantages over the sample-then-process design used for initial investigations in Seguin. Long-duration chirps, which exceed one second in length, can be used without difficulty. Troubleshooting physical problems, such as antenna leakage or cross-coupling, is vastly simplified when the detector statistic updates quickly. The matched filter detector program offers an easy-to-understand demonstration of the stimulated emissions technique. Although the hardware used in Seguin was commonly available, and more than adequate for a preliminary study, the SDR platform resulted in a much simpler, easy-to-use system.

Software-Defined Radar

Locating superheterodyne receivers using the time-of-arrival method, as discussed in prior sections, requires high-precision timing. The SDR must be capable of accurately measuring the time difference between the transmission of the stimulation and the reception of the emissions. For speed-of-light signals, a timing error of just ten nanoseconds translates into one meter of range error. This is a strict real-time synchronization demand which cannot be met using general-purpose computer programs. Designing an SDR to meet these demands is a challenging task.

From Stagner et al. (2011), it is known that superheterodyne receivers are highly responsive to linear FM chirps. Using a technique known as frequency-modulated continuous wave (FMCW) radar, it is possible to use similar chirp signals for ranging in addition to detection. In continuous-wave radar, the power of the transmitted stimulation is kept constant. Constant-power signals perform well with systems that use solid-state, low-noise amplifiers—as superheterodyne receivers typically do (Stove, 1992). FMCW has a computationally-efficient implementation which makes it ideal for SDR.

In Levanon (2004b), it is demonstrated that delaying a linear FM chirp in time is equivalent to shifting it in frequency. In radar systems, the time-delayed return signal—in this case, the emissions from the target device—appears to be slightly shifted in frequency. This frequency shift, as shown in Figure 14, can be estimated

Figure 14. Delaying a linear FM chirp in time by some amount dt is equivalent to shifting it in frequency by some amount df. This relationship is easy to visualize from the proportional triangles given below. By estimating the frequency difference df, it is possible to estimate the time delay dt

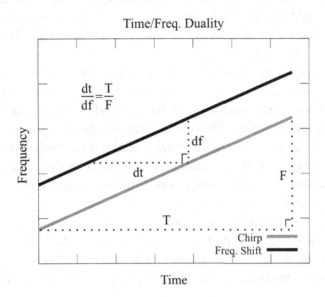

by finding the instantaneous difference in frequency between the transmitted stimulation and the received emissions. This difference can be found using mixers.

In the mixer implementation, the received emissions are mixed with a time-reversed version of the transmitted stimulation. The result is a low-frequency "beat" signal which contains the range information. Traditional estimators of frequency, such as the Fast Fourier Transform (FFT), can be used to estimate the beat signal's frequency—and thus the range. This design is ideal for use on software-defined radio platforms: The mixing is a mathematically simple—but time-sensitive—operation, whereas the frequency estimation can benefit from the processing power of a general-purpose computer.

To fulfill the real-time requirement, an FMCW front-end was added to the USRP. The front-end generates the linear FM chirps and performs a simultaneous de-chirp of the received emissions. To guarantee a fixed delay, these operations were implemented in the USRP's field-programmable gate array (FPGA). The FPGA typically performs the high-speed digital down-conversion (see Figure 12), but it supports loading user-customized instruction sets as well. This customization is made possible, in part, by the USRP's open-source design. After de-chirping, the resulting beat signal is down-converted and sent to the host computer.

The host computer then estimates the frequency of the beat signal. A two-dimensional FFT, as per Wojtkiewicz (1997), simultaneously estimates both the range to and Doppler shift of a target. The entire software-defined radar system is depicted in Figure 15. Since it was designed for stimulated emissions, this radar system has one additional feature: it can transmit and receive on different, arbitrary frequencies. This enables the radar system to receive and detect up-mixing emissions from superheterodyne receivers.

This prototype system demonstrates the extensibility of software-defined radio platforms. Owing to their advanced computer software and re-programmable circuitry (i.e., FPGAs), such platforms can be modified to function far beyond their original design specifications. The system described above was successfully tested in Stagner et al. (2013), where it accurately measured the range to various superheterodyne receivers. While isolation problems between the transmitter and receiver substantially reduced the system's performance, these problems occurred in the analog front-end and are not specific to SDR.

As this case study demonstrates, software-defined radio products greatly increase the accessibility of the radio spectrum to academic researchers. These devices can facilitate the development of novel communications and signal processing techniques, and it is worthwhile to consider them whenever rapid prototyping is desired.

Figure 15. Block diagram of the software-defined radar. A chirp generator, and a synchronized de-chirp function, were added to the USRP's FPGA firmware. The range-doppler processing is carried out on the host PC. Adapted from (Stagner et al., 2013), © 2013 IEEE. Used with permission

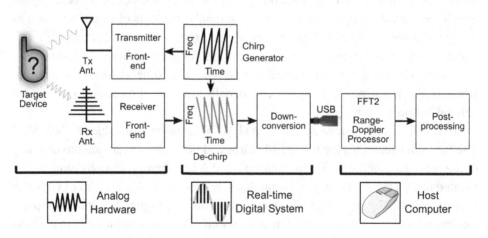

CURRENT CHALLENGES

The ALERT project has successfully developed numerous radio-receiver detectors, but many technical questions still remain. The super-regenerative receiver emissions, as shown in Figure 2, are a nearly-periodic on-off keying (OOK) signal. These emissions are very nearly cyclostationary and can thus be analyzed using techniques such as the spectral-correlation density (SCD) function (Gardner, 1991). Cyclostationary methods have been used for many years to detect similar radar and communications signals (Gardner, 1988), and they may be capable of detecting super-regenerative receivers as well. The SCD could serve as a more robust alternative to the filter bank in the cascading correlation algorithm.

This project does not undertake a thorough study of direct-conversion receivers. Unlike superheterodyne receivers, direct-conversion receivers do not require multiple stages or off-chip analog filters, and their popularity has grown in recent years (Mirabbasi & Martin, 2000). Since this new design also uses high-frequency RF mixers, it is expected to have electromagnetic emissions which are similar to those found in a superheterodyne receiver. While stimulated detection is possible, further testing is required to determine if they can be located using time-of-arrival.

Although the stimulated emissions technique has been thoroughly field-tested and proven, much work remains before it can be integrated into deployable national-security products. A sensor network should be constructed to prove the accuracy of the time-difference-of-arrival technique. A more comprehensive study of performance, with more target devices, would greatly benefit and re-enforce the ALERT project's findings. The demonstration and test-bed systems documented herein, while functional, are not field-ready; a deployable hardware system is required.

SOLUTIONS AND RECOMMENDATIONS

Researchers at Missouri S&T have developed new techniques for detecting and locating radio receivers. This approach, which is known as stimulated emissions, enhances and complements existing techniques for locating potential explosive threats. The work was conducted by a multidisciplinary team of faculty and students, with both electromagnetic compatibility (EMC) and digital signal processing (DSP) backgrounds. The team collaborated over a five year period to author several papers and one patent and a patent disclosure.

Several real-time detectors were also developed for software-defined radio systems—the use of which greatly expedited research and testing. While these systems serve as adequate functional prototypes, university research programs are ill-suited to producing ready-to-use products. The time-limited nature of funding contracts, high turnover rate of researchers (i.e., graduate research assistants), and lack of dedicated fabrication facilities greatly impacts the ability of academic institutions to produce such products.

Due to these limitations, the final phase of most university projects consists of technology transfer to industry partners. At Missouri S&T, the establishment of a dedicated technology transfer office has proven to greatly improve the rate at which cutting-edge research is brought to market (Bruns, 2009). As of late 2012, the ALERT Center was collaborating with Firestorm Emergency Services to develop a commercial product for detecting radio receivers. The final product of this research, undertaken by the ALERT Center of Excellence, offers new counter-IED capabilities to checkpoint operators, law enforcement, and war-fighters.

ACKNOWLEDGMENT

This material is based upon work supported by the U.S. Department of Homeland Security under Award Number 2008-ST-061-ED0001, the National Science Foundation under Grant No. 0855878, and the Wilkens Missouri Endowment. The views and conclusions contained in this document are those of the authors and should not be interpreted as necessarily representing the official policies, either expressed or implied, of the U.S. Department of Homeland Security or the National Science Foundation.

The authors would also like to thank the tireless efforts of our graduate students, Andrew Conrad, Matthew Halligan, and Christopher Osterwise, without whom this project would not be possible.

REFERENCES

Bard, J. D., & Ham, F. M. (1999). Time difference of arrival dilution of precision and applications. *IEEE Transactions on Signal Processing, 47*(2), 521–523. doi:10.1109/78.740135

Beetner, D., Seguin, S., & Hubing, H. (2008). *Electromagnetic emissions stimulation and detection system*. Academic Press.

Bracewell, R. (1999). *The Fourier transform and its applications* (3rd ed.). New York: McGraw-Hill.

Bruns, A. (2009). Talent by design. *Site Selection Mag.*, 475–490.

Chuchmach, M. (2013). *Boston marathon bomb made with toy car parts?* ABC News. Retrieved from http://abcnews.go.com/Blotter/boston-marathon-bomb-made-toy-car-parts/story?id=18991380#.UXCWPdeFGoM

Dai, J., Clough, B., Ho, I.-C., Lu, X., Liu, J., & Zhang, X.-C. (2011). Recent progresses in terahertz wave air photonics. *IEEE Trans. Terahertz Science and Tech., 1*(1), 274–281. doi:10.1109/TTHZ.2011.2159550

Davidson, A. J., Chellappa, Raja, S., Dattelbaum, D. M., & Yoo, C.-S. (2011). Pressure induced isostructural metastable phase transition of ammonium nitrate. *The Journal of Physical Chemistry A, 115*(42), 11889–11896. doi:10.1021/jp207754z PMID:21902257

(2008). *Department of Homeland Security Appropriations Bill, 2009*. Washington, DC: GPO.

Dourbal, P. F. (1998). Method and apparatus for detecting and locating a concealed listening device.

Ferrari, P., Flammini, A., & Sisinni, E. (2009). Introducing the wireless ultra smart sensor. In *Proceedings of IEEE I2MTC* (pp. 1304–1308). IEEE.

Flintoft, I. D., Marvin, A. C., Robinson, M. P., Fischer, K., & Rowell, A. J. (2003). The re-emission spectrum of digital hardware subjected to EMI. *IEEE Transactions on Electromagnetic Compatibility, 45*(4), 576–585. doi:10.1109/TEMC.2003.819058

Gardner, W. A. (1988). Signal interception: a unifying theoretical framework for feature detection. *IEEE Transactions on Communications, 36*(8), 897–906. doi:10.1109/26.3769

Gardner, W. A. (1991). Exploitation of spectral redundancy in cyclostationary signals. *IEEE Sig. Proc. Mag., 8*(2), 14–36. doi:10.1109/79.81007

Giacoletto, L. J., & Landee, R. W. (Eds.). (1977). *Electronics designers' handbook* (2nd ed.). New York: McGraw-Hill.

Gleason, S., & Gebre-Egziabher, D. (2009). *GNSS applications and methods*. Artech.

Griffith, C. M. (2007). *Unmanned aerial vehicle-mounted high sensitivity RF receiver to detect improvised explosive devices*. Naval Postgraduate School.

Jankiraman, M. (2007). *Design of multi-frequency CW radars*. SciTech Publishing.

Kumar, T., et al. (2012). *2012–2013 factbook* (Tech. Rep.). Missouri S&T. Retrieved from http://ira.mst.edu/factbook/1213/

Lee, J.-Y., & Scholtz, R. A. (2002). Ranging in a dense multipath environment using an UWB radio link. *IEEE Journal on Selected Areas in Communications, 20*(9), 1677–1683. doi:10.1109/JSAC.2002.805060

Levanon, N., & Mozeson, E. (2004). *Radar signals.* Wiley. doi:10.1002/0471663085

Mirabbasi, S., & Martin, K. (2000). Classical and modern receiver architectures. *IEEE Communications Magazine, 38*(11), 132–139. doi:10.1109/35.883502

Moseley, F. (1955). The automatic radio direction finder. *IRE Trans. Aeronautical and Navigational Electronics,* (4), 4–11.

Nambayah, M., & Quickenden, T. I. (2004). A quantitative assessment of chemical techniques for detecting traces of explosives at counter-terrorist portals. *Talanta, 63*(2), 461–467. doi:10.1016/j.talanta.2003.11.018 PMID:18969454

Noble, D. E. (1962). The history of land-mobile radio communications. *Proc. IRE, 50*(5), 1405–1414.

Oppenheim, A. V., Schafer, R. W., & Buck, J. R. (1999). *Discrete-time signal processing* (2nd ed.). Pearson.

Orfanidis, S. J. (1988). *Optimum signal processing: An introduction* (2nd ed.). New York: McGraw-Hill.

Pacheco-Londoño, L., Ortiz-Rivera, W., Primera-Pedrozo, O., & Hernández-Rivera, S. (2009). Vibrational spectroscopy standoff detection of explosives. *Analytical and Bioanalytical Chemistry, 395*(2), 323–335. doi:10.1007/s00216-009-2954-y PMID:19633965

Patwari, N., Hero, A. O. III, Perkins, M., Correal, N. S., & O'dea, R. J. (2003). Relative location estimation in wireless sensor networks. *IEEE Transactions on Signal Processing, 51*(8), 2137–2148. doi:10.1109/TSP.2003.814469

Pinsky, M. A. (2002). Introduction to Fourier analysis and wavelets. In *Graduate studies in mathematics* (Vol. 102, pp. 131–133). American Mathematical Soc.

Seguin, S. A. (2009a). *Detection of low cost radio frequency receivers based on their unintended electromagnetic emissions and an active stimulation.* Missouri S&T. Retrieved from http://scholarsmine.mst.edu/thesis/pdf/Seguin_09007dcc80708216.pdf

Seguin, S. A. (2009b). Detection of regenerative receivers based on the modulation of their unintended emissions. In *Detection of low cost radio frequency receivers based on their unintended electromagnetic emissions and an active stimulation* (pp. 37–52). Missouri S&T. Retrieved from http://scholarsmine.mst.edu/thesis/pdf/Seguin_09007dcc80708216.pdf

Sekiguchi, H., & Seto, S. (2008). Proposal of an information signal measurement method in display image contained in electromagnetic noise emanated from a personal computer. In *Proceedings of IEEE Instrum., & Measure. Tech. Conf.* (pp. 1859–1863). IEEE.

Shaik, A., Weng, H., Dong, X., Hubing, T. H., & Beetner, D. G. (2006). Matched filter detection and identification of electronic circuits based on their unintentional radiated emissions. In *Proceedings of IEEE ISEMC* (Vol. 3). IEEE.

Skolnik, M. I. (1960). Theoretical accuracy of radar measurements. *IRE Trans. Aeronautical and Navigational Electronics*, (4), 123–129.

Smith, I., & Coderre, M. (2008). The continuing war against IEDs. *WSTIAC Quarterly*, *8*(2), 3–6.

Spencer, Q., Rice, M., Jeffs, B., & Jensen, M. (1997). Indoor wideband time/angle of arrival multipath propagation results. In *Proceedings of IEEE Vehicular Tech. Conf.* (Vol. 3, pp. 1410–1414). IEEE.

Staelin, D. H. (1969). Fast folding algorithm for detection of periodic pulse trains. *Proceedings of the IEEE*, *57*(4), 724–725. doi:10.1109/PROC.1969.7051

Stagner, C., Conrad, A., Osterwise, C., Beetner, D. G., & Grant, S. (2011). A practical superheterodyne-receiver detector using stimulated emissions. *IEEE Transactions on Instrumentation and Measurement*, *60*(4), 1461–1468. doi:10.1109/TIM.2010.2101330

Stagner, C., Halligan, M., Osterwise, C., Beetner, D. G., & Grant, S. L. (2013). Locating noncooperative radio receivers using wideband stimulated emissions. *IEEE Transactions on Instrumentation and Measurement*, *62*(3), 667–674. doi:10.1109/TIM.2012.2219141

Stove, A. G. (1992). Linear FMCW radar techniques. In Proceedings of Inst. Elect. Eng.—Radar and Signal Process. F (Vol. 139, pp. 343–350). Academic Press.

Swinyard, W. O. (1962). The development of the art of radio receiving from the early 1920's to the present. *Proc. IRE, 50*(5), 793–798.

Thotla, V., Ghasr, M. T. A., Zawodniok, M., Jagannathan, S., & Agarwal, S. (2012). Detection and localization of multiple R/C electronic devices using array detectors. In *Proceedings of the IEEE Int'l. Instrum. Meas. Tech. Conf.* (pp. 1687–1691). IEEE.

Turin, G. (1960). An introduction to matched filters. *I.R.E. Transactions on Information Theory, 6*(3), 311–329. doi:10.1109/TIT.1960.1057571

Ulversoy, T. (2010). Software defined radio: Challenges and opportunities. *IEEE Comm. Surveys & Tutorials, 12*(4), 531–550. doi:10.1109/SURV.2010.032910.00019

Van Trees, H. L. (2001). Detection, estimation, and modulation theory. Wiley.

Wild, B., & Ramchandran, K. (2005). Detecting primary receivers for cognitive radio applications. In *Proceedings of the IEEE Int'l Symp. DySPAN* (pp. 124–130). IEEE.

Wilson, C. (2006). *Improvised explosive devices (IEDs) in Iraq: Effects and countermeasures* (Congressional Research Service Report No. RS22330). Washington, DC: Library of Congress.

Wojtkiewicz, A., Misiurewicz, J., Nałecz, M., Jedrzejewski, K., & Kulpa, K. (1997). Two-dimensional signal processing in FMCW radars. In *Proceedings of XX KKTOiUE* (pp. 475–480). KKTOiUE.

Zheng, L., & Tse, D. N. C. (2003). Diversity and multiplexing: A fundamental tradeoff in multiple-antenna channels. *IEEE Transactions on Information Theory, 49*(5), 1073–1096. doi:10.1109/TIT.2003.810646

Zimmerman, T. G. (1999). Wireless networked digital devices: A new paradigm for computing and communication. *IBM Systems Journal, 38*(4), 566–574. doi:10.1147/sj.384.0566

KEY TERMS AND DEFINITIONS

Local Oscillator: The main high-frequency radio signal generated by a superheterodyne receiver. This signal can radiate into the environment as unstimulated emissions.

Matched Filter: The optimal linear filter for detecting a known signal in additive white noise. Such filters are often used for detecting known electromagnetic emissions.

Range-Doppler Processing: A method for simultaneously extracting both range and range-rate from a radar signal. The processor outputs a two-dimensional matrix with range on one axis and range-rate (doppler) on the other. For stimulated emissions, the "doppler" output is the mutual frequency drift between the transmitter and the target device.

Software-Defined Radio: A radio transmitter or receiver which has signal processing functions that are defined by computer software.

Stimulated Emissions: A method for inducing changes in a device's unintended electromagnetic emissions by using specially-crafted radio signals.

Superheterodyne Receiver: A radio receiver design used for high-quality speech or high-rate data signals. They are common in two-way radios, broadcast receivers, and cellular or cordless telephones.

Super-Regenerative Receiver: A simple radio receiver design used by many low-cost devices, such as toy cars and keyless entry systems.

Target Device: An electronic device that has stimulated emissions. Devices tested in this study include toy cars and narrow-band FM radio receivers.

Up-Mixing Component: The high-frequency stimulated emissions of a super-heterodyne receiver. These emissions contain a nearly-perfect copy of the signal that the device is receiving.

Chapter 5
Maritime Security Summer Research Institute

Beth Austin-DeFares
Stevens Institute of Technology, USA

Julie Pullen
Stevens Institute of Technology, USA

Barry Bunin
Stevens Institute of Technology, USA

EXECUTIVE SUMMARY

In its efforts to respond to national workforce imperatives and central to its mission as a Department of Homeland Security (DHS) Center of Excellence in Port Security, the Center for Secure and Resilient Maritime Commerce (CSR), led by Stevens Institute of Technology, has created an intensive summer research program tailored to undergraduate and graduate-level students. The Summer Research Institute (SRI) is designed to engage multidisciplinary student teams in rigorous, hands-on research in collaboration with the Center's researchers and industry and government partners. The research fields include maritime security, remote sensing technologies, emergency response and management, and Marine Transportation System (MTS) resilience. The program aims to enhance the professional development of students while increasing their interest in advanced academic study and careers in the maritime/homeland security domain.

DOI: 10.4018/978-1-4666-5946-9.ch005

ORGANIZATION BACKGROUND

In 2008, Stevens Institute of Technology was designated as the lead university in the National Center for Secure and Resilient Maritime Commerce (CSR), a Department of Homeland Security Center (DHS) of Excellence (COE) in Port Security. CSR is one of two DHS centers (the other is led by the University of Hawaii) that together form the National Center of Excellence for Maritime, Island, Remote and Extreme Environment Security (MIREES). The Center supports DHS efforts to provide for the safe and secure use of the nation's maritime domain and a resilient Marine Transportation System (MTS), through the advancement of the relevant sciences and the professional development of the current and prospective maritime security workforce.

Central to CSR's mission is the transfer of its research and expertise into innovative educational programs designed to enhance maritime domain awareness and MTS resiliency, and the interest, knowledge, technical skills and leadership capabilities of the nation's current and future maritime security workforce.

Since the Center's inception, CSR in collaboration with its academic partners, Stevens Institute of Technology, Rutgers University, University of Miami, University of Puerto Rico–Mayaguez (UPRM), Massachusetts Institute of Technology (MIT) and Monmouth University, have worked together to develop a comprehensive portfolio of maritime security-centric educational programs. These include:

- The Summer Research Institute,
- Professional development programs, seminars, and certificates tailored to maritime security practitioners,
- The Maritime Systems Master's Degree program, including the DHS-funded Maritime Systems Master's Degree Fellowship program.

CSR leverages the existing programs, research assets and teaching talents of its academic partners to develop, support and deliver the Center's educational programs. Committed to advancing the Center's educational portfolio and outreach to current and prospective maritime/homeland security practitioners, CSR hired a full-time Director of Education in 2010 to coordinate and evolve its programs.

To date, the Center has successfully delivered multiple professional development courses and seminars to stakeholders, it has been awarded three consecutive DHS Career Development Grants to support nine full-time students in Stevens Institute of Technology's Maritime Systems Master's Degree program and has engaged 70 high-achieving engineering and science students from 16 U.S. universities in its Summer Research Institute.

The eight-week intensive Summer Research Institute (SRI) brings together CSR's academic partners, together with its robust partnerships in industry and government, to provide a rigorous, hands-on, multidisciplinary research program for undergraduate and graduate-level engineering and science majors.

The concept and framework for the SRI was modeled after a Maritime Security Summer Institute pilot program coordinated by CSR researcher Dr. Scott Glenn, Director, Rutgers University Coastal Ocean Engineering Laboratory. The ten-week pilot program leveraged funding support by DHS, National Science Foundation (NSF), National Oceanic and Atmospheric Administration (NOAA), Office of Naval Research (ONR) and the Vetlesen Foundation, to expose undergraduate students to ocean sensing and modeling technologies used in maritime security applications. Nineteen students representing four U.S. universities participated in the experiential research program.

THE NEED: MARITIME/HOMELAND SECURITY WORKFORCE DEVELOPMENT – EXPERIENTIAL LEARNING

Preparing students to compete and be successful in the global economy and workforce is of paramount concern and interest to the U.S. government, business community, policy makers, citizens, and academic institutions. Studies conducted by the National Academy of Sciences, Committee on Prospering in the Global Economy of the 21st Century (2007, 2010) and reports prepared for the U.S. Department of Labor (Jobs for the Future, 2007) suggest that the strength of the U.S. economy relies heavily upon the nation's ability to make long-term investments in the research capabilities and the science, technology, engineering, and mathematics (STEM) skills of our next generation workforce.

Experiential learning programs have become a cornerstone of higher-learning institutions in their efforts to enhance the real-world skill competencies and professional development of their students.

To meet this need, CSR has created a summer research program, the Summer Research Institute, designed to enhance the STEM skill competencies and professional development of college-level students while exposing them to the complex challenges of securing the nation's ports, maritime borders and inland waterways, and to the significance of the MTS as a critical factor in the nation's economic infrastructure.

Recent and emerging threats against the U.S. maritime system, both man-made (e.g., oil spills, terrorist attacks, and pollution) and natural (e.g., hurricanes, earthquakes, and tsunamis) have created new and complex challenges for today's maritime safety and security professionals. The evolving complexity of these challenges strongly suggests that our current and next generation of maritime leaders and security workforce practitioners must be well grounded in the emerging science and technologies needed to inform and support the nation's maritime security policies and directives. To effectively enhance the security of the U.S. maritime domain, maritime professionals must possess the skills needed to develop new strategies for mitigating threats and disasters, and must be highly adept at developing and/or evaluating new methods and tools for efficient and effective emergency response and recovery, and maritime system resilience.

Other similar homeland security-focused programs have been established and successfully delivered by DHS Centers of Excellence, including the National Center for Border Security and Immigration (NCBSI), co-led by the University of Texas El Paso (UTEP) and the University of Arizona, in Tucson, AZ. NCBSI's Homeland Security Summer Scholars Academy engages students in emerging and on-going research projects aimed at enhancing U.S. border security and addressing complex immigration issues within a global context. Like the CSR's Summer Research Institute, the Homeland Security Summer Scholars Academy, is a practical, highly-collaborative research program for college-level students. Established in 2010, the Scholars Academy has engaged 39 students from diverse academic disciplines, in hands-on research projects, including Behavioral Game Theory Analysis, Game Theory for Border Security, and Human Trafficking.

Out of the Scholar Academy's participants to date, nearly 18% percent have gone on to pursue careers and employment in homeland security and/or law enforcement professions, 74% percent are continuing to complete their undergraduate degrees or are currently attending law school or graduate study, and 8% are employed in non-homeland security related careers. (Talavera, 2013)

SUMMER RESEARCH INSTITUTE

The CSR Summer Research Institute is a multidisciplinary summer research program designed to provide high-achieving undergraduate and graduate-level engineering and science students with the unique opportunity to collaborate with CSR researchers and industry and government homeland security practitioners, on research projects focused on critical issues in maritime domain awareness, emergency response and preparedness, and maritime system resilience.

The program was developed as a collaborative effort across the entire CSR research enterprise, leveraging the research assets, teaching talents and expertise of its industry, government and academic partners. The SRI was created with the following program objectives:

- Expose a diverse group of students from a broad range of engineering and science disciplines, to the maritime domain, the MTS, and the tools and technologies used to secure our nation's ports, coastal borders, inland waterways and extreme and remote island environments.
- Encourage students to think along the same lines as public and private industry and government stakeholders and homeland security practitioners to understand the complex challenges in maritime and port security operations.
- Engage students in rigorous research activities that produce innovative solutions and novel approaches to address maritime security issues of national significance.
- Cultivate a strong and active alumni network to promote professional connections and support on-going SRI programs.
- Enhance the interest of students to pursue advanced academic study and/or careers in the maritime and homeland security domain.

Research members from each of the six CSR partner universities, including Stevens Institute of Technology, Rutgers University, University of Miami, University of Puerto Rico-Mayaguez (UPRM), Massachusetts Institute of Technology (MIT) and Monmouth University, participate at various stages throughout the eight-week program, providing a comprehensive and cohesive student research experience. The research members collaborate shoulder-to-shoulder with the student research teams, providing subject matter expertise, mentorship, and unparalleled access to state-of-the-science tools and technologies, including Stevens Passive Acoustic Detection System and radar and electro-optics systems; Rutgers University's and UPRM's HF Radar coastal networks; University of Miami's CSTARS Synthetic Aperture Radar and Electro-Optics Satellite Systems; and MIT's Port Mapper visualization and decision support tool (Pullen, 2013), to name a few.

PROGRAM LOCATION

The Stevens Institute of Technology campus, located in Hoboken, NJ, provides an exceptional research venue for the Summer Research Institute, allowing students access to a robust suite of research assets and laboratory facilities. At the forefront of its facilities is the CSR's Maritime Security Laboratory (MSL). Established through support by the Office of Naval Research, MSL is organized to conduct real time research and technology development and evaluation in support of the detection and characterization of present and emerging maritime threats. MSL's assets include acoustic and infrared sensors; manned and unmanned ocean vehicles; and ocean and weather observation and forecasting tools; and access to research vessels.

Stevens Center for Maritime Systems (CMS), located within the Department of Civil, Environmental and Ocean Engineering in the Charles V. Schaefer Jr. School of Engineering and Science, also provides students with access to the university's Davidson Lab, where experiments and modeling and simulation exercises are conducted to address problems varying from swimmer detection to coastal flooding, to specialized marine craft design. Work conducted by CMS is supported by industry and federal agencies, including the Office of Naval Research (ONR) and other Navy organizations, DHS Science & Technology, U.S. Coast Guard (USCG), Federal Emergency Management Agency (FEMA), and the National Oceanic and Atmospheric Administration (NOAA).

Through the leveraged use of Stevens, CSR and CMS facilities and technologies, SRI participants are afforded a broad set of resources to facilitate and inspire innovative research.

Located adjacent to the New York-New Jersey Harbor and few short miles from the Port of New York/Newark, the nation's third largest port, Stevens Institute of Technology's geographical location provides unique opportunities for students to visit with port and terminal operators and to conduct in situ field experiments and observational studies of the heavily trafficked Hudson River estuary.

STUDENT RECRUITMENT / STUDENT PARTICIPANTS

Efforts to recruit students for the Summer Research Institute begins in the late fall of each academic year. CSR's recruitment efforts include the following initiatives:

- Hardcopy and electronic distributions of the SRI program brochure is sent to CSR academic partners, DHS Science & Technology education representatives and CSR contacts.

CSR is committed to promoting enhanced opportunities for students from underrepresented communities and makes special efforts to target students from Minority Serving Institutions (MSI) and Historically Black Colleges and Universities (HBCU), through its MSI and HBCU faculty contacts and its DHS S&T Office of University Programs' academic channels.

Since the program's inception in 2010, more than half of the program's 70 participants have been women and/or students from underrepresented communities.

To be considered for admission students must meet the following criteria:

- Students must be enrolled in an Engineering or Science related discipline at an accredited U.S. college or university.
- Undergraduate students must possess a GPA of 3.0 or better.
- Graduate student applicants must possess a GPA of 3.5 or better.

In addition to the above stated criteria, students are required to complete an online application form, prepare a statement of interest and submit one letter of recommendation from a current academic advisor or faculty member. Student applicants from CSR partner universities are given priority in the application process.

Exceptions to the admission criteria are made, however, for students who come highly recommended by CSR's academic partners and for whom external funding support is provided through a scholarship, fellowship or by sponsorship. In cases such as these, CSR will waive the one letter of recommendation requirement.

CSR has modified its admission criteria over the past four years. At the time of the inaugural program in 2010, only graduate-level students and students in their junior and senior years of undergraduate study were qualified to attend the SRI. Due in large part to budget cuts in the Center's funding and the inability of the Center to provide student stipends and housing allowances, CSR has changed its criteria to allow high-achieving externally funded students in their freshman and sophomore years to participate.

Table 1 shows the student demographics for each of the four years the SRI program has been delivered.

STUDENT HOUSING AND STIPENDS

During the first two years of the Summer Research Institute, CSR was fortunate to have received additional funding from DHS to allow for stipend and housing support for students. Students in the 2010 and 2011 programs were provided with up to $4,500 in summer stipends and were provided free accommodations in Stevens Institute of Technology's off-campus housing complex.

Cuts to the CSR's budget over the past three years have instigated a significant shift in the Center's funding of student participants. Lacking the necessary funds to provide stipend and housing support, CSR reached out to its academic partners for assistance in identifying students who could attend the program through fellowship, scholarship or external sponsorship support. In 2011, eight out of the 21 SRI student participants attended the program with external funding, in 2012 nine out of the ten student participants were externally supported, and in 2013, each of the 13 student participants attended the program through external funding sources.

Table 1. Student participant stats and demographics

Program Year	Students	Undergrad	Grad	Male	Female	Minority	University
2013	13	12	1	10	3	6	Stevens, Elizabeth City State Univ., Essex County College, UPRM
2012	10	7	3	8	2	6	Stevens, Drexel Univ., UPRM
2011	21	13	8	17	4	10	Stevens, Jackson State, Norfolk State, SUNY Binghamton, Univ. of Hawaii, Univ. of Miami, UPRM
2010	26	16	10	16	10	6	Stevens, John Jay College of Criminal Justice, Monmouth Univ., Morgan State, Rutgers Univ., Univ. of Guam, Univ. of Miami, UPRM
TOTAL	70	48	22	51	19	28	16 U.S. Colleges/ Universities

Details regarding CSR's SRI funding issues will be discussed in the "Challenges" section of this chapter.

PROGRAM CURRICULUM AND FORMAT

The introductory curriculum for the summer research program draws upon graduate courses from Stevens Institute of Technology's Maritime Systems Master's Degree and Maritime Security Graduate Certificate programs. The curriculum is designed to provide students with an intensive overview of the maritime domain, the MTS, and the tools and technologies used by CSR researchers to help enhance the maritime domain awareness, maritime system resilience and the surveillance capabilities of first responders and maritime security practitioners.

Throughout the eight-week intensive program, students engage in the following activities:

- Attend seminars and lectures by CSR researchers and maritime industry and government homeland security experts and practitioners.

- Participate in collaborative multidisciplinary (e.g. acoustics, electro-optics, HF radar, synthetic aperture radar and earth observation satellite imaging) hands-on research, through modeling and simulation projects, data collection, and real-time analysis.
- Engage in field visits to local ports, laboratories, and industry and government homeland security facilities.
- Participate in professional development activities, including weekly oral presentations, report writing, teamwork, and networking.
- Work as part of a multidisciplinary team to prepare final reports and present research findings to CSR researchers, DHS S&T officials, and maritime industry and government stakeholders.

FIELD VISITS AND GUEST SPEAKERS

Field visits and interactions with guest speakers are a key facet of the Summer Research Institute. Off-campus field trips and one-on-one discussions with guest speakers provide students with a contextual framework and unique insight into the real-world implications of their research projects. (see Figure 1)

Figure 1. SRI 2013 students met with customs and border protection (CBP) officers and agricultural specialists during a field visit to CBP facilities at Port New York/ Newark.

Drawing upon its relationships within the public and private maritime community and leveraging its vast partnerships among local, state and federal DHS affiliate agencies, CSR has facilitated guest lectures and visits by senior level practitioners from CBP, DHS S&T Borders and Maritime Directorate, DHS Homeland Security Advanced Research Projects Agency (HSARPA), the Federation of American Scientists (FAS), New Jersey Office of Homeland Security and Preparedness (NJOHSP), Port Authority of New York and New Jersey (PANYNJ), U.S. Navy Strategic Systems Programs (SSP), U.S. Navy Sealift Commands, and the U.S. Coast Guard (USCG).

CSR guest speakers provide personal and professional insight into current issues in the field, including emergency response and management, situational awareness, capability gaps and high-priority technology needs. Students are encouraged to ask questions and take advantage of the opportunity to engage practitioners and homeland security experts as it pertains to their respective research projects and general academic and career interests.

Field visits to port environments and locations where maritime and homeland security practitioners conduct their day-to-day operations is another key feature of the Summer Research Institute. SRI administrators and researchers actively arrange for on-site tours of public and private, local, municipal and state maritime and emergency management facilities. The physical experience of visiting a new location and going behind the scenes to observe and learn the roles and responsibilities of practitioners and their organizations, provides students with a frame of reference and enhanced connection to their research projects.

Over the past four years, SRI students have had the opportunity to participate in field visits to the following locations: APM Terminals at the Port of NY/Newark, CBP security facilities at the Port of NY/Newark and the International Mail Facility at JFK Airport, Fire Department of New York City (FDNY), Marine Battalion in NYC, Maher Terminals at the Port of NY/Newark, the National Urban Security Technology Laboratory (NUSTL) in NYC, the New York City Office of Emergency Management (OEM) in Brooklyn, NY, the Regional Catastrophic Planning Team (RCPT) in NYC, U.S. Coast Guard Sector New York in Staten Island, NY, and the U.S. Coast Guard Ft. Hancock in Sandy Hook, NJ.

Since 2012, CBP has hosted an annual half-day trip for the SRI students to visit the agency's security operations at the Port of New York/Newark and has arranged for the students to meet with the Chief of the Anti-Terrorism Contraband Enforcement Team for a first-hand overview of the agency's operational units and day-to-day security procedures.

CBP is the Department of Homeland Security division responsible for keeping terrorists and weapons out of the U.S., enforcing immigration laws, drug laws and other regulations, and securing and facilitating trade and travel. According to Federal law, all incoming containers to the U.S. must be scanned for radiation and contraband.

During the visit to CBP at Port New York/Newark, the SRI student participants are able to observe the operational areas containing x-ray equipment, radiation detection portals, infrared cameras and other high-tech equipment used for detecting threats. The visit also includes a behind the scenes tour of the agency's warehouse where agricultural imports are combed for pests and counterfeit merchandise and items used to smuggle drugs are confiscated and analyzed.

The annual trip to CBP provides unique insight into the agency's range of responsibilities and highlights the many security considerations and practices that they must employ each day to safeguard the nation's ports, airports and border crossings.

Field visits and meaningful conversations with guest speakers have had collective benefits for SRI students, researchers and CSR stakeholders. Some of these benefits include:

- Students get exposed to a range of career and employment opportunities in the maritime/homeland security domain that many of which would never have known about or have ever considered in the past.
- Students are able to ask questions and receive informed answers about current issues, capability gaps and technology needs in the field.
- Stakeholders are able to tap into the innovative capabilities and fresh perspectives of aspiring engineers and scientists.
- Stakeholders are afforded the opportunity to engage with prospective new hires and future employees.
- CSR researchers are able to keep informed of the current state of affairs and the current-state-of-practice in the field.
- CSR researchers are able to leverage partnerships and collaborations with stakeholders, to help keep their educational program curricula up-to-date and relevant.

Other positive unintended benefits have included program recognition by organizations including the U.S. Navy SSP and the USCG as a fast track into student internships and employment opportunities, and invitations to participate in local and regional emergency response training exercises hosted by the USCG and the New Jersey Office of Homeland Security and Preparedness.

These exercises have included a multi-jurisdictional emergency response exercise at an oil refinery along the New York Harbor and full-scale hypothetical crisis events at the Newark International Airport and the George Washington Bridge. CSR and Stevens student and researcher participation at these events have contributed to the program's reputation and growing awareness within the emergency response and first responder communities.

Additional positive benefits have included increased stakeholder engagement and involvement in the ongoing curriculum development of Stevens Maritime Security graduate courses.

SRI PROGRAM SCHEDULE

The Summer Research Institute is held each year at the Stevens Institute of Technology campus in Hoboken, NJ, from June - July. Students are required to participate Monday – Friday, from 9am to 5pm, not including field experiments and observational exercises that might begin and end beyond the typical program hours.

CSR administrators and researchers have established a program format that aims to balance in-class lectures and field visits, with sufficient time allocated for student research project time. Lessons learned over the past three years have taught CSR administrators to be flexible and agile in regards to the program structure. Each week, administrators assess student needs for research time and modify the weekly program activities and lectures accordingly. Table 2 reflects the generalized weekly schedule for the SRI.

The first week of the Summer Research Institute is devoted entirely to providing students with a comprehensive overview of the maritime domain and the significance of the MTS to global trade and the U.S. economy. Faculty members from Stevens Institute of Technology's Maritime Systems and Maritime Security graduate programs tailor material from their graduate courses to develop a framework in which SRI students can begin to understand the relationships between public and private maritime stakeholders, and the complexities of safeguarding and securing the nation's coastal borders, ports, inland waterways and remote island environments.

During week one, students are also organized into their respective research teams and are paired with a CSR research mentor(s). Student teams will either operate under one common research challenge, with shared objectives (e.g., Methods and approaches for detecting small vessel threats), or will focus on individual teams, as

Table 2. SRI generalized weekly schedule

Monday	Tuesday	Wednesday	Thursday	Friday
Faculty Lectures	Faculty/Guest Lectures	Field Visits/ Guest Speakers/ Research Project Time	Student Research Team Status Update Presentations	Research Project Time
	Research Project Time		Research Project Time	Research Project Time

was the case in the 2012 and 2013 programs. Over the past two-years, the students have been organized into teams, each working on separate research projects with different objectives.

Student teams are typically organized according to student research interest, skill sets, degree levels, and general representation across the participating schools. Much effort is given to ensure that each team is well balanced and represents diversity (e.g. degree level, gender, school representation) and multidisciplinary academic majors. Exceptions have been made, however, for students who have been sponsored to attend the SRI with the intent that they will return to their home university to continue the research they started during the summer research program. An example of a prearranged student team includes students from the University of Puerto Rico-Mayaguez (UPRM) who were selected to participate on the 2012 HF Radar team under the mentorship of CSR researchers from Rutgers University. The student team was purposefully organized with the intent that they would later return to UPRM and continue their research in collaboration with CSR's academic partners to advance the center's Caribbean HF Radar test bed in Puerto Rico.

Week Two of the program is focused on giving students an intensive overview of the center's sensor tools and technologies. During Week Two, students receive in-class lectures by CSR academic partners on the science behind and uses of Acoustics and Electro-Optics, HF Radar, Plume Modeling, and Satellites. For general knowledge purposes and to encourage cross team interactions, all student participants are expected to attend in-class faculty and guest lectures, as well as all organized field visits.

Starting Weeks Three - Seven, the SRI program format shifts from time spent in the classroom, to more time spent engaging in research project time with faculty mentors and field visits to meet with working practitioners. During Weeks Three – Seven, student teams also begin to provide organized status updates on their research in the form of oral presentations and power point slides. Each team is responsible for providing a twenty-minute weekly presentation describing their research project, the challenges they are addressing and/or encountering, the activities and experiments they are conducting, and the progress they are making. The status update presentation's contribute to a dynamic exchange of information and ideas across the student research teams and also provides a forum for the SRI students to practice their presentation skills.

Week Seven of the program, student teams begin to synthesize their research and start compiling their final team research reports.

During Week Eight, the last week of the SRI program, students submit their final reports and provide team presentations to an audience of CSR researchers and representatives from DHS S&T, USCG, NJOHSP, Stevens Institute of Technology, and other invited guests.

At the end of each summer's program, the student team's final presentations are made available to the general public on the CSR Website at www.stevens.edu/csr/SummerInstitute. Students also engage in a formal commencement event and receive certificates of achievement and participation.

Table 3 provides a sample of the weekly activities, field visits and topics of discussion for the eight-week summer research program.

PROFESSIONAL DEVELOPMENT

A critical component of the Summer Research Institute is the professional development of its student participants. According to the National Association of Colleges and Employers (NACE), 2012 and 2013 Job Outlook reports, the top attributes

Table 3. Sample SRI weekly activities: topics, guest speakers and field visits

SCHEDULE	TOPIC	FACULTY/ GUEST SPEAKERS	SRI ACTIVITIES
Week One	MDS /MTS- Intensive Overview	Stevens Maritime Systems/Security faculty Guest speakers: USCG/ PANYNJ	Faculty/student introductions, tours of Stevens labs & facilities. Research team assignments.
Week Two	Sensor Technologies	Passive Acoustics HF Radar Satellite Systems	Acoustic and AIS observation experiment.
Week Three	Team research projects with research mentors	Guest Speakers from Maritime Industry / Federal Agencies	Field visit to NUSTL. Student research status update presentations.
Week Four	Team research projects		Field visit to CBP Port New York/Newark. Student research status update presentations.
Week Five	Supply Chain & Port Resilience	Guest Speaker: U.S. Navy Strategic Systems Programs	Simulation project/class exercise.
Week Six	Team research projects	Guest Speaker: DHS S&T HSARPA	Student research status update presentations.
Week Seven	Program Synthesis/ Team research projects		Attend CSR Stakeholder Engagement Meeting. Student research status update presentations.
Week Eight	Team research projects - final reports and presentations.		Visitors from DHS, CBP, NJOHSP, CSR & Stevens attend final research project presentations.

that employers seek most in college graduates are the ability to communicate, both written and verbally, the ability for candidates to work in team environments, and the ability for graduates to problem solve. (NACE 2012, 2013)

For its part, CSR has organized the SRI curriculum to include activities that inherently enhance student communication skills, teaming capabilities, and critical thinking and problem solving abilities. CSR also engages faculty members from Stevens Writing and Communications Center to provide lunch and learn seminars on presentation skills, tips for preparing power point slides and report writing.

PROGRAM THEMES AND STUDENT RESEARCH PROJECTS

SRI program themes and research projects focus on current issues of national significance in the maritime domain. Over the past four years, the program themes of the SRI have included: Detecting and Tracking Small Vessel Threats, Consequence Assessment and Threat Detection, Stakeholder/End-User Engagement, and Technology Transition.

A list of the SRI program themes and the corresponding student research projects is provided in Table 4.

PROGRAM IMPACTS AND OUTCOMES

SRI student research outcomes have resulted in significant and notable achievements that have contributed to new knowledge and the creation of new tools and technologies for homeland security practitioners and emergency responders. These achievements include:

- Development of a new Web-based portal called Magello. Magello provides first responders and emergency management personnel with real-time high-resolution environmental and oceanic data needed to make informed decisions during emergency and crisis situations. The system was employed during a massive sewage spill in the Hudson River on July 20, 2011. A fire at the North River Wastewater Treatment Plant in upper Manhattan had disabled the plant and caused the facility to shut down and subsequently result in the spill of millions of gallons of untreated wastewater into the Hudson River. With assistance from Dr. Alan Blumberg, Director, Stevens Center for Maritime Systems, Magello was able to generate a sewage transport forecast and provide the critical flow data to the New York City Department of Environmental Protection (NYCDEP) and the New Jersey State Department

Maritime Security Summer Research Institute

Table 4. SRI program themes and projects

Program	Theme	Research Teams and Project Outcomes
2013	Stakeholder Engagement and Data Integration	**CBP Trade Facilitation** – Students conducted a case study on the effectiveness of CBP's new Centers of Excellence and Expertise (CEEs) to enhance safety and security and trade processing within the pharmaceutical industry. **Detection Technology Synergies** – Students assessed the tipping and cueing of sensor technologies, utilizing the Stevens Passive Acoustic Detection System and Rutgers University's HF Radar detection systems. **HF Radar Integration into USCG Operating Systems** – Students assessed the use of advanced algorithms for integrating HF Radar data feeds into Coast Guard operational systems.
2012	End-user Engagement and Technology Transition	**Sensor Technologies** – Students utilized Machine Learning Algorithms in a novel approach to automatically classify acoustic signatures of vessels transiting the Hudson River. **HF Radar Vessel Detection** – Students developed algorithms to increase the probability of vessel detections in multi-ship environments. **Magello Emergency Response Tool** – Students advanced the functionality & assessed end-user data needs for the transition of Magello to stakeholders. **Port Mapper Tool** – Students developed port closure scenarios to advance the decision support capabilities of the Center's Port Mapper Tool.
2011	Consequence Assessment and Threat Detection	**Consequence Assessment and Management** – Students developed a new Web interface called Magello. Magello is designed to pull together ultra-high resolution high-fidelity oceanic and atmospheric real-time data feeds into one easy to use Web interface. The Web interface was developed as a decision support tool to assist first responders and decision makers in emergency and crisis events. Magello was selected as a top ten finalist in the National Security Innovation Competition in 2012. **Sensor Technology Applications in Port Security** – Students developed a database of acoustic vessel signatures and created a graphical user interface designed to assist in identifying vessel traffic abnormalities.
2010	Small Vessel Threats	**Acoustics & Electro-Optics** – Students analyzed the use of passive acoustic systems to detect, track and classify vessels in the New York Harbor. **HF Radar** – Students assessed the capabilities and limitations of HF Radar to detect small vessels in the New York Harbor. **Satellite** – Students assessed the use of satellite applications for port security applications. **Systems Thinking** – Students developed a detection, response and resilience strategy focused on vessel threat scenarios outlined in the 2008 DHS Small Vessel Security Strategy.

of Environmental Protection (NJDEP) for their remediation and response efforts. In 2012, Magello was selected as a top ten finalist in the National Security Innovation Competition (NSIC) and was showcased at the 2011 USCG Innovation Expo in Tampa, FL. The USCG continues to be interested in the advancement of Magello and has recently provided funding support for the continued development of the tool's capabilities and functionality.

- Development of a new database used to characterize and archive acoustic signatures of vessel traffic in the New York Harbor and Hudson River Estuary. The database assists Stevens researchers in their efforts to detect, classify, and track small vessel threats. In 2012, SRI students leveraged the data collected during the 2011 program, to explore the use of Machine Learning Algorithms, to automatically process and classify vessel acoustic signatures in the multi-vessel environment of the New York Harbor.
- Advancement of MIT's Port Mapper to include scenario based assessments for decision support purposes. The Port Mapper tool was used during Hurricane Sandy to assist USCG senior leadership in the redirection of cargo, during the weeklong closure of the Port of New York/Newark.
- DHS S&T University Programs Best Student Paper Awards and recognition as panelists and presenters at the DHS 4th and 5th Annual University Summits.

Positive unplanned impacts have included the SRI being written into other academic institutions grants and proposals, as the summer research and experiential learning component of their proposed projects. Such instances have included DHS Scientific Leadership proposals prepared separately by the University of Puerto Rico-Mayaguez and Elizabeth City State University that have each designated funding support for their students and faculty to participate in the Summer Research Institute.

STUDENT BENEFITS

Students gain invaluable professional experience by working on real-world homeland security issues in collaboration with leading academic researchers and industry and government homeland security practitioners. The rigorous hands-on Summer Research Institute is designed to provide students with the following experiential learning benefits:

- Students enhance their STEM skill competencies, technical capabilities and leadership qualities by engaging in complex problems of national interest.
- Students learn to interact and engage in professional relationships with industry and government practitioners and develop long-standing professional networks.

- Students enhance their professional communications and presentation skills through presentations and report writing.

PROGRAM ASSESSMENTS

An assessment of the SRI is conducted at the end of each year's program in the form of a student survey. The survey is designed to provide feedback on the following key areas: 1). Program strengths and weaknesses; 2). Skills and professional knowledge learned; 3). Impact on career and academic interests; 4). Areas for program improvement.

Collectively, student assessments have rated the SRI "Excellent" in the following areas:

- Faculty Mentor Guidance and Assistance
- Quality of Program Coordination/Administration
- Quality of Teamwork
- Quality of Research Outcomes
- Quality of Research Facilities

When asked to identify the top three takeaways from the SRI, students commonly mentioned the following items:

- Team work and student diversity,
- Improved communications & presentation skills, and
- Knowledge and experience

When asked how best to describe their experience in the SRI, student survey responses have said:

- *Extremely educational; it opened me up to areas I probably wouldn't have otherwise considered for the future.*
- *Very powerful experience. I came to the program wanting to understand the professions of maritime and homeland security. I have a much better grasp what it takes to get into those fields and also what is involved in pursuing a career in research. I greatly enjoyed my time here. I've learned not only academically but career wise and life lessons as well.*
- *I feel for the first time since starting school that I (and my team) am contributing something important to the "real world" and not simply performing an academic exercise.*

- *It is highly rewarding to feel as though we are contributing something to the greater community which may improve the country's ability to protect itself from catastrophic events.*
- *The student and faculty interactions define the experience more than anything. There was so much interaction while researching, before and after lectures and during field trips.*

Relative to professional development skills, most students ranked the following skills as "improved substantially": Ability to conduct research, Communications skills, Leadership skills, Networking, Oral presentation skills, Professional confidence, and Teamwork/collaboration.

In a testament to the effectiveness of the SRI in enhancing student interest in maritime and homeland security, close to 90% of the students said that they would consider advanced academic study and/or a career in homeland security because of their experience in the program, and 100% of the survey respondents said that they would recommend the SRI to their friends and colleagues at their respective universities.

LESSONS LEARNED

The most salient lesson learned during the SRI has been the need to engage students in their research projects from Week One of the program and to provide them with increasing amounts of time to conduct their research and field experiments. Conversations with students and researchers from the inaugural program, together with their survey responses, indicated that student project outcomes had been constrained and adversely affected by excessive time spent attending in-class lectures.

While CSR administrators initially discussed the option of extending the length of the SRI from eight weeks to 10-weeks, it was determined that such a change would significantly increase the program's operational costs and would conflict with the availability of Stevens on-campus student housing.

The lessons learned throughout the delivery of the SRI, have taught CSR administrators that when students are given flexibility in their schedules and dedicated time to conduct research and hands-on experiments, they are more likely to produce higher quality and more substantive research outcomes. Examples of this include the development of the Magello Web interface and the unique application of Machine Learning Algorithms to automatically classify acoustic signatures of vessels, in the 2011 and 2012 SRI programs respectively.

Each year, CSR administrators work to achieve balance between structured group activities (in-class lectures and field visits) and unstructured time for independent research activities and experiments. Over the past four years, administrators have learned to adjust the program schedule and vary the number of program activities (e.g. lectures, guest speakers, and field visits) according to student research needs.

ALUMNI NETWORK AND STUDENT ACHIEVEMENTS

CSR has actively worked to maintain relationships and on-going communications with its SRI alumni. Since the start of the program in 2010, CSR's director of education has continued to engage SRI alumni through email communications, including CSR newsletters and notifications of internship and employment opportunities, and through follow-up surveys. It is through these communications that CSR has been able to track the impacts of the SRI on the activities and career choices of its alumni participants.

Many of the SRI program alumni are now employed in the workforce and continue to credit the SRI as an important factor in their professional development and their ability to successfully obtain high-level internships, fellowships and employment.

Some of the relevant and notable SRI alumni achievements include:

- Gregory Sciarretta, SRI 2011, was selected as a top-ten finalist in the 2012 National Security Innovation Competition for the work he and his team completed on Magello during the 2011 Summer Research Institute.
- Brandon Gorton, SRI 2011, is currently employed as a Deputy Physical Protection Specialist, at the Pacific Northwest National Laboratory.
- Hamid Darabi, SRI 2011, collaborated with Stevens faculty members, Drs. Alex Gorod, Mo Mansouri and Thomas Wakeman, to prepare the paper entitled *Using hybrid modeling to simulate Maritime Transportation System of Systems (MTSoS)*. The paper was selected for presentation at the 2012 IEEE International Systems Conference, in Vancouver, BC, Canada.
- Hardik Gajjar, SRI 2010, is currently working as a Ports and Intermodal Planner at Parsons Brinkerhoff in Virginia, while completing his doctoral dissertation at Stevens Institute of Technology in the area of Economic Resiliency for Marine Terminals.
- Danielle Holden, SRI 2010, was awarded a DHS-funded Stevens Maritime Systems Master's Degree Fellowship based on her work and experience in the SRI.

- Three out of the four SRI 2010 student research teams submitted abstracts to the DHS University Network Summit. All three were selected to present their SRI research at the 5th Annual event held March 29 – April 1, 2011. Student papers included: *A Study of Small Vessel Threats Using Acoustic and Electro-optic Technologies* (Student authors: Andreas Graber, Qing Li, Saiyam Shah, Walter Seme, Ariel Marrero, and Wojciech Czerwonka), *Aiding in the Prevention of Terrorist Attacks in the Hudson River Through Detection of Small Vessels with UHF Radar* (Student authors: Angelica Sogor, Lenny Llauger, Omar Lopez, Shankar Nilakantan, Danielle Holden, and Dakota Hahn), and *Systems Thinking Approach to Small Vessel Security* (Student authors: Leonid Lantsman, Hardik Gajjar, Nazanin Andalibi, Blake Cignarella, Tanaira Cullens, Jose Mesa, and Tiffany Walter).
- Talmor Meir, SRI 2010 participant, received the 5th Annual DHS University Network Summit "Best Paper Award" for her paper submission entitled *Decision Learning Algorithm for Acoustic Vessel Classification.* Her work was later published in the April 2012 edition of Homeland Security Affairs, the peer-reviewed online journal of the Naval Postgraduate School Center for Homeland Defense and Security.

CURRENT CHALLENGES

Funding support for the SRI is an on-going challenge for CSR administrators. As with many of the Center's stakeholder organizations, budget cuts have limited the Center's ability to provide stipend support and housing for students participating in the SRI. As a result, CSR administrators have submitted proposals for external sponsorship and funding support to industry and government agencies and have pursued private foundations for operational support. Given the current state of the economy and the budget sequestration, CSR has had little success to date with external sponsor support.

Fortunately, however, CSR has been able to leverage existing Stevens scholarship and fellowship programs and those of its academic partners to recruit students who can attend the SRI fully-funded through external resources. In 2013, each of the 13 student participants attended the program with funding support leveraged from DHS Scientific Leadership Awards, Stevens Scholar's program and sponsorship by CSR's sister research center, the Center for Island, Maritime and Extreme Environment Security (CIMES).

CONCLUSION

The Summer Research Institute is a world-class summer research program designed to engage high-achieving engineering and science students in maritime and port security research. The program's curriculum inspires students to develop innovative and novel solutions to some of the nation's most complex maritime security related issues. Established in 2010, the program has had tremendous impacts on student achievements and has inspired academic and career interests in the maritime/homeland security domain.

Collaborations between students and researchers, field visits, and activities involving industry and government practitioners are key features of the SRI program.

Student participants are given unparalleled opportunities to interact one-on-one with representatives from a broad range of maritime security focused organizations and federal emergency response agencies including, CBP, NJOHSP, DHS S&T, PANYNJ, U.S. Navy, and the USCG. These unique interactions and networking opportunities afford students a real-world context in which they can frame their research and enhance their experiential learning.

Student survey responses reflect the success of the CSR in meeting its' objectives. In a testament to the programs' impact on student academic and career interests, close to 90% of the student respondents said that the SRI had enhanced their interest in pursuing advanced academic study and/or a career in the maritime/homeland security domain, and 100% of the students said that they would recommend the SRI to their friends and colleagues at their respective schools.

Similar DHS-funded summer research programs, including the Homeland Security Summer Scholars Academy, delivered by the National Center for Boarder Security and Immigration at the University of Texas El Paso, have also demonstrated comparable student impacts and program outcomes as the CSR's Summer Research Institute.

DHS ACKNOWLEDGEMENT AND DISCLAIMER

This material is based upon work supported by the U.S. Department of Homeland Security under Grant Award Number 2008-ST-061-ML0002. The views and conclusions contained in this document are those of the authors and should not be interpreted as necessarily representing the official policies, either expressed or implied, of the U.S. Department of Homeland Security.

REFERENCES

Committee on Prospering in the Global Economy of the 21st Century (U.S.) & Committee on Science, Engineering, and Public Policy (U.S.). (2007). *Rising above the gathering storm: Energizing and employing America for a brighter economic future*. Washington, DC: National Academies Press.

Committee on Prospering in the Global Economy of the 21st Century (U.S.) & Committee on Science, Engineering, and Public Policy (U.S.). (2010). *Rising above the gathering storm, revisited, rapidly approaching a category 5*. Washington, DC: National Academies Press.

Jobs for the Future. (2007). *The STEM workforce challenge, the role of the public workforce system in a national solution for a competitive science, technology, engineering, and mathematics (STEM) workforce*. Washington, DC: U.S. Department of Labor, Employment and Training Administration.

National Association of Colleges and Employers. (2012). *Job outlook report*. Bethlehem, PA: Author.

National Association of Colleges and Employers. (2013). *Job outlook report*. Bethlehem, PA: Author.

Pullen, J., & Bruno, M. (2013). The center for secure and resilient maritime commerce: A DHS national center of excellence in maritime security. In *Cases on research and knowledge discovery: Homeland security centers of excellence*. Hershey, PA: IGI Global.

Talavera, V. (2013). *The national center for border security and immigration*. El Paso, TX: University of Texas El Paso, Homeland Security Summer Scholars Academy, Program Summary.

KEY TERMS AND DEFINITIONS

Center of Excellence: DHS Center's of Excellence are designated research centers led by experts and researchers to conduct multidisciplinary homeland security research and education. Each center is university-led or co-led in collaboration with partners from other institutions, agencies, national laboratories, think tanks and the private sector.

Consequence Assessment: The process of identifying or evaluating the potential or actual effects of an event, incident, or occurrence.

Experiential Learning: The process of learning from hands-on experience.

High Frequency Radar: High frequency (HF) radar systems measure the speed and direction of ocean surface currents in near real time. The Rutgers University/University of Puerto Rico–Mayaguez HF radar system is a multi-use system. The first is to measure ocean currents via Doppler effects on the radar signal due to the currents, and the second is to detect and measure position, velocity, and bearing of vessels, via Doppler shift techniques.

Marine Transportation System: The Marine Transportation System, or MTS, consists of waterways, ports, and intermodal landside connections that allow the various modes of transportation to move people and goods to, from, and on the water.

Maritime Domain Awareness: The effective understanding of anything associated with the maritime domain that could impact the security, safety, economy, or environment. The maritime domain is defined as all areas and things of, on, under, relating to, adjacent to, or bordering on a sea, ocean, or other navigable waterway, including all maritime-related activities, infrastructure, people, cargo, and vessels and other conveyances.

Passive Acoustics: The action of listening for sounds generated by targets of interest, often at specific frequencies or for purposes of specific analyses. These may be water or airborne vessels, or intruders, among other things.

STEM: Science, Technology, Engineering and Mathematics.

Chapter 6
Frienemies:
Assessing the Interactions between Native American Tribes and the U.S. Government in Homeland Security and Emergency Management Policy

Leigh R. Anderson
The Ohio State University, USA

EXECUTIVE SUMMARY

The working relationships between Native American tribes, the states, and the federal government have been strained for centuries. These intergovernmental interactions have led to a fragmented system whose attempt to deliver public service is consistently met with opposition. One area where this has become increasingly evident is within homeland security and emergency management policy. Guided by Agranoff (2012), this study used a cross sectional survey to gather information about the beliefs tribes held about the various aspects of their working relationships with states and the federal government within the context of homeland security and emergency management.

DOI: 10.4018/978-1-4666-5946-9.ch006

BACKGROUND: NATIVE AMERICAN TRIBES WITHIN THE UNITED STATES OF AMERICA

This study will help to provide a foundation upon which to build future studies in the field of public policy and homeland security focused on Indian country. As sovereign nations within the borders of the United States, Native American tribes hold a very distinct political and legal position. Native American tribes entered into agreements and compromises with the United States government; however, tribal nations never forfeited their sovereignty when entering into those agreements and as a result remain independent, occupying a position of sovereign immunity (Evans, 2011; McGuire, 1990) on U.S. soil.

Being sovereign nations within another sovereign nation, Wilkens (1993) acknowledges that from a theoretical and political perspective, tribes are in a legal and political quandary. As a result of these sovereign positions, much of the interaction between tribal nations and levels of the American government has been grounded in intergovernmental conflict for centuries. The conflict has consistently pit tribal governments against state, local, and the federal government regarding jurisdiction, gaming regulations, natural resources, tax obligations, and most recently, homeland security funding. In theory, tribes are to be sovereign, but in practice, they hold many other conflicting positions. As separate nations within another politically functioning nation they also simultaneously play subordinate roles.

Much of the existing literature on this topic paints a picture of hostility that is seated within the U.S. government, namely the states, and is directed towards tribal nations (Evans, 2001; Bays & Fouberg, 2002). In fact, the interactions between states and the tribal nations have been cited as one of the most divisive intergovernmental conflicts within United States history (McCool, 1993; Mason, 1998, 2002; Wilson, 2002; Steinman, 2004). Scholars have sought to increase awareness of these conflicts and their harm to intergovernmental relations between the two systems of governance. They have classified the historical and contemporary components of these relationships as crucial. In this study's effort to explain ways to move past this conflict in the area of homeland security emergency management policy, it is important to engage the information put forth by these authors.

Aside from various treaties, Presidential Executive Orders, and Supreme Court rulings, the Constitution is the only formal document that acknowledges tribal governance as a system apart from the American system of federalism. Native American tribes are referred to in the Commerce and the Apportionment Clauses of the Constitution. Based upon the wording, the relationship between the federal government and tribes is one between sovereign nations and exclusive authority over Native American affairs lie with the federal government, not the state (Ortiz, 2002; Jarratt-Ziemski, 1999; National Council of American Indians, n.d.). However, there is concern that decision-making powers are shifting from the federal government to the states; this shift is giving states control over federal dollars and more say in how and where those dollars should be spent at the expense of the tribes (Ortiz, 2002).

Despite the existence of federal tribal policy, which intends that states should have no control over affairs in Indian Country, the federal government has often delegated many responsibilities to the states; thus, giving states decision-making and fiduciary control over many policy areas including emergency preparedness and homeland security. The creation of this indirect line of authority between tribes and the states has further complicated existing disagreements. It begs the question of whether or not the same interactions are taking place in the area of emergency management and homeland security.

In addition to tribes sitting outside the parameters of the federalist system, differences in culture and identity also influence the interactions between tribal nations and the U.S. government. Tribal governance incorporates such issues as tribal culture, history, social interactions, laws, jurisdiction, and sovereignty; therefore, it is critical to understand why Indian country wishes to retain their ways of governance (Ortiz, 1999). There is indeed a difference between the cultural and traditional aspects of American governance and that of tribal governance. These differences present very real barriers to conflict resolution between these two governance systems.

The culture and identity differences that make interactions difficult and conflict highly probable are not just about differences between Indian county and the U.S., but also include variations in culture and identity amongst tribal nations themselves. As Bays and Fouberg (2002) articulate, culture, population, land base ownership, histories, languages, governance structures, and traditions, all vary amongst Native American tribes themselves. Understanding how culture and identity can impact public policy is essential, especially in emergency management. Changes in culture and identity are not negotiable nor should they be jeopardized. If culture and identity are impacting the success of intergovernmental relationships in a negative way, then it is necessary to figure out ways to look beyond this influence.

SETTING THE STAGE: NATIVE AMERICAN TRIBES AND U.S. HOMELAND SECURITY AND EMERGENCY MANAGEMENT POLICY

Understanding how important unified systems are to the nation's ability to prevent, protect, mitigate, respond to, and recover from all hazards, the Department of Homeland Security (DHS) has the responsibility of creating a seamless preparedness and response system across the U.S. Ranking high on the nation's list of priorities, effective homeland security has come to be synonymous with strong coordination;

the prevention of an attack is a function of tightening and strengthening coordination across agencies and governments (Kettl, 2007). In a quest to fulfill their mission of achieving an integrated and unified system of homeland security and emergency management, the DHS, and more specifically, the Federal Emergency Management Agency (FEMA), has decided that the best way to accomplish this goal is to advise the sharing of emergency management resources and coordination amongst all government actors and jurisdictions including tribal nations.

To encourage the establishment and maintenance of resources, and eventually, the sharing of those resources, DHS created initiatives such as the Homeland Security Grant Program (HSGP). Established in 2003 and consisting of three separate, yet interrelated programs: the State Homeland Security Program (SHSP), the Urban Areas Security Initiative (UASI), and Operation Stonegarden (OPSG), the HSGP provides grant funds to state and local governments to increase funding for first-responder equipment, planning, training, exercises, and the collection of intelligence about natural hazards and potential attacks. One of the key requirements of these grants is that the state and local governments must put forth efforts to establish and maintain intergovernmental relationships with neighboring governments. To further demonstrate how integral the establishment of a unified system of homeland security was to the priorities of the United States, there have been other initiatives such as The National Incident Management System and The National Response Framework that have helped to specify the parameters of these collaborative relationships as well as the procedures behind creating and sustaining these partnerships. On March 30, 2011, President Obama signed Presidential Policy Directive 8 – National Preparedness (PPD-8). The document directs the federal government to ensure that the nation is working towards the use of an integrated and strategic approach in achieving national security objectives. Efforts to coordinate emergency preparedness initiatives can be a daunting task across the nation; and can become even more overwhelming when 566 Native American tribes must be included in those efforts.

Executive Order 13084: Consultation and Coordination with Indian Tribal Governments was issued in 1998 by President Clinton; also covering the same topic. Executive Order 13175: Consultation and Coordination with Indian Tribal Governments was issued as well by President Clinton in 2000. It was later enforced in November 2009 by President Obama. American Indian and Alaska Native Education, Executive Order 13336 was issued by President George W. Bush in 2004. Each of these Presidential Executive Orders support and mandate government-to-government interactions between the U.S. government and tribal nations. Executive Order 13175 strongly encourages that each of the Executive agencies reach out to tribal nations "in order to establish regular and meaningful consultation and collaboration with tribal officials in the development of federal policies that have tribal implications, to strengthen the United States' government-to-government relationships with Indian tribes (Executive Order 13175, 2000)." In response to Executive Order 13175, FEMA reassessed and re-released their tribal policy to better address the needs of tribal nations. Additionally, the Department of Homeland Security created the Tribal Homeland Security Grant Program (THSGP) in 2008 which provides funding directly to the tribal nations to help strengthen their preparedness efforts and reduce any risks associated with natural hazards and potential attacks. This grant, however, requires tribes seeking funding to have already established relationships with neighboring governmental units. Being able to provide this evidence comes at a high price for many tribal nations.

Despite the creation of the THSGP, the tribes still found themselves unable to meet the demands of the federal criteria for the program; namely the ability to establish and maintain effective intergovernmental relationships in homeland security. If they did not have proof of these relationships, they were not eligible for the federal grant program. This forced many tribes to turn to those same neighboring governments for assistance with homeland security related efforts. The situation was one in which the tribes felt as though they had to choose between protecting their sovereign rights from their respective states and taking steps to protect the lives of their members from natural and manmade disasters. For many tribes, these two objectives were mutually exclusive.

Like many of the federal Indian policies of the past, current homeland security and emergency management policies are extremely ambiguous with relation to the position of the tribes. At times, they are considered politically independent and at other times, they are required to go through their respective states to seek assistance. For example, the ambiguous nature of these policies is illustrated within the National Response Framework. Initially published in 2008 by the Department of Homeland Security, the National Response Framework (NRF) is a guide to help governments plan and prepare for the ability to provide a unified response across jurisdictions to any manmade and natural disasters.

The policy states that it recognizes the trust relationship and acknowledges the right to self-government for tribes. It also explains that as sovereign entities, tribes can *elect* to deal *directly* with the Federal government. Yet, at the same time, the policy makes it extremely clear that tribes *must* go through the states if they wish to seek emergency assistance after a disaster, by way of a Presidential declaration. This policy not only demonstrates the ambiguity that exists within federal policies regarding tribal nations in general, it also illustrates a blatant attempt by the federal government to disregard the trust relationship. Following the January 29, 2013 signing of Sandy Recovery Act by President Barack Obama, which amongst other changes, amended the Stafford Act to allow federally recognized tribal governments to seek a federal emergency or major disaster declaration directly from the President of the United States, the National Response Framework was updated. While the updated guidance from the 2013 National Response Framework no longer explicitly states that a governor must request a Presidential Declaration on behalf of a tribe and while it gives tribes the option to elect to seek assistance from states and/or the federal government, issues of ambiguity remain; primarily, the conditions under which tribes are required to work with states for "certain types of federal assistance."

This policy supports the tribal claims that despite having agreements which exclude state power over tribal lands, federal responsibilities to tribal nations are in fact being delegated to states. According to the American Indian Policy Center (2010), "the devolution of authority to the states in the last two decades has impinged on the government-to-government relationship Indian tribes have with the federal government." Organick and Kowalski (2009) argue that by deferring its powers to the state level, the Federal government is subverting and undermining the tribal-federal trust relationship and forcing tribes to engage in decision making with states that should be reserved only for the federal government. This re-delegation of power is not only unfair to the tribes; it further drives a wedge between the two systems of government.

The national emergency management framework does not take into consideration the possibility of conflicts existing between tribes and states. It disregards statutes, legislation, and executive orders which prohibit states from asserting any type of relative power over tribes. It presupposes that tribes, and the states in which they are situated, have open and clear lines of communication. It forces tribes to comply with the state in order to have a *chance* to be considered for inclusion into the states' request for a Presidential Declaration and further emergency management assistance. There is no way that such a policy, as it is written, can be effective. While tribes are forced to go through the state, many tribes assert that they have no working relationship with the state in which they are situated. It has become clear that the federal government contributes to potential conflicts between tribes and states by ignoring the rules and laws they set forth.

As the National Congress of American Indians (2013) explains, "Tribal nations represent a unique and important sector of the United States homeland security and emergency management system…nineteen tribal nations are each larger than the state of Rhode Island…twelve have a land base larger than the state of Delaware... tribal governments have extensive border-security responsibilities, including immigration, anti-terrorism, and anti-smuggling." In an interview with National Public Radio on February 15, 2013, Executive Director of the National Congress of American Indians, Jacqueline Pata (2013), a member of the Raven/Sockeye clan of the Tlingit tribe, explained that currently, there are a total of 40 tribes that border either Mexico or Canada and that have tribal members on both sides of those borders. Pata described immigration policy as being of great concern to Indian country because as guardians of the borders, they are the first to come into contact with the negative impacts stemming from ineffective U.S. immigration policies.

Recent reports published by the Congressional Research Service and authored by Immigration Policy Specialist Chad C. Haddal (2010) infer that federal homeland security agencies have implemented policies which might be increasing the burden specifically on tribes in terms of homeland security obligations. This includes using their own local resources to deter international crimes targeted at the U.S., but not necessarily providing them with resources to combat the high risk terrorism levels or other organized criminal activity. This is particularly true for those 40 Native American border tribes of which Pata spoke. Many of those border tribes have reported dealing with high rates of traffic from illegal immigration and drugs, amongst other crimes. An example of these policies is the Department of Homeland Security's U.S. Border Patrol "Prevention through Deterrence Policy." First adopted in 1994 and currently being practiced, this operational strategy seeks to "push unauthorized migration away from population centers and funnel it into more remote border regions (Haddal, 2010, p. 19)." These remote border regions, to which migration is funneled, happen to be in areas where southwest tribal nations are situated. Along with this migration come reports of increased drug trafficking and the fear that terrorists will soon begin to take advantage of the ill-regulated and ill-prepared tribal borders.

Fulfilling these demanding border-security responsibilities has proved difficult for border tribes such as the Tohono O'odham. The Tohono O'odham Nation lies in both the United States and Mexico. Residing in the Sonoran Desert, located in southeastern Arizona and northwest Mexico, as William R. Di Iorio explains in his piece *Mending fences: the fractured relationship between Native American tribes and the federal government and its negative impact on border security* (2007), the Tohono O'odham are responsible for almost 700 to 1,000 illegal and undetected border crossings per year. In an article entitled *Victims in Waiting: How the Homeland Security Act Falls Short of Fully Protecting Tribal Lands*, Jessica Butts (2003, 2004) states that more than 25 tribes govern land that is adjacent to international borders or is accessible directly by boat and more than tens of thousands illegal migrants use these ill-protected borders to gain access to the United States; making entry through Indian country a potential option for future terrorists organizations.

CASE DESCRIPTION

On February 12, 2013, just thirty-three days after his second Presidential Inauguration, President Barack Obama delivered the State of the Union Address. It was during this time that President Obama not only detailed the current conditions with which the nation was grappling, but he also laid out a vision which would help to guide the nation's efforts to address current and anticipated challenges over the next four years. Just two days later in Washington, D.C., there was a second State of the Union Address delivered. The president of the National Congress of American Indians, Jefferson Keel, of the Chickasaw Nation of Oklahoma, delivered the 7th annual State of Indian Nations Address. Like President Obama, Keel outlined current challenges within Indian Country.

Amongst the many challenges that faced both groups, one of the main concerns stemmed from both Indian Country's and the United States' ability to ensure that homeland security policy implementation remained a high priority. Despite goal congruence, evidence of historical and contemporary barriers to collaboration pose significant problems for these systems of governance in homeland security and emergency management policy.

There are constant struggles amongst the various units of governance within the United States, and although the most familiar occur between the federal government and state governments, the most complicated and historically persistent may be those that involve Native American tribes (Mason, 1998; Ortiz, 1999; Steinman, 2004; Organick & Kowalski, 2009). Rooted in issues surrounding differences in cultural, philosophical, legal, and historical identities, the sometimes volatile interactions between tribes and levels of the American government can threaten basic human values and needs if not addressed (Wondolleck & Bryan, 2003; Coleman & Morton, 2000). This is certainly the case when considering U.S. homeland security and emergency management policy. Understanding that disasters and emergencies do not stop at geopolitical boundaries, it is important for tribal nations to ensure that they have access to the same resources as sectors of the U.S. government with similar land bases. Tribal nations have not been exempt from the same threats and hazards that have tormented the U.S. In fact, in 2010, tribes experienced both natural and man-made disasters that damaged critical tribal infrastructure and personal property (National Congress of American Indians, 2011). In spite of having similar risk levels as sectors of the U.S. government, tribes have consistently argued that they have often been less prepared than state and local governments. A disadvantage they claim is a direct result of their unique geopolitical positioning (Adams, 2012) which has significantly limited their access to resources. This includes preparedness, response, and recovery networks, already available to sectors of the U.S. government. This limited access to resources has caused and, in some cases, increased a rift between tribal nations and their U.S. government counterparts within the same and/or neighboring geographic region(s). The quest for a unified system of homeland security relies heavily upon the concept of unification amongst all governments present on American soil. If the United States is to attain an integrated national homeland security system, it is imperative to incorporate our country's various social and cultural groups into the total national effort.

It is clear that tribal nations face the same dangers as states and local governments. What is not as clear is why tribal governments are adamant about neglect by the federal government and states under these policies and why there appears to be a lack of progressive interactions amongst these governmental systems in the area of emergency management and homeland security policy. The foundation of this case study lies in attempting to understand *how* these government units are interacting and what other factors might be intervening and impacting the formation or lack thereof of cooperative partnerships. Documents presented by the representative congress of the American Indians suggest that their interactions with sectors of the U.S. government have been less than satisfying; however, more information about the nature of these interactions within this specific context is needed. In order to get to that understanding, an assessment of the perspectives of tribal governments and how they view their interactions as actors within this system is integral.

Guided by Agranoff (2012), this chapter assesses how tribal nations view their interactions with the U.S. government and how these interactions have impacted the mission for integrated protection, preparedness, and response efforts for all government entities on American soil. Gathering data and analyzing these relationships will help to (1) explore elements of these partnerships that are necessary to achieve effective interactions, and (2) understand the extent to which tribes believe effective interactions have or have not been taking place.

Within the area of homeland security policy, this project aims to produce the following results: (1) provide insight into the manner in which tribes and the U.S. government relate to each other in the context of homeland security and emergency management, and (2) advance understanding of how tribes view their relationships with the U.S. government and how these relationships impact the federal and state government's understanding of tribes' unique needs.

CONCEPTUAL FRAMEWORK

As has been discussed, the merging of federal, state, local, and tribal government units into one cohesive unit will not be an easy task. In fact, for highly multifaceted policy areas like homeland security and emergency management, at first glance collaborating resources across multiple jurisdictions can seem more like a problem rather than a solution.

In *Collaborating to Manage: A Primer for the Public Sector*, Agranoff (2012) explicates key characteristics that must be present in order to yield beneficial and effective collaborative relationships when addressing policy concerns and seeking goal congruence. Those key qualities are as follows: (1) the policy problems must be complex and the solutions must lie across different agencies and jurisdictions, (2) there must be extreme complexity in the decision making process, (3) there must be an opportunity to promote effective working relationships and mutual support amongst parties, (4) participants must be willing to confront and manage potential conflicts, (5) there must be a willingness to treat all participants as equals, and (6) effective communication must be present. Agranoff emphasizes that effective intergovernmental partnerships, even between governments with conflicting views, are possible.

Based upon the background presented concerning the complex geopolitical and legal positioning of tribal nations within the U.S., it is clear that the first two requirements of Agranoff's theoretical model for effective collaborative partnerships are met: (1) the problem of achieving a homeland security system has proved extremely complex and difficult for the nation (Wise & Nader, 2008) and as the basis for the system relies upon creating a unified and seamless configuration, it is evident that its solutions lie across different agencies and jurisdiction. The first requirement leads very well into the second which necessitates (2) that the policy problem provide all potential partnering governments with an opportunity to promote and form effective working relationships while acknowledging that the solution will be as complex as the problem.

Using the above theoretical framework as a guide, effective cooperative partnerships between tribes, the state, and the federal government should depend upon the presence of all or some combination of the remaining four characteristics: (1) tribes must be able to state that they are satisfied with their communication with the state and federal government, (2) tribes must be able to state that they are satisfied with state and federal government willingness to understand unique tribal needs and treat them as equal partners, (3) tribes must be able to state that they are satisfied with the willingness of the state and federal government to confront possible conflicts by responding to tribal needs regarding U.S. Homeland Security policy on tribal lands, and (4) tribes must be able to state that they are satisfied with the ability of state and federal government to promote effective working relationships through the offering of technical assistance to tribes. Utilizing the criterion put forth by Agranoff (2012) for establishing and maintaining effective and cooperative partnerships, this case study will assess whether or not the interactions between tribes and the U.S. government in homeland security and emergency management qualify.

METHODS

The data for this case study were collected from a survey that was administered by the Federal Emergency Management Agency (FEMA) in March of 2002. The survey was required under the Disaster Mitigation Act of 2000 (Public Law 106-390) Section 308 (b) (1), which amended the Robert T. Stafford Disaster Relief Act. The results of the survey were to be reported to the U.S. Congress and used to advance the relationship between FEMA and Tribes in hazard preparation. The questions administered in this particular survey were designed to ask respondents from tribes that were federally recognized in March 2002 (N=562), about their impressions regarding the tribe's participation in homeland security and emergency management activities within their community and in coordination with the U.S. government. Of the 562 federally recognized tribes, there were a total of 85 respondents for the open-ended response section of the survey.

The units of analyses for this case study are be the perspectives and reports of tribal nations surrounding their relationships with states and the federal government. The open-ended responses were analyzed using an *a priori* coding process. *A priori* codes were gathered based upon themes from existing research associated with homeland security, emergency management, and intergovernmental relations. There were four a priori codes: (1) communication with tribes, (2) acknowledgement and understanding of the unique cultural needs of tribes, (3) responsiveness to tribal needs, (4) technical assistance offered to the tribes. These codes are the result of the four areas that the research is addressing and evaluating and are rooted in the theoretical constructs presented here in the case study. In the survey, the tribes were asked the following question:

What can FEMA do to assist in improving your Tribe's capability to plan and respond to disasters? (Please be specific about your individual tribal needs such as training, pre-disaster mitigation, technical/financial assistance, etc.)

RESULTS

The information provided below illustrates the nature of the interactions between tribes, state, and federal government with regards to homeland security and emergency management.

A Priori Code #1: Communication

When examining the area of communication, tribes asserted that a lack of communication existed between their systems of government and units of the U.S. government. Supporting Agranoff's (2012) claims surrounding the importance of communication in producing effective partnerships, one tribe acknowledged that when it came to communication between the tribe and FEMA, that there was "[n]ot enough communication to establish an effective and consistent emergency management program." This same tribe went on to comment that "tribal partnerships must be strengthened to have national emergency management continuity."

Feelings of alienation in the area of emergency management also surfaced under the topic of communication. One tribe replied that it would be appreciated if FEMA could assist with "open[ing] the lines of communication and let[ting] other governments know [they] suffer from disasters too." This notion of alienation of the tribes by the sectors of the U.S. government threads throughout the qualitative responses.

A Priori Code #2: Understanding of Tribes' Unique Needs

One of the key areas that this case study has sought to explore has been how important it is for units of the U.S. government to understand the unique geopolitical and cultural aspects of tribal nations in order to form and maintain effective cooperative partnerships in homeland security and emergency management. Many of the respondents used the open response portion of the survey to explicate the unique positions of their tribal lands and how that position complicates how they approach efforts to provide emergency management on tribal lands. The survey captured that a great majority of the tribes reported that FEMA could provide assistance through acknowledging these unique positions and helping to tailor emergency preparedness training to those unique positions. The tribes pinpoint areas of concern such as the duty of the federal government to acknowledge and fulfill the trust responsibility, the problems that arise when the states become involved in the intergovernmental partnerships, and consideration of the barriers that exist when tribal lands lie across multiple jurisdictions.

The issue of honoring the trust responsibility relationship continued to rise to the top among the responses. As one tribe explained, "FEMA could assist by simply do[ing] a needs assessment and fulfill[ing] the trust responsibility." According to another tribe, it is imperative that FEMA take seriously, the government-to-government conditions set forth in the trust responsibility instead of using state governments as middlemen, stating: "FEMA needs to stand behind their partnership with the tribes directly, without the State involvement which only complicates, side tracks, and undermines the very concept of a 'partnership'." An additional tribe underlined the importance of the differences that they saw in the emergency management training offered by units of the U.S. government and how it does not meet the unique geopolitical and cultural requirements of the tribe, noting that "the courses offered by State emergency management agencies often do not meet the needs of the tribes." This respondent goes on to highlight that "FEMA needs to communicate directly with the program manager [of the tribes] rather than through the state," again emphasizing the importance of upholding the government-to-government conditions of policy communication that the federal government established long ago with tribal nations.

Those tribes located in more than one contiguous county and/or state also explained how their unique geopolitical position has significantly impacted how they carry out emergency management and homeland security efforts. Stating that they would like FEMA assistance in all homeland security and emergency management areas, one tribe acknowledges that their tribe is "uniquely located on the U.S/Mexico border which places it in an inevitable position of hazards resulting from illegal immigrant activity"; bringing to life the difficulties that tribes are facing across the country, with a special emphasis on border tribes. Another tribe also explained their unique geopolitical position, expanding across "a three state area" and "getting a lot of shipments of radioactive material"; their request from FEMA was for training in dealing with potential hazardous spills in their community.

Acknowledging the sovereignty of tribes was also revealed as a necessary condition to assisting tribes in establishing and maintaining an emergency management partnership. As one tribe explained, they recently found out that they were not covered by a neighboring fire department which was a U.S. government unit. The tribe disclosed that they were hesitant to enter into agreements with the neighboring government because of the fear that the U.S. government unit would try to annex the tribe. The tribe justified their trepidation to sign any agreements by stating that they "want to stay as independent as humanly possible." This illustrates one of the principle challenges that tribes face. For this tribal nation, entering into any mutual aid agreements must take into account the fear of tribes losing their sovereign rights and provide protection for those rights.

In terms of providing FEMA with guidance on how to assist tribes in the area of homeland security and emergency management, one tribe recommends that FEMA seek to gain an understanding of all of these unique aspects of the tribes. The tribe suggests that FEMA, "coordinate with federal and state representatives to meet with Tribe[s] to gain a comprehensive understanding of needs" and insisted that FEMA establish meetings between tribes and "federal and state agencies or visit [the tribe] to understand [their] needs."

A Priori Code #3: Responsiveness to the Needs of the Tribe

In the area of responsiveness to the needs of the tribes, one tribal nation bluntly stated that FEMA must be "more responsive to the training needs of tribal emergency management personnel." Another tribe advised that "returning [their] calls would be a good start." The same tribe also alludes to differential treatment and/or alienation of the tribes in the forming of intergovernmental relationships in homeland security and emergency management, stating that "Tribes are left out of government decisions and [with] recent funding for homeland security-Tribes were left out."

However, sentiments towards FEMA under this topic area were not all negative. In fact, when it came to FEMA, one tribal government exclaimed that FEMA was "very responsive to the needs of the tribe and timely in assisting [them]." Yet, this particular tribe also maintained that "[o]utside of FEMA, no other organizations, local, state, or federal ha[d] approached the Tribe regarding disasters," adding more evidence to solidify tribal claims of being ignored and not acknowledged by certain units of the U.S. government system in the area of homeland security and emergency management.

A Priori Code #4: Technical Assistance Offered to the Tribe

With regards to the area of technical assistance offered, respondents noted that FEMA could assist in providing technical assistance in a variety of ways from planning and training, to assistance with grant development and funding. However, returning back to the significance of the unique positioning of tribes, some of the respondents requested that FEMA seek to provide technical assistance to tribes with an understanding of the geopolitical and cultural qualities of tribal communities. In one instance, a tribe suggested that FEMA "consider going to the reservation and/or Rancherias and do local training so all of the Tribes who want to attend can do so." They go on to explain that their "[t]ribe is small and [they] don't have a large budget," so it would be helpful if "FEMA could organize a training session where two or three Tribes could attend at once." Evidence of a lack of coordination and communication between tribes and units of the U.S. government is also demonstrated by one respondent's request to FEMA in seeking assistance with their "strategic response program development [which is] in need of coordination among local, state, and federal jurisdictions." Another respondent did report on a positive experience with FEMA. It noted that "FEMA Region 9 held its first Tribal Emergency Preparedness workshop in 2001, Reno, NV" and explained that it was "a great workshop & a beginning for FEMA and Tribes in Region 9 to work together." The experiences of this particular tribe illustrate that there is hope for intergovernmental partnerships to form across the two government systems in the area of homeland security and emergency management.

DISCUSSION

As has been previously discussed, the unified system of homeland security and emergency management is based upon elements of coordination, communication, and cooperation amongst and between different jurisdictions here in the U.S. Evidence of collaborative partnerships is the bedrock for many of the homeland security grant programs. A concrete example of the successful inclusion of tribes into these networks would be the presence of effective cooperative partnerships. Determining whether or not tribes have been integrated into this system consisted of investigating how tribes have felt about being included into these networks and to explore the interactions between these groups. The greater part of the literature that has covered the interactions between Native American tribes and units of the U.S. government has characterized these interactions as intensely volatile. The presence of conflicts between these groups has been a clear indicator of problems with the integration of tribal nations into this system. It has been an even clearer sign of the presence of barriers to the overall goal of the U.S. government to provide safety and protection on American soil.

As learned from Agranoff (2012), there are six key defining characteristics of an effective collaborative relationship. Overall, the results showed that there was indeed evidence of a lack of communication between the two systems of governance, a lack of responsiveness on behalf of states and the federal government to the unique needs of tribes, a lack of cultural understanding, and a lack of technical assistance being offered to tribal nations by units of the U.S. government. The qualitative data also revealed that a large majority of tribal nations seek to enter into cooperative agreements in the area of homeland security and emergency preparedness, but are hesitant to do so for fears of conceding inherit sovereign rights.

After applying the results of the data analyses to Agranoff's guiding theoretical framework, based upon the data collected in 2002, it appears as though the working relationships between tribal nations and units of the U.S. government do not meet the criterion for effective cooperative partnerships. It was apparent throughout the data analyses that tribal nations do not perceive that they are being treated as equal partners within the homeland security and emergency preparedness system and believe that they must compromise their social and political identities in order to be included.

Tribal governments have been adamant about neglect by sectors of the U.S. in the area of emergency management and homeland security policy. Unfortunately, based upon the results, their experiences are valid. There is extensive evidence that suggests that they have been overlooked and excluded from many of the homeland security and emergency management networks operating around the U.S. Suggestions for solutions have been routinely biased against either government, prompting the other to respond with a lack of participation. These historical rifts are having contemporary effects on policies that seek to protect and save lives.

The relationship between tribes and the U.S. has changed course over time (Bays & Fouberg, 2002) and with the shared goal of protecting lives here on American soil, the relationship must continue to evolve; taking in both the good and the bad while setting the willingness to reach a collective goal as the focus of their relationships.

SOLUTIONS AND RECOMMENDATIONS: POLICY RECOMMENDATIONS FOR INTERACTIONS BETWEEN NATIVE AMERICAN TRIBES AND THE U.S. GOVERNMENT WITHIN HOMELAND SECURITY AND EMERGENCY MANAGEMENT POLICY

If continued progress is going to be made, tribal nations and sectors of the U.S. government will have to adopt a comprehensive approach to creating a governance structure amongst and between each other. Despite the cultural and political differences between these two systems of governance, there have been multiple neighboring jurisdictions with diverse cultural and political identities that have been successful in creating and maintaining a functioning network within the area of homeland security and emergency management such as the Saint Louis Area Regional Response System (STARRS).

The Saint Louis Area Regional Response System (STARRS) was created as an Urban Area Security Initiative (UASI) with funding awarded by the Homeland Security Grant Program in 2003. STARRS' objective is to help coordinate planning and response for large-scale critical incidents within the Saint Louis Urban Area. The region that STARRS serves consists of Franklin, Jefferson, Saint Charles, and Saint Louis, all counties located in the State of Missouri; as well as, Madison, Monroe, and Saint Clair counties located in the State of Illinois. Within the borders of the Saint Louis urban area, the represented counties all possess different forms of local government. Each county differs in its approaches to policy making culturally, politically, and legally. In addition to the inherent differences that make up the governance systems represented in the Saint Louis urban area, in order to accomplish the goal of providing effective prevention, protection, mitigation, response, and recovery for the region, the counties must work to coordinate the efforts of 171 fire agencies,

146 law enforcement agencies, 42 Emergency Medical Services (EMS), and 193 different municipalities nested throughout the eight counties.

STARRS has operated for over a decade working to organize and coordinate meaningful and effective collaboration for the Saint Louis urban area within homeland security and emergency management. Throughout this time, the region and the STARRS organization have learned many lessons. One of their greatest lessons has been discovering how to build effective governance structures across multiple jurisdictions. When considering the extreme levels of diversity amongst and between the counties in the Saint Louis region and comparing that to the differences that exist between tribes and sectors of the U.S. government, it is apparent that the Saint Louis urban area could certainly provide a template for the interactions between tribes and the U.S. government across the country. According to STARRS and the Saint Louis urban area, there are seven basic principles that must be adopted if multiple jurisdictions are to develop and maintain a successful governance structure within homeland security and emergency management.

Each of the stakeholders must seek to accomplish the following:

1. **Build Consensus:** Achieving effective cooperative relationships requires consideration of the different concerns and interests amongst the stakeholders in order to reach a broad consensus about what is in the best interest of the group. Before consensus can be achieved, trust must be achieved so that each stakeholder is comfortable with expressing their beliefs and viewpoints. Building trust is a process and it must be approached with patience and perseverance. They have to develop trust for each other and trust that their government counterparts are apt to handle complex, overarching policy issues as well. There needs to be more communication that is focused on sharing information about the differing governing styles of each party as well as their decision making processes and available resources; all of which could vary from tribe to tribe, and state to state as well. Cultural sensitivity training is going to be a necessary investment for the representatives from the two government structures. As was discussed in the qualitative data, it is clear that a great majority of the conflict is stemming from a lack of familiarity with the cultural differences between the groups. Once they have been able to share, the group can work to find common ground amongst their perspectives so that agreements can be made where consensus exists, compromises can be discussed, and unrelenting disagreements between members can be further explored as a group. In this particular context, all parties must agree that the area of homeland security and emergency management is an area of shared concern and must seek joint ventures to help in the achievement of a unified system of homeland security. The interactions between these governments should be guided by efforts to

achieve the mission of the Department of Homeland Security. A method of ensuring that this focus remains at the forefront of the Tribal-U.S. partnerships is to seek out joint funding opportunities such as the Urban Areas Security Initiative (UASI) or Operation Stonegarden (OPSG). This process will increase opportunities for collaboration, help to protect the nation in a unified and inclusive manner, and strengthen intergovernmental partnerships within the area of homeland security and emergency management.

2. **Ensure Participation:** Encouraging participation must be at the core of the group's overall objectives. When they are present, stakeholders remain informed, interested, and involved. It is important for the stakeholders to hold each other accountable and for each stakeholder to *do* just that, hold a stake in the conversations being had, the plans being developed, and the implementation processes being completed.

3. **Ensure Equity and Inclusiveness:** Each member of the group must feel welcomed and included in the processes taking place and the decisions being made. All parties must be intimately involved in the process of creating, developing, and implementing policies and other collaborative agreements. Tribal nations have not been a part of a great deal of the conversations and decisions that have progressed to policies that have impacted tribal lands. After forming collaborative partnerships, it should be expected that each government entity will work to find a balance in both giving to and receiving from the network.

4. **Be Responsive:** Being responsive includes efforts on behalf of tribes and units of the U.S. government to be receptive to the initiation of contact made by other tribal leaders and U.S. government actors to express key needs and concerns in the area of homeland security and emergency management. Responsiveness was one of the key variables that were explored within the case study with tribes claiming that sectors of the U.S. government have not been as responsive as their needs require. In a theoretical context, Agranoff (2012) cites the importance of responsiveness amongst cooperative partnerships and STARRS and the Saint Louis urban area have cited its importance within a practical context. As it has been shown, communication is integral to forming and sustaining relationships.

5. **Be Transparent:** Any and all decisions made by the group or sections within the group should be easily accessible to all members and stakeholders. Transparency helps to alleviate any remaining issues of distrust amongst group members. This will also assist in increasing the amount of shared information while working to foster an increased sense of ownership for each member.

6. **Be Effective and Efficient:** The partnerships must seek to meet the needs of all of the stakeholders while making the best use of the shared resources. In the case of tribal nations and the U.S. government, this must always be the

case regardless of past volatile interactions. The group must always place great significance on the overall effectiveness and efficiency of the group's decisions. Protecting citizens cannot wait until all intergovernmental disputes are resolved. Each governmental actor must be committed to moving beyond their disputes. To accomplish this, adopting an incremental approach to addressing past grievances while retaining a focus on homeland security is required.

7.   **Be Accountable:** Stakeholders must be accountable to themselves, each other, and to the public. These public representatives must be willing to answer for good decisions made for their jurisdiction and cooperative partnerships, but also be willing to discuss and learn from any decisions that proved contradictory to that goal.

CURRENT CHALLENGES: INVESTIGATING INTERACTIONS BETWEEN NATIVE AMERICAN TRIBES AND THE U.S. GOVERNMENT IN HOMELAND SECURITY AND EMERGENCY MANAGEMENT POLICY

To date, there has been very little research conducted that has assessed the impact of the turbulent relationship between states, tribal nations, the federal government and its affect on public policy making processes in the area of homeland security and emergency management. Empirically, how participants within these specific intergovernmental relationships are viewing, acting, and perceiving the system has not been extensively examined. This case study sought to provide insight which would be used to help fill those particular gaps in the literature.

The study of intergovernmental affairs is housed within the field of public policy and management; a discipline that unfortunately has not seized the opportunity to fully investigate the parameters of the working relationships between Indian country and the U.S. government. There is extensive literature in the fields of law, sociology, education, mental health, and environmental disciplines with topics that are relevant to tribal nations; however, the topic of Native American governance and intergovernmental relations is not as prevalent in public policy literature. In his article entitled *MISSING: Native American Governance in American Public Administration Literature,* Aufrecht (1999) asserts that "public administration literature almost completely ignores the topic of Native American governance" (p. 370). He goes on to note that "despite a rich legal literature on Native American rights; the public administration literature is almost silent in regard to Native American governance" (Aufrecht, 1999, p. 371). This is especially the case in the area of intergovernmental relations. Aufrecht is later echoed by researchers like Ortiz (2000), who not only agree with Aufrecht, but also argues that tribes are excluded for the very reason that they should be included in public administration studies: their unique political positioning as sovereign nations on U.S. soil.

Ortiz (2000) suggests that the field of public administration needs to do more to be made aware of the presence of tribal nations, their importance to the American public administration system, and the nature of their existence. Ronquillo (2011) explains that "as organizations, institutions, and the relationships between American Indian tribes and communities evolve and progress, so must the academic studies that revolve around them" (p. 288). Despite calls to focus more attention on tribal governance and its relationship to the U.S. system of governance, it has also been argued that there are some scholars in the field that know how important the positioning of Native American tribes is to the American system of governance and as a result have *intentionally* sought to exclude these groups from mainstream public administration literature.

In their study entitled *Superficiality and Bias: The (Mis)treatment of Native Americans in U.S. Government Textbooks*, Ashley and Jarratt-Ziemski (1999) explain that in an examination of 18 of the most commonly used American Government textbooks for introductory college courses, all of them discussed federalism and the relationship between the national government and subnational governments (in this case the states) as the foundation for the U.S. system. However, with the exception of two, the textbooks examined made no mention of American Indian governments within the context of federalism and intergovernmental relations; areas which according to the authors were logical to include Native American governance topics. According to the authors, this was an intentional act to avoid addressing the complexity of the federal-tribal-state relationship and the conflicts that have characterized these relationships. The authors mention that some of the textbooks even went so far as to "alter or paraphrase constitutional clauses to omit recognition of tribes and treaties" (Ashley & Jarratt-Ziemski, 1999, p. 56).

Any mention of tribes inherently forces scholars to address their position outside of the American system of federalism. Unfortunately, leaving Native Americans out of much of the discourse surrounding federalism and intergovernmental management within the field of public administration has come to be viewed as elitist and racist. "One of the most insidious forms of elitism, racism, and prejudice comes through simply ignoring the existence of those who are different...it is the belief here that the amount of coverage given to certain topics will inherently determine importance in the minds of readers (Ashley & Jarratt-Ziemski, 1999, p. 51)." In addition to running the risk of stigmatizing tribal governments, their absence from the literature is also seen as providing incomplete and misinformation to budding public administration students and scholars; eventually resulting in a disservice to their education and research progress throughout policy areas such as homeland security and emergency management. While there is not a wide variety of literature that exists on this topic, nearly most of it mentions the absence of tribal governance from mainstream public administration; however, more recently, another point of view has been presented.

In *American Indian Tribal Governance and Management: Public Administration Promise or Pretense?* author John C. Ronquillo (2011) takes on much of this literature that contends that the public administration field has not paid much attention to the topic of Native American governance. Ronquillo (2011) argues that tribal governance is not *missing* from the field of public administration, but rather it is "merely unassembled or often unrecognized by certain groups" (pp. 285). Ronquillo (2011) notes that the goal of his article is not to refute the works of Aufrecht and Ortiz, but rather to present evidence that this particular subject area may be present in other areas of the social sciences, prompting a more interdisciplinary approach to assessing its salience and importance.

Although Ronquillo (2011) makes some compelling points, suggesting that public administration scholars look elsewhere in the social sciences for the presence of research conducted on Native Americans in the field of public administration actually proves the points of authors like Aufrecht and Ortiz. While Ronquillo's work certainly addresses the lack of Native American representation in the field, it does not address the issue head on. Rather than contributing to the work of authors like Aufrecht and Ortiz, which seek to hold the field of public administration accountable for not widening their scope to include this group, Ronquillo (2011) instead advises readers to look elsewhere for evidence that such research exists in other fields.

Ronquillo's article certainly highlights the interdisciplinary nature of both the field of public administration and topics concerning Native American tribes, however, it does not directly discuss *why* readers *must* look elsewhere. To this point, Ronquillo (2011) does however point out that negative stereotypes of Native American tribes still exist and in fact hinder the inclusion of this group in mainstream research journals namely, within the field of public administration. This provides more support to the points of contention articulated by authors like Ashley and Jarratt-Ziemski (1999) and the viewpoint that the lack of presence is rooted in forms of intentional, racial undertones.

After identifying these key concerns regarding interactions between tribal nations and the U.S. government, the reality remains that there is still more work to be done. As illustrated here, the importance of incorporating tribes into the system of homeland security will only continue to grow. Research on tribes and their experiences within this system must continue to be tracked. As questions continue to loom about the progress that the DHS has made in working to solidify cooperative partnerships in homeland security and emergency preparedness across the U.S., the experiences of tribal nations will remain fundamental to answering those questions.

Taking into consideration the complexities of the position of tribes outside of the American governance system and seeking to discover ways to reduce volatile interactions the following toolkit, which discusses the core values that should guide all research endeavors concerning Native Americans, may prove helpful.

The National Congress of American Indians has produced a toolkit entitled *Research that Benefits Native People-- Foundations of Research: An Indigenous Perspective*. The toolkit provides Tribal leaders and other research scholars with five suggested core values that are related to research in Native Communities: (1) indigenous knowledge is valid and should be valued, (2) research is not culturally neutral (research that has been designed to not be influenced by culture has actually harmed Indigenous people), (3) research should be used to enhance community well-being and not be harmful to the Tribes, (4) expression of Tribal sovereignty (tribal sovereignty includes the right to regulate research and unguided research relinquishes tribal power over the results and diminishes tribal sovereignty), (5) beneficial to Native People (the researcher has an ethical obligation to build the Tribe's research capacity).

While this toolkit provides a basic foundation on how to establish a research agenda in this area, it also sets a precedence of cultural relativism that has been ignored in other research topic areas on Native Americans.

CONCLUSION

After experiencing terror attacks and natural disasters, it is imperative that citizens witness their leaders coordinating operationally and working to help the public understand anticipated threats to their safety and steps being taken to ensure their protection (Kettl, 2007; Agranoff, 2007). It is the responsibility of government actors to provide effective and efficient service delivery across numerous policy areas regardless of how complex the task. In the wake of recent natural disasters, terrorists' attacks, and attempted terrorist attacks on U.S. soil, perceptions of what it takes to achieve effective homeland security and emergency management has become even more salient throughout society. As the public seeks to ensure that their protection remains a top priority for government officials, it is no longer acceptable to continue to place political conflicts before promising the safety of citizens. As Lester and Krejci (2012) explain in their article *Business 'Not' As Usual: The National Incident Management System, Federalism, and Leadership*, the nation is extremely aware of the leadership needs as well as the failures that must be fulfilled in order to meet expectations in the area of homeland security and emergency management. It is clear that these expectations lie within coordination and cooperation amongst acting governments across multiple jurisdictions.

Data from this case study has shown that communication, sensitivity to the unique political, legal and social positioning, responsiveness to needs, and the offering of technical assistance are all integral factors in helping to lay the foundation for effective working relationships between tribes and the U.S. government. The data was collected in 2002 and being one of the first empirical studies of its kind, it can be used as a basis upon which to examine the evolution of the cooperative partnerships between the U.S. and tribal nations in the area of homeland security and emergency management over time.

With the creation of the Tribal Homeland Security Grant Program in 2008, the creation of Executive Orders 13084,13175, 13336, and the development of tribal policies across federal agencies, there is evidence that the interactions between these two systems of government is progressing incrementally. FEMA's Emergency Management Institute (EMI) now offers a total of five courses specific to preparedness and response training on tribal lands. To help those tribal nations located on international borders and struggling to meet the security demands placed upon them, Operation Stone Garden (OSG), a part of the HSGP, allocates money to cooperative homeland security and emergency management partnerships between states, tribes, and local governments along the Mexican and Canadian borders. At the 2012 annual National Congress of American Indians conference, Department of Homeland Security Secretary Janet Napolitano supported the knowledge that disasters and emergencies do not stop at geopolitical boundaries.

Furthermore, on January 29, 2013, more than a decade after tribes expressed their concerns on the FEMA survey; President Barack Obama signed the Sandy Recovery Act which, amongst other policy changes, amended the Stafford Act to allow federally recognized tribal governments to seek a federal emergency or major disaster declaration directly from the President of the United States.

The unwavering persistence of tribal nations to not have their sovereignty jeopardized in order to participate in the U.S. system of homeland security and emergency management yielded them a milestone victory. The amending of the Stafford Act serves as evidence that true and meaningful advancement is being made and that it is not at the expense of the unique political, legal, and cultural identities. The presence of ambiguous policies that violate the rights of tribal nations are being reviewed and promises of government-to-government communication between the federal government and tribes without state involvement are finally on the path to being honored.

The purpose of this case study is to help establish a solid foundation upon which leadership in units of the U.S. government and tribal governments could base future interactions. That foundation addressed past and present issues between actors in the homeland security and emergency management system and provided information on how to use past conflicts to propel cooperative partnerships forward. The amendment of the Stafford Act is not where this story ends. It is where it begins.

ACKNOWLEDGMENT

This case study is based upon a more expansive study that was completed for the dissertation work entitled: *An Assessment of Intergovernmental Relationships between Native American Tribes, the States, and the Federal Government in Homeland Security and Emergency Management Policy by* Leigh R. Anderson, Ph.D. The author is grateful to the Department of Homeland Security (DHS)Federal Emergency Management Agency (FEMA) for allowing the use of the data analyzed herein.

REFERENCES

Adams, H. (2012). Sovereignty, safety, and security: Tribal governments under the Stafford and homeland security acts. *American Indian Law Journal, 1*(1), 127–146.

Agranoff, R. (2012). *Collaborating to manage: A primer for the public sector.* Washington, DC: Georgetown University Press.

American Indian Policy Center. (2002). *Brief history of U.S. tribal relations.* Retrieved 2011 from http://www.airpi.org

Ashley, J. S., & Jarratt-Ziemski, K. (1999). Superficiality and bias: The (mis) treatment of Native Americans in U. S. government textbooks. *American Indian Quarterly, 23*(3/4), 49–62. doi:10.2307/1185828

Aufrecht, S. E. (1999). Missing: Native American governance in American public administration literature. *American Review of Public Administration, 29*(4), 370–390. doi:10.1177/02750749922064481

Bays, B. A., & Fouberg, E. H. (2002). *The tribes and the states: Geographies of intergovernmental interaction.* Rowman & Littlefield Publishers, Inc.

Butts, J. (2003/2004). Victims in waiting: How the homeland security act falls short of fully protecting tribal lands. *American Indian Law Review, 28*(2), 373–392. doi:10.2307/20070712

Caruson, K., & MacManus, S. A. (2006). Mandates and management challenges in the trenches: An intergovernmental perspective on homeland security. *Public Administration Review, 66,* 522–536. doi:10.1111/j.1540-6210.2006.00613.x

Coleman, P. T., & Morton, D. (2000). *The handbook of conflict resolution: Theory and practice*. San Francisco: Jossey-Bass Publishers.

Companion Site to the McGraw Hill Homeland Security Handbook. (2007). Retrieved 2011 from http://www.homelandsecuritybook.com/book/table-of-contents.html

Di Iorio, W. R. (2007). Mending fences: The fractured relationship between Native American tribes and the federal government and its negative impact on border security. *Syracuse Law Review, 57*(2), 407–428.

Donley, M. B., & Pollard, N. A. (2002). Homeland security: The difference between a vision and a wish. *Public Administration Review, 6*, 138–144. doi:10.1111/1540-6210.62.s1.23

Eisinger, P. (2006). Imperfect federalism: The intergovernmental partnership for homeland security. *Public Administration Review, 66*, 537–545. doi:10.1111/j.1540-6210.2006.00614.x

Evans, L. E. (2011). *Power from powerlessness: Tribal governments, institutional niches, and American federalism*. New York: Oxford University Press. doi:10.1093/acprof:oso/9780199742745.001.0001

Executive Order 13175. (2000). *Coordination and consultation with Indian tribal governments*. Retrieved 2010 from http://ceq.hss.doe.gov/nepa/regs/eos/eo13175.html

Federal Emergency Management Agency. (1999). Final agency policy for government-to-government relations with American Indian and Alaska native tribal governments. *Federal Register, 64*(7).

FEMA. (2002). *About NIMS*. Retrieved 2011 from http://www.fema.gov/emergency/nims/AboutNIMS.shtm

Haddal, C. C. (2010, August 11). *Border security: The role of the US border patrol* (RL32562). Washington, DC: United States Congressional Research Service.

Kettl, D. F. (2007). *System under stress: Homeland security and American politics* (2nd ed.). Congressional Quarterly Press.

Lester, W., & Krejci, D. (2007). Business not as usual: The national incident management system, federalism, and leadership. *Public Administration Review, 67*, 84–93. doi:10.1111/j.1540-6210.2007.00817.x

Mason, D. W. (1998). Tribes and states: A new era in intergovernmental affairs. *Publius: The Journal of Federalism, 28*(1), 111–130. doi:10.1093/oxfordjournals. pubjof.a029943

McCool, D. (1993). Intergovernmental conflict and Indian water rights: An assessment of negotiated settlements. *Publius: The Journal of Federalism, 23*, 85–101.

McGuire, T. R. (1990). Federal Indian policy: A framework for evaluation. *Human Organization, 49*(3), 206–216.

Menzel, D. C. (2006). The Katrina aftermath: A failure of federalism or leadership? *Public Administration Review, 66*, 808–812. doi:10.1111/j.1540-6210.2006.00649.x

Moynihan, D. P. (2005). Homeland security and the U.S. public management policy agenda. *Governance: An International Journal of Policy, Administration and Institutions, 18*, 171–196. doi:10.1111/j.1468-0491.2005.00272.x

National Congress of American Indians. (2011). *An introduction to Indian nations in the United States*. Retrieved 2011 from http://www.ncai.org/fileadmin/initiatives/ NCAI_Indian_Nations_In_The_US.pdf

National Congress of American Indians. (2011). *NCAI commends FEMA support for direct authority of tribal governments to apply for presidential disaster declaration*. Retrieved 2013 from http://www.ncai.org/policy-issues/tribal-governance/ emergency-management

National Congress of American Indians. (2013). *Homeland security*. Retrieved 2013 from http://www.ncai.org/policy-issues/tribal-governance/homeland-security

Organick, A. G., & Kowalski, T. (2009). From conflict to cooperation: State and tribal court relations in the era of self-determination. *Court Review, 45*, 48.

Ortiz, J. (2002). Tribal governance and public administration. *Administration & Society, 35*(5), 59–481.

Pata, J. (2013). *The state of Indian country: Global tribes?* National Public Radio. Retrieved 22 February 2013 from http://www.npr.org/2013/02/15/172102688/the-state-of-indian-country-global-tribes

Posner, P. L. (2002). *Combating terrorism: Intergovernmental partnership in a national strategy to enhance state and local preparedness (GAO-02-547T)*. Washington, DC: General Accounting Office.

Ronquillo, J. C. (2011). American Indian tribal governance and management: Public administration promise or pretense? *Public Administration Review, 71*, 285–292. doi:10.1111/j.1540-6210.2011.02340.x

Steinman, E. (2004). American federalism and intergovernmental innovation in state-tribal relations. *Publius: The Journal of Federalism, 34*(2), 95–114. doi:10.1093/oxfordjournals.pubjof.a005031

United States Constitution. (1787). *Article 1, section 8: Commerce clause.*

Wilkins, D. E. (1993). Breaking into the intergovernmental matrix: The Lumbee tribe's efforts to secure federal acknowledgement. *Publius, 23*(4), 123–142.

Wilson, P. I. (2002). Tribes, states, and the management of lake resources: Lakes Coeur d'Alene and Flathead. *Publius: The Journal of Federalism, 32*(3), 115–131. doi:10.1093/oxfordjournals.pubjof.a004951

Wise, C., & Nader, R. (2002). Organizing the federal system for homeland security: problems, issues, and dilemmas. *Public Administration Review, 62*(Special Issue), 44–57. doi:10.1111/1540-6210.62.s1.8

Wise, C., & Nader, R. (2008). Developing a national homeland security system: An urgent and complex task in intergovernmental relations. In T. Conlan, & P. Posner (Eds.), *Intergovernmental management for the 21st century* (pp. 77–101). Washington, DC: The Brookings Institution.

Wise, C. R. (2002). Organizing for homeland security. *Public Administration Review, 62*(2), 131–144. doi:10.1111/0033-3352.00164

Wollendeck, J. M., Gray, B., & Bryan, T. (2003). Us versus them: How identities and characterizations influence conflict. *Environmental Practice, 5*(3), 207–213.

KEY TERMS AND DEFINITIONS

Homeland Security Grant Program (HSGP): Established in 2003 and consisting of three separate, yet interrelated programs: the State Homeland Security Program (SHSP), the Urban Areas Security Initiative (UASI), and Operation Stonegarden (OPSG), the HSGP provides grant funds to state and local governments to increase funding for first-responder equipment, planning, training, exercises, and the collection of intelligence about potential attacks.

Intergovernmental Relations: The codependent and multifaceted relationships that exist between and amongst different levels of governments.

National Response Framework (NRF): A guide to help governments plan and prepare for the ability to provide a unified response across jurisdictions to any manmade and natural disasters.

Native American Tribes: The term "tribe" is used interchangeably with "American Indian," "Native American," and "tribal nations." As used throughout this study, these terms refer to "any Federally-recognized governing body of an Indian or Alaska Native tribe, band, nation, pueblo, village, or community that the Secretary of Interior acknowledges to exist as an Indian tribe under the Federally Recognized Tribe List Act of 1994, 25 U.S.C 479a (FEMA, 2010)." For clarification purposes as designated by the Department of Interior, Bureau of Indian Affairs (2013), "federally recognized tribes are recognized as possessing certain inherent rights of self-government (i.e., tribal sovereignty) and are entitled to receive certain federal benefits, services, and protections because of their special relationship with the United States."

Tribal Governance: Incorporates tribal culture, history, social interactions, laws, jurisdiction, and sovereignty.

Trust Responsibility: The responsibility of the federal government to honor treaties, compromises, and other bound agreements by inheriting the expectation to honor those agreements for the best interests of the tribes and its members.

Unified System of Homeland Security and Emergency Preparedness: The unified approach to homeland security and emergency preparedness has included efforts to "provide a systematic, proactive approach to guide departments and agencies at all levels of government, nongovernmental organizations, and the private sector to work seamlessly to prevent, protect against, respond to, recover from, and mitigate the effects of incidents, regardless of cause, size, location, or complexity, in order to reduce the loss of life and property and harm to the environment" (FEMA, 2010). According to the Department of Homeland Security's National Response Framework (2007), to be able to achieve an effective system of unified command, there needs to be unity of effort which must extend across multiple geographic and legal jurisdictions. FEMA made it clear that emergency management is a difficult function that must frequently cross jurisdictional boundaries (Waugh, 1994). Like the foundation for achieving a unified system of command, in order to be able to execute effective emergency management strategies, it is crucial that there be cooperation and coordination across jurisdictions. To be more specific, FEMA's agency policy warns that within the field of emergency management, the agency expresses that problems are shared and so too should responsibility. It goes on to note that the agency refrains from providing assistance to only one jurisdiction or government and consequently placing in jeopardy the interests of needs of another government (Federal Registrar, FEMA Tribal Agency Policy, 1999).

Chapter 7
Visual Analytics for Students and Teachers (VAST) Model at a Minority Serving Institution:
A Department of Homeland Security Project for Strengthening STEM Teaching and Learning

Timothy Akers
Morgan State University, USA

Douglas Gwynn
Morgan State University, USA

Kofi Nyarko
Morgan State University, USA

Willie D. Larkin
Morgan State University, USA

EXECUTIVE SUMMARY

This chapter focuses on a model for the teaching and learning of STEM by undergraduate students, teachers, and faculty at Morgan State University that focuses on visual analytics. This project represents an interdisciplinary approach to the teaching and learning of STEM at a Minority Serving Institution funded by the Department of Homeland Security. The chapter also outlines salient strategies associated with challenges at the university. In addition, the chapter discusses partnerships developed with Visual Analytics for Command, Control, and Interoperability Environments (VACCINE), a DHS Center for Excellence at Purdue University that supports DHS priority research in the area of visual analytics.

DOI: 10.4018/978-1-4666-5946-9.ch007

I hear and I forget. I see and I remember. I do and I understand. —Confucius

ORGANIZATION BACKGROUND

Morgan State University is a public urban research university in the state of Maryland that focuses on excellence in teaching, interdisciplinary research, effective public service and community engagement and outreach. Morgan State University prepares diverse and competitive graduates for success in a global, interdependent society. Morgan State has a Carnegie Foundation classification as a doctoral research university.

SETTING THE STAGE

In 2008, the U.S. Department of Homeland Security's (DHS) Science and Technology Directorate, Office of University Programs, provided funding to Morgan State University to "*Increase the Pipeline of STEM Majors among Minority Serving Institutions.*" This was a three year project that employed diverse methodologies designed to enhance both the teaching and learning of early career faculty and minority students engaged in science, technology, engineering, and mathematics education, also referred to as STEM. Part of this project also called for the introduction of cybersecurity into various aspects of the university curriculum. The ultimate purpose was to address the disparities gap within the STEM field (Flores, 2007).

During this time, fifteen (15) students were introduced to a diversity of approaches that would later broaden their tapestry of knowledge by introducing them to some of the best and most creative methodologies, processes, technologies, and training available. These ranged from smartphone app development and geospatial analysis to interdisciplinary informatics and data visualization. For example, after their training, a number of the students began helping to create and conceptualize what the Director of Residence Life and Housing, Douglas Gwynn, called "SMART Suites."

Through their effort, they began learning what we collectively agreed is systems and concept mapping, and critical thinking. In essence, the work and training of the students demonstrated a hierarchy of thinking in how we should lay out the SMART Suite labs, systems, structure, function, and operation. Concurrently, five STEM professors were also supported by DHS, to varying degrees, to enhance and disseminate their research in order to help determine how their scientific acumen and hierarchical thinking could benefit the broad needs of the DHS and STEM education.

Throughout this time period between Fall 2008 to Fall 2011, Morgan State University embraced the fiscal, technical, programmatic, and scientific resources and expertise provided by DHS, its program officials and the *Visual Analytics for*

Command, Control, and Interoperability Environments (VACCINE). VACCINE is a DHS Center of Excellence collaborator based at Purdue University. In addition, MSU also actively engaged two other leading institutions in order to help our students receive additional training in electrical engineering and physics. Specifically, additional training opportunities were provided by The Athena Group out of Gainesville, Florida, and the Florida Institute of Technology, located in Melbourne, Florida.

It was through these interactions that the students selected to work on the DHS projects began to experience a renewed sense of excitement, a manifested zeal for learning, and a thirst for wanting to create technologies that would benefit DHS priority areas. In short, DHS's focus on university programs has served as a catalyst for ingenuity and creativity, innovation and technological development for both students and faculty alike.

CASE DESCRIPTION

This chapter provides a brief summary as to how new and engaging teaching and training models were introduced into the learning process of students, faculty, and teachers (Jackson & Wilson, 2012). Based on our experience and extensive interactions with the students and faculty, a significant body of thematic issues rose to the forefront in this analysis. In addition, this chapter further discusses how the DHS supported students taught STEM teachers in data visualization while, in turn, the teachers taught students how to create STEM lesson plans. The threads running through this symbiotic relationship were partnerships and collaborations that lead to the development of unique and innovative models for STEM teaching and learning of minority students at a Historically Black College and University.

Engaging Interdisciplinary Students Interested in STEM

Through the support provided by the DHS, the project team began a systematic assessment of what were critical, essential characteristics needed to engage the science, technology, engineering and mathematics students, relative to their other student colleagues. The team quickly came to realize that student engagement is more than simply flipping a switch and proclaiming that "*I am now engaging our students.*" Quite to the contrary, student engagement—especially when working with a diversity of disciplines and students—is a dynamic and fluid process, full of twists and turns, barriers and unanticipated challenges, along with some rewarding opportunities.

Foundational to this review is the body of literature posited by George Kuh and Alexander Astin. Their theories suggest that successful student development is rooted in the reciprocal efforts put forth by the student and the institution (Astin, 1993; Kuh et al., 2005a). This theory speaks to the responsible actions of the institution in the holistic development of the student. Additionally, it is this *engagement* that guides, supports, and assists students to be participants in their own personal and academic maturation through college (Astin, 1993; Kuh et al., 2005a).

Conceptually, how students are engaged by their institution has been shown to be an important indicator in the ways students are successful while in college. This relationship or engagement, between the student and their academic institution, is a critical component in building an environment that supports and nurtures positive experiences. These experiences for the student are vital to successful developmental and educational outcomes (Astin, 1993; Kuh et al., 2005a; Pascarella & Terenzini, 2005; Tinto, 1993). Additionally, true engagement, or intentional interaction, is another essential instructional component for African American students. In essence, a mentor's ability to be able to adapt to an ever changing landscape of student opportunities (and unanticipated challenges) is paramount.

In coming to some of these realizations, the project team began to conceptualize, develop and implement a unique and innovative model that would help to guide student STEM teaching and learning strategies. The goal was to blend the best within the university as well as outside the student's comfort zone away from the university. This approach required that the project team view the students completely differently. Their approach was to change the student's perceptions so as not to view themselves as passive learners, which is the conventional educational model (Maton, 2004).

This new model, defined as "VAST-MSI" for minority serving institutions, which stands for *Visual Analytics for Students and Teachers at a Minority Serving Institution*," required that we identify challenges/difficulties experienced by students followed by strategies, solutions, and opportunities that would help them to overcome some unanticipated problems. Table 1, for example, provides a list of some of the more salient challenges and strategies we identified and resolved.

Apart from the fact that some of the students were encountering technical and academic challenges, they were still thrust into new situations in which they had little or no experience. This approach was deliberate and calculated and required a close assessment of behaviors and academic performance, especially when they were interacting with students from other disciplines who spoke entirely different technical jargon. In other words, their scientific lexicon did not match. Needless to say, this was an initial hurdle that had to be overcome. The close monitoring of peer to peer interactions further helped the mentors to better assess how quickly they accomplished and mastered their tasks, along with other criteria.

Table 1 further illustrates the challenges the team encountered and had to overcome, while, at the same time, considering a number of strategies that would be employed to help change their mindset to embrace technical tasks that were considered

Table 1. Challenges and strategies

Challenges	Strategies
Retention Rate	Use Visual Analytics / Visualization informatics
Graduation Rate	Provide Hands-on Training Opportunities
Progression Rate	Create a Train-the-Trainer Mindset
Resource Limitations	Seek Government Support
Institution Barriers	Seek Corporate Support (Fiscal, Technology, Expertise)
Perceptual Barriers	Interdisciplinary Students Work Together
Lack of Fiscal Resources	Keep Students Busy! Busy! Busy!
Lack of Technology	Teach Students to Conceptualize
Lack of Opportunities	Encourage/Expect Extreme Thinking!!!!!!!!
Lack of Mentorship	Build Student Credibility / High Expectations
Math & Science Deficits	Be Available to Students Unconditionally

difficult, such as statistics, data visualization (e.g., Many Eyes™, Tableau™, and others), mapping data spatially, mathematical modeling, and computer programming, among others). This required that the mentor approach student growth, development, and learning in the context of identifying individualized learning styles, identify what makes the students comfortable and—at the right moment—turn their world upside down.

In other words, we wanted to get the students to challenge their very nature; change their environment and problem associates; and provide challenging (yet achievable) opportunities that would "explode" their thinking by provoking (and invoking) critical thinking that tested their very assumptions, their cultural norms, and their academic complacency (Keefe, 2010). Quite literally, the team wanted to dare them to *think outside the box*; to determine just how realistic or unrealistic their ideas were was not relevant, not important.

The project team did not necessarily care whether the students' ideas were achievable or farfetched. Rather, the purpose was more intended to stimulate their thinking alter their perceptions of self by changing their perceptions from one of normal thinking of self to extraordinary thinking of self. The team worked very strategically, calculatingly, and deliberately to have the students embrace and perceive themselves as great, exceptional, incredible, and extraordinary.

The team already realized that we were working with highly impressive students that simply needed to be brought out of their shell. The students needed to change what may have been inculcated within them, such as singular disciplinary thinking, normal achievements (versus extraordinary achievements), and a sense of mediocrity as being acceptable. Quite literally, the team wanted to create, nurture, and cultivate within the students a renewed sense of pride, while, at the same time, bringing out the genus from within each of them as individuals, and allowing their individual and collective brilliance to begin shinning through in whatever project they may have been undertaking.

With respect to environment, it has been described as having the ability to exert characteristic, qualities and pressures in the developmental exchange between the student and their environment (Astin, 1993, Kuh et al., 2005a). Further, environment has also been described, for example, as the institution's capacity to develop and cultivate many developmental factors impacting students' experiences (Astin, 1993; Pascarella & Terenzini, 2005). Examples of environmental factors include, developing relationships and social networks with other students, faculty and staff, participation in campus events, embracing the educational experience, academic support services, and residential facilities (Astin, 1993; Kuh et al., 2005a).

In essence, the broader goal was to remind them that innovation is oftentimes by accident, or when a person has a "Wow!" moment, an epiphany, a passion, or is simply willing to take a risk and step out on a limb, or "outside the box." The team wanted to teach each of our students that sometimes ideas are not always so regimented, structured, planned in a methodical way, or contrived; though the scientific method serves a vital purpose in helping to structure our thinking. However, we wanted the students to internalize that some of the most extreme, impacting, and innovative ideas emerge from—more often than not—fluid, organic, and almost ridiculous thoughts; they do not necessarily always follow a conventional scientific method, pathway or comply with grounded assumptions.

In summary, we are reminded that factory teaching and learning styles, methodologies, approaches, and environments do not work in an era where information is king; data are fluid and alive; environments are forever changing; systems and technologies are active and observing; and attention span and ambidextrous skills are fleeting. Yet, the need for the student (and mentor) to touch one's environment, technologies, and toys, are more akin to jumping inside the computer and become a "ghost in the machine." Such is the case of the new millennial youth. That is, the mentor must be adaptive, resilient, creative, impassioned, and uniquely devoted to keeping the student active, engaged, stimulated, interested, and, quite literally, extremely busy. Otherwise, the attention span of the student wanes and their desires become only *shadows in thought*. These characteristics and qualities are essential when solidifying a mentorship structure.

Lastly, a critical point to note has been to stress to each individual student that while collective thoughts and ideas have a vital role in STEM research, it also requires, first and foremost, that the individual to be more strongly embraced and nurtured. Hence, individualized teaching and mentorship is paramount; because, if a student is studying STEM, or any other discipline for that matter, and views them self as unique and exceptional, they will, in turn, and without question, enhance and actively infuse into the entire group a sense of greatness, limitless potential, and create a can do attitude.

To paraphrase the late Steve Jobs, founder of Apple™, the team was only as good as the greatness of each individual, or going from "average to the best." During an interview, Jobs stated that when you find gifted people don't settle for "B" and "C" players. He further went on to note that "A" players really like working with other "A" players. They don't want to work with "B" and "C" players and it becomes "self-policing" and you build up pockets of "A" players and it propagates (Cringely, 1995). That is, if each individual student sees their individual selves and achievements as extraordinary, innovative, incredible, and great, than the group will see its collective effort as amazing thereby becoming self-replicating.

Student Training Approaches

Experience has taught us that learning, creativity, and idea generation do not necessarily occur within a vacuum (Sanders, 2009); that is, a closed space where little interactions occur, or in isolation where everyone looks, thinks, dresses, and trains alike. Rather, as we reflect on the past three years, our research and experience have helped to validate and identify salient characteristics and qualities inherent in college students—particularly at minority serving institutions—including the process we developed and implemented to ground our understanding. Recognizing the importance of implementation is critical (Hall, 2010).

Figure 1 illustrates the process we conceptualized and implemented. Other sections in this chapter further summarize our approach across these various phases. For example, Figure 1 shows how the students were initially given a problem, such as how to better understand data—conceptually, theoretically, methodologically, computationally, developmentally, empirically, spatially, and visually. Through this research process we were able to determine that if an educator simply provides a student a mathematical equation, with all of the parameters and Greek symbols, they run the risk of the student experiencing a mental road block.

In other words, it is not because they do not necessarily understand the logic, procedures, and assumptions of the equation (which might be the case), but rather, it may be because they forgot different aspects or procedures in solving the equation. More likely than not, the students were only taught the equation in relation to a specific use, procedure, purpose or approach. Hence, their ability to apply and adapt or create an equation relative to other specific or critical problem sets may be one of their stumbling blocks or greatest challenges.

Figure 1. Student/teacher training module

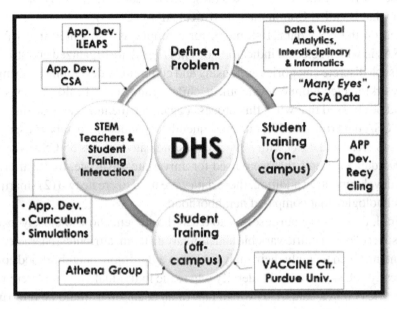

To address this deficit, the team implemented an entirely new and innovative approach by showing the students how to better understand an equation, its application, and exactly where the data (or variable) within a structured dataset actually fits relative to a particular mathematical equation. In addition, the students were, at the same time, shown visual representations of the equation along with the dataset (e.g., the Community Statistical Area (CSA) database, to be discussed more later) so that they might better understand the relationship among an equation and its elements (e.g., radical sign, integers, variables, binary operators, power, function, and other attributes), relative to a dataset (e.g., CSA), and the various visualization types and outputs that can be generated, such as a bar, pie, line, spatial, tree, or radar chart, among many others.

The approach undertaken was a combination of deductive and inductive teaching methods. That is, the students were provided many diverse tools used to visualize data, data elements, data characteristics, and their application to the organization of a functional dataset/data warehouse. More specifically, we introduced the students to a comprehensive database that had selected indicators about the city of Baltimore—or, more commonly referred to as "Vital Signs." This was important because it provided data they could immediately relate to thereby feeling a sense of ownership and identity. Moreover, these data were not from some faraway unknown source, but rather, were organized by the Jacob Francis Institute (JFI) at the University of

Baltimore, whereby the JFI integrated these diverse data and spatially standardized them to what is called Community Statistical Areas (CSAs).

Based on the CSA data, Baltimore, for example, is segmented into fifty-five (55) CSAs in which selected indicators (or *Vital Signs*) are organized and structured around such discrete categories as housing and community development, crime and safety, workforce/economic development, children and family health, among others. It should be stressed that when this process began, the mentors and students identified the CSA data from the JFI, but subsequently expanded the database used by the students to create a dataset with 309 variables/indicators across 55 CSAs for a total of 16,995 data elements that were used for univariate, bivariate, multivariate, and indices development. In addition, these data were used to create two (2) smartphone apps technologies that compared neighborhoods.

Overall, the primary purpose was to teach the students how to closely examine every aspect of one specific variable and its many different attributes, characteristics, and elements, then to apply their analysis within a Baltimore neighborhood context. Specifically, the student would identify where the individual variables were within 1) a specific cell in a dataset, 2) which part of an equation it would be referring to, and 3) what part of a visualized graphic is exactly being displayed relative to one specific cell/variable. For their equation exemplar, the students were introduced to the United Nation's Human Development Index where they were taught how to cre-

Figure 2. STEM teaching constructs

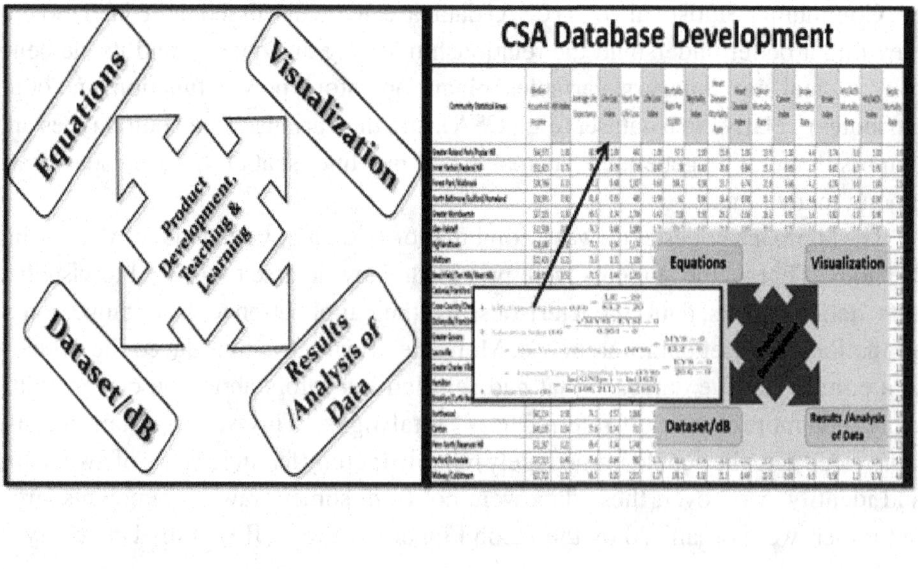

ate new variables for computing other analyses and applying this index to Baltimore CSA data. Figure 2a and b illustrate visually the main constructs taught.

To summarize this section, oftentimes universities, middle and high schools teach STEM topics the same way it has always been taught—as separate and independent concepts, such as a mathematical equations/formulas, visualizations/ graphic representation, database/datasets, and results/analyses, as though they are separate and distinct events, in which they firmly expect the students to be able to synthesize these relationship. While this may have been the best practice methods in the past, given the *zeitgeist* of the time, the new millennial generation views these as one and the same, not as distinct elements. This is due, in part, to the way they look at the world—in diagrams, pictures, relationships, and patterns. As Daniel Pink scripted in his book *A Whole New Mind: Moving from the Information Age to the Conceptual Age (2005)*

The future belongs to a very different kind of person with a very different kind of mind—creators and empathizers, pattern recognizers and meaning makers. (pg. 1).

Off-Campus Training

Many a STEM student, especially undergraduates, endures a rigorous curriculum while going through their course work at their home institution. The tendency to overlook off-campus training opportunities is all too common. The need for mixing training up across institutions is an important strategy to expand perspectives, ideas, and stimulate innate excitement for the desire to learn and create. It is critical to note that changing a student's environment expands their capacity for learning, while, at the same time, demonstrates the student-mentor relationship to engagement. As briefly mentioned, through support and guidance provided by the DHS, the VAST project team entered into three unique relationships with off-campus mentors, consisting of Purdue University's VACCINE Center of Excellence, The Athena Group (TAG), and Florida Institute of Technology (FIT).

Figure 3 and 4 shows a few examples of different types of training. For example, one of our physics students went through a summer training course at FIT, which provided engineering and astrophysics training, resulting in his contribution in helping to design a camera mount that is currently being used at an observatory. The other photos in Figure 3 and 4 were taken at Purdue University's VACCINE Center, where the students manipulated the CSA data to learn techniques in visualization of data and how to conduct multi-level analysis that blended both qualitative and quantitative data for mixed-methods analysis and interpretations, as well as learning how to analyze 3-dimensional imagery. In addition, the students were also brief on machine learning and its application through the use of smartphone app development.

Figure 3. Morgan STEM students at VACCINE at Purdue University

Figure 4. VACCINE 2012 summer institute

Through this training, the students learned a number of important lessons. First, how to learn and appreciate learning from a diversity of educators, comprising many different disciplines, styles of teaching, and cultures. Secondly, the students gained insight and different perspectives from both professors and graduate students in how to understand visual analytics and informatics across diverse disciplines, spanning computer science and engineering, among other disciplines, such as education, physics, and the behavioral sciences.

Other extraordinary training, which was provided off-campus in a residence program, was at The Athena Group (TAG), in which students learned how to develop STEM training simulations for middle, high school, and college students, such as those currently available by TAG online at http://www.athenaed.com/. In short, these various off-campus programs would not have been possible had it not been for the U.S. Department of Homeland Security's Office of University Programs that established a system whereby the federal government recognized that minority serving institutions would benefit through other forms of interactions with scientists and engineers at various institutions was spot on to the learning modality of the students.

Students Become Teachers: Lessons Learned

It has often been said that the best way to learn is to teach. This adage cannot be more accurate than what was witnessed, firsthand, through the training provided by the DHS scholars. In summer 2011, upon returning back from their off-campus training, the students underwent additional training at Morgan State University (MSU) Center of Excellence in Math and Science Education (CEMSE) in learning how to teach math and science teachers.

Through a joint collaboration, CEMSE and the project team of students engaged in additional training on the MSU campus in learning how to teach twenty-four (24) Baltimore Public School teachers about visual analytics, databases, mathematics, and analysis of data. Figure 5 shows the students hovering over and near the math and science teachers that were learning how to understand and analyze the CSA data—visually, computationally and spatially.

In turn, what was also unique about the VAST training program was that during the training, the teachers, in response, taught the students how to develop academic curricula in order to incorporate this training into their STEM modules for their public school courses. Another unique, but almost overlooked observation, was that most of the DHS students conducting the training were African American while the race and ethnicity of the school teachers were primarily Black and Filipino. This cultural exchange across diverse age cohorts, race and ethnicity, and the exchange of training lessons proved to be some of the most important observa-

Figure 5. STEM student/teacher summer institute

tional interactions the team experienced. There was, without question, learning going on with no subtle or observable biases or prejudices being witnessed.

In summary, during the training, the students divided the teachers into groups by topical areas, such as education, crime, health, and housing, among other areas. While the students were conducting the training, the teachers, at the same time, incorporated what they were learning into lesson plans that were later presented. This symbiotic relationship has, to the best of our knowledge, never been undertaken with respect to visual analytics for curriculum development in STEM middle and high school courses. The lessons learned reflect the importance of blending middle, high school, and college research and training programs across systems of education (NRC, 2011).

The most unique and critical innovation in this student-teacher and teacher-student approach to learning STEM was the shared exchange of information and innovations that occurred across both cohort groups. The potential model for introducing DHS relevant topical areas provided to diverse STEM constituents was extraordinary. The teachers that taught rote mathematical formulas and standard scientific equations were introduced to visual analytics and visualization of static data as innovative methods in teaching students. The teachers learned better techniques in illustrating how data could be understood and analyzed. In turn, students then learned how to incorporate visual analytics into middle and high school curricula.

Conclusion

This project spanned undergraduates, public school teachers, and early-career faculty. Because of space limitations, we were not able to focus on early-career faculty; but the projects that have been undertaken by early-career faculty, through support provided by the U.S. DHS, have proven to be extraordinary, as many of the faculty have been able to enhance their teaching and research skills as well as obtain other support in order to continue to fund students on projects that are important to the homeland.

Lastly, other innovative initiatives are underway that are resulting in the distributive impact of visualization technologies throughout the campus of Morgan State University, as in the case of the establishment of a new and innovative visual analytics laboratory. Combined with the integration of the first Smart Suites tutorial programs in residence life and housing, MSU students will be able to receive academic enhancements through the use of large screen display technologies and distributive learning systems across venues. In other words, one high level tutor can bridge training across various technological platforms relative to the students' needs.

The need for future research and training programs supported by such federal agencies as the DHS, or other agencies as NSF, NIH, CDC, DoD, EPA, etc., is pivotal as the nation pursues innovative methods and means to educate our primary and post-secondary student, teachers, and early career faculty researchers. Following yesterday's approaches to educate a new cohort of highly skilled, innovative, and critical thinking young scientists, engineers, and mathematicians is no longer optional, but rather, is a matter of national security.

CONCLUSION AND RECOMMENDATIONS

In 2012, the U.S. Department of Homeland Security provided additional support to Morgan State University in the area of STEM research and training of early career faculty and students, with a particular focus on cybersecurity and product development. In pursue of this Phase 1 project, the principal investigators of this new DHS award sought input from faculty, students, and government in order to begin to structure an emerging research agenda around cybersecurity, visual analytics, and environmental informatics. In theory, the plan has been to create, cultivate, and nurture a new cohort of faculty in such disciplines as computer science, electrical engineering, and civil engineering to find and identify common ground, a synergy, where their research and training areas can or might overlap.

In addition, what is also intriguing is that the principal investigators have, quite literally, created a brain trust of faculty, staff, and administrators on the campus of MSU. The most recent cohort jointly participated in visual analytics training at Jackson State University, in collaboration with Purdue University's VACCINE Center of Excellence. During their residency training program as JSU, the MSU contingent were actively engaged in visual analytics training that taught them how diverse roles in the academy can enhance the overall learning process for students on campus as well as strengthen the institutional infrastructure in support of DHS priority areas.

Figure 6, for example, shows faculty and administrators from electrical engineering, residence life and housing, economics, architecture and planning, computer science, and civil engineering all embarking on this training. In theory, the goals is to help ensure that there is a contingent of faculty and administrators on campus who will champion the clarion call for visual analytics across the entire university over sustained periods of time.

The unique qualities inherent in the administrators and early career faculty are their shared interest in visual analytics and student innovation. Since their return

Figure 6. Morgan faculty and administrators at Jackson State (2013 Summer Institute)

Figure 7. Morgan VAST Student Interns at the DHS Career Pathway Conference

back to the MSU campus, they have been instrumental in conceptualizing the creation of a visual analytics working group whereby open exchange and dialogue around ideas can stimulate thinking and action in the area of product development, teaching and learning, and research. It is anticipated that this group will be pivotal in helping to strengthen the anticipated outcomes of the early career faculty.

As Phase 1 begins a series of research and training initiatives and strategies, the initial four students selected to receive significant DHS sponsorship bring with them a tapestry of diversity in experience and expertise, comprise such areas as biology, computer science, transportation and civil engineering, economics, food safety, and public health. Upon their selection, this new cohort of DHS student scholars were sent to the DHS Center of Excellence, VACCINE, on the campus of Purdue University whereby they received extensive training in hands-on projects that examine such areas as analytical reasoning and critical thinking, data transformation and statistics, Google maps tutorial, temporal and spatial statistics, and cognition in visual analytics, among other topics. (see Figure 7)

The unique expectations surrounding this new cohort of students will be their ability to move beyond conventional visual analytics by embracing the importance of interdisciplinary thinking and learning. The future direction for this Phase 1 (and subsequent Phase 2) will be for the students to gain new insight and in-depth thinking in how to effectively view visual analytics training from the perspective of informatics across their individual disciplines, expertise, and interest. Cybersecurity, for example, will be introduced to the students from a number of innovative perspectives within the context of integrated data and visual analytics.

It is anticipated that this new cohort of students will experience some extreme innovative thinking exercises that build upon their individual and collective insight. The purpose of their role as DHS scholars is to help ensure that the nation can start to inculcate into this new cohort of scientists, policymakers, and educators a new world view of threats to the nation and our communities. Ideally, the project team anticipates creating an emerging and innovative model for teaching STEM across diverse disciplines that both directly and indirectly serve in protecting the homeland.

ACKNOWLEDGMENT

Special thanks and deep appreciation goes to the U.S. Department of Homeland Security's Science and Technology Directorate, Office of University Programs, and the program director, Ms. Stephanie Willett, and her colleagues, Ms. Patty Mayo, and Sheena Cochran, for their continued mentorship and tireless effort in helping to guide our project in a way that has the greatest and most beneficial impact on the people of the United States of America. Thank you! We would also like to thank and acknowledge our off-campus collaborators, Purdue University's VACCINE, a DHS Center of Excellence, The Athena Group, and Florida Institute of Technology, for each institution's willingness to provide opportunities for our students through guidance, mentorship, and training. Thank you!

REFERENCES

Astin, A. W. (1993). *What matters in college*. San Francisco, CA: Jossey-Bass Inc.

Cringely, R. X. (1995). *Personal interview with Steve Jobs: The lost interview*. Available on Netflix, 2012.

Flores, A. (2007). Examining disparities in mathematics education: Achievement gap or opportunity gap? *High School Journal, 91*(1), 29–42. doi:10.1353/hsj.2007.0022

Hall, G. E. (2010). Technology's Achilles heel: Achieving high-quality implementation. *Journal of Research on Technology in Education, 42*(3), 231–253. doi:10.1080/15391523.2010.10782550

Jackson, K., & Wilson, J. (2012). Supporting African American students' learning of mathematics: A problem of practice. *Urban Education, 47*(2), 354–398. doi:10.1177/0042085911429083

Keefe, B. (2010). *The perception of STEM: Analysis, issues, and future directions. Survey*. Entertainment and Media Communication Institute.

Kuh, G. D., Kinzie, J., Schuh, J. H., & Whitt, E. J. (2005a). *Assessing conditions to enhance educational effectiveness: The inventory for student engagement and success*. San Francisco, CA: Jossey-Bass.

Maton, K. (2004). Increasing the number of African American PhDs in the sciences and engineering: A strengths-based approach. *The American Psychologist, 59*(6), 547–556. doi:10.1037/0003-066X.59.6.547 PMID:15367090

National Research Council. (2011). *Successful K-12 STEM education*. Washington, DC: The National Academies Press.

Pascarella, E., & Terenzini, P. (2005). *How college effects student: A third decade of research* (Vol. 2). San Francisco: Jossey-Bass Higher & Adult Education.

Pink, D. (2005). *A whole new mind: Moving from the information age to the conceptual age*. New York: Riverhead Books.

Sanders, M. (2009). Integrative STEM education primer. *Technology Teacher, 68*(4), 20–26.

Tinto, V. (1993). *Leaving college: Rethinking the causes and cures of student attrition* (2nd ed.). Chicago, IL: University of Chicago Press.

KEY TERMS AND DEFINITIONS

CDC: Center for Disease Control.

CHIPP: Center for Health Informatics, Planning and Policy.

COE: Center for Excellence affiliated with the Department of Homeland Security.

DHS: Department of Homeland Security.

MSI: Minority Serving Institution.

MSU: Morgan State University, a historical Black University and minority serving institution (MSI).

OUP: Office of University Programs within the Department of Homeland Security.

VACCINE: Visual Analytics for Command, Control, and Interoperability Environments, a DHS Center for Excellence.

VAST MSI: Visual Analytics for Science and Technology at a Minority Serving Institution.

Chapter 8
Critical Infrastructure Higher Education Initiative

Kendal Smith
George Mason University, USA

EXECUTIVE SUMMARY

As an essential element of homeland security, critical infrastructure protection requires a professional, highly educated workforce and community of leaders at all levels of government and in the private sector. Yet there are few structured and comprehensive higher education programs in critical infrastructure protection. This case study reviews an education initiative that partners the U.S. Department of Homeland Security with the Center for Infrastructure Protection and Homeland Security at the George Mason University School of Law in an effort to develop and distribute critical infrastructure protection courses and materials that will become part of a comprehensive, unified approach to homeland security education.

INTRODUCTION

The notion of protecting things that are essential to one's livelihood is not novel. It's common sense. Whether Mother Nature, malicious intent, or sheer accident, there have always been forces at work that threaten to destroy the things on which we depend. Yet it is only within the past twenty years that the protection concept has become a national policy focus. While the term *critical infrastructure protection*

DOI: 10.4018/978-1-4666-5946-9.ch008

was first used in a 1996 Executive Order, it was the tragic attacks of September 11, 2001 that woke the nation to its necessity. Beyond the devastating loss of life, the cascading failures and long-term economic impacts demonstrated the far-reaching consequences of destruction in the networked and interdependent world in which we now live.

Infrastructure protection became a primary focus of the newly created U.S. Department of Homeland Security (DHS), and in 2006, its Office of Infrastructure Protection (IP) released the first National Infrastructure Protection Plan (NIPP) to guide the integration of protection and resilience efforts across multiple critical infrastructure sectors. The framework designates roles and responsibilities, and outlines a risk management strategy to deter threats, mitigate vulnerabilities, and minimize consequences. Proper implementation requires professionals skilled not only in specific sectors, but in risk analysis, partnership building, and collaboration across Federal, State, local, tribal, and territorial (FSLTT) governments, as well as private industry. Accordingly, the 2006 NIPP also includes long-term goals to guarantee the program's continued success, including "education, training, and exercise programs to ensure that skilled and knowledgeable professionals and experienced organizations are able to undertake NIPP-related responsibilities in the future" (p. 6).

To that end, in 2008 IP produced the NIPP Education and Training Assessment Report and Implementation Plan (NIPP Education Report). The report identifies seven core competency areas that "together define the elements required for performance" (2008, p. 10) as a critical infrastructure professional. (See Figure 1)

The report also recognizes the different groups comprising the critical infrastructure community, including FSLTT government officials; DHS personnel; sector-specific agency and other federal employees; and private industry owners and operators. Based on these target audiences, the resulting model expresses the core competencies that characterize the scope of the critical infrastructure field and establishes the requirements for a comprehensive education training program. (See Figure 2)

The updated 2009 NIPP reinforces the competency model, particularly emphasizing the importance of partnering with universities to create new academic programs resulting in specialized degrees from accredited institutions (pp. 84-85). This case study examines the efforts of such a partnership—between DHS and George Mason University—to develop and distribute courses and materials that will become part of a complete, unified critical infrastructure higher education program.

Figure 1. CIP core competencies (Adapted from NIPP, 2009, p. 84)

Area	Includes Knowledge & Skills To....
Risk Analysis	• Perform accurate, documented, objective, defensible, transparent, and complete analyses. • Support executive and managerial decision-making related to CIP programs.
Protection Measures/Mitigation Strategies	• Establish CIP program goals and objectives based on risk-analysis and risk-reduction return on investment. • Plan, develop, and implement CIP-related projects, measures, and activities. Take advantage of existing emerging and anticipated methods and technologies in order to develop effective strategies, projects, and activities. • Implement continuous feedback mechanisms.
Partnership Building/Networking	• Understand the roles and responsibilities of all partners. • Establish mechanisms for interacting with partners and exchanging information and resources (including best practices).
Information Collection &Reporting (Information Sharing)	• Use systems, tools, and protocols to collect, analyze, organize, report, and evaluation information. • Communicate and share information with sector partners at each tier of governance, including sector-specific, across sectors, and within the private sector.
Program Management	• Establish sector-specific or jurisdictional CIP goals and plans. • Identify and prioritize CIP projects, strategies, and activities for a sector or jurisdiction. • Manage a CIP program on schedule, within budget, and in compliance with performance standards. • Design and implement continuous feedback mechanisms at the program level. • Develop and implement CIP training plans.
Metrics & Program Evaluation	• Define and establish CIP metrics based on goals and objectives. • Establish data collection and measurement plans, systems, and tools. • Collect and analyze data. • Report findings and conclusions.
Technical & Tactical Expertise (Sector-Specific)	• Note: This area includes the specialized (sector-specific) expertise required to plan, implement, and evaluate technical and tactical activities, measures, and programs.

Figure 2. CIP core competency model (Adapted from NIPP, 2009, p. 83)

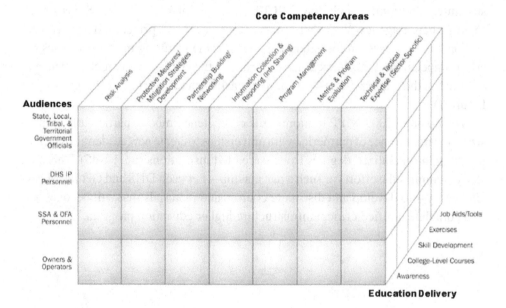

BACKGROUND

Anticipating the need for a new comprehensive approach to infrastructure protection, in the spring of 2001 several leaders at George Mason University began discussing the possibility of a research center devoted to the intersection of law, policy, economics, and technology as it concerned critical infrastructure protection (CIP). With the need evidenced by all on September 11, the conversation quickly became a reality. The CIP Project was founded in early 2002 with the goal of building one of the first multidisciplinary and collaborative research initiatives to treat critical infrastructure as a discipline. Funded by a grant administered through the National Institute of Standards and Technology, in its first year, the CIP Project sponsored over 50 individual research initiatives among 14 institutions. It also launched *The CIP Report*, a monthly electronic publication highlighting current infrastructure protection issues for government, industry, and academic professionals.

The Project continued to expand, with additional funding generated to address unexplored areas of infrastructure protection. Renamed the Center for Infrastructure Protection and Homeland Security (CIP/HS) in 2008, the program has developed an extensive network of subject matter experts and partnerships with industry; academia; and Federal, State, and local officials.

From its inception, education has been a primary objective of CIP/HS research efforts, with education and outreach listed as the first of four program goals in the July 2002 inaugural issue of *The CIP Report*. With this focus embedded in its history, the Center's affiliation with a respected academic institution that is recognized as a Center of Excellence in information assurance, and its advantageous location in the National Capital Region, the groundwork for a DHS-collaboration in this area was already in place. Consequently, shortly after the NIPP Education Report identifying the CIP core competencies and the subsequent updated NIPP were released, a partnership was born.

The Critical Infrastructure Higher Education Initiative (CI HEI) began in 2010 with a goal of creating and disseminating critical infrastructure higher education materials. All courses would be non-proprietary, designed for use in academic institutions across the nation, with the seven core competencies serving as the framework for development. Initially a two year contract, DHS underscored its commitment to the effort and to the importance of critical infrastructure education with five years of incremental funding awarded in September 2012.[1]

CASE DESCRIPTION

The CI HEI began with a four month assessment that surveyed and evaluated existing CIP instructional material. The assessment identified current best practices in higher education, compared CIP curricula with the DHS critical infrastructure professional core competencies, and discussed unmet CIP educational needs. Based on the assessment findings, CIP/HS developed seven stand alone CIP courses that include introductory and capstone courses, as well as courses focused on risk management; information sharing; systems analysis; methods, policies, and strategies; and cybersecurity.

The project's second year saw the creation of a five course CIP certificate program adapted from the base year curricula, as well as the modification of an existing Public Administration program to include an eight course CIP concentration. In addition, the second year expanded upon initial efforts by developing supporting materials such as a library of CIP reading materials, a roster of relevant subject matter experts, and a case study and accompanying instructor materials on the 2007 I-35W Minnesota bridge collapse. To ensure that all of these courses and supporting materials meet the needs of current and future professionals in the infrastructure protection community, CIP/HS conducted multiple reviews through structured roundtables and on individual bases with experts from the public and private sectors as well as the academic community. Following this extensive evaluation process, each course was made publicly available for use in academic institutions across the country.

Assessment

The first step in the project consisted of a four month survey and assessment of existing instructional CIP material within higher education institutions across the United States. The purpose was to identify programs and courses that focus on CIP and compare them with the seven core competencies identified in the NIPP Education Report as well as with best practices in higher education and curriculum development. Gaps and weaknesses were identified and recommendations made to strengthen CIP higher education efforts.

The survey was conducted in two phases and included (a) institutions identified by the Naval Postgraduate School's Center for Homeland Defense and Security (CHDS) and the Federal Emergency Management Agency's (FEMA) Emergency Management Institute (EMI) as offering higher education programs in homeland security and emergency management, and (b) a random sampling of other accredited academic institutions throughout the country. CHDS and EMI are recognized leaders in homeland security and emergency management education and training, and have compiled lists of relevant programs through extensive outreach efforts.

The random sampling was taken from a master list of institutions accredited by associations and regional agencies recognized by the U.S. Department of Education, minus those focusing on fine arts, specialty medical disciplines, and seminaries. In total, 785 institutions were surveyed, 260 from the CHDS and EMI lists, and 525 from the random sampling.

In Phase One, the project team searched for the terms "critical infrastructure" and "infrastructure protection" in the search engine and the course catalogue of each institution's website. For each institution, an Institution Report was generated to detail the actions taken by the project team (e.g., whether a course database, PDF, or website pages were available for search), as well as the results. Initially, 114 of the 785 schools were found to have CIP material—100 from the CHDS and EMI lists and 14 from the random sampling. Upon further analysis, the team determined that only a portion of the 114 institutions possessed significant CIP material, with 46 offering CIP courses, 3 offering a CIP degree and/or certificate, 2 offering seminars or training programs, and 1 offering a CIP concentration.

Phase Two reviewed the institutions on the CHDS and EMI lists with homeland security degrees, programs, certificates, and concentrations but did not limit the search to CIP terms. The project team instead looked for material that, while not specifically referring to "critical infrastructure" or "infrastructure protection," referenced relevant topics such as public-private partnerships, information sharing, or risk management. This phase ensured that all materials in homeland security programs were thoroughly searched. The Phase Two review included 108 institutions and the results were included in the Institution Reports. An additional 5 institutions and 18 courses were found to incorporate CIP material.

In total, Phase One and Phase Two revealed 80 courses within 52 institutions containing CIP material. This number was reduced to 69 after further research revealed 1 program no longer in existence, another on hiatus, and several courses no longer offered. The courses were hosted within various academic fields and programs, including: homeland security; criminal justice; emergency/disaster management; public policy/administration; public safety; engineering; government/national security; business administration; and urban planning. Instructor backgrounds were equally diverse.

The project team was able to collect 32 course syllabi[2] from the remaining institutions—14 taught at the undergraduate level and 18 taught at the graduate. The content was delivered in the classroom for 17 courses, online for 12, and in a hybrid manner for 3. These syllabi were evaluated for higher education best practices and core competency integration. (see Figure 3)

While a curriculum provides the framework for learning, the effective communication of curricular content occurs via educational best practices. Such practices ensure learner retention and integration of new knowledge, as well as learner mo-

Figure 3. Assessment results

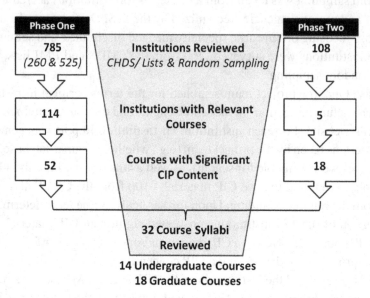

tivation and engagement. For this reason, the project team analyzed the collected syllabi for commonly recognized best practices in higher education, including:

- Clearly stated objectives,
- Clear expectations,
- Learner-Centered Principles,
- Authentic, real-world assessments and rubrics,
- Use of technology,
- Different instructional modalities,
- Flexible grouping practices and cooperative learning.

All 32 syllabi included course objectives, while 17 expressed clear expectations for student performance and guidelines for completion of assignments. Many courses also incorporated Learner-Centered Principles. Such principles endeavor to establish positive personal relationships, honor learners' ideas and opinions, address learners' individual needs and beliefs, and facilitate higher order thinking (McCombs and Lauer, 1997). Twenty-three courses focused on facilitating higher-order or critical/reflective thinking, with 5 courses utilizing critical thinking exercises such as reflective journaling. Seventeen courses addressed individual learner needs by stating the course rationale, allowing learners to gauge the relevance of the class to their specific goals or interests. Seven syllabi included an authentic or real-world assessment, such as analyzing a real-world CIP incident or conducting a CIP risk assessment. Twenty of the courses required the use of technology in learning course content, including viewing online videos and podcasts, and 1 course required development of a video presentation. While the majority of the courses employed the traditional method of direct teacher instruction and lecture, 8 courses utilized a variety of modalities such as workshops, seminar-style discussions, short faculty presentations, and videos. Finally, 14 courses included flexible grouping practices, which enable active learning and promote collaboration and shared understanding.

While it is essential to implement best practices in the learning environment to ensure academic rigor, professional core competencies must also be integrated, as they provide students with the expected knowledge that is required for the workforce. Yet, the CIP core competencies were not specifically referenced in any of the syllabi reviewed by the project team and the NIPP was included in only 9 courses. However, several core competencies were highlighted in the course content. Risk analysis was emphasized in 29 syllabi, with nearly that many focusing on certain protective measures/mitigation strategies. Sixteen courses dedicated lessons and/or assignments to specific sectors, the most common being water, transportation, energy, communications, and nuclear materials. Only 15 courses discussed the roles and responsibilities of CIP partners and even fewer focused on information sharing. Metrics and program evaluation was found in some syllabi, though it was unclear whether it related more to risk analysis than to the separate core competency identified by the NIPP Education Report. Program management was largely lacking within the syllabi.

Based on the syllabi review and the overall assessment process, the project team identified several gaps in CIP higher education and made four recommendations:

1. **Career paths in CIP should to be developed and marketed:** A career path in CIP has not been developed in either the public or private sector. The number of courses and/or programs in infrastructure protection is not extensive, confirming the hypothesis that a critical infrastructure curriculum should be developed. In addition, many of these courses and/or programs are offered only on demand. In some cases, courses and/or programs are no longer offered or are temporarily on hiatus. Without clearly defined career paths in CIP, there is little demand on the higher education system to provide courses. Therefore, outreach is needed to familiarize young professionals with the potential opportunities in government and the private sector. This includes job fairs, open houses, recruiters, guest lecturers, etc.

2. **Guidance on course content in CIP programs is required:** Course content varied greatly among reviewed syllabi and often did not align with the core competencies identified in the NIPP Education Report. To properly educate a cadre of CIP professionals, the basic educational content conveyed must be

uniform across different institutions. As with any academic discipline, individual programs can and should remain unique, highlighting certain areas or offering additional courses in specific topics. Yet the fundamental framework for a CIP education program should remain the same for learners attending any institution. While there were some commonalities among the reviewed courses, the differences were widespread and further illustrated the need for a comprehensive CIP curriculum.

3. **The critical infrastructure core competencies must be continuously validated:** Because CIP is inherently multidisciplinary and constantly evolving in response to emerging technologies and threats, the core competencies should be continually validated to ensure they remain a relevant and effective framework. This is a recurrent process that can be accomplished through annual conferences and/or workshops, commentaries in peer reviewed national and international journals, and discussions with the academic community, the private sector, DHS, and other stakeholders. Disseminating information and generating discussion about the core competencies in such venues will ensure the competencies continue to reflect knowledge areas and skills applicable to the infrastructure protection field.

4. **Best practices in CIP higher education need to be implemented:** Several best practices were found in a significant portion of the reviewed CIP courses such as clearly stated objectives, use of technology, rationale for course content listed on the syllabus, and different grouping practices. However, other best practices were not evident in courses and may contribute to lack of enrollment. Less apparent were the use of authentic or real-world assessments, different teaching modalities, reflective practices, and application of knowledge. Many courses provided few guidelines, such as rubrics, for evaluating student products or for student self-assessment. These practices are the key to developing and sustaining links to workforce competencies and must be integrated in the CIP learning environment.

This project builds upon the achievements of these institutions that have implemented critical infrastructure into their curriculum and/or training programs. Their pioneering efforts in combination with effective best practices in higher education and the CIP core competencies provided the framework used by the CIP/HS project team in efforts to develop a robust CIP educational curriculum. With insight into existing programs and gaps in content and best practices identified, the project team began the process of developing CIP higher education materials that are both comprehensive and academically rigorous.

Curricula Development

Proper design of course objectives and integration of best practices in higher education ensure that the end result is not just a training program, but an educational curriculum. Generally speaking, training imparts the *how* of something, while education is concerned with the *why* behind it. Training emphasizes practice and acquiring skills. Education focuses on principles, theory, and critical thinking. It is possible to have one without the other. A person trained in construction need not have any knowledge of civil engineering, nor does one need to understand the inner-workings of a car in order to drive it. Conversely, there are those who could theorize at length about aerodynamics and the Constitution, but would be at a loss if placed in a cockpit or a courtroom. Yet success in most professions requires both the "know-how" and the "know-why". While it is impossible to perform a task without knowing how it is done, understanding the why behind it engenders flexibility and inspires innovation.

Producing a community of professionals capable of protecting our nation's critical infrastructure requires education as well as training. By its very nature CIP is constantly in flux. It must evolve in relation to emerging technologies, incorporate the latest laws and policies, and respond to new threats and vulnerabilities—all across multiple infrastructure sectors. Hence, the "know-how" within the CIP field is at once incredibly vast and exceedingly limited. As a result, the "know-why" becomes even more essential, ensuring professionals acquire the critical thinking skills necessary to evaluate and respond to new situations. While this does not minimize the importance of training or its place in the working environment, the aim of this project is to produce comprehensive CIP *educational* materials, and consequently, the courses are designed with that goal in mind.

To accomplish this, in addition to internal research and expertise, the CIP/HS project team cultivated a pool of subject matter experts (SMEs) from government, industry, and academia to assist with curricula development, evaluation, and deployment. SME roundtables were held to discuss assessment findings, determine course content, evaluate developed syllabi, and suggest outreach and implementation strategies. The balance of theory and practice was a continual topic of debate during the development process, with roundtable participants returning to the question several times. The resulting consensus was that there should never be a place in the courses where theory is "left hanging" without practical application. Hence, the syllabi should include discussion questions and exercises throughout. At the same time, it is important to avoid getting bogged down in the weeds of any particular subject or sector. The goal is not to create SMEs in specific CIP areas, but to provide an overall framework of understanding. Moreover, analyzing case studies and struggling with authentic CIP issues in class is essential because it provides learners with a practical awareness of the government and private sector responsibilities associated with the CIP field.

However, while an instructor may try to impart practical skill in the classroom, CIP's expansive and evolutionary nature, the needs of different students, the deployment method being used, and the instructor's personal limitations all pose significant challenges to this process. Despite these difficulties, if learners invest in this program they will expect a return on that investment—namely, employment. Thus, whatever the balance between theory and practice that exists in the classroom, learners have to leave these courses with the skills necessary to obtain a job within the CIP community. Those skills—the core competencies—must be validated by course objectives and exercises.

Further discussion about curricular goals involved accounting for the diverse background of CIP learners. Some of the individuals taking these courses will be young professionals who have recently completed their undergraduate degree. Others may already be practicing in the field, such as emergency management professionals or counterintelligence analysts. Some may have a strong background in mathematics and statistics while others may only be comfortable with basic math. Background diversity makes it difficult to address the needs of each learner in the classroom. How will new learners as well as those from the fields of emergency management, engineering, intelligence, law, and technology work together in a course? Will all learners be able to successfully complete course goals and objectives?

After discussing this challenge, the project team determined that learner diversity is beneficial to the CIP learning environment. The various perspectives generated in a diverse learning environment simulate the reality of a field that is inherently interdisciplinary. For example, a group project or table top exercise invites various viewpoints and helps develop the cross-collaboration essential for the CIP profession. CIP education *should* reflect this diversity. It is the educator's responsibility to provide a guiding framework that any learner from any background can utilize as a CIP professional.

Because the CI HEI is creating courses for use in various academic institutions and every class and instructor will be unique, the curriculum was designed to be as comprehensive as possible. Thus, an extensive amount of readings, both fundamental and advanced, are included in the course syllabi, allowing an instructor to tailor it to fit the needs of her particular students. The course syllabi also incorporate opportunities for learner and instructor feedback, ensuring course expectations and progress are evaluated throughout the semester. Accordingly, the courses cater to a diverse group of potential students.

Each course underwent a substantial review process, including draft, revised, and final versions. All drafts were reviewed by DHS IP personnel, as well as by private sector and education SMEs. The curriculum evaluation guide (Figure 4)

Figure 4. CI HEI curriculum evaluation guide

Curriculum Evaluation Guide		
Name of Reviewer		
Title of Course Reviewed		
Date Reviewed		

Curriculum	Goals	Comments/ Recommendations
Alignment to Critical Infrastructure Core Competency Areas	The curriculum aligns with the critical infrastructure core competency areas: ☐Risk Analysis ☐Protective Measures/Mitigation Strategies Development ☐Partnership Building/Networking ☐Information Collection & Reporting (Information Sharing) ☐Program Management ☐Metrics and Program Evaluation ☐ Technical & Tactical Expertise (Sector-Specific)	
Learner Expectations	☐ The learner expectations clearly describe what students should know and be able to do at the end of the course	
Pacing	☐ The skills and concepts are sequenced along a continuum of development.	
Learning Activities	☐ The learning activities reflect current higher education best practices; align with expected course outcomes; and apply to the field of critical infrastructure protection	
Assessments	☐ The ongoing assessments, including tracking the process of individual learners and providing improvement to the course design, are evident and aligned with expected course outcomes and the critical infrastructure core competency areas	
Learning Resources	☐ The curriculum contains relevant, sufficient, and timely materials that support learning issues related to critical infrastructure protection	
Course Design	☐ The curriculum is academically rigorous, organized, and easy for instructors and learners to use	
Professional Development	☐ The courses meet the current and future needs of the critical infrastructure protection profession	

was designed to assist reviewers in critiquing the course syllabi and pinpoint areas for improvement.

Utilizing this collaborative process, the CI HEI developed 20 CIP courses in its first two years. They are grouped in three separate curricular packages. The first consists of seven stand alone, graduate level CIP courses available for deployment in various schools, such as Business, Engineering, Government, Health and Human Services, Information Technology, Public Policy, and Management. They are:

1. **Introduction to Critical Infrastructure Protection and Resilience:** Provides an introduction to the policy, strategy, and practical application of CIP and resilience from an all-hazards perspective.
2. **Critical Infrastructure Protection and Information Sharing:** Provides an overview of information sharing processes necessary to protect and make the nation's critical infrastructure more resilient, with a focus on promoting subject matter understanding, critical analysis of issues, and insight into senior leader decision-making in both the public and private sectors.

3. **Critical Infrastructure Protection and Risk Management:** Provides an introduction to the policy, strategy, and practical application of risk management and risk analysis from an all-hazards perspective.

4. **Critical Infrastructure Protection Systems Analysis:** Introduces the notion of systems analysis in the context of infrastructure protection; provides learners with tools and techniques for describing a system in terms of its internal parts and dependencies with other systems, and for uncovering risks affecting systems.

5. **Critical Infrastructure Protection Methods, Policies, and Strategies:** Facilitates student-centered learning, integrates critical decision-making, and uses historical event case studies to reinforce national security and homeland security policies governing the protection, identification, and resilience of the nation's critical infrastructure from an all-hazards context with emphasis on the prevention, mitigation, and response to adversary attack scenarios against single or multiple critical infrastructure sectors.

6. **Critical Infrastructure Protection: The Cyber Dimension:** Provides a careful examination of the methods necessary to identify and address risks to critical information infrastructure from a variety of human and natural threats.

7. **Critical Infrastructure Protection Capstone Seminar:** Designed according to a building block approach that fosters the development of an advanced baseline of relevant learner knowledge and applies this baseline to "hands-on" CIP and resilience strategy through case studies and incident management exercises.

Academic institutions may customize these courses for use as electives or as required courses, or they may be bundled as a CIP concentration.

The stand alone courses were followed by a five course graduate certificate program. The certificate can be offered in conjunction with other degrees or deployed separately. Some of the material parallels that found in the stand alone courses, though the certificate package was designed as an integrated course series. The courses include:

1. **Foundations of Critical Infrastructure Protection and Resilience:** Provides an introduction to the policies, strategies, and practical application of CIP and resilience from an all-hazards perspective.

2. **Partnering and Information Sharing for Critical Infrastructure Protection and Resilience:** Provides an overview of partnerships and information sharing within the homeland security enterprise with a focus on the collaboration and information products, processes, and systems necessary to protect and enhance the resilience of the nation's critical infrastructure.

3. **Assessing and Managing Risk to Critical Infrastructure Systems:** Provides an introduction to the policy, strategy, and practical application of all-hazards risk assessment and management in the context of CIP and resilience.
4. **Critical Infrastructure Protection and Resilience and Cybersecurity:** Provides an introduction to the policy, strategy, and operational environment of cyberspace in the context of the critical infrastructure protection and resilience mission area.
5. **Advanced Topics in Critical Infrastructure Protection and Resilience:** Provides an advanced focus on CIP and resilience policy, strategy, planning, and incident management operations in an all-hazards context while fostering "hands-on" development through case studies and group activities.

Finally, the project team took eight courses from George Mason University Master's of Public Administration and modified them to create a CIP concentration. The courses are built on the foundation of courses commonly found in public administration and policy programs but designed around existing literature and materials that focus on CIP. Six of the modified courses were taken from those that comprise the core courses in the Public Administration curriculum. The remaining two courses focus on strategic planning and interagency coordination for homeland security and emergency management. They include:

1. **Public Policy Process and Critical Infrastructure/Domestic Security Policy:** Provides an assessment of how public programs are developed through the policy-making process, with specific focus given to the formation of CIP policy, including the roles of the Congress, the President, interest groups, media, and political parties.
2. **Third Party Governance and Critical Infrastructure Protection:** Focuses on how Federal CIP programs use grants, contracts, regulations, and other governance tools to engage State and local governments, the private sector, and nonprofit entities in carrying out major national programs to protect infrastructure.
3. **Organization Theory and Behavior: Organizing for Critical Infrastructure Protection:** Uses CIP case studies as models of organizational theory to provide an analysis of how organizations are structured and managed to meet the expectations of various publics in the political and social environment.
4. **Program Evaluation:** Provides learners with skills necessary to evaluate public programs; builds on general knowledge of statistics to enable learners to apply criteria for effectiveness, efficiency, and equity to CIP programs.
5. **Federal Budgeting:** Analyzes the Federal budget process over time and what the future holds for Federal deficits, debt, and the allocation of resources across

agencies and programs, specifically focusing on CIP initiatives; examines the formation of budget proposals and the fiscal and performance accountability requirements faced in implementing CIP programs.

6. **Project Management:** Provides learners with a detailed understanding of tools and techniques for managing the implementation of large projects requiring substantial investments of public and private funds and long time frames for planning, design, construction, and operations.

7. **Infrastructure Protection and Emergency Response – Interagency Communication/Coordination:** Focuses on coordination and collaboration in settings where numerous agencies, levels of government, and sectors of the economy are summoned to work together on public goals; examines intergovernmental management and inter-organizational relations to discern best practices and lessons learned for managers who must work in networked environments.

8. **Critical Infrastructure – Emergency Planning and Preparedness:** Focuses on how managers at Federal, State, and local levels, as well as the private sector, develop plans and protocols for emergencies, whether natural disasters, terrorism, or other forces.

When the project received additional funding in 2012, it was decided that two supplementary courses would be developed per year for five additional years, subject to the same rigorous review process. Thus far, the project team has developed two additional CIP stand alone courses that may be treated as electives or used as part of a core requirement for a CIP concentration or degree. They are:

1. **Critical Infrastructure Protection and Resilience – Sector Approaches and Cross-Sector Interdependencies:** Compares and contrasts the different approaches vis-à-vis protection and resilience utilized within the various critical infrastructure sectors, including those that operate within a defined regulatory space and those that do not, and examines the nature of critical dependencies and interdependencies across the sectors.

2. **Critical Infrastructure Protection and Resilience – The International Dimension:** Focuses on CIP and resilience from the international perspective, including examination of: government-private sector policy approaches; governance/organizing structures, partnerships, and information sharing mechanisms; best-practices for risk assessment, risk management, and performance measurement; infrastructure and supply chain dependencies and interdependencies; the cybersecurity landscape; and the future of infrastructure risk and operating environments.

All CI HEI courses are structured following a standard 15-week academic semester for 3 credit hours. Individual institutions and instructors can adapt the courses to fit an alternative format as necessary. Each syllabus includes:

- **Course Description/Overview:** The course description provides the learner with a course rationale, a higher education best practice that enables the learner to gauge the relevance of the course material to his or her own interests.
- **Learner Outcomes/Objectives:** Course objectives are mapped against the core competencies identified in the NIPP Education Report.
- **Delivery Methods:** This section informs learners of the various instructor modalities utilized within the course, such as mini-lectures, structured collaborative projects and exercises, guest speakers, and interactive classroom discussions.
- **General Course Requirements:** Information about class attendance and participation, reading requirements, classroom policies, etc., is included here.
- **Grading:** All course assignments are broken down by total grade percentage.
- **Activities, Exercises, and Research Projects:** The purpose and requirements for each assignment are detailed here, making learners aware of course expectations and evaluation criteria.
- **Incorporation of Feedback:** This section explains how learners can provide and receive feedback throughout the course, ensuring collaboration in the learning process.
- **Textbooks:** If utilized, primary textbooks are included here; however, the majority of course readings can be found online and links are provided in the corresponding lesson.
- **Course Outline:** Each course includes 15 lessons complete with objectives, discussion topics, in-class exercises, and required readings.
- **Attachments:** All courses include authentic or real-world assessments such as case studies and table top or incident management exercises. These are generally included as attachments at the end of the course.

Both course and lesson objectives are aligned with Revised Bloom's Taxonomy on learning domains.[3] Bloom's categorizes cognitive processes according to a hierarchical framework that assists in measuring educational goals (Bloom, 1956). Cognitive behavior begins with remembering, and then moves to understanding, applying, analyzing, evaluating, and creating (Anderson and Krathwohl, 2001). A learner cannot move to the next level without mastering the one before it. (see Figure 5)

Figure 5. Revised Bloom's Taxonomy

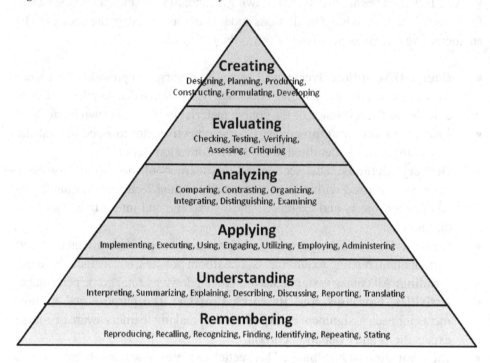

In the CIP curriculum, Bloom's was used to formulate course objectives and activities that encourage learners to move beyond knowledge retention into higher levels of thought. For example, in one of the stand alone courses, a Lesson 1 objective reads: "Distinguish between what constitutes a threat, vulnerability, and consequence from different perspectives." Corresponding discussion topics ask the learner, "What role do perspectives play in labeling a particular event or phenomenon as a threat, vulnerability, or consequence?" and "How does the quality of your understanding about a system affect the credibility of your analysis?" These questions compel the learner to grapple with the material and go beyond the realm of remembering to understanding and application. To further aid this process, this lesson includes an in-class activity, where the instructor presents to learners a set of 8-10 images. For each, the learner must identify whether what they are seeing is a threat, vulnerability, or consequence, and from whose perspective it is seen that way. This exercise brings learners to even deeper levels of cognition, and encourages collaboration and varied thinking.

All course lessons are structured to reinforce this type of critical thinking, successively building to ultimately validate the overall course objectives mapped against the core competencies. The highest levels of thinking—including analyzing, evaluating, and creating—are emphasized by class exercises and research projects.

For instance, the risk management classes require learners to conduct a risk methodology analysis, the systems course requires learners to create a YouTube video analyzing a CIP system, and several courses include table top exercises requiring learners to assume roles as key public and private individuals with CIP responsibilities during a simulated event.

Several additional higher education best practices are utilized throughout the courses to create activities designed to further CIP learning objectives, such as the "quick prompt," requiring learners to quickly write down the potential threats and vulnerabilities to a particular infrastructure or brainstorm a response to a threat or scenario; the "pair share," where learners gather in small groups to discuss a CIP topic and then report to the class; and structured dialogue examining real-world case studies, further discussed *infra*. These practices not only integrate varied learning modalities, but help develop the skills that are most useful for a CIP professional, such as risk assessment and collaboration.

After going through the final review process and receiving DHS approval, the courses were released for public use and placed on the CIP/HS website. Other distribution efforts are described *infra*.

While the courses comprise the foundation of the CI HEI, with an aim of cultivating a truly comprehensive approach to CIP education, the project team also created supplementary materials to assist with the project goal. The results of these efforts are detailed below.

Case Studies

Commonly recognized as a best practice and often utilized in disciplines such as law, medicine, and business, case studies require learners to use inductive reasoning to analyze real-world scenarios and develop solutions. Boehrer & Linsky give an excellent summation extolling the advantages of the case method:

Case discussion is interactive, student centered exploration of realistic and specific narratives that provide grist for inductive learning. The students engage in the intellectual, and emotional, exercise of facing complex problems and making critical decisions within the constraints imposed by reality, e.g. limited time and information, and pervasive uncertainty. Considering them from the protagonist's perspective, which calls on analysis to inform action, the students strive to resolve questions that have no single right answer. Their differing views and approaches produce a creative tension that fuels the enterprise and a synergistic outcome that both recognizes and exceeds their individual contributions. In their effort to find solutions and reach decisions through discussion, they sort out factual data, apply analytical tools, articulate issues, reflect on their relevant experience, and draw conclusions they can carry forward to new situations. In the process, they acquire substantive knowledge, develop analytic and collaborative skills, and gain in self-confidence and attention to detail. (1990, pp. 42-43)

Useful in most any field, cases are especially valuable in the CIP learning environment. They model the challenges faced by CIP professionals and allow learners to apply knowledge in a meaningful way, thereby "bridg[ing] the gap between theory and practice and between the academy and the workplace" (Barkley, Cross, and Major 2005, p. 182).

The CI HEI relies on the case method as a teaching technique in many of its courses, where authentic and simulated incidents are used to foster discussion around a complex problem. In addition to smaller case vignettes, the project team has developed detailed supplementary case studies keyed to course learning objectives and designed to reinforce the core competencies. The content and requirements for the case studies were discussed at a roundtable comprised of Federal and private sector CIP SMEs. Participants unanimously identified the key case study requirement in graduate education as the development of critical thinking and analytic evaluation skills. Federal participants further emphasized the importance of cases that assist in generating flexibility, effective communication skills, and successful collaboration. Cases should also create an awareness of the dependencies and interdependencies between sectors, and the additional complexity created by the contextual nature of criticality, where for instance, a non-critical asset might become so in the wake of an incident. Furthermore, cases should demonstrate the multi-disciplinary nature of the field, consider its inherent lack of uncertainty, and incorporate the importance of long-term planning. Private sector participants stressed the importance of objectivity and realism in creating case studies, particularly an accurate description of threats faced by different assets and sectors, using information from action reports, Congressional testimony, and Federal investigations. Overall, participants agreed that an effective case study should leverage existing data on successes and failures in CIP to provide a realistic example that facilitates critical thinking and collaborative analysis.

Like the courses, the cases studies were reviewed by DHS IP personnel and private sector and academic SMEs, and were further tested among students and CIP/HS staff. Thus far, two supplemental case studies are available for public use, with plans to develop two per year for the duration of the contract.

Each case begins with key questions to orient the learner to principal issues, and then provides a case narrative detailing the scenario, recommended additional reading, and three step-by-step learner exercises. Separate instructional materials were also created that include annotated exercise instructions, describe the value added for each exercise, and provide notional exercise solutions and a case conclusion. The cases are:

1. **Collapse – A Case Study of the I-35W Minnesota Bridge Disaster with Exercises:** This case highlights the challenges of planning and response in a high-vulnerability, multi-threat environment that is a nexus of multiple infrastructure modes. Exercises include: 1) Structured Planning Using Structured Brainstorming; 2) Effective Response Using Hypothesis Generation and Paired Comparison; and 3) Understanding Secondary Effects Using Starbursting. The exercises model robust critical thinking and small group processes to provide a blueprint for tackling the types of challenges faced by CIP professionals. They also reinforce the learners' ability to recognize critical infrastructure, identify man-made and natural threats and vulnerabilities, prioritize hypotheses, pinpoint potential secondary affects, and think creatively to adapt risk management principles to a changing environment.

2. **Blackout – A Case Study of the 2003 North American Blackout with Exercises:** The 2003 North American Blackout was a widespread incident that serves as a comprehensive case study of the Energy Sector, illustrating the unique characteristics of the Electricity Subsector and the effects of cascading failures and interdependencies for CIP professionals. Given the importance of planning activities for CIP professionals, the exercises center on strategy and planning activities in an interdependency-rich environment and include: 1) Strategic Planning Divergent Thinking Phase: Elements of Future Resilience for the Electricity Subsector; 2) Strategic Planning Convergent Thinking Phase: Creating a Forward-looking Strategy; and 3) Strategic Planning: Strengths-Weaknesses-Opportunities-Threats (SWOT) Analysis.[4]

Reading Library, SME List, and Speakers Bureau

The foundation of any academic field is its literature. While there is less to be found in an area as young as CIP as in other long-standing disciplines, its interdisciplinary nature again ensures no shortage of information. To assist both educators and learners in locating relevant CIP instruction, the CI HEI project team has compiled a comprehensive electronic listing of historical and professional CIP reading materials from multiple government and academic sources. Updated quarterly, it contains links to over 700 sources, arranged by topic. Each entry includes the title, author/publisher, publication date, and a brief summary. In addition to sector-specific topics, the library has categories devoted to bridges, disaster and emergency management, education, Federal budgeting and CIP, general CIP, information sharing, interdependencies, international CIP, policy, program management, resilience, risk analysis, supply chain security, and terrorism.

To create this library, the project team began with a list of all the required readings used in the course development process, including CIP legislation and policy documents. Topics were designated from this base list. The team then searched applicable academic journals using topic terms. Links to journals and reports focusing exclusively on CIP received separate entries. Academic publishers such as Springer Link, Inderscience, John Wiley & Sons, Taylor & Francis, and Westlaw were also searched. Finally, a Google search was conducted for each of the chosen topics and the first 100 hits were reviewed.

Alongside the reading library, under the project's first contract the team developed a list of infrastructure protection SMEs. This list includes over 400 individuals from government, industry, and academia with notable CIP expertise. It includes the person's title and professional affiliation, educational information, and a link to any available biographical information. To create this list, the project team began with CI HEI roundtable participants and invitees, as well as CIP/HS research fellows. The team also searched the archived issues of *The CIP Report* for contributing authors with applicable expertise and added authors of materials included in the reading library. The search expanded to include speakers at relevant conferences such as the Critical Infrastructure Symposium, the Annual IFIP Working Group 11.10 International Conference on Critical Infrastructure Protection, the Annual Homeland Defense and Security Education Summit, the Defense Industrial Base Critical Infrastructure Protection Conference, the Critical Infrastructure Security Summit, the Royal United Services Institute's Critical National Infrastructure Conference, and other sector-specific events. CIP course instructors identified during the assessment were also included. As with the reading library, a Google search was then conducted using specified key terms.

Under the second contract, the project team used the SME list to create a speakers bureau listing of CIP subject matter volunteers who are willing to contribute to higher education initiatives, seminars, conferences, and classroom courses. Individuals from the SME list were contacted, informed about the project goals, and invited to be included in the speakers listing. Each listed SME provided contact information as well as his or her areas of expertise. The listing is updated monthly as additional contacts are made.

Course Updates

Because CIP is such a dynamic and interdisciplinary field, it experiences change at a much faster rate than many other disciplines. Legislation, directives, and regulations, as well as global, national, regional, and local events can all substantially affect CIP practices in a short time frame. This makes it difficult to keep course content current. With the additional DHS funding provided to continue this effort, the project team is able to conduct bi-annual comprehensive reviews and updates of all course materials.

The first review was completed in March 2013. All twenty courses were updated to reflect recent policy changes, including the release of Presidential Policy Directive 21-Critical Infrastructure Security and Resilience—which replaced Homeland Security Presidential Directive 7 and reorganized the critical infrastructure sectors so that there are now 16 instead of 18—and Executive Order 13636-Improving Critical Infrastructure Cybersecurity.[5] These documents were added to appropriate reading lists and incorporated into lesson discussion topics, and terminology was changed where necessary. Updates also included discussions and readings on relevant CIP events such as Hurricane Sandy. Outdated readings were substituted and broken links replaced. Furthermore, the courses were sent to DHS for additional SME evaluation. Various personnel reviewed the updates, and as in the original development process, made additional comments or recommendations. The updated materials then replaced the former courses on the CIP/HS website and notices were sent to inform key contacts of the changes.

Following updates, the project team also conducts a core competency evaluation. This evaluation analyzes the competencies in light of the review process, identifying any potential modifications, additional competencies, knowledge areas, or skills that are applicable to the CIP field. This ensures that all project materials remain comprehensive and continue to accurately reflect the needs of the changing CIP environment.

Distribution

As stated, the goal of the CI HEI is to develop *and distribute* CIP higher education materials. The project team began generating awareness at the outset with an article introducing the program and outlining its objectives in the August 2010 issue of *The CIP Report* (p. 12). The seven stand alone courses were made publicly available at the end of the base year, followed by the certificate and modified courses at the end of the second. Another *CIP Report* article summarized all developed project materials and announced their availability on the CIP/HS website at the conclusion of the first contract (June 2012, p. 2). Key contacts made during the assessment process and at SME roundtables were also leveraged to assist with distribution initiatives. Each institution listed on the CHDS and EMI websites with degrees and/ or programs in homeland security and related areas was sent information about the project, including links to all developed materials. Finally, during the first contract the project team gave four CI HEI presentations at relevant conferences, including:

the 2011 Homeland Defense and Security Education Summit, the 2011 and 2012 Critical Infrastructure Symposiums, and the 2012 Transportation Research Board Annual Meeting. CIP/HS was able to co-host the 2012 Critical Infrastructure Symposium, and offered a three-hour opening workshop focused on the CI HEI that not only gave a comprehensive project description, but invited audience feedback and included a demonstration of the supplemental case study.

Under the second contract, although curriculum expansion remains an essential program objective, with twenty foundational CIP courses and supporting materials created, outreach has become a priority. An outreach strategy was created to guide distribution initiatives—emphasizing events, written products, as well as targeted meetings, phone calls, and emails. The strategy calls for annual participation in multiple conferences, symposia, and workshops targeting the CIP community, and a CI HEI Curricula Guide with course and case study descriptions was created for distribution at outreach events. This includes sector specific forums, industry meetings, and other gatherings of individuals likely to generate future course demand.

As such, the project team again presented at the 2013 Critical Infrastructure Symposium, this time focusing on effective best practices in CIP higher education, and gave presentations as part of the National Military Intelligence Association's Intelligence Education and Training Day, the Security and Risk Management Association's 6th Annual Meeting, and as part of a CIP/HS sponsored resilience workshop. Furthermore, the team has been asked to speak to the Association of Contingency Planners and to co-lead a four-hour workshop at the 6th Annual Homeland Defense and Security Education Summit.[6]

The project team is also identifying opportunities for written outreach products, particularly in academic journals and scholarly publications such as the *Journal of Homeland Security Education, Journal of Homeland Security Affairs,* and *International Journal of Critical Infrastructure Protection.* Recognition of this type will not only raise program awareness and assist in validating the curriculum content, but will generate dialogue within the academic community on the need for CIP higher education programs in general.

In February of 2012, an SME roundtable was held to discuss course deployment and implementation strategies and challenges. Once again, representatives from government and industry participated, though special effort was made to include CIP SMEs with experience in the academic community. This includes individuals who have taught graduate level CIP courses or successfully piloted an academic program in a related area. The roundtable objective was to garner input from SMEs with an understanding of both the complexities of CIP and academic processes, and thus obtain recommendations for how best to deploy the CI HEI courses in institutions of higher learning.

These experts agreed that a focused effort targeting key individuals would be a more effective strategy than a broad-based method aimed at numerous organizations. It was suggested that the project team target individuals who have already made some investment in a CIP course or program, whereby CI HEI courses could be used to further their involvement. Even in a program with existing CIP courses or degree programs, CI HEI courses might be used to supplement or replace current material. Moreover, the project team should target existing degree programs where certain CIP courses can be used as electives, such as business, engineering, law, or public policy, while also finding pioneers willing to create new specialized degrees that will use the courses in their core curriculum.

Several of the participants themselves indicated a willingness to take on these roles. Currently, one professor is planning to teach two of the stand alone courses in the upcoming semester, another has presented the introductory course to his curriculum committee for approval, and a third is looking to start a full CIP program based on the CI HEI material. These efforts are key, as these individuals are experienced homeland security educators, and their support will go a long way towards building a recognizable foundation in CIP higher education.

The project team is also focused on building collaborative partnerships with leading organizations. For instance, the University Agency Partnership Initiative (UAPI), a CHDS online portal, "brings together institutions nationwide dedicated to advancing homeland security education... and provide opportunities for collaboration that create an intellectual multiplier effect that furthers the study of homeland security" (UAPI homepage). The site offers curriculum development support and provides a forum for partners to share course syllabi, instructor resources, teaching methodologies, and subject matter expertise. To date, UAPI includes program and contact information for 306 member institutions. The site allows users to browse by institution, educator, forum posts, curricula materials, or subject matter.

Recognizing shared objectives, the CI HEI has utilized UAPI partners to collaborate on several project goals. All of the courses are posted on the UAPI website. As UAPI is a centralized venue for homeland security educators, this ensures that the courses are accessible to those most likely to utilize them. Project team members monitor forum posts and have been able to send course materials directly to instructors wanting to add a CIP class to their curriculum. UAPI educators have also contributed to CI HEI course evaluation and attended project roundtables. Additionally, the site lists upcoming conferences and meetings and announces calls for papers, helping the project team to identify outreach venues. It also monitors new releases in a wide array of homeland security literature, enabling team members to more easily pinpoint CIP materials to add to the reading library.

CURRENT CHALLENGES FACING THE ORGANIZATION

Despite the aforementioned efforts, course distribution and deployment remains the greatest project challenge. Beyond considerations of course content and design, this project entails rationalizing the purpose, relevance, and marketability of a new curriculum, as institutions require justification before granting approval. The CI HEI's primary goal is to begin the process of institutionalizing a core CIP curriculum, and a basic requirement to achieving this aim is institutional support. Generally speaking, colleges and universities are slow to embrace change. One must navigate through numerous administrative bodies, departmental requirements, faculty expectations, and resource demands. This process is further complicated when a course or program is not only new to an institution, but the subject matter itself is in its infancy.

On a fundamental level, to offer a new course, there must be students to take it and someone to teach it. Academic institutions will not tender these courses if they do not generate demand. While CIP has certainly experienced massive growth over the past decade, in the academic landscape it is only just emerging. The literature is sparse, and as this project's assessment showed, there is currently no identifiable CIP career path—i.e., students do not have plans to become CIP professionals, as that is generally not understood as an option. Consequently, the demand might not be obvious because the end-users are not aware of the product or even that CIP exists as a field of study.

Additionally, given that CIP is such a diverse field, no one person can be an expert in everything it covers. This can be problematic for a potential CIP instructor. Perhaps an engineering, business, or public policy professor would like to teach a CIP course, but feels she lacks the requisite knowledge beyond her individual area of interest. Without faculty expertise, a course will not acquire the necessary institutional support to make it through a university's curriculum committee or other approval board.

Insufficient expertise may still be a concern even if a course is successfully deployed. These courses are in the public domain. Neither DHS nor the CIP/HS project team can ensure quality control. Public access also makes it difficult to track course deployment and thereby evaluate project success. Although the project team encourages course instructors to provide feedback, there is no established mechanism to ensure this occurs.

SOLUTIONS AND FUTURE RESEARCH DIRECTIONS

To assist in overcoming institutional challenges to course adoption, the project team plans to create and deliver workshops for potential faculty. These workshops will address obstacles to developing, deploying, and institutionalizing a CIP course or program. They will identify and assess the obstacles and provide tools and techniques to surmount them, including the CI HEI course offerings, strategies for overcoming administrative hurdles, and a guiding framework for self-study that will prepare faculty to offer instruction in this continually evolving field. Workshops will conclude with participants developing a strategic plan, specific to their institutions, outlining the necessary steps for effectively implementing a CIP course or program. The first of these workshops will take place at the 6th Annual Homeland Defense and Security Education Summit. Further workshops will be offered via webinar and at other conference venues.

The speakers bureau listing can also be used to alleviate concerns caused by lack of instructor expertise. These individuals have volunteered to help with CIP educational initiatives, including guest lectures. If there is a topic that an instructor is unsure of, he can consult the listing, find an expert in that area, and arrange a guest lecture. Though the project team is attempting to include SMEs from around the country and internationally, geographical limitations may well be an issue. Thus, a future goal is to obtain recorded lectures for various lesson topics and make them available as well. Supplementary instructor materials such as lecture notes and PowerPoint presentations would be additionally beneficial.

The project team also hopes to develop a more comprehensive method for tracking course deployment and conduct another assessment of CIP courses, concentrations, and degree programs before the conclusion of this effort. This assessment would improve upon previous methodology to include a wider sample of institutions, discussions with instructors, and international programs. Continual tracking of CI HEI courses and assessment of the overall CIP educational landscape are necessary to measure project success, identify curricular gaps, and ensure course content evolves with professional needs.

This initiative exists because both DHS and CIP/HS recognized a need for CIP higher education programs. Numerous jobs have been created within the past decade in efforts to implement the NIPP and secure infrastructure across governments and throughout industry. Sustaining these efforts requires comprehensive education, and while new programs might be slow to infiltrate the university landscape, the project team remains hopeful that the adoption of these courses by even a few key individuals will open the door to universal acceptance of this essential field of study.

REFERENCES

Anderson, L. W., & Krathwohl, D. (Eds.). (2001). *A taxonomy for learning, teaching, and assessing: a revision of Bloom's taxonomy of educational objectives*. New York: Longman.

Barkley, E. F., Cross, K. P., & Major, C. H. (2005). *Collaborative learning techniques: a handbook for college faculty*. San Francisco, CA: Jossey-Bass.

Bloom, B. S. (1956). *Taxonomy of educational objectives, handbook I: the cognitive domain*. New York: David McKay Co Inc.

Boehrer, J., & Linsky, M. (1990). Teaching with cases: Learning to question. *New Directions for Teaching and Learning*, 41–57. doi:10.1002/tl.37219904206

George Mason University School of Law's National Center for Technology and Law, in Conjunction with James Madison University, Launches Critical Infrastructure Protection Project. (2002). *The CIP Report, 1*(1), 2.

Joint George Mason University and Department of Homeland Security Initiative on Critical Infrastructure Higher Education Programs. (2010). *The CIP Report, 9*(2), 12.

McCombs, B. L., & Lauer, P. A. (1997). Development and validation of the learner-centered battery: Self-assessment tools for teacher reflection and professional development. *Professional Educator, 20*(1), 1–21.

Review and Revision of the National Infrastructure Protection Plan, 78 Fed Reg. 109 (Thursday, June 6, 2013), 34112-34115.

The 2012 Critical Infrastructure Symposium. (2012). *The CIP Report, 10*(12), 2.

U.S. Department of Homeland Security. (2006). *National infrastructure protection plan*.

U.S. Department of Homeland Security. (2008). *National infrastructure protection plan: Education and training assessment report and implementation plan*.

U.S. Department of Homeland Security. (2009). *National infrastructure protection plan*.

ENDNOTES

[1]   While many have contributed to this effort, special thanks must be given to Ms. Devon Hardy, former CIP/HS Education Program Manager.

2   Several institutions elected not to share syllabi due to university policy and intellectual property concerns. Syllabi were also unavailable for new courses, courses under modification, and courses available only on student demand.

3   The original Bloom's Taxonomy, developed by Benjamin Bloom in 1956, was revised in the 1990's by one of his students. The CI HEI utilizes the revised version, or Revised Bloom's Taxonomy, which uses verbs instead of nouns to categorize learning domains.

4   Cases were developed by Sarah Miller Beebe, CIP/HS Senior Fellow and President, Ascendant Analytics, LLC.

5   Presidential Policy Directive 21 further "changes the lexicon by using critical infrastructure security and resilience in place of critical infrastructure protection…The new terminology supports the move toward a more comprehensive approach to overall national preparedness, of which critical infrastructure security and resilience are major components" (Review and Revision of the NIPP, p. 34114). Accordingly, the project team is also updating the curriculum to reflect this change.

6   LTC Steven Hart, Ph.D. will co-lead this workshop.

Chapter 9
An Examination of Challenges Faced by First Responders in the Midst of Disaster

Terri Adams
Howard University, USA

EXECUTIVE SUMMARY

The ineluctable threat of future natural and manmade disasters makes it imperative to advance the understanding of key issues that first responders face in the midst of disasters, and to develop meaningful strategies for preparing them for disaster response. The potential conflicts between professional and personal responsibilities that first responders may face in responding to an incident can represent a distinctive feature of a catastrophic event. This project examined the issues of role conflict and resilience among first responders who have participated in major disaster events. Answers to the project's research questions provide an understanding of the human dynamics experienced by first responders when they are personally impacted by a disaster. This work advances the mission of the Science and Technology Directorate of the Department of Homeland Security (DHS) by providing information needed for advancing the development of simulation models and effective training curricula to assist first responders in their quest for preparing and responding to future disaster events.

DOI: 10.4018/978-1-4666-5946-9.ch009

ORGANIZATION BACKGROUND

The Principle Investigator (PI) for this project is an Associate Professor of Criminology in the Department of Sociology and Criminology at Howard University. Howard University is considered the nation's top-ranked historically black college or university. The main campus, located in Washington, DC, houses the undergraduate and graduate programs, Howard hospital, medical school, and dental school. The university also has three additional campuses that include: the School of Divinity, the Law School, and the Beltsville Center of Climate Systems Observations. Howard University is a comprehensive research university, with a commitment to educating youth for leadership and service to our nation and the global community. The Carnegie Foundation classifies Howard University as a "Doctoral Research University-Extensive." It is one of only 88 institutions, one of only 25 private institutions, and the only historically black college/university with this designation.

SETTING THE STAGE

The Department of Homeland Security (DHS) began offering Summer Research Team opportunities to faculty members at Minority Serving Institutions (MSI) in 2005. This program provides an avenue for MSI faculty to engage in research germane to the mission of the DHS at one of the many Centers of Excellence that are supported by the agency. Selected faculty members are invited to bring with them up to two students to participate in their research endeavor; all participates are award a stipend to support their summer expenses. Faculty members can either select an independent topic that relates to the mission of their selected Center of Excellence, or participate in one of the pre-established research teams. The affiliation of this PI with DHS began with participation in this program.

During the summer of 2006, the PI worked at the Johns Hopkins' Preparedness and Catastrophic Event Response (PACER) Center of Excellence in Baltimore, Maryland. The research project undertaken for the DHS Summer Team Program was an independent project lead by the PI that focused to examining the challenges faced by first responders during disasters. While working with the PACER Center of Excellence, the PI was able to network with faculty members at the Johns Hopkins Division of Public Safety Leadership, and gain insights about public safety professionals, and fostered networking opportunities through these connections. This opportunity leaded to additional funding through DHS that supported the expansion of the project.

The additional DHS funding provided the resources necessary to expand the original research conducted during the PI's participation in the Summer Research

Team Program. The original study focused on the organizational challenges faced by the New Orleans Police Department during the Hurricane Katrina disaster. Findings from this work lead to focusing on issues that personally impacted police officers in New Orleans. Upon completion of this funding cycle, the PI solicited funds through PACER, and Howard University became one of their institutional partners. This funding allowed the project to include an analysis of the impact of Hurricane Katrina on the Gulfport Police Department (GPD) in Mississippi. The project then went on to receive additional funds through PACER to incorporate Santiago, Chile as a study site and expanded the range of responders that were being examined to include fire fighters and emergency medical personnel. The project then expanded to include an examination of some of the first responders impacted by Tōhoku earthquake and tsunami disasters in Japan. Details associated with the evolution of this work are explained below as case studies.

In addition to providing resources for conducting the research on first responder challenges and behaviors, a number of students were provided with opportunities. Students from underrepresented groups, as well as other students, were able to receive training and participate fully in the research process. The details associated with the student training are provided in the student training section below.

CASE DESCRIPTION 1

In the early spring of 2006, the PI applied for the DHS Summer Research Program, and was selected to participate in the program along with two Howard University students -- one graduate and one undergraduate (see Figure 1). The research team took up the task of examining an issue that received a great deal of coverage in the press, and remains an important issue for the security of the nation. Most of the nation's preparation, response, and recovery plans for potential man-made and natural catastrophic events presuppose that first responders will respond in the event of a disaster. However, media reports of neglect of duty among police officers in New Orleans during the Hurricane Katrina crisis challenge this assumption and force a conclusion that an examination of this issue is important. The New Orleans' crisis presented a unique opportunity to study what can be expected when those society relies upon in the midst of a disaster are personally impacted by the disaster. The project sought to examine the organizational challenges faced by this department during the Katrina crisis. This research was designed to build a foundation for understanding the divergent responses of law enforcement officers to the disaster. The research findings shed light on the nature and impact of the crisis on the organizational structure of the NOPD and on the response strategies employed by

Figure 1. Summer research team: Nicole Branch, Terri Adams, and Leigh Anderson

upper management to maintain the functions of the department during and after the height of the crisis.

Originally the project was met with skepticism by some of the scholars within the Division of Public Safety Leadership at Johns Hopkins. However, overtime the program of research was accepted and some of the scholars provided useful networking opportunities to the PI as well as useful insights regarding the research. During the summer the research team was able to travel to New Orleans to interview some of the top ranking officials with the NOPD. The officers proved to be advocates of the research and were open about their experiences during the Katrina crisis. The team also interviewed other professionals who had insights on the challenges faced by the department including a City Councilman and the person who was serving as the lead psychiatrist for NOPD. The PI was also able to interview the former Superintendent of NOPD, who was at the time serving as a Chief of Police with the Atlanta Police Department.

The collected data provided unique insights into the operational challenges posed by the Katrina disaster, and the internal struggles of the department. Hurricane Katrina presented New Orleans with a unique set of chaotic circumstances. The widespread impact of the disaster and particularly its impact on the infrastructure of the city, and the police department, underscore the chaotic and destructive nature of natural disasters. While law enforcement officers are the least likely to receive notoriety for their efforts during a disaster, they are often the first responders called to a scene, and they are expected to have significant involvement in disaster related activities (Wenger et al., 1989). The Katrina disaster was no exception. Regardless of the enormity of the situation, society expects the police to live up to their professional responsibilities. As Nylés (1996) states, "Society demands that the police shall function even in unexpected and dynamic situations" (p.23). However, the damages caused by the disaster to the infrastructure of the NOPD severely hampered the functions of this first responder agency during the Katrina disaster, and challenged their abilities to fully function as a department.

The research found that the media underreported the challenges faced by the NOPD during the Katrina crisis and instead focused on the aberrant behaviors of some of the officers. While there were instances of police misconduct and abandonment of duty, much of the media reported accounts of abandonment of duty were reported out of context. The findings also revealed that the interpersonal issues the officers faced during the crisis were in need of deconstruction for further examination to delve into the dynamics associated with their response to the Katrina disaster. While some of officers participated in police misconduct and a number left their post during the crisis, other officers suffered in silence from a number of challenges as a result of the disaster, and two committed suicide during the early days of the crisis.

Some of the findings suggested that additional research was necessary to understand the challenges faced by individuals within the department to assess what lead to the divergent responses of the officers. It was reasoned that the investigation of the interpersonal challenges faced during the disaster was germane to advancing society's understanding of the human dynamics experienced by first responders when they are personally impacted by a disaster. Additionally, the preliminary findings indicated that the response of law enforcement during a catastrophic event is highly informal and disconnected from other law enforcement agencies and responding entities. In an effort to fully understand the challenges faced by responders it was important to seek to continue the research to fully understand the informal networks. This quest to further the research was met with approval from DHS and follow-up funds were awarded to continue the work. This work was also supported by a small grant from PACER to support two graduate students.

CASE DESCRIPTION 2

This study, "Dilemma in the Midst of a Crisis: Case Study of the Divergent Responses of New Orleans Police Officers during the Hurricane Katrina Crisis" expanded the original research by examining factors that influenced the divergent responses of

NOPD law enforcement officers of all ranks during the Hurricane Katrina crisis. The first phase of the project, conducted in summer 2006, focused on the perspectives of those officer holding high-level management positions. The reported neglect of duty among the NOPD highlights an important concern that all future plans involving disaster management must address. Adequate preparation for future crisis events requires a better understanding of the critical issues that will impact the behavior of the first responders who are mostly relied upon in the midst of a crisis. Specific attention needs to address the dilemmas confronted by responders when they, responders and their families, are personally impacted by the very disaster to which they are expected to respond.

It was believed that the project contributed to the body of knowledge regarding human dilemmas that can affect the preparedness and response of law enforcement personnel to catastrophic events. Specifically, the project provided key data for three of PACER's research domains: Preparedness Theory and Practice, Response Networks, and Analysis Modeling and Simulation. The potential conflicts between professional and personal responsibilities that law enforcement personnel can face in responding to a catastrophic event can represent a distinctive feature of a catastrophic event. Planners and emergency program managers will be able to use the findings from this project for self-assessment and improved planning.

The new study extended the research project to patrol officers and first level management, and sought to answer the following questions: (1) What factors contributed to the "lapse of duty" during the Katrina disaster? (2) What coping strategies were employed by officers at the height of the disaster? and (3) What motivated adaptive responses despite the dilemmas and hardships faced at the height of the disaster? It was reasoned that answers to these questions would help advance society's understanding of the human dynamics experienced by first responders when they are personally impacted by a disaster; and advance the mission of the Science and Technology Directorate of the DHS by providing information needed to develop more accurate simulation models and more effective training curricula to reduce dereliction of duty in future disasters.

The project took a case study approach to examine the divergent responses of NOPD officers, and both quantitative and qualitative data was collected. Case study analysis allows researchers to investigate the real-life context of an observable phenomenon, and can utilize both quantitative and qualitative evidence (Yin, 2000). The quantitative component of this study used a questionnaire to capture data by posing reflective questions to assess the degree to which various factors impacted the divergent responses among the officers. Key concepts associated with response behavior in the midst of disaster were measured, these included, but are not limited to: (1) threat perceptions, (2) feelings of isolation, (3) coping mechanisms, (4) motivational factors, (5) major concerns emerged during the height of the disaster (e.g.

whereabouts of loved ones), (6) major problems encountered, (7) perceptions of crisis management strategies employed by NOPD, (8) perceptions of cohesiveness or isolation among personnel, and (9) perceptions of professional responsibility. Experienced professionals in law enforcement (JHU's Division of Public Safety Leadership) and experienced methodologists in the fields of sociology and psychology at Howard University were consulted in developing the questionnaire.

The instrument was administered to officers of all ranks, including those who were released from the department for neglecting their responsibilities during the crisis. The research team sought to have the instrument included with the in-service training program of NOPD. However, some of the instruments were administered during role call in the police districts across the city. Attempts were made to include the entire universe of officers (1,500); however, officers who joined the department after the crisis were excluded from this study.

While, the questionnaire yielded rich data, the study also included the collection of qualitative data through in-depth interviews with law enforcement officers of each rank. These interviews served to provide the study with an opportunity to probe greater into the research questions. The data provided much needed contextual information to the study.

While the project focused on the police officers that worked during the Hurricane Katrina crisis and were still on active duty during the time period of the data collection, the project also sought to include individuals who were released from the department, to complete a mail-survey. The department sanctioned offices that were accused of abandoning their post during the disaster. Many were suspended without pay, but those whose infractions were considered to be the most egregious were fired from the department. In total 51 NOPD employees were fired - 45 officers and six civilian employees - for post abandonment before or after Hurricane Katrina (MSNBC, 2005). It was believed that this group of offices could shed light on the depths of how the challenges faced caused them to leave their post for an extended period of time. However, this part of the project proved to be quite difficult and was not completed due to the complications associated with distributing the survey. The police department needed to protect the identity of officers who were released from the department, and other possible alternatives to reaching the officers (e.g. snowball sampling techniques) were not sought due to time and monetary constraints. While this element of the data would have added to the understanding of abandonment of duty among the officers, the data elements that were collected provided a sufficient source of data.

While not all of the targeted data was collected, the program of research was successful in meeting most of its objectives. The findings revealed that NOPD faced a great deal of organizational challenges that were a result of the damages caused by the storm which complicated the ability of the department to function based on normal operational protocols. The study also revealed that many of the officers were beset with personal challenges that caused them to experience conflict between their professional and family obligations. As one officer stated:

There was chaos, no communication. The situation was Hell - we were stuck in the hospital. Captain said before we go, we have to save the people, I didn't want to at first, but it was the best decision. The Captain was strong... Hardest part was not knowing where my family was...helping people but could not help my family.... police helped my Momma. (Adams et al., 2011)

Hence, these officers were dealing with heart wrenching situations that impacted the ability of many to function effectively during the disaster.

The findings for this project were presented to the Undersecretary of DHS and after the presentation the Undersecretary noted that the work of the project was important and should be continued. That recommendation prompted the PI to seek funding from PACER to expand the study to examine resilience and role conflict among the police officers in Gulfport, Mississippi. This quest for funding was approved and provided funds to extend the scope of the project.

CASE DESCRIPTION 3

This project "Divergent Responses in the Midst of a Disaster: Hurricane Katrina" specifically examined the challenges faced by law enforcement officers who become torn between preservation of self and family and their professional responsibilities in the midst of disaster. There was a dearth of contemporary literature examining the divergent responses of first responders in the midst of a crisis, as most of the previous literature presupposed that abandonment of duty among first responders was a non-issue; however the Katrina crisis challenged this assumption and brought to light the need for continued investigation into the challenges of first responders (Adams & Turner, 2014). This study addressed a gap in the literature by examining the factors that influenced the divergent responses of police officers in Gulfport Police Department (GPD) during the Hurricane Katrina crisis.

Similar to the reception the team experienced with NOPD, the GPD was also accepting of the research project. Teams members conducted a program of study similar to the one conducted with NOPD accept all of the kinks that were found in the survey design were worked out and adjusted for this project site. The study design also included personal interviews that were collected within months after the collection of the survey data.

Figure 2. Summer research fellow: Nishaun Battle, Howard University Ph.D. student

This program of research included Howard University students, PACER selected research fellow (see Figure 2), as well as research interns from other universities that worked with the PI during the summers of the project period (see student training section for more information). The research fellows diversified the research team, providing the team with additional perspectives on the research questions. The addition of the students from other universities slightly changed some of the inter-personal dynamics of the research team that extended the professional growth experience for all of the students.

The findings for this project proved to be quite interesting. It appears that the officers with the GPD experienced similar challenges as those of the NOPD, but their situational factors were different which impacted how the challenges were manifested. The findings suggested that the traditional definition of role conflict as it relates to first responder communities should extend beyond the expression of it through role abandonment (Adams & Turner, 2014). This and other findings prompted the PI to seek to expand the study to examine first responders within other cultural and disaster context. The team competed for additional funds through PACER and was awarded these funds to expand the study to include other first responders (i.e., fire fighters and emergency medical personnel) that have experienced major disasters.

CASE DESCRIPTION 4

This project "Examination of Resilience and Role Conflict among Police, Fire, and Emergency Medical Service Personnel in the Midst of Disaster" provided information on "what can be expected" from those whom society relies upon in the midst of a disaster -- police, fire and emergency medical service (EMS) personnel -- when they are personally impacted by the catastrophe to which they are expected to respond. Specifically, the project addresses the following research questions: (1) How were first responders impacted by role conflict during their previous disaster experience? (2) What issues and concerns impede professional responses? (3) What coping strategies are useful in fostering resilience among first responders at the height of a disaster? (4) What motivated adaptive responses despite the dilemmas and hardships faced at the height of the disaster? and (5) What issues may impede police, fire, and EMS personnel from responding to a future disaster? To address the research questions the study employed a mixed method approach utilizing quantitative and qualitative research methodologies. These methods included: (1) collection of archival data for background information; (2) collection of survey data; and (3) collection of face-to-face interview data.

The project examined the challenges faced by police, fire, and EMS personnel who served as first responders during the Hurricane Katrina crisis in New Orleans, Louisiana and Gulfport, Mississippi (2005), and the earthquake in Santiago, Chile (2010). Although data was collected already on the police officers in New Orleans and Gulfport, the project sought to collect data on the experiences of fire fighters and emergency medical personnel at these sites. The team was readily accepted to collect data on the additional first responders in New Orleans. On the other hand, the Gulfport site proved to be quite the challenge. After repeated attempts over the course of several months to connect with the head of the fire and emergency response department went unanswered, it was deemed necessary to drop this site from the study.

The reduction in the number of study sites allowed the team to consider alternative sites for data collection. During this time the nation experienced one of the worst tornado disasters -- the Super Tornado Outbreak of 2011. A total of 14 different states were impacted by the outbreak of tornadoes; but the number of deaths in Alabama accounted for 234 of the 316 deaths related to the storm, and Tuscaloosa, Alabama was particularly hit hard by the disaster. This led the PI to conduct a cursory analysis of the site to see if the impact of the disaster was comparable in scope to the Katrina disaster. The PI and two graduate students traveled to New Orleans to collect background information on the disaster and interviewed leaders of the first responder agencies. This investigation revealed that while the disaster resulted in a number of deaths and loss of property over a wide area, the scope of the damages did not cause the first responder agencies to endure the type of chaos and uncertainty experienced by the responders of the Katrina disaster. Hence, this site was not selected as a comparable study site.

While the PI was making decisions about whether or not to include Tuscaloosa, Alabama as a study, the possibility of examining the earthquake and tsunami disaster in Japan became acutely apparent. The size and scope of this disaster was comparable to the disaster experienced in Chile and the Katrina disaster. Hence, the PI sought approval to add this site to the study. In order, to add this study site, it was necessary to get approval from PACER and DHS officials to add this international site to the study.

As the team was waiting for approval to examine the Tōhoku earthquake and tsunami disaster, the PI, a former student, and a translator traveled to Santiago, Chile to collect data at this study site (see Figure 3). Making arrangements to collect data at this study site was a bit challenging as two issues had to be overcome, language differences and organizational differences. These challenges were met with hiring a former student as a consultant who spoke the language and was able to collect background information and establish contacts in Chile to seek approval for the study. Eventually she was able to set-up all of the logistical arrangements for the study. The Chilean officials were very cooperative and appeared to be honored that an American team of researchers were interested in understanding the nuances associated with their experiences with the disaster. While collecting data in Santiago, Chile, the team was made aware that one of the towns of major destruction needed to be included in the study, Constitución. This was not originally a part of the data collecting plans; however, after becoming aware of the level of devastation at this site, the team traveled to Constitución to interview members of the police department about their experiences with the disaster.

The data collection mission in Chile provided a unique experience for the team members. The team had to make quick on the spot decisions about data collecting plans that proved to be useful for the mission of the project. Adding this site to the study provided a unique international perspective to the project.

After several months of seeking approval to add Japan as a study site, the project was granted approval to add the site to the research project. Although there were language barriers associated with seeking approval for the study in Chile, the challenges of seeking approval in Japan were even more daunting because of the 12 to 13 hour time difference. However, the PI has a graduate student from Japan who was interested in conducting research on a similar topic for her dissertation. Consequently, the student joined the research team and provided invaluable assistance to the project. She was able to make contacts with first responder agencies, gain approval for the study, and set-up all of the logistical arrangements. She also participated fully in the collection of data for the project, as she served as an interpreter during the trip (see Figure 4).

The process of collecting data in Japan was very similar to the experience of collecting data in Chile. The Japanese officials were very open and willing to share

Figure 3. Research consultant Yasmine Detrés with members of the Carabinero Gope Force

Figure 4. Howard University student Makiko Toge-Lawson surveying damages caused by the Tōhoku earthquake and tsunami

their experiences, and similar to the officials in Chile they appeared to be honored to have an American researcher interested in collecting data on the challenges they faced during and after the disaster. The experience of going to Japan also provided a unique cultural experience and expanded the scope of the research to include two different international perspectives on the challenges faced by first responders during disasters.

The addition of the international study sites provided the project with the unique ability to examine how first responders deal with the challenges associated with disasters within different cultural contexts. The preliminary findings of this study show that there are both similarities and differences in how first responders across the various agencies and countries deal with organizational and individual challenges.

Project Summary

In the event of a manmade or natural disaster, police, fire, and emergency medical service (EMS) personnel are essential front-line first responders. The ability of police, fire, and EMS agencies to provide adequate services is contingent upon critical response personnel working and functioning in an efficient manner. Although trained to respond under pressure, first responders are susceptible to the same fear induced cognitive processes that are associated with human response to extreme stress. The degree to which individuals can effectively respond to threats is heavily influenced by the amount of fear elicited by the threatening stimuli (Leventhal & Niles, 1964; Leventhal & Watts, 1966). Research has shown that being reminded of our own mortality can lead to negative decision-making and behavioral responses (Arndt, Greenberg, Solomon, Pyszczynski, & Schimel, 1999; Pyszczynski, Greenberg, & Solomon, 1999). Widespread impact of a disaster can lead to anxiety about the safety and wellbeing of loved ones, leading to role conflict. These concerns can pose a real challenge to disaster response, and this program of research explored the issue of what can be expected when those society relies upon in the midst of a disaster are personally impacted by the disaster in which they are expected to respond to professionally.

The project has been able to successfully address the major research questions, and additional research questions relevant to the security of the nation have grown out of this work. The data from the project is informing the development of a planning and decision support tool, that will be useful for local officials, State and Federal emergency planners and managers, as well as non-government and private security disaster planners. The PI has established a number of contacts that have provided useful information. The PI is hoping to solicit additional funds from other resources to provide a Web-based platform to make this information available to first responder communities.

While the overall program of research was successful, the project did experience a few challenges. One of the major issues faced by the project was the challenge of getting all of the study sites on board to participate in the project. First responder communities are sometimes closed communities, and they can be difficult to navigate. As noted earlier one of the targeted agencies appeared not to be receptive to the program of research, even after repeated attempts to try to forge a relationship with the leadership of the organization. In response to this, the PI adjusted the program of research to accommodate a new study site. It should be noted that all of the other targeted agencies were open to participating in the research and these agencies are greatly appreciated for the work they do and their willingness to share their challenges to help improve preparedness, response, and recovery plans for other first responders. The agency leaders at the international study sites were particularly hospitable and open to sharing information with the project team.

Additionally, the time spent in the study sites provided the project team members with invaluable experiences that are measurable beyond data collection metrics. The ability to travel provided the opportunity to get a sense of the massive nature of the disaster that country experienced, and to place into context how the disaster impacted the infrastructure, geology, and social and cultural dynamics of the various study sites. It is one thing to view stories about it through the media but quite another to see the land where the destruction took place and to hear peoples survival stories. This background information provided the team members with a great depth of knowledge about the nuances associated with the disasters and the impact of these events on the organizational features of the first responder agencies and the individuals who work as first responders.

Project Products

The study's findings have been disseminated through: conference presentations, conference papers, journal article publications, as well as the forthcoming book *Policing During Disasters*. It should be noted that the book is being co-authored by the PI and the former student mentioned earlier in this chapter, who is now a Ph.D. candidate specializing in Emergency Management at Ohio State University. An additional product that is in the works includes a Website designed to share best practices with the first responder communities. The PI is also seeking additional funds to expand the work to include the development of a theoretical and mathematical model for computer simulations.

Student Training

The funding for this work provided opportunities to a number of students. A total of 11 Howard University students have been trained to conduct research through their participation in the PACER project, seven graduate students and 4 undergraduate students. One of the Howard University students who participated in the program of research was involved as a research fellow. For three years PACER allowed students from the PIs home institution to compete for a research fellowship that allowed the selected person to work with the PI over the course of the summer. The PI also participated in DHS's Summer Internship Program that paired undergraduate students and graduate students up with volunteer PIs associated with DHS Centers of Excellence. Three students from other universities, including the University of Puerto Rico, the University of Maryland, and the University of Chicago participated in the research project. The students who participated in the research were provided the opportunity to expand their research skills, and some of the students were afforded the opportunity to travel and collect data with the PI to various study sites.

All of the students were able to participate in a number of the project's phases, including: the development of the survey instrument design, literature reviews, data collection, manuscript production, presentations, and proposal writing. Most of these students participated in the program of research during the summer months. Each summer the assembled team of students ranged from three to five students, and each team was charged with a set of responsibilities to be accomplished for the summer.

In addition to encouraging the students to gain research and professional skills during their participation in the project, the PI also encouraged the students to take advantage of the resources made available to those who live and work in the nation's capital, including visiting some of the nation's repositories of research and information (see Figure 5). The PI sought to provide the students with opportunities for personal and professional growth. Originally the PI did all of the training and monitoring of student activities, but as the project grew in size and scope so did the experience and knowledge base of the core group of students who participated in the project, and student lead training began to take place. The students' were all managed by the PI but those who remained with the project over an extended period of time, began to serve as first line supervisors for the project.

Of all the opportunities provided to the students, the most rewarding for them appeared to be the hands on training they received with data collection. As previously noted, the project required the collection of two types of data, qualitative and quantitative data. Each of these data sources was pertinent to the objectives of the project and student participation was necessary in order to complete the full range of objectives. Hence, many of the students were trained on how to develop survey questions and administer surveys to study participants. The students were also trained

Figure 5. Howard University student Milinika Turner, with University of Maryland students Anna Burton and Mark Jubar at the National Library of Congress

on how to conduct face-to-face interviews and deal with participants' reactions to survey questions. The multi-method approach to collecting data allowed the students to be trained on these approaches to research and to learn how to integrate these sources in social science research to create a comprehensive view of the phenomenon being examined.

While the students appeared to appreciate gaining experience on various aspects of the research process, the most cherished was participation in collecting face-to-face interview data. Many of the students talked about connecting with the study participants, and feeling empowered from the experience. Ultimately, these data sources proved to be the most interesting to the students. An additional benefit to the project for the students was the ability for many of them to travel to participate in the data collection. The project team took several trips to New Orleans and Gulfport to interview key stakeholders, distribute and collect surveys, and conduct face-to-face interviews. The team also traveled to Tuscaloosa, Alabama to survey the damaged areas of the communities impacted by the super outbreak of tornadoes that occurred in 2011 and to interview heads of first responder agencies. On this trip the students seemed particularly fascinated with the ability to see the damages of the disaster and to learn about the first responder efforts immediately after the tornado outbreaks.

In addition, to the domestic travel, a couple of the students were able to travel to the international study sites of Chile and Japan to collect data. These opportunities provided them with the ability to experience different cultures outside of their own and to see how research can be conducted within a different cultural framework. It is believed that travel provides intellectual growth and stimulates the imagination (Stone & Petrick, 2013). The students appeared to be empowered by their experiences and their growth as professional social science researchers was evident in the work that they produced as a result of their experiences.

Another rewarding component associated with working on the project was the ability to receive support to attend and participate in professional conferences. A few of the students presented the study's findings at a variety of different conferences and first responder workshops. These opportunities provided them with the ability to develop and fine-tune professional presentation skills and effective networking skills. Participation in professional conferences and workshops provided the students with the ability to see how the work applies to academics and professionals in the fields of homeland security, criminal justice, and emergency management.

Lastly, several of the students were afforded the ability to assist the PI in drafting proposals for funding and manuscripts for publication. This provided them with the ability to experience firsthand how an idea gets transformed into a product that can be used to solicit funds or add to the existing body of literature. Three of the students have been co-authors on selected publications, and other students are currently working with the PI to complete additional manuscripts for publication.

Additionally, one of the original undergraduate students affiliated with the project was awarded a DHS scholarship that provided her with five years of funding for graduate school. This student is currently scheduled to defend her dissertation in Public Administration, and is currently working in the field of homeland security. Another of the original students who worked on the project as an undergraduate is in the process of completing her Ph.D. Her MA thesis examined the role of social support as a buffer to occupational stress after a disaster.

CONCLUSIONS AND RECOMMENDATIONS

As a side note, it is important to share my experiences of being the PI on a DHS related project, as it may shed light on the process of conducting research for other scholars. As an African American woman, I find that people are surprised to see a woman conducting research in a male dominated enterprise. It also may be the case that they are surprised to see an African American women in this position, but I believe my gender has played a larger role in the process of conducting research than my race. While some women may have been met with hostility while operating in a male dominated profession, this has not been my experience. I believe that on some level my gender allows people to relax their guard when being interviewed for the project.

It has also been brought to my attention that some of the officials at the international sites were pleased to see a woman investigating issues that are relevant to them as it is not the norm within their culture. My advice to anyone collecting sensitive data is to approach your subjects with respect and with an open mind to see them beyond being subjects in your research study, but to embrace the experience of seeing their humanity. I cannot say that my gender accounts for the success I have had with conducting this work, but I do believe that it did not serve as a hindrance.

ACKNOWLEDGMENT

The author would like to thank DHS and PACER for providing grant funds for the program of research. A special thank you goes out to Matthew Clark the Director of the Science and Technology Directorate, Office of University Programs at DHS who has been encouraging; and Desiree Linson of DHS who was particularly encouraging during the beginning stages of the project. Additionally, I should also acknowledge the hard work of many of the students who worked with me on the program of research over the years. Two students in particular stand out as exemplary team members who appeared to be as dedicated to the project as the PI -- Ms. Leigh Anderson and Ms. Milinika Turner, who are both nearing the completion of their doctorates (see student training session above). It is also important to thank the first responders who participated in this program of research, as their willingness to lend their voices to the project is what has made this endeavor possible.

REFERENCES

Adams, T., Anderson, Turner, & Armstrong. (2011). Coping through a disaster: Lessons from Hurricane Katrina. *Journal of Homeland Security and Emergency Management, 8*(1), 19. doi:10.2202/1547-7355.1836

Adams, T., & Anderson, L. (Forthcoming). *Policing during natural disasters.* Boulder, CO. *FirstForumPress.*

Arndt, J., Greenberg, J., Solomon, S., Pyszczynski, T., & Schimel, J. (1999). Creativity and terror management: Evidence that creative activity increases guilt and social projection following mortality salience. *Journal of Personality and Social Psychology, 77,* 19–32. doi:10.1037/0022-3514.77.1.19

Leventhal, H., & Niles, P. (1965). Persistence of influence for varying durations of exposure to threat stimuli. *Psychological Reports, 16,* 223–233. doi:10.2466/pr0.1965.16.1.223 PMID:14283967

Leventhal, H., & Watts, J. C. (1966). Sources of resistance to fear-arousing communications on smoking and lung cancer. *Journal of Personality, 34,* 155–175. doi:10.1111/j.1467-6494.1966.tb01706.x PMID:5939211

Nylés, L. (1996). Disaster prevention and management. *Bradford, 5*(5), 23-25.

Pyszczynski, T., Greenberg, J., & Solomon, S. (1999). A dual-process model of defense against conscious and unconscious death-related thoughts: An extension of terror management theory. *Psychological Review, 106,* 835–845. doi:10.1037/0033-295X.106.4.835 PMID:10560330

Stone, M., & Petrick. (2013). The educational benefits of travel experiences a literature review. *Journal of Travel Research, 52*(6), 731–744. doi:10.1177/0047287513500588

Wenger, D. E. Quarantelli, & Dynes. (1989). Disaster analysis: Local emergency management offices and arrangements. Newark, DE: University of Delaware, Disaster Research Center.

Yin, R. (2000). *Case study research: Design and methods*. Thousand Oaks, CA: Sage Publications.

KEY TERMS AND DEFINITIONS

DHS: Department of Homeland Security.
GPD: Gulfport Police Department.
NOPD: New Orleans Police Department.
PACER: Preparedness and Catastrophic Event Response Center of Excellence.
PSL: Johns Hopkins Division of Public Safety Leadership.

Chapter 10
DHS Minority Serving Institution (MSI) Programs:
Research Linked to DHS Centers of Excellence (COE)

Kevin A. Peters
Morgan State University, USA

Nira C. Taru
Morgan State University, USA

EXECUTIVE SUMMARY

This chapter highlights seven (7) DHS programs/research that involved faculty and students at Morgan State University, a Minority Serving Institution (MSI) that was linked to a DHS Center for Excellence. The programs were developed in part from partnerships and collaborative efforts from researchers and principal investigators at Morgan State University and several DHS Centers of Excellence. Researchers from Morgan State University submitted summaries of their DHS-funded programs and activities. In addition, information was gathered from DHS Websites pertaining to their collaborative work with a DHS Center of Excellence (COE). This chapter emphasizes the importance of collaborative research and programs that support the overall mission of DHS in providing opportunities for MSIs to work with COEs in DHS priority research areas. These efforts have enhanced faculty as well as students at Morgan State University with regard to education, research, professional development, and training related to a DHS priority research.

DOI: 10.4018/978-1-4666-5946-9.ch010

ORGANIZATION BACKGROUND

Morgan State University is the premier public urban research university in Maryland, known for its excellence in teaching, intensive research, effective public service and community engagement. Morgan prepares diverse and competitive graduates for success in a global, interdependent society. The University serves the community, region, state, nation, and world as an intellectual and creative resource by supporting, empowering and preparing high-quality, diverse graduates to lead the world. The University offers innovative, inclusive, and distinctive educational experiences to a broad cross section of the population in a comprehensive range of disciplines at the baccalaureate, master's, doctoral, and professional degree levels. Through collaborative pursuits, scholarly research, creative endeavors, and dedicated public service, the University gives significant priority to addressing societal problems, particularly those prevalent in urban communities.

SETTING THE STAGE

The Department of Homeland Security (DHS) Office of University Programs (OUP) attempts to link and facilitate the expertise of the country's colleges and universities to address pressing homeland security issues and needs through its program activities. With this overall goal in mind, the Minority Serving Institutions (MSI) Programs attempts to ensure the diversity of America is reflected in the future of Homeland Security science and technology work force. Centers of Excellence engage the academic community to deliver tools, technologies, knowledge products, training and talent to enhance the Department's homeland security capabilities. The OUP education programs engage, educate and support academically high achieving students as well as early career faculty and other individuals toward choosing Homeland Security-Science, Technology, Engineering, and Mathematics (HS-STEM) related careers. It is with these efforts that Morgan State University and other MSIs are able to support the mission of DHS. Table 1. is a summary capsule of collaborative efforts with a DHS, COE and Morgan State University, a Minority Serving Institution. It is important to note that the Science and Technology (S&T) Directorate has strongly supported collaborative efforts between the Minority Serving Institutions (MSIs) and the Centers for Excellence Program through summer programs and various research initiatives.

Table 1. Summary capsule of collaborative efforts between Morgan State and a DHS COE

MSI	COE	DHS ACTIVITY	MSI Faculty	OUTCOME
Morgan State	VACCINE	Visual Analytics	Timothy Akers	Student Internship/Training
Morgan State	START/ PACER	Natural Disasters/ Terrorism	Randoph Rowell	Summer Research Experience
Morgan State	IDS-UAC	Bioterrorism	Asamoah Nkwanta	Summer Research Experience
Morgan State	IDS	Bioterrorism	Asamoah Nkwanta	Summer Research Experience South African Experience
Morgan State	CCICADA	Terrorism	Manoj K. Jha	Summer Research Experience
Morgan State	OUP	DHS Career Pathway	Kevin Peters Timothy Akers	DHS Career Information
Morgan State	VACCINE	Visual Analytics	Timothy Akers Kevin Peters	. Faculty Research/Student Research

CASE DESCRIPTION 1: BUILDING A STEM INTERDISCIPLINARY RESEARCH ENTERPRISE FOR STEM RESEARCH TRAINING AND TECHNOLOGY TRANSFER (MORGAN STATE UNIVERSITY AND VACCINE)

Since 2008, Morgan State University (MSU) has worked toward building on the resources provided by the *Department of Homeland Security's Scientific Leadership Award grant*. The following is a synopsis of activities that have yielded tremendous outcomes based on important resources provided by DHS. Thanks to the advice and input provided by program officers at DHS in the Office of University Programs, Morgan State University has been instrumental in advancing significant outcomes in the fulfillment of grant opportunities.

In 2011, MSU initiated a dialogue with Purdue University, a DHS Center of Excellence (COE) – "*VACCINE*." This introduction resulted in the establishment of a formal memorandum of Understanding (MOU) that was developed and signed by senior administrators across both institutions. The purpose of the MOU was to support collaborative research efforts between institutions with particular focus on student training in *visual analytics*. What further developed through this collaboration was MSU's first remote student training program in visual analytics, where fifteen (15) Morgan State Interdisciplinary STEM students studied and received intensive training during the summer. The students received their training at Purdue's DHS supported VACCINE Center in how to incorporate visual analytics and data analysis in science, technology engineering, and mathematics (STEM) fields of study. MSU students also learned how to apply their training to development of technologies that could benefit DHS priority research areas.

The intellectual growth and technical skills development of the students upon their return from Purdue University's VACCINE Center was nothing short of extraordinary. They returned to MSU where they transferred their knowledge, skills, and training to Baltimore City Public STEM high school teachers. During the summer of 2011, MSU hosted a DHS Summer Professional Development Institute to train Baltimore Public School teachers in the area of STEM content and research. Teachers learned about DHS priority research and were engaged in the utilization of visual analytics and data analysis in the preparation of STEM lessons. The outcome of this Institute was an innovative way of teaching and training by having MSU students that just returned from Purdue University's VACCINE Center served as facilitators / trainers to public school teachers in data analysis and visualization. The teachers in turn used their knowledge base of instructional delivery practices to train MSU students with regard to STEM pedagogy.

An important goal of the professional development activities was for teachers to apply visual analytics and data analysis in their instructional strategies in teaching students about STEM research. The training resulted in cohorts of teachers developing lesson plans in which they made presentation at the end of the Institute. The strategy to employ students as catalysts in training the teachers was developed and conceptualized by Drs. Tim Akers (P.I.) and Kevin Peters, Director of the Center for Excellence in Mathematics & Science Education (CEMSE).

The Summer Institute also included faculty from Chemistry and Bioinformatics. Dr. Angela Winstead, Professor of Chemistry faculty, provided innovative research strategies that were included in STEM research curriculum development. Dr. Winstead in 2011 from DHS support was cited in the authorship of a book chapter entitled, *"Application of Microwave Assisted Organic Synthesis to the Development of Near-IR Cyanine Dye Probes"* (Winstead, Williams, Zhang, McLean, & Oyaghire, 2010).

An additional session in Professional Development Institute was led by Dr. Ric Ledbetter, Director of Educational Technologies, and his associate from The Athena Group, Gainesville, Florida is another DHS supported project site. Dr. Ledbetter was instrumental in introducing to teachers and students simulation modules for curricula and science fairs kits. These modules were also supported by a DHS supported project. An outcome of this collaborative partnership between MSU and The Athena Group has been the development and utilization of science fair research kits that assist students in developing quality research projects that have been submitted to the Morgan State University Science-Engineering-Mathematics Fair held annually.

CASE DESCRIPTION 2: ASSISTING TARGETED POPULATIONS TO PREPARE FOR NATURAL DISASTERS AND TERRORISM (START / PACER CENTERS AND MORGAN STATE UNIVERSITY SCHOOL OF PUBLIC HEALTH AND POLICY)

Natural disasters are random events that can affect the lives of diverse populations globally. There is a growing need to educate low-income populations and communities on how to react prior to, during and after a natural disaster. In addition to the potential for unexpected terrorist events, the need to educate underrepresented populations is paramount for their survival. Addressing special populations' emergency preparedness and first response needs, the research team from Morgan State University, consisting of Assistant Professor Dr. Randolph Rowel and doctoral candidates Shanita Wooten and Lakaisha Barber, spent time during at the START Center of Excellence to analyze the problem and to come up with research strategies for addressing the need. Dr. Rowel is also an investigator with PACER Center for Excellence. The focus of the research has been to further develop the Special Populations Response to Emergency Health Threats Survey (SPRETS) Instrument. This unique instrument assists health departments and emergency management agencies in measuring a community's levels of understanding, attitudes and behavior associated with appropriate preparedness, recovery, and response to natural disasters. The target audiences addressed in this study were Spanish speaking and African American populations that have limited knowledge on how to respond to natural disasters.

An expert panel of researchers from START and the team from Morgan State University has worked to increase the reliability and validity of SPRETS instrument. It was discovered that key factors to increasing the validity of the SPRETS instrument was to identify the impact of such variables as: family / personal income, educational level, gender and geographic location of other "non-special-population" groups. An additional factor for enhancing SPRETS has been identifying the differences between preparedness for potential terrorist events and natural disasters.

As a follow-up to the summer research, the team will develop a more rigorous research design to assist, political and community leaders and educators in utilizing the SPRETS instrument in understanding the knowledge, attitudes and behavior of a more diverse and larger sample population. They participated in a START Annual Conference and an 8-day DHS Summer Workshop on Teaching Terrorism at Morehouse College in Atlanta. In Atlanta, the team toured the Centers for Disease Control and Prevention to learn more about CDC's role in terrorism preparedness, response, and recovery. Further activities include the publication of a manuscript entitled, "Reflections of Isabel and Katrina: A low-income perspective."

CASE DESCRIPTION 3: CUTTING THROUGH THE NOISE TO DETECT BIOTERROR EVENTS (IDS-UAC CENTER - MORGAN STATE UNIVERSITY WITH HOWARD UNIVERSITY)

Associated with threats of bioterrorism in the United State are incidences of disease and are considered a part of numerous homeland security issues. While attempting to minimize human injury and the loss of life resulting from any kind of contamination, an early detection process is vital for the overall safety and health of injured victims. A major challenge connected to early detection is differentiating true signals of an outbreak versus the decrypting noise detected by current surveillance procedures. Attaining more efficient early-detection signals that "bi-passes the noise" has been the focus of two research teams from MSIs that collaborated with the Center for Discrete Mathematics and Theoretical Computer Science (DIMACS) at Rutgers University, a DHS IDS-UACs Center of Excellence member.

A team from Howard University was led by Dr. Abdul-Aziz Yakubu, and a second team from Morgan State University, was led by Dr. Asamoah Nkwanta, partnered with DIMACS to explore the theoretical effects of entropy in resolving this homeland security issue. Entropy for this project was defined as measuring the uncertainty associated with a particular variable signal and the amount of information noise. The two teams and DIMACS researcher Dr. Nina Fefferman hypothesized that the signal to noise ratio will increase during an outbreak. If the increase in this ratio is large enough to be measured, this could indicate that an outbreak is occurring. The results of this study could improve the speed in which outbreaks are detected. A highlight of the teams' experience was a trip to a conference in South Africa that addressed the mathematical modeling of infectious diseases. The conference gave the Howard and Morgan State research teams the opportunity to share their research with a global audience, while gaining additional knowledge associated with modeling of diseases. Howard students involved in the research included Ashley Crump and Devroy McFarlane. Students from Morgan State engaged in the research included Nakeya Williams and Anthony Ogbuka. The student researchers gained invaluable knowledge of challenging issues facing the country linked to homeland security.

CASE DESCRIPTION 4: ANSWERS TO U.S. HEALTH THREATS FOUND IN AFRICAN STUDENTS IN SCIENCE AND TECHNOLOGY MINORITY-SERVING INSTITUTIONS

Student researchers from Morgan State University and Howard University gained knowledge and understanding of HIV and tuberculosis as an epidemic crisis in parts of Africa gained additional knowledge on how to prevent naturally-occurring and bioterror threats in the U.S. This project was a part of a DHS sponsored Summer Research Program for Minority Serving Institutions. Howard University students, Ashley Crump and Devroy McFarlane, and Morgan State's Anthony Ogbuka and Nakeya Williams joined students and researchers in South Africa to address disease spread in Africa. The students developed mathematical models to assess the spread of disease and examined data linked to preventing future disease outbreaks.

Several diseases of interest included SARS and the avian flu in addition to bio-terrorism threats. Student researchers identified several issues that included privacy concerns and inconsistencies across groups in health data reported. These issues posed, created gaps in data that created "noise" in the data and analysis. Mathematical calculations were applied to account for the noise and the existence of an outbreak. Abdul-Aziz Yakubu of Howard and Asamoah Nkwanta of Morgan State guided the research of the students. Nina Fefferman of the Center for Discrete Mathematics and Theoretical Computational Science at Rutgers University assisted the team in creating algorithms to analyze and the proposed research problems. The Center is linked with the Center for Dynamic Data Analysis, part of the DHS Institute for Discrete Sciences Center of Excellence.

In Africa, research teams partnered together that included fifteen (15) American student researchers with corresponding numbers of African students. Discussions took place that addressed government policies and procedures associated with the spread diseases to epidemic proportions. The knowledge and information gained from the experience was valuable as the U.S. is challenged by unknown diseases and the ease of diseases passing across borders via humans and animals. Observation were made by a Morgan graduate of the Public Health Department their African peer students were using mathematical and computational skills to address public health issues.

Another Morgan student suggested the modeling experience helped the Morgan team with their research. The consensus view was that the African professors demonstrated how their life was linked to the research. The student research teams achieved promising outcomes while at Rutgers, and the research continued as they sought to establish techniques to detect disease spread as rapidly as possible. This information was collected and summarized from an article written by Carl Blesch, Rutgers University.

CASE DESCRIPTION 5: DHS SUMMER FACULTY AND STUDENT RESEARCH

In the Summer of 2005, a Morgan State University research team led by Dr. Manoj K. Jha, Professor of Civil Engineering and three undergraduate civil engineering students Kimberly Freeman, Michael Jones, and Turkessa Parker, were competitively selected by the Office of University Programs in the DHS's Science and Technology Directorate to participate in its Summer Faculty and Student Research Team Program. The Morgan State University team worked on a conceptual research project to model uncertainty associated with terrorist strikes using an innovative probabilistic technique called Bayesian Networks. In order to develop a robust model that would have real-world applicability it was critical that the model was tested with various group-based and event-based terrorism datasets. In subsequent years, Dr. Jha extended the Bayesian network application for developing simulation models for understanding the trends of terrorism and other extreme events. In April 2011, he led another research team consisting of a doctoral student Francis Udenta and faculty research associate Dr. Min Wook Kang, and made a presentation titled, "A Dynamic Capacitated Arc Routing Problem for Optimal Evacuation Strategies in Disasters: Formulation and Solution Algorithms " at a research retreat of another DHS Center of Excellence entitled, "Special Event: Command, Control, and Interoperability Center for Advanced Data Analysis (CCICADA)" located at the Rutgers University. The research retreat was held at Morgan State University located in Baltimore, Maryland.

CASE DESCRIPTION 6: VISUAL ANALYTICS FOR SCIENCE AND TECHNOLOGY AT A MINORITY SERVING INSTITUTION (VAST MSI) – INCREASING THE PIPELINE FOR STEM RESEARCH IN PRODUCT DEVELOPMENT AND DHS WORKFORCE OPPORTUNITIES

This current project for the Department of Homeland Security (DHS) builds on a previous DHS awarded grant (2008-2011) to Morgan State University entitled "*Increasing the Pipeline of STEM Majors Among Minority Serving Institutions*." This recently completed project was directed toward interdisciplinary STEM students and early career faculty with a specific focus on training, course development, and research in the areas of database security (cybersecurity), advance programming, biovisualization, bioinformatics, and scientific visualization. Additionally, the previous project helped to develop a foundation for research in the areas of wireless data acquisition systems for video, voice, and data sensors from diverse sensor sources that efficiently acquire and disseminate data from simple sensor networks and combines these data for analysis.

This project builds on past research by introducing a new cohort of students and early career faculty to new tools, techniques and technologies in advanced data analysis and visual analytics, both within the university and through our DHS

Center of Excellence partner, Purdue University's *Visual Analytics for Command, Control, and Interoperability Environments* (VACCINE) Center VACCINE Center. This project is in the process of interpreting large volumes of data while, at the same time, developing innovative ways of examining complex terabytes of data that can lead to new opportunity for product development technologies critical to DHS and the marketplace.

The overarching goals of this project are twofold: 1) introduce STEM undergraduate students to research opportunities and curriculum that are focused on visualization informatics; and 2) to cultivate early career STEM faculty in DHS related research linked to DHS Centers of Excellences (COEs). Based on these overarching goals, the VAST MSI project will address five (5) measurable objectives that are described below and linked to the overarching goals:

- Recruit and train 5-10 STEM undergraduate students per year that will have a concentration in homeland security;
- Develop curriculum for STEM majors with a concentration in homeland security specializing in visual analytics and data analysis (visual informatics);
- Established DHS research priorities and faculty training linked to visualization informatics in partnership with DHS COE (VACCINE / Purdue Univ.);
- Develop and train early career faculty in the use of new technologies acquired through VAST with senior faculty collaboration; and
- Develop and acquire the visualization technology necessary for continued research, instruction, faculty and student development, and product development.

Based on the two overarching goals and five measurable objectives, the VAST MSI project team estimates outcomes resulting from this project over the course of phase 1 and phase 2 will result in the following:

- Increase the knowledge and awareness of STEM students who are more highly trained in DHS priority research areas. Specifically, this planned outcome is targeted for students who are recruited will be provided with specialized training and hands-on development of DHS priority research areas in visualization and data analysis.
- Develop a new STEM curriculum that focuses on DHS priority research areas, such as cybersecurity as it relates to visual analytics and data analysis. The awareness of students will be significantly enhanced through this curriculum development.
- Strengthen the working relationship with a DHS Centers of Excellence (VACCINE). This planned outcome builds upon and strengthens the relation-

ship with a highly sophisticated COE, such as Purdue University's VACCINE Center in which Morgan State has been working hard to expand.

- Increase the skill set and advanced resources for faculty in the area of advanced visual analytics and data analysis. Students as well as other early career faculty and mid-career faculty interested in changing their research focus will benefit from being able to use and develop new tools and technologies in this area of research and data analytics.
- Develop an advanced state-of-the-art visual analytics laboratory. Based on work currently underway MSU has identified on-campus space in which visualization technology can be deployed and incorporated into existing infrastructure.

Undergraduate Student Recruitment and Retention (Objective 1)

To date, Morgan State University has been instrumental in recruiting four (4) top interdisciplinary STEM students that include majors in computer science, civil engineering, biology, and economics. These students were the first cohort to be selected during the first half of the year through a rigorous selection process. Given the timing from the initial award, other competitive students have been placed in various academic and research programs. Aside from these challenges, the VAST project team, during Phase 1, was instrumental in identifying the four highly competent and competitive students. During the second half of year 1 award, the project team will select a second cohort of interdisciplinary STEM students.

During this first year, the students selected as DHS scholars have undergone training in DHS priority areas. They have met with early career faculty and the project team for whom they will be working alongside. During this process, the students were also part of the DHS Pathways Conference where they received over the course of three days extensive training in DHS priority areas nationally. During the beginning of summer, students underwent further training with Drs. Akers and Peters, along with a few of the original 15 students that were previously supported by DHS. The on-campus training they received over the course of a week focused on DHS priority projects, informatics, database development, basic statistics, the use of EXCEL as a data analysis tool, and protocol while studying at Purdue University's DHS Center of Excellence, VACCINE. The preliminary on-campus training helped to serve as the foundation for the training the students received while at Purdue University.

During a two-week intense training, the students enhanced their education through lectures and hands-on projects that examined areas that included: analytical reasoning and critical thinking, data transformation and statistics, Google maps tutorial, temporal and spatial statistics, and cognition in visual analytics.

Student Retention

Within the past 3½ years, Morgan State University has seen the hiring of a new president, Dr. David Wilson, former Chancellor at the University of Wisconsin. Upon his arrival, he has made retention one of MSU signature priority area. On behalf of the VAST MSI project team, we require that each of our STEM students recruited for this project, either directly or indirectly, receive close, hands-on supervision with respect to course work and academic standing.

Curriculum Development (Objective 2)

Regarding concentration in homeland security, in less than one year, the project team has been able to pull together key members across the entire university to better assess the impact the project has had across the academic training of homeland security related topics, with cybersecurity being at the top of the list. Throughout this process, we have learned and been able to identify and become part of a university-wide effort to focus resources in the area of NSA / DHS certifications in cybersecurity. This initiative in combination with other activities is being addressed by interdisciplinary faculty across the campus by including homeland security relevant issues in their classroom discussions.

During this process, one of the lessons learned concerning concentrations associated with STEM fields of study was that the Maryland Higher Education Commission (MHEC) does not allow concentrations without prior approval, though faculty are continuing to include topical areas relevant to DHS priorities within their individual class lectures and course syllabi. However, to keep the momentum, the project team has worked with key faculty who are working to create DHS research priority areas, namely, cybersecurity. Specifically, the university has formed a cybersecurity working group/advisory panel to assist in this area. What has evolved, under the leadership of one of our faculty cybersecurity mentors, has been to work towards developing the first NSA/DHS certified certificate program, with a goal of completion and approval by August 2014. Figure 1 shows the conceptual framework for interdisciplinary research and educational activities.

Conceptually and theoretically we have brought together highly qualified faculty and students that has enabled the project to utilize an interdisciplinary approach to the teaching and learning of STEM. Based on a previous DHS award, we were able to conceptualize and implement an interdisciplinary approach in achieving outcomes. This has resulted in students from across the campus with an interest and skill set in STEM that include: biology, computer science, engineering (electrical, civil, industrial, and transportation), chemistry, physics, physical therapy, history, psychology, and other disciplines. These students make up "*Morgan Xtreme*." Their

Figure 1. Conceptual basis and unifying aspect of the interdisciplinary research and educational activities offered

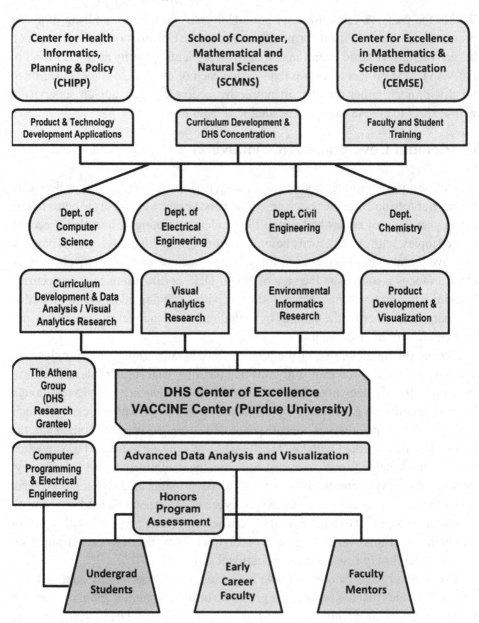

interdisciplinary skill set has enabled MSU students to introduce new ideas and technologies. For example, the *Morgan Xtreme* students and the previous team developed Smartphone APPs relevant to DHS priority areas. These APPs have been introduced and presented to: classes, university administrators, business leaders, teachers, and, most recently, the entire State of Maryland Legislature during the Morgan Innovation Day in Annapolis, Maryland (February 9, 2012). These strategies unify our interdisciplinary research approach to the teaching and learning of STEM.

Faculty Training (Objective 4)

Faculty selected to attend the visual analytics training on behalf of Purdue University's VACCINE Center underwent training at Jackson State University. Their intense training was facilitated by VACCINE faculty and staff. This two day "boot camp" training provided a depth and breadth of knowledge in visual analytics to the seven (7) MSU faculty and administrators that attended the training. As a result of the training, the administrators and faculty proposed to establish a university-wide visual analytics working group at Morgan State University. This is critical and has resulted in administrators working with early career faculty and immersing themselves into the science of visual analytics and informatics at the university.

With the advent of cybersecurity as a university and national priority, along with other critical infrastructural issues that include: roads, bridges, physical structures and educational systems, administrators from the School of Architecture and Planning and senior administrators from Residence Life and Housing (who are responsible for STEM tutoring across campus), and early career faculty are working to develop innovative STEM curriculum utilizing the visual analytic training received at Jackson State. It is through these educational opportunities for early career faculty and administrators that will ultimately institutionalize a sustainable system of visual analytics at Morgan State University.

Acquiring New Technologies (Objective 5)

The VAST research team acquired space for a *Visual Analytics for Science and Technology* (*VAST*) laboratory as a major research component for the VAST project. The focus of this laboratory will be visual analytics and interdisciplinary STEM concentration on DHS priority research initiatives, training, as well as faculty and student development. In addition, the project team has been actively acquiring the necessary and needed technologies, equipment, and supplies to provide mentorship, training, research and product development activities that are outcomes of the project. Additionally, because of the significance of this project, university administrators in the Office of Information Technology and the Office of Residence Life and Housing have provided Smart-board projector technology, and ordered an 88" large screen LCD display for the same location. With the advent of the other large screen visualization screens pending, this venue will serve as a research and training laboratory for large data systems that are suited for visual analysis.

Other technologies have been ordered, received, and are currently being utilized by early career faculty members. These technologies, such as remote sensing, will enable the overall project team a vast amount of data for latent (or real-time) analysis. Ideally, the VAST Laboratory will be the venue for teaching, training, tutoring, and research. Case in point, the Office of Residence Life and Housing has already approached the team and extend resources (88" LCD Interactive Display) to become actively engaged in the DHS project in order to enhance the tutoring needs of the students in residence life and housing facilities. In year 2, data will be pushed across other locations throughout residence life and housing facilities. The use of visual analytics is being completely integrated throughout the entire university by linking these large screen displays.

University faculty selected for this project are from STEM interdisciplinary fields that include: computer science, electrical engineering, and civil engineering, and education. While our previous award introduced DHS into a number of courses, there still exist a major gap between what is learned by students about DHS and how projects are being developed around DHS priority research areas. The proposed interdisciplinary DHS curriculum will blend what is being taught in the classroom with creative visual analytic tools, techniques and technologies. For example, when a student reads about an intentional act of terrorism versus being able to see the statistics or epidemiology of such acts visually and creatively, the process of learning and actions become more enhanced and predicable—based on previous lessons learned.

Education and Training

The project is divided into four components that include: undergraduate student recruitment and retention; curriculum development; undergraduate and faculty training; and product / technology development and research. These four components will form the basis of the four year proposed project involving Phase I and Phase II. The project applies an interdisciplinary approach to teaching, learning and research that includes the STEM disciplines of computer science, chemistry, engineering, and mathematics.

The project will support 7-10 undergraduate students for phases 1 and 2. However, students will be phased into the project as systems develop over the course of the project. As was accomplished in the previous project, we were able to leverage the resources from DHS and obtained other federal resources from the U.S. Centers for Disease Control and Prevention (CDC) in which resources were also provided to help support students in the DHS research projects that were also CDC priority areas as well. Other resources will be identified to fund additional students.

Developing Career Opportunities for Students

One strategy for supporting the career development of students has been to introduce students to DHS program officials, such as Ms. Stephanie Willett and others who have provided guidance and advice to students related to career development. From the start of the new continuation grant, we will be request to host DHS officials on the campus of MSU for site visits as well as to make presentations to faculty and students pertaining to programs in the Office of University Affairs. The focus will be targeted specifically towards DHS STEM focus on visual analytics and data analysis. The project also works closely with other graduate programs on campus to encourage collaborations with our students in the computer science master's program and the Ph.D. bioenvironmental sciences programs. All of the students will

Figure 2. Morgan Xtreme research students and faculty presenting a DHS supported project

be constantly encouraged to work across diverse teams of scientists and engineers, as well as those in the liberal arts, humanities, and social and behavioral sciences.

The VAST administrative team is working closely with the Career Development office towards identifying student placement opportunities which is an outcome of the project. VAST research students have been supported under the DHS VAST MSI program to Purdue University's VACCINE Center for summer research training programs. This training, combined with our in-house training with our early career faculty, can provide critical synergy to this process. Figure 2 shows Morgan undergraduate research students at a DHS supported presentation.

Early career faculty researchers have the opportunity and are encouraged to participate in a VACCINE Center residency program, specifically designed for this project. The project is focused on visual analytics and data analysis where faculty arrive at Purdue University in early summer and returns back to Baltimore after two or three weeks of training, and return back to Purdue University prior to the end of the summer and the start of the Fall semester at Morgan.

Proposed Faculty Research

Dr. Schinnel Small (Computer Science)

Schinnel Small, D. Eng. is a recent graduate of Morgan State University's doctoral program in engineering, and a current instructor in the Computer Science Department. Her research experience began with her participation in the HP technologies program, where she assisted instructors with the integration of technology to traditional courses, and established a network in which students could interact with their instructor using notebooks and/or tablets. The concept of integration remains a constant theme with the research that she conducted during her stint with the Chesapeake Information Based Aeronautics Consortium (CIBAC). There, she applied computer visualization and simulation, data analysis, and algorithm development to avionic research. Her doctoral dissertation focused on the feasibility of a commercially available optical tracker that could be installed as part of an Integrated Intelligent Flight Deck (IIFD), in order to alleviate issues such as limited visibility and reduced situation awareness during flight. In addition to this, she developed an adaptable smoother to reduce tracking jitter that may be experienced by the tracker while in the cockpit of a General Aviation (GA) aircraft. Dr. Small has maintained her interest in visual analytics while expanding her research interests to include concepts in bioinformatics and cryptography. In this context, Dr. Small represents an early career faculty member whose participation can be beneficial in her career development.

Dr. Small's students will participate in the establishment of a Homeland Security Biotechnology Lab which will focus on visualization and simulation concepts for biodefense and biosecurity. This effort highlights the necessity of preparing for (and preventing) bio-terrorism, as well as ensuring that biodefensive countermeasures evolve as well as technology. Students will be actively involved in the development of computer simulations that will model the proliferation and cessation of potential threats as well as the analysis of both scenarios.

Since students will require extensive training with programming and software development, this exposure offers an opportunity to demonstrate how the core concepts they learn can be applied to DHS related research, which will prepare them for tasks in the DHS workplace. Furthermore, a portion of the students' experience will be devoted to the development of applications on mobile devices which will enhance the capabilities of biodefensive measures. This objective will require the use of tablets that support android and Mac platforms so that applications can be tested.

In the second objective, Dr. Small will be involved in the development of an undergraduate Computer Science track that includes a concentration or some other certification in Homeland Security. This includes the assessment of current Computer Science concepts in this track, as well as the establishment of courses designed specifically for the Homeland Security concentration / certification such as Cryptography and Statistical Methods for Intrusion Detection. New courses would be created using course models outlined by the Cyber watch Educational Center, and existing and new courses will be reviewed by consultants from the Maryland Alliance of Information Security Assurance (MAISA).

Dr. Small will receive mentorship from the Chairperson of the Computer Science Department, as well as training to prepare her for instructing some of the electives pertinent to the Homeland Security Track. She will also assist with the mentorship of students who are actively pursuing this track. Students who participate in this track are expected to be fulltime students and will complete their curriculum requirements within four-years. The intent is to produce at least 3-5 students with this concentration in the first year and to double enrollment in the following years.

For objectives 3 and 4, Dr. Small will rely on the assessment from senior faculty of the current DHS research to ensure that the primary objectives are met. Following the assessment, the senior faculty will offer mentorship as the research goals are expanded to address other pertinent issues in biosecurity, biodefense, or other DHS research. In addition, Dr. Small will actively participate in training offered by COEs, as well as any additional training facilitated by the senior faculty. The fifth objective will ensure that the Homeland Security Biotechnology lab will be well equipped for students and early faculty members to handle the research requirements.

A Biotechnology lab will require high performance computers for conducting the simulations, as well as switches to ensure interactivity. A particular goal will be to set up an 'attack versus defense' simulation, where half of the lab is set up for simulating the propagation of bio-attacks, and the other half of the lab is programmed to execute counter measures against them. This environment could serve as a useful tool for both students and early faculty as they learn how to simulate and analyze the scenarios.

By receiving training, Dr. Small will be able to assist with the curriculum development as well as the development of new research. The curriculum development and research will then be introduced to new students, who will apply their concepts in the Homeland Security Biotechnologies Lab. Results and findings from the research will be presented as means of validating the faculty training. In this manner, the cyclic model ensures the continued evolution of existing junior faculty, as well as the fulfillment of student preparation for the DHS workforce.

Dr. James Hunter (Civil Engineering)

Dr. James Hunter, a doctorate in civil engineering from Purdue University, DHS research project is entitled "*Environmental Informatics and Visual Analytics for the Development of Decision Support Systems for Urban Infrastructure Resilience.*" Dr. Hunter has noted that many signs point towards our country's interest in promoting sustainable practices, infrastructure, and systems. Security, economic, environmental, health, and quality of life are essential for evaluating the sustainability of U.S. cities (NRC, 2010). To be sustainable, infrastructure needs to be physically resilient, environmentally viable, cost effective and able to protect human health and well-being, particular in the face of disasters and security threats. The incidents of natural disasters such as earthquakes, hurricanes, floods, and tsunamis, along with man-made threats, demonstrate that urban areas are susceptible to devastating environmental, social, and economic disturbances. DHS and other stakeholders face mounting challenges presented by protecting critical urban civil infrastructure and the function of natural ecosystems. Local, state, and federal agencies face tough decisions to make wise investments in sustainable approaches to quickly and effectively respond to ecosystem/environmental injury, and to make informed decisions to improve the ecological resilience of the environment.

In response to these increasing demands for information and tools to quickly and easily assess loss of ecosystem services, an adequate timely response to environmental dangers and ecological calamities, decision support system (DSS) tools need to be developed to evaluate the data, benefits of practices and retrofits to existing infrastructure. Of particular interest is the loss of ecosystem services (ES). Ecosystem services are goods or services provided by natural, green infrastructure. Water and filtering/natural treatment of water through wetlands are recognizable services that benefit humans from ecosystem processes. Several stressors include water quality, water availability, and soil and land degradation threaten to reduce

234

significantly these services, especial under threat from man-made or natural disasters. To prevent further degradation and loss of these services provided, it is important to identify, quantify them, and assess the benefits so that economically efficient decisions can be made.

In response to these increasing demands for information and tools to quickly and easily assess loss of ecosystem services and adequate, timely response to environmental dangers and ecological calamities, decision support system (DSS) tools need to be developed to evaluate the data, benefits of practices and retrofits to existing infrastructure. DSS tools enable users to define goals, input parameters data, run models, review performance indicators, and obtain feedback pertaining to management scenarios. The overall goal of the "sustainability" DSS will be to holistically help users decide the best course of action to reduce their environmental footprint through demonstrated metrics (such as recognized measurements for energy, waste tonnage, gallons of water), thus enabling informed decisions about environmental, economic, and social impacts.

The background gained from previous DSS development projects (Engel et al., 2003; (Choi et al., 2005), allows Dr. Hunter to be uniquely positioned to explore innovative, interdisciplinary applied research targeting the difficult urban challenges which will require interdisciplinary approaches, from individuals of diverse backgrounds to provide research that demonstrates ecologically innovative and sustainable actions that promotes a successful paradigm shift for the future. Those systems were designed in promoting watershed management approaches, such as the identification of critical areas for placement of best management practices (BMPs) and water quality prioritization, as well as for analyzing runoff and pollution reduction from low impact development (LID) practices.

Drawing upon this past success, the intended model will enable regulatory agencies, organizations, and practitioners to quickly: (1) locate their area(s) of interest for evaluation; (2) evaluate the baseline scenario and effects events on a particular area; and (3) screen actions and practices given a particular response. The endeavor of this research is to develop DSS tools that may be implemented to allow government agencies to establish and optimize a Web-based spatial decision support systems (DSSs) to receive feedback and data from participatory sensing, community involvement, and other dynamic sensing systems to provide a comprehensive, versatile tool for promoting, sustaining and recovering urban infrastructure resilience through effective management and sound decision making following potential natural disasters and catastrophic events. The data acquired through research will provide opportunities to develop models to measure the benefits, understanding the tradeoffs, and assess the ecosystem services yielded by integrating "green" into everyday function. This research will influence many the functions for operating and maintaining the built environment and will play a significant role with the planning, design, construction, and operation of future systems for energy, transportation, buildings, water, and waste.

In summary, Dr. Hunter proposes the development, testing and implementation of a DSS model, as a decision-making and educational tool for integrated management of urban infrastructure and ecosystem function. The integrated management DSS model uses a systems approach, taking into account the various data sets and sources. This research is targeted to help stakeholders with establishing baseline data and scenarios, while developing the capabilities to tracking real time, remotely sensed data to yield information on the quantity and quality on resource and ecosystem services yield. Dr. Hunter proposes to establish a model/system that will be comprehensive targeting water management, infrastructure, and associated ecosystem services.

Research Objectives

The overall goal of this research is to protect and enhance the flow of ecosystem services from agricultural landscapes. In the objectives that follow, Dr. Hunter proposes to develop an integrated ecologic-economic scientific framework to identify, quantify and value crop production, water quantity and water quality, soil, and carbon services; use this framework to assess how stressors such as climate change, water availability and soil and land degradation and management practices interact to change quantities and their corresponding values to humans; and embed this scientific framework in user-friendly, public decision support tools that allow resource managers, policy makers, and producers to estimate site-specific changes in ecosystem services of proposed impacts of land use changes and management practices.

The *primary research objectives* include:

- Measure the potential vulnerability of an area of interest to natural disasters;
- Quantify provisioning and regulating ES in existing stand-alone models;
- Identify potential environmental stressors and means to "sense" and relay these parameters to the DSS;
- Identify actions and management practices that promote urban infrastructure and green infrastructure resilience; and
- Estimate the economic value of selected provisioning and regulating ES.

The *objective of the decision support tool* developed through this project will:

- Enable DHS and other stakeholders to easily evaluate management options for crisis and recovery scenarios by accounting for ecosystem services lost, maintained, or recovered due to action or inaction.

Finally, Dr. Hunter further builds upon his research by working towards the development of a Web-based DSS tool(s) that can be developed for the analysis and planning of response and prioritize infrastructure approaches. Such tools can enable users to define goals, input parameters data, run models, review performance indicators, and obtain feedback pertaining to the management of built landscapes, thus enabling informed decisions about economic and environmental impacts. Data acquired through research should provide opportunities to develop models to measure the benefits, understand the tradeoffs and ecosystem services yielded by integrated green infrastructure components and management practices.

The establishment of the DSS will need clearly identified data essential for analysis, design, operation, maintenance, and related costs. Various databases, GIS data layers, and monitoring systems will be incorporated to allow users to evaluate issues pertaining to effective management in times of crisis and reconstruction. Ultimately, the Web-based DSS will disseminate information and will allow users to transfer integrated technologies, sensors, live and legacy data, and sustainable concepts into practice, inform policy, and educate the designers and users of these green buildings.

Dr. Kofi Nyarko (Electrical Engineering)

Dr. Nyarko's research focuses on building more advance visualization capability at Morgan State University. He has indicated that over the past twelve years, the Engineering Visualization Research Laboratory (EVRL) at Morgan State University has engaged students in funded research encompassing various STEM fields. With support from the Department of Energy, Department of Defense, Army Research Labs, National Aeronautics and Space Administration and many others, EVRL has played an instrumental role in introducing 41 young engineering students to the rigor and discipline of research and development (R&D), which, in turn, has prepared them for productive careers in STEM industries. Under the proposed objective 1, introducing undergraduate STEM students to research focused on visualization informatics, product development, and DHS workforce development opportunities, EVRL will involve students in the development of a cyber-security visual analytics system.

The Department of Homeland Security has identified the growing number of attacks on U.S. cyber networks as one of the nation's most series economic and national security threats. Significant progress continues to be made in deploying systems capable of monitoring every facet of the nation's network communications with a primary objective of detecting and mitigating threats on these networks. However, not enough progress is being made on tools and techniques that effectively analyze and visualize the voluminous amounts of data generated by these systems.

The proposed visual analytics system will employ flexible techniques for data gathering, aggregation, and interpolation to provide a common operating picture through several visual models of the security state of one or more networks under test. This visual analytics system, as illustrated in Figure 3, will advance prior work involving network representation and intrusion visualization of tactical ad hoc mobile networks and the development of an intrusion detection visual and haptic analyzer. Through user interactivity, the visual models will dynamically configure to support advanced information queries and critical analysis and verification in a manner that facilitates the discovery of trends and patterns through direct observation and induction of underlying laws. Under a cyberspace attack, the system will facilitate a timely response as well as effective mission execution.

It is anticipated that, across all three phases, about ten undergraduate research students will be selected to be involved in the proposed research topic. The students will be required to learn new skills in the areas of computer programming, algorithm development, system engineering, data visualization, statistics, pattern recognition and classification, and machine learning. It is anticipated that some students will be recruited at a higher skill level than the others, and consequently will be heavily involved in student training. This process will ensure they become familiar with

Figure 3. Visual analytics system framework

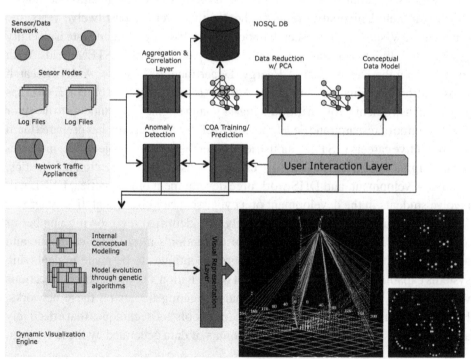

effective methods for communicating technical knowledge, which should help prepare them for postgraduate endeavors.

All students will be required to attend suitable IEEE conferences and seminars, similar to *IEEE Conference on Technologies for Homeland Security (HST)*. While all students will be required to be involved in original poster sessions and technical papers, select students will be trained to attend relevant conferences as presenters. Existing partnerships with Army Research Labs in Aberdeen, Johns Hopkins and others, will be leveraged to provide students with related internship opportunities. Lastly, existing resources for tracking student academic progress will be leveraged to track student progress towards careers in HS-STEM research and development.

While student involvement in research will be the central focus of this project, further consideration will be given towards shaping computer science and engineering curriculum to include some of the visualization techniques and analytical processes that will be applied towards the cybersecurity domain. Subjects such as visual representations of multivariate data, data complexity reduction and pattern recognition will be incorporated into the curriculum. In a similar manner to prior efforts, software tools and applications will be developed to aid students visualize and comprehend complex STEM principles related to this effort. Furthermore, EVRL will hold faculty-training sessions in which MSU faculty from various disciplines will be exposed to this visual analytics for cybersecurity project. Additionally, they will be instructed on how the field of visual analytics can be applied to their own DHS related domains. Special effort will be made towards collaboration with one or more DHS Centers of Excellence (i.e. Purdue University) in order to disseminate visualization techniques and models, author joint publications, incorporate existing research applicable to cybersecurity and provide further training opportunities for faculty.

A core aspect of this research effort will require the use of advanced visualization equipment beyond what is currently available. Facilities are required where large-scale data sets can be quickly and efficiently displayed in a large screen format to facilitate comprehension of complex patterns and trends in addition to facilitating collaboration. Facilities must support advanced interaction paradigms in which both traditional mouse and keyboard input methods are supported alongside gesture based techniques, and tracked head and wand movement. Stereoscopic projection will offer an additional dimension of freedom where complex three-dimensional models of network traffic and threat data can be expressed and easily navigated.

Additionally, mobile tablets will serve to provide individuals with personalized and interactive information displays that may be easily shared with the primary large form displays when needed and information displayed on the large format displays may similarly be transferred to an individual's mobile display for further examination. These mobile tablets will also serve as the primary means for ink annotations with a stylus since it will be impractical to support traditional white boards within this visualization space. Members will be able to generate text and handwritten notes over new or existing display content and have that information automatically displayed on one or all of the primary large format displays. This advanced visual analytics facility will ensure that the proposed objectives will be met in a timely and comprehensive manner.

This aspect of the project is also well established. For VAST MSI, the team has already received confirmation from the Director of the MSU Honors Program who as agreed to actively participate in the selection, recruitment, tracking process. Moreover, as we have previously learned and developed, we will also identify a cohort of high achieving STEM students who will help to identify and recruit other students who will participate in the VAST MSI Project. Again, we have a strong track record of cohort selection, especially given our previous project. Based on the strategy we developed through our previous DHS grant, our former STEM students have created what they call "Morgan Xtreme." They number over 18 currently. They are routinely traversing campus looking for other STEM students who are already interested in DHS priority areas. We will continue to cultivate this process as well as use the "Open House" process.

Project Management

The VAST MSI project is organized and managed by Drs. Timothy Akers and Kevin Peters. Both co-principal investigators have extensive STEM organization and management experience and expertise, especially focusing on faculty mentorship and student development. In addition, both co-PIs have extensive management experience with federal agency grants, contracts, and cooperative agreements. Specifically, Dr. Akers is a former Senior Behavioral Scientist with the U.S. Centers for Disease Control and Prevention (CDC), where he was responsible for managing prevention research for eight of the nation's leading minority health professions schools. Additionally, he has served as the PI for the former DHS Scientific Leadership Awards grant and is currently serving as Director for a recent CDC project to establish the Center for Health Informatics, Planning and Policy (CHIPP), in which he co-founded. Dr. Akers is also co-PI on a National Science Foundation (NSF) grant entitled iTIERS (Informatics for Targeted Infusion of Education and Research in the Sciences). A significant part of his career has focused on data, data visualizations, and informatics with respect to public health and criminology.

Dr. Peters is a Senior Science Administrator at MSU and is currently the Director for the Center for Excellence in Mathematics and Science Education (CEMSE) at Morgan State University where he has served as co-PI for several STEM focused Maryland Higher Education Commission (MHEC) Grants. In addition, he has served as co-PI for an NSF Mathematics-Science Partnership Grant. He has extensive experience in the management and implementation of STEM programs. Dr. Peters serves as the university's key contact for all STEM school-based professional development training of public school teachers.

The organization and management of the VAST MSI project is structured to where if something unforeseeable happens to either co-PI, the other will take full responsibility and assume the duties of the other principal investigator until such time that they return or a replacement is provided. In addition, the VAST MSI project has established an advisory board to ensure that the project is ran according to the objectives and outcomes set forth in the proposal.

CASE DESCRIPTION 7: CAREER PATHWAYS CONFERENCE FOR FUTURE HOMELAND SECURITY SCIENCE AND TECHNOLOGY PROFESSIONALS

On April 11-13, 2013, Morgan State University's (MSU) honor students, LaShaunda Johnson, Derek Riley, Benjamin Hall, and Astrid Garrison, participated in the Career Pathways Conference for Future Homeland Security Science and Technology held in Washington, DC, and sponsored by the U.S. Department of Homeland Security's Office of University Programs, Science and Technology Directorate. The Conference focused on career opportunities at DHS, under the leadership and guidance of Ms. Stephanie Willett, Education Director, with the DHS Office of University Programs.

The initial cohort of students were competitively selected to participate in DHS relevant research projects under the direction of DHS principal investigators, Dr. Timothy Akers and Dr. Kevin Peters, as part of the DHS scholars for the Visual Analytics for Science and Technology (VAST) at a Minority Serving Institution grant awarded to MSU. The students will also work alongside early career faculty Drs. Kofi Nyarko (electrical engineering), James Hunter (civil engineering), and Schinnel Small's (computer science).

CONCLUSION AND RECOMMENDATIONS

Increasing the representation of minorities in STEM is important for the U.S. in becoming more competitive in global STEM research. Having more citizens of U.S. origin engage in research that is focused on DHS priorities is a national security priority. Including MSIs in developing partnerships and collaborations with DHS Center for Excellences (COE) institutions of higher education will be one of many keys to future success as the nation attempts to get a full understanding of issues associated with homeland security. The programs highlighted in this chapter clearly demonstrate significant outcomes in collaborative efforts between MSIs and COE. Students and faculty who participated in the seven MSI programs linked to Morgan State University and COE benefitted from the research experiences. Without such programs students and faculty will not get exposure to cutting edge research that is focused on the nation's security.

The Department of Homeland Security (DHS) Office of University Programs (OUP) has been key in linking the talent that exists at MSIs to COEs so that each institution can share knowledge and information. This inclusiveness of talent has benefitted MSIs in unlimited ways. The ability to acquire research equipment, connecting with DHS COE faculty researchers, acquiring professional development through internships has fostered new opportunities at MSIs. Additionally, this partnership has created opportunities for continued research and scholarship for faculty and students. These programs have fostered collaborative research between Universities that otherwise may not have taken place. The opportunity and exposure for collaborative research has been invaluable. Morgan State University faculty and students appreciate this unique and innovative approach to collaborative research

ACKNOWLEDGMENT

The author would like to acknowledge the DHS Office of University Programs (OUP) in its continued support of MSIs and for the opportunity to connect with DHS COE. This office has played a key role in working with PIs to develop important partnerships and collaborations. In addition, I would like to thank the following faculty from Morgan State University for their input and review of the seven (7) MSI programs highlighted in this chapter: Dr. Timothy Akers, Dr. Randoph Rowell, Dr. Asamoah Nkwanta, Dr. Manoj K. Jha, Dr. Kofi Nyarko, Dr. Schinnel Small, and Dr. James Hunter.

REFERENCES

Choi, J. Y., Engle, B. A., & Farnsworth, K. (2005). Web-based GiS and spatial decision support system for watershed management. *Journal of Hydroinformatics*, 7(3), 165–174.

Engle, B. A., Choi, J. Y., Harbor, J., & Pandley, S. (2003). Web-based DSS for hydrologic impact evaluation of small watershed land use changes. *Computers and Electronics in Agriculture*, 39, 241–249. doi:10.1016/S0168-1699(03)00078-4

Jha, M. K., Udenta, F., & Kang, M. W. (2011). *A dynamic capacitated arc routing problem for optimal evacuation strategies in disasters: Formulation and solution algorithm presentation.* Retrieved from http://ccicada.rutgers.edu/Workshops/ResearchRetreat2011/Jha.pdf

National Resource Council. (2010). *National resource council report: The national research council's assessment of research-doctoral programs.* Retrieved from http://www.gsas.harvard.edu/faculty/national_research_council_report_2010.php

Network, D. H. S. (2007a). *DHS centers and MSI research teams partner on critical security need.* Retrieved from http://www.dydan.rutgers.edu/Files/Aug07-MSISummerresearchteamfeature_002.pdf

Network, D. H. S. (2007b). *DHS student and alumni network.* Retrieved from http://www.dydan.rutgers.edu/Files/DHSOctober2007networknewsletter.pdf

START. (2005). *START hosts DHS faculty/student research teams.* Retrieved from http://www.start.umd.edu/start/announcements/announcement.asp?id=3

Winstead, A., Williams, R., Zhang, Y., McLean, S., & Oyaghire, S. (2010). Application of microwave assisted organic synthesis to the development of near-IR cyanine dye probes. *The Journal of Microwave Power and Electromagnetic Energy, 44*(4), 207–212. PMID:21721469

KEY TERMS AND DEFINITIONS

CDC: Center for Disease Control.

CCICADA: Command, Control, and Interoperability Center for Advanced Data Analysis, a DHS Center of Excellence.

CHIPP: Center for Health Informatics, Planning and Policy.

COE: Center for Excellence affiliated with the Department of Homeland Security.

DHS: Department of Homeland Security.

DSS: Decision Support System.

EVRL: Engineering Visualization Research Laboratory.

IDS-UAC: Institute of Discrete Sciences- University Affiliate Sciences, a DHS Center for Excellence.

iTIER: Informatics for Targeted Infusion of Education and Research in the Sciences.

MSI: Minority Serving Institution.

MSU: Morgan State University, a historical Black University and minority serving institution (MSI).

NSF: National Science Foundation.

OUP: Office of University Programs within the Department of Homeland Security.

PACER: The National Center for the Study of Preparedness and Catastrophic Event Response, a DHS Center for Excellence.

MAISA: Maryland Alliance of Information Security Assurance.

DIMACS: Discrete Mathematics and Theoretical Computer Science.

START: National Consortium for the Study of Terrorism and Responses to Terrorism.

SPRETS: Special Populations Response to Emergency Health Threats Survey.

VACCINE: Visual Analytics for Command, Control, and Interoperability Environments, a DHS Center for Excellence.

VAST MSI: Visual Analytics for Science and Technology at a Minority Serving Institution.

Chapter 11
Homeland Security Information Technology and Engineering (ITE) Professional Development Training for Educators in Urban High Schools

Cecelia Wright Brown
University of Baltimore, USA

EXECUTIVE SUMMARY

This chapter focuses on an Information Technology and Engineering (ITE) professional development training project designed to increase the number of teachers in an urban school district with proficient skills, tools, and content knowledge in computer/information technology, engineering technology, and technical certifications that will support students in Science, Technology, Engineering, and Mathematics (STEM) fields. Through this process, high school teachers will use tools, resources, and training to understand homeland security issues and career opportunities for students in their schools. A cohort of STEM teachers from an urban school district located in Baltimore City participated in a professional development workshop that included information technology, engineering, and homeland defense education to support students pursuing technical careers in these areas. The training addressed

DOI: 10.4018/978-1-4666-5946-9.ch011

deficiencies in content knowledge of homeland security issues and research linked to the high school STEM curriculum homeland security career opportunities available to high school students. The overall goal of the ITE profession development training was designed to increase the technical proficiency of STEM teachers in urban high schools serving historically underserved students to support students in Information Technology (IT), engineering, and homeland security careers, thus nurturing a homeland security science and engineering workforce.

SETTING THE STAGE

Today's students require educators who understand and know how to use technology in the classroom. Local Urban Public Schools are committed to graduate all students with the necessary science, technology, engineering, and mathematics (STEM) competencies that are needed to become part of the global work force of problem solvers and innovators, (Maryland State Department of Education, 2001). The National Strategy for Homeland Security support information systems contributions to the country's national defense. It is imperative that present and future educators learn to use information technology and systems in its most advanced capacity to adequately support the homeland security mission.

The use of instructional technologies as applied to homeland security applications in the classroom will cultivate key components of student learning that include active engagement, participation in group discussions, frequent interactions, feedback, and connections to real-world applications. Instructional technology through the use of computers and the Internet have changed the world rapidly and irreversibly (Gardner, 1993). Our society is in transition from an industrial economy to an information economy and these paradigm shifts will have an impact on the way individuals live, work and educate students.

CASE DESCRIPTION

During the first week, the teachers were given an introduction to Homeland Security, 21st Century Skills and project base learning, (Hmleo-Silver, Duncan, & Chinn, 2007). Teachers were awarded an opportunity to interact with various professionals in the Homeland Security industry and learn insightful methods of implementing elements of Homeland Security into their existing curriculum. Teachers were also granted an opportunity to visit the Cryptologic Museum and furthermore expand their knowledge on yet another Homeland Security topic. Finally, teachers began to work on developing project base curriculum that infused Homeland Security topics, projects and elements (Powers & DeWaters, 2004).

Instructional Technology Linked to Homeland Security and the STEM Curriculum

Instructional technology as applied to homeland security and the state Voluntary State Curriculum (VSC) in science, mathematics and technology education applications in the classroom is linked in the following ways (Maryland High School Assessments, 2009):

- Students are motivated, engaged and learning actively based on real word applications;
- Collaborative student learning is authentic;
- Instruction and learning can be integrated across curriculum;
- Assessments are performance based;
- Effective technology integration is achieved through teacher professional development in technology making it routine and transparent in the classroom in order to support curricular goals;
- Instructional technology tools enable students to be intellectually challenged while providing a realistic outlook of homeland security technologies;
- Students acquire and refine their analysis and problem-solving skills as they work individually and in teams to find, process, and synthesize information;
- Podcasting connects students and teachers with world experts and provide numerous opportunities for expressing understanding through images, sound and text;
- Visualization and modeling tools offer students ways to experiment, observe phenomenon, and view results in graphical ways that aid in understanding; and
- Utilization of instructional technology with students help them to stay engaged and on task, reducing behavioral problems in the classroom.

Project Design

The University of Baltimore information technology and engineering (ITE) professional development training project was designed to increase the number of teachers in an urban public school system with proficient skills, tools, and content knowledge in computer and information technology, engineering technology, and technical certifications that support students in science, technology, engineering and mathematics (STEM) fields (Zeidler, 2002) . Through this process, teachers used tools, resources, and training to support homeland security in their schools. The program consisted of a cohort of twenty (19) STEM teachers from urban schools located in

Baltimore City who participated in professional development training in information technology, engineering and homeland defense which supports students pursuing technical careers in these areas. The specific problem this program addressed was the lack of knowledge of homeland security issues linked to the high school STEM curriculum and the lack of homeland security career awareness for high school students. The overall goal of the ITE profession development training was to increase the technical proficiency of STEM teachers at two urban high schools serving historically underserved students to support students in information technology (IT), engineering and homeland security careers, thus, nurturing a homeland security science and engineering workforce. Two distinct areas of research were highlighted to achieve three proposed technical goals. These included: 1) human factors, 2) biological threats, and 3) countermeasures. This research originated from the following homeland security-STEM fields that included: biology, chemistry, mathematics, and computer science. All of these subject areas are taught in the targeted schools that were selected for this project. Teachers received professional development training in these subject areas linking DHS content information and career development to the curriculum that enabled them to prepare students to pursue DHS careers.

Three major activities took place to achieve the research oriented professional development training goals that included:

1. **Individual Plan and Orientation (IPO):** A professional development needs assessment was planned before the closing academic school year at each partner school location. Each teacher completed an assessment questionnaire designed to assess individual needs of teachers. Teachers were required to complete an IPO. The IPOs needs assessment questionnaire allowed instructors/ facilitators the opportunity to address individual needs within the scope of the professional development activities. Each teacher signed a memorandum of understanding that committed them to completing the training. Additionally, the IPO provided teachers with an opportunity to express their teaching goals as applied to the integration of instructional technology in their classrooms.

2. **Summer Technology Institute:** The professional development activity supported increasing teachers' content knowledge and skills in STEM areas involving pedagogy, media technology, and virtual learning. Teachers worked on individual and group projects that developed into lesson plans/curriculum in digital portfolios that were used during the academic year. Assessments were made outlining individual strengths and weaknesses by instructors/facilitators. The IPOs and needs assessment questionnaires completed by teachers were used by facilitators and instructors to accommodate special needs of teachers during daily sessions. Evaluations included regular assessment of participants' knowledge of homeland security issues and research linked to the STEM cur-

riculum through the development of lesson plans as well as pre- and post-tests administered by the instructors / facilitator (School Improvement in Maryland Report, 2010).

3. **Saturday Academies:** Designed to strengthen teacher's content knowledge in STEM areas by providing advanced digital learning applications. Teachers were given the opportunity to cast podcasts that were added to the digital learning community.

The ITE program applied science, technology, engineering and mathematics (STEM) concepts to realistic conditions in industry that technical professionals would experience in a profession. Teachers from Urban High Schools in the technology and engineering education tracks were introduced to homeland security applications, information technology and engineering theory and concepts. Teachers participated in interdisciplinary laboratory experiences that developed practical skills complementing the classroom theory.

Hands-on exercises improved mathematics and science proficiency in addition to, problem-solving and critical thinking skills. Information technology undergraduate students from the University of Baltimore and the industry partner facilitated a progressive learning environment. The integration of hands-on applications, technical projects with partnering agencies, field trips to facilities, speaker roundtable discussions with volunteers from technical professional organizations, industry and government installations bridged the gap between academia and the professional workforce (Moseley & Utley, 2006). Teachers participated in technical professional development workshops with the partners to develop competency-based learning.

Proposed Outcomes:

- Produce a multi-skilled teacher who can adapt to a modern technical environment;
- Instill a sound technical proficiency to pursue higher education in teachers and students;
- Adopt an integrated, collaborative teaching strategy and active learning technique to educate students through cross-departmental collaborative activities;
- Provide an opportunities for students to be trained in technology and increase minority representation in technical areas;
- Collaborate with partners creating a pathway of producing new technical educators; and
- Provide hands-on cognitive learning in media technology that will convey tangible knowledge to students in a digital learning environment making knowledge visible.

Evaluation Results

A post-workshop questionnaire was presented to participating teachers with a 100% response rate for the two-week Academy, and a 50% response rate for the Saturday Academy and follow-up activities. The overall response by teachers was extremely positive and reflected the overall success of the project in meeting the established goals and objectives.

Below are the responses made by teachers to the post-workshop questionnaire:

Question 1: How satisfied were you with the workshop content, facilitators, and presenters?
Response 1: 100% of the teachers were either satisfied or very satisfied.

Question 2: How satisfied are you with the method of combining presentations with participatory discussion/ activities?
Response 2: 100% of the teachers were either satisfied or very satisfied.

Question 3: How satisfied are you with the training materials and resources from the workshop?
Response 3: 100% of the teachers were either satisfied or very satisfied.

Question 4: Did this workshop increase your knowledge of homeland security, information, issues and career information?
Response 4: 90% of the teachers were fully satisfied.

Question 5: How much do you think you can apply what you learned from the workshop to teaching?
Response 5: 90% of the teachers were fully satisfied.

Question 6: To what extent have you shared the workshop with colleagues?
Response 6: 90% of the teachers shared information with colleagues.

The following are summary responses to open-ended qualitative evaluation questions:

Question 7: Have you been able to use the workshop content in your teaching? If so, how?
- I fully applied numerous applications of science and technology including robotics and computer technology.

- ○ When I discussed communication and information technology, we used the concepts of DHS to communicate with others for safety. Students presented PowerPoint presentations on output.
- ○ I have been able to implement very little at this time.

Question 8: What part of the summer workshop or Saturday academy session(s) did you find most useful and effective to your classroom instruction?
- ○ Research programs at NASA, DHS, and DOD
- ○ Movie making techniques
- ○ Biometrics
- ○ Vodcast production
- ○ DHS and other STEM career opportunities
- ○ PowerPoint training

Question 9: How much did this workshop help increase your instructional technology skills?
- ○ Excellent opportunity in the area of video presentation for instructional technology.
- ○ Very much!
- ○ It improved my skills in using instructional technology and added more ideas, techniques, and strategies.
- ○ Helped me in improving my PowerPoint producing techniques.
- ○ Introduced me to Video movie maker and Vodcast techniques.

Question 10: Would you be interested in attending other homeland security professional development workshops?
- ○ Absolutely!
- ○ Yes, if given a chance I need to have full knowledge and mastery of the skills of integrating technology into the curriculum.

Question 11: Do you have any additional comments and/or suggestions?
- ○ I would love to see an increase in funding for this program, and I am extremely grateful for the opportunity to participate.
- ○ The workshop enhanced teachers' skills and exposed them to new career opportunities for students.
- ○ I would like to see the career opportunities for students expanded.
- ○ I hope we can be given a software package to make podcasting easier and more efficient.

DHS PROFESSIONAL DEVELOPMENT TRAINING PROGRAM: WEEK 1 EVALUATION RESULTS

The two-week workshop took place at the University of Baltimore. The following are the results of the first week of evaluations in the Professional Development Workshop for science and mathematics teachers through a grant funded by DHS. The overall evaluation of the week 1 workshop was rated by fifteen (15) participant teachers. The participants were teachers from urban public schools. The overall evaluation rating for week 1 activities was 4.88 on a scale of 2 to 5; five (5) being the highest and 2 the lowest (poor).

Table 1 shows the quantitative results of week 1.

Eight questions comprised the quantitative portion of the evaluation instrument. Generally, the questions focused on the perceptions of the participants on the issues of the Department of Homeland Security, curriculum development, the STEM content curriculum, ratings of the speakers, perceptions of the multimedia instructions, and web / technology training. Table 1 shows the details.

The quantitative evaluation results are supported by the qualitative data presented in teacher responses and comments regarding the workshop. Overall, the respondents felt the week 1 workshop experience was educational. The teacher responses indicated that teachers were enriched professionally through the workshop activities. Based on the responses, teachers valued the information and materials shared by the speakers as well as facilitators as important in integrating the content into daily classroom activities.

Table 1. Quantitative results table for week 1

Items	M	Description
1. Intro to Homeland Security	4.89	Close to Excellent
2. Intro to Podcasting	4.67	Close to Excellent
3. Curriculum Development	4.44	Good
4. Curriculum in Math, Science & Eng.	4.00	Good
5. Rate: Speaker "Energy Preparedness"	5.00	Excellent
6. Rate Speaker: "Project Scope"	5.00	Excellent
7. Multi-media: Web-Based Tech	4.81	Close to Excellent
Overall Evaluation for Week One	**4.88**	**Close to Excellent**

Detailed scale: 4.75-5.0 Excellent; 4.50 - 4.74 Very good; 4.0 -.4.49 Good; 3.5 – 3.9 Fair 2.0-2.9 Poor; 1.0 N/A

Qualitative Analysis

The qualitative analysis is supported by the following direct comments from teachers. Seven out of eight (88%) of the participants felt the workshop was very informative and useful to them.

The following are direct quotes from the respondents:

- "Everything is so informative and useful to me as a teacher."
- "I like the information shared with us by the guest speakers."
- "I enjoyed the various facts/information shared by the presenters."
- "I like the information about the real world."
- "The workshop was very informative and productive."
- "The information I got was great, I learned a lot."
- "New information about school staff and homeland security is very useful."

The participants also expressed what they liked most about the workshops. These items included the content of the workshop, the format of the workshop plan, guest speakers, and presenters.

The following are direct quotes from the participants:

- "I liked the interactive lecture about Biometrics and podcasting."
- "I liked the content, preparations, presentations and applications of materials."
- "It was very interesting to learn the importance of cyber security, emergency situations and handling, and most importantly, the need for the protection of students' lives."
- "The presentations were well done."
- "The speakers were really expert in their fields."
- "The curriculum and the topic on homeland security were very motivating and inspiring."
- "Biometrics presented great applications, and were most challenging."
- "The computer is indeed a very useful tool for human identification."
- "It was great, I learned a lot."

The following are comments that teachers liked least of the Week 1 workshop:

- "The time was not enough."
- "It seemed too short to get things done."
- "I suggest that for the next time, we will extend the time, even if it will mean 'overtime.'"
- "Absence of hand outs, hard copies."

- "Perhaps, breakfast every morning."

The following suggestions / recommendations were made by participants that may provide insights for future workshops. Most of the suggestions are related to the comments they liked least:

- "We need to extend the time, especially when we are practicing the application of new technology."
- "I think it will be advantageous for us to receive hard copy hand-outs."
- "Sometimes copies forwarded to us through email failed."
- "These materials are too important to be left to chance."
- "The workshop is too good. I don't want to miss this kind of activity. I look forward to week # 3."
- "Although it is not yet time to do a podcast, I think I need to know more about this instrument before I start using it."
- "What about having access to onsite visits to the labs and facilities to actually see and observe science at work?"
- "I am interested to hear more about Homeland Security problems and issues."

DHS PROFESSIONAL DEVELOPMENT TRAINING PROGRAM: WEEK 2 EVALUATION RESULTS

This following is an evaluation of Week 2 of the workshop conducted by the University of Baltimore funded by DHS. There were 16 participants in this workshop. All of the participants were STEM teachers from urban public schools. The goal of the Week 2 workshop was to provide professional development training utilizing technology in teaching and to highlight homeland security issues related to classroom instruction. Eight items were included in the evaluation, with the 8th question the overall assessment of the week 2 workshop. On a scale of 5 to 2; 5 the highest (excellent) and 2 the lowest (poor), the 16 participants rated the workshop. The quantitative results are presented in Table 2.

The participants were also asked to assess the Week 2 workshop qualitatively from open-ended questions. There were three general questions from which the participants made their comments, suggestions, and recommendations that may later serve as guidelines for preparing future workshops. Utilizing a qualitative software package called Atlas Ti, eight codes were created / generated based upon the comments of the participants. Table 3 shows the codes and the number of times the statements appeared in the transcript.

The Complete codes for each theme is enumerated:

Table 2. Quantitative Results Table for Week 2

Items	M	Remark
1. Field trip (Cryptologic museum)	5.00	Excellent
2. Homeland Security scenario (STEM curriculum)	4.62	Very Good
3. PowerPoint (HLS Scenario)	4.79	Excellent
4. Podcast & Portfolio Development/Learning Community Development	4.86	Excellent
5. Value of Final Podcast Portfolio Development to STEM classroom instruction	4.87	Excellent
6. Overall, how would you rate the instructors	4.94	Excellent
7. Digital Learning Community presentation	4.47	Good
8. Overall All assessment by the participants	**4.93**	**Excellent**

Detailed scale: 4.75-5.0 Excellent; 4.50 - 4.74 Very good; 4.0 -.4.49 Good; 3.5 – 3.9 Fair 2.0-2.9 Poor; 1.0 N/A

What did you like most in this workshop?

1. I liked the hands on video and podcast production
2. I liked developing video.
3. I liked movie making and video vodcasting process.
4. I liked making vodcast and podcast.

Table 3. Themes

Themes	No. of times found in the transcript
A source of confidence building	2
Workshop Value	4
More time for lab work	3
Speakers	5
Liked most	11
Like least	5
Recommendations	4
Total	34

5. I liked the making of podcast because I believe it will help my teaching career.
6. I liked learning how to download, edit, and produce videos for lessons.
7. I liked working with audio files.
8. I liked the movie making vodcast.
9. I learned so much about making class movie.
10. I liked podcasting and vodcasting.
11. I liked editing the video and audio files using "audacity and windows" live movie.

There were five items that the participants like least that included:

1. I would like to have learned Smart Board.
2. Just the food – although we are thankful for having it during lunch, but we just don't have a choice as discussed earlier.
3. There was not enough time to apply finishing details of our projects.
4. We had few presenters.
5. The lack of retaining shots for the production of the vodcast.

Comments concerning the speakers and facilitators:

1. Speakers were motivating and inspiring.
2. The guest speakers were all essentials in making the workshop meaningful.
3. Presentation by one of the speakers who told his story was very inspiring.
4. The engagement of the tutors proved very effective for interpretation and application of theories.
5. I like everything because I learned a lot from the presentations of the speakers and facilitators.

Overall comments included the following:

1. Everything was valuable.
2. Everything is valuable, and there's something to think about.
3. Everything was excellent, including the food.
4. The workshop was generally good.

The following are recommendations by the participants:

1. Teach us how to use Smart Board.
2. Extend time in order for us to complete the given tasks.

3. More time is needed to include the topics on Science.
4. There is a need to support us in developing and maintaining the skills we learned from this workshop.

Data

Table 4. Teacher demographics data

Gender	Male	Female	Total(s)
Total(s)	**6**	**11**	**17**
Ethnicity	**Male**	**Female**	**Total(s)**
Asian	0	8	8
Black or African American	5	1	6
White	1	1	2
N/A	0	1	1
Total(s)	**6**	**11**	**17**
Citizenship	**Male**	**Female**	**Total(s)**
U.S. Citizen	6	3	9
Working Visa	0	8	8
Total(s)	**6**	**11**	**17**

Table 5. Years of teaching service

Number of Years	3-5 Years	6-8 Years	9-11 Years	12-15 Years	15+ Years	Total(s)
Male	1	1	0	0	4	**6**
Female	1	2	1	1	6	**11**
Total(s)	**2**	**3**	**1**	**1**	**10**	**17**

Table 6. Needs assessment

Question	Poor	Below Average	Average	Above Average	Excellent	Total(s)
1	1	5	9	1	1	17
2	1	1	12	2	1	17
3	3	6	5	2	1	17
4	2	5	7	2	1	17
Total(s)	**7**	**17**	**33**	**7**	**4**	**68**

Table 7. Level of education

Highest Level Completed	BA or BS	Multiple MA or MS	MA or MS	Ph.D. or Ed.D.	Other	Total(s)
Male	4	0	2	0	0	6
Female	5	1	4	0	1	11
Total(s)	9	1	6	0	1	17

College/University Major	Mathematics	Science Education	Physics	Other Disciplines	Total(s)
Male	2	2	1	1	6
Female	1	6	1	3	11
Total(s)	3	8	2	4	17

Other Disciplines Included: 1 Special Education Major, 1 Engineering Major, 1Business Administration Major and 1 Unknown Major

Current type(s) of Certification	Secondary [Other than Mathematics]	Secondary Mathematics	National Board Certification	Total(s)
Male	3	3	0	6
Female	12	1	1	14
Total(s)	15	4	1	20

Note: Number of certifications may exceed the number of people(may hold more than one certification)

Table 8. Formal course preparation

Degree Courses	0	1-2	3-4	5-6	7-8	9-10	11-12	13-14	17+	Total(s)
Refresher Mathematics (e.g., Algebra, Geometry)	1	4	5	2	2	0	0	0	0	14
Advanced Mathematics (e.g., Calculus, Statistics)	0	6	6	3	0	0	0	0	2	17
Mathematics Education	2	2	3	3	1	0	0	0	0	11
Refresher Science	2	2	2	0	0	1	1	2	1	11
Advanced Science	2	1	1	1	1	0	2	1	6	15
Science Education	2	2	1	0	1	0	0	3	6	15
Total(s)	9	17	18	9	5	1	3	6	15	83

Note: The totals are an estimate of semester courses taken at the undergraduate and/or graduate level in each area.

Table 9. Current knowledge of technology

Technology	None	Minimal	Some	Considerable	Extensive	Total(s)
Basic Operating System Techniques	0	2	4	10	1	17
Telecommunications (e.g. Internet)	0	0	6	8	3	17
Email/ Collaboration (e.g. Outlook)	0	2	7	8	0	17
Word Processing	0	0	5	6	6	17
Spreadsheet/Database	0	7	5	4	1	17
Presentation (e.g. PowerPoint)	1	2	4	8	2	17
Desktop Publishing (e.g. Publisher)	8	3	0	5	1	17
Hypermedia Development (Hyperstudio, etc.)	11	2	2	2	0	17
Internet Browsers	0	2	4	8	3	17
HTML/Web Page Development	8	4	3	2	0	17
Photo Editing Software (e.g. Photoshop)	7	3	5	2	0	17
Video Editing Software (e.g. Movie Maker)	9	3	3	2	0	17
Scanners, Digital Cameras	4	3	2	7	1	17
TV/Audio/ Video	0	1	7	5	4	17
SMART Board Interactive Whiteboards	8	5	3	1	0	17
Virtual Learning Environments	7	2	6	1	1	17
Student Management (e.g. Grading)	0	2	3	7	5	17
Student Information (e.g. Records)	0	1	8	6	2	17
School Management (Budget, Personnel, Scheduling, etc.)	7	2	6	2	0	17
Curriculum- specific applications	3	3	6	5	0	17
CD-ROM/ Multimedia Applications	2	4	5	4	2	17
Electronic Research	0	3	5	6	3	17
Podcasts	10	4	2	1	0	17
Webquests	8	4	2	2	1	17
Total(s)	93	64	103	112	36	408

Table 10. Classroom implementation of technology

Computer- Aided Instruction or Technologies	Never	Occasionally	Frequently	Total(s)
Drill and Practice and/or Tutorial	0	5	12	17
Simulation or Educational Games	2	13	2	17
Problem Solving	10	6	1	17
Webquests	11	6	0	17
Internet Research	11	5	1	17
CD-ROM based Research	9	8	0	17
Electronic Database Research (e.g. Galileo)	13	4	0	17
Media Center on-line Circulation Catalog	13	3	1	17
Email	5	6	6	17
Internet Communities (Forums, Message Boards. Blogs)	11	4	2	17
Word Processing	4	9	4	17
Spreadsheet/ Database	7	8	2	17
Presentation (PowerPoint, etc.)	1	8	8	17
Desktop Publishing	12	4	1	17
Hypermedia	16	1	0	17
HTML/ Web Page Development	14	3	0	17
Photo Editing Software	11	5	1	17
Video Editing Software	12	5	0	17
Digital Cameras	7	7	3	17
Camcorder	10	6	1	17
Scanners	10	4	3	17
Total(s)	190	120	47	357

Question 1: How would you rate your knowledge concerning "homeland security issues" and the educational environment in general?

Question 2: How would you rate your knowledge concerning homeland security issues in general?

Question 3: How would you rate your knowledge concerning cybersecurity in the educational environment?

Question 4: How would you rate your knowledge base of homeland security careers related to STEM?

Qualitative Reponses to Open-Ended Questions

The following questions required written responses and selective replies have been listed:

1. Describe how the flu epidemic in schools could be a homeland security issue.
   - It could attack the immune system and the survival rate.
   - If the flu epidemic is the result of a planned biological attack then it qualifies as a homeland security issue.
   - Could be attributed to immigrant students.
   - The flu epidemic can fall under preparing your family under "preparedness, response, and recovery" category.
   - Homeland security might be involved in finding out its origins and how it spreads.
   - It's a public health and safety issue and that in turn makes it a security threat.
   - Any epidemic needs a known response plan for intervention and containment to maintain public health.
2. What do you see as a major homeland security issue in your school?
   - Lack of emergency plans for security issues other than fires.
   - Prohibited cell phone use is an issue because not managing communication systems can lead to a homeland catastrophe.
   - School should instill in students and staff that homeland security is everyone's business.
   - Open access to school building.
   - Bomb threats.
   - School transportation security.
   - Students who commit acts of targeted violence.
   - Cybersecurity
   - Electronic gadgets.
3. What technology would you suggest the school needs? Are there any new technologies you would like to learn more about?
   - Latest versions of software such as video editing and podcasts.
   - An instrument that would allow only registered mobile phones to operate.
   - How to circumvent or prevent daily computerized threats.
   - Smartboards, whiteboards, and computers in every class room.
   - Smart cameras and emergency buttons in all classrooms to report serious activities instantly.
   - Digital display boards to show safety rules.

- Social networking integration into the curriculum.
- Expanded multimedia center.
- Website development.

4. How do you like to learn technology and software applications (formal training, independently, from peers, etc.)? What have you found to be most effective?
    - Presentations and peer group reviews of lesson activities.
    - Read background information then complete formal training tasks.
    - Real-World experiences.
    - Most effective has been peer training.

5. How do you feel about the access your students currently have to technology? Do you think they are receiving the access they need?
    - Students need additional access to computer labs.
    - Not enough access the school needs to provide adequate resources to meet the student's needs.
    - Most access internet through cell phones which is not appropriate.
    - Need camcorders to record developmental stages and results.
    - They need to have better access. There have been scheduling and over-booking issues in the school's multimedia center.
    - They have minimal output of the work if the project or work is related to technology.

6. Do you feel that your students can benefit from knowledge concerning home-land security careers? Please give examples.
    - Yes, many of them have very little direction career wise and their inter-est may be sparked and help them gain focus and direction.
    - Absolutely, for inner city youth, staying out of trouble is a critical con-cern. Knowing about keeping a "clean record" will certainly help youth to get the security clearance needed to work for Homeland Security.
    - Yes, students could go into career pathways leading to Intelligence Analysis, Criminal Justice, Emergency Response and Management, etc.!
    - Yes, they can choose various technical educational majors so that they can use their expertise in any number of DHS areas such as Aviation, Medical, and Engineering jobs, etc.
    - Yes and so can a lot of the teachers because their teachers do not know.
    - Yes, very much such as cybersecurity, chemical and biological defense, health, information sharing, interoperability and people.

7. Do you find it difficult or time consuming to incorporate homeland security issues as part of the high school curriculum?
    - No. The applications of homeland security are numerous.
    - No, as long as the tasks are not too time consuming.

○   No. Knowledge is key!

○   No. Homeland security is everywhere!

○   If materials, equipment, and resources are provided then this incorporation of homeland security issues to the curriculum is not difficult.

8.   Could you benefit from professional development workshops focused on content as well as pedagogy in your discipline and homeland security issues?

○   Yes, the programs applicable to the science curriculum.

○   Yes, such workshops would bring significance and applications to Algebra topics, especially word problems.

○   Yes, but a very knowledgeable professional from DHS is key.

○   Most definitely!

○   Yes. Especially since I am a foreign teacher here and I am still in the process of learning my students' culture and behavior and learning more about homeland security issues and how they relate to my classroom would be very useful.

○   No. Although, the present curriculum is still not current. It has been made by textbook authors to district standards and incorporating homeland security issues would take time to implement and would affect the pacing guide of the present curriculum.

9.   Can you describe any IT issues in your school that could be linked to homeland security?

○   Any weakness in IT security that would allow cyber viruses to attack the network is a homeland security issue.

○   Any time the internet fails and people are not properly logged out of the system (i.e. unsecure computers).

○   The public address system in the school is old and unreliable so students and staff cannot receive instructions in the event of an emergency.

○   Use of cell phones and computers to send messages outside which can sometimes trigger serious problems in the school building.

○   Any security breach that would allow access to student records and employee data.

10.   Describe how you might infuse homeland security into a specific lesson/unit in your curriculum?

○   The discipline of chemistry offers the opportunity to explore chemical terrorism, preparedness for chemical accidents and technological hazards.

○   Homeland security includes use of a lot of linear and exponential data. This data can be represented with proper equations, inequalities and graphs giving students real-world simulations.

- A lesson on "Momentum and its conservation" as it relates to rifle recoil might be a good platform to link DHS's firearms training issues.
- Experimental equations to model the spread of toxins.
- Covering kinematics and projectile motion to teach students to use the concepts to figure out the best methods of hitting enemy targets.
- Nuclear physics, related to nuclear attacks, radioactivity testing, etc..
- Linking pathogenic diseases and genetics and evolution of these diseases that could make it a threat to public health and safety.
- When preparing students for the Biology HSA, the scientific method including data collection, sampling procedures and analysis would be taught and reinforced using homeland security materials.
- Ecology unit is one of the units that homeland security issues can be infused into since it tackles the environment and all organisms that interact within it (i.e. how homeland security ensures coordinated responses in natural disasters such as forest fires, earthquakes, tsunamis, etc.).

11. Describe your experience with project based learning.
    - Served as the Math, Science and Engineering Coordinator and Robotics liaison for the school system and the students participation in science and engineering competitions is one the most effective project based learning activities.
    - Created short term projects to help students with systems of equations to express possible purchase combinations given an amount of money. Students expressed the data as equations, graphs, and complete sentences by the end of the project.
    - The feedback gained from each project yields more in-depth knowledge about that subject and also a chance to discover the next steps of the process.
    - Worked extensively with the HSA Bridge projects with 12th grade students.
    - Implemented in an afterschool program where students were taught how to build remote operated vehicles.
    - This makes my students more curious. Helps them develop more challenges and imagine the future world.

CONCLUSION

The technical goals of this project were in line with the research, creation, development/ evaluation of innovative educational tools, and approaches that resulted in strengthening the U.S. scientific leadership in homeland security research in public institutions in an urban school district. The project strengthened scientific leadership in homeland security research in public institutions through professional development workshops and Saturday Academy workshops with teachers from targeted public schools in Baltimore City. This was accomplished by introducing teachers to homeland security research and issues important to education. This accomplishment was measured through quantitative responses made by teachers in evaluation questions. The dissemination of information and knowledge of technology and career opportunities of students interested in pursuing STEM careers was introduced to teachers. This accomplishment was important in the dissemination of knowledge and the expansion of the mission of the DHS in creating a more competitive workforce.

The DHS funding of such educational activities that involve teachers is critical in STEM students developing skills that support the mission of DHS and that support the STEM workforce.

The professional development activities were extremely important in linking DHS priority issues to the STEM curriculum. This was clear through the development and dissemination of information through a detailed web page created that introduced several homeland security lessons and resources that teachers can utilize in their classrooms. An extension of the professional development is the nurturing of a homeland security science and engineering workforce. This was initiated through introducing teachers to homeland security careers at the state and national levels that they in turn can share with students during classroom instruction. With these outcomes in mind, the following technical goals were achieved: 1) increased the content knowledge of STEM teachers linking information and engineering technology with the high school curriculum; 2) assisted STEM teachers in developing model STEM lesson plans that connect to IT education and homeland security applications. This was accomplished through the development of homeland security lesson plans that were linked to the STEM curriculum. A novel approach was used to put the lesson plans on a web page. Teachers at the targeted schools can now access the website for curriculum incorporation into classroom lessons. The website for program lesson plans, courses and links in Homeland Security was created specifically for participants. 3) Assisting in the facilitation of IT career pathways for students that include private and government employers in the Department of Defense, Homeland Security and the many Base Realignment and Closure (BRAC) initiatives.

Finally, this project was effective in linking to IT career pathways of programs at the National Aeronautics and Space Administration (NASA), Department of Defense (DOD) as well as DHS career opportunities. These opportunities were discussed with teachers as STEM pathways for students. The professional development activities provided a combination of theory and hands-on instruction through a variety of computer applications, media technology and virtual learning in homeland security applications linked to the STEM curriculum. The culmination of the applications, media and virtual resources were compiled into a competency-based program with measurable outcomes designed to meet the proposed technical goals. The professional development activities/training included the following: 1) Summer Technology Institute, 2) Saturday Academy Workshops and 3) an On-line Digital Learning represents a unique approach in nurturing a homeland security workforce by training STEM teachers in urban public high schools that support an increase in knowledge and awareness of homeland security issues as well as career opportunities for students.

REFERENCES

Gardner, H. (1993). *Framework of mind: The theory of multiple intelligences* (Rev. ed.). New York: Basic Books.

Hmleo-Silver, C., Duncan, R., & Chinn, C. (2007). Scaffolding and achievement in problem-based and inquiry learning: A response to Kircshner, Sweller and Clark (2006). *Educational Psychologist, 42*(2), 99–107. doi:10.1080/00461520701263368

Maryland High School Assessments. Test Support. (2009). *Practice test.* Retrieved from http://hsaexam.org/support/practice.html

Maryland State Department of Education. (2001). *Keys to math success a report from the Maryland mathematics commission.* Retrieved from http://www.msde.state.md.us/Special_ReportsandData/keys.pdf

Moseley, C., & Utley, J. (2006). The effect of an integrated science and mathematics content-based course on science and mathematics teaching efficacy of pre-service elementary teachers. *Journal of Elementary Science Education, 18*(2), 123–132. doi:10.1007/BF03174684

Powers, S. E., & DeWaters, J. (2004). Creating project-based learning experiences university-K-12 partnerships. In *Proceedings of the American Society for Engineering Education Frontiers in Education Conference.* Savannah, GA: ASEE.

School Improvement in Maryland. (2010). *HSA test performance status.* Retrieved from http://mdk12.org/data/HSA/TestPerformanceStatus.aspx?Nav=1.5:5.1:10.99:15.10#bargraph-all

Zeidler, D. L. (2002). Dancing with maggots and saints: Visions for subject matter knowledge, pedagogical knowledge, and pedagogical content knowledge in science teacher education reform. *Journal of Science Teacher Education, 13*, 27–42. doi:10.1023/A:1015129825891

KEY TERMS AND DEFINITIONS

DHS: Department of Homeland Security.

DOD: Department of Defense.

IPO: Individual Plan and Orientation.

IT: Information Technology.

ITE: Information Technology and Engineering.

NASA: National Aeronautics and Space Administration.

STEM: Science, Technology, Engineering and Mathematics.

Chapter 12
Conclusion:
Perspectives on Effective Collaborative STEM Research Experiences Linked to DHS Centers of Excellence (COE)

Kevin Peters
Morgan State University, USA

Cecelia Wright Brown
University of Baltimore, USA

Kofi Nyarko
Morgan State University, USA

EXECUTIVE SUMMARY

The previous chapters in this book demonstrate how collaborative research linked to DHS Centers for Excellence support the overall mission of DHS, while at the same time support research by faculty and students at institutions of higher education. The value added and success of these programs highlight the importance of developing effective partnerships that can lead to quality research experiences for faculty, students, and teachers. In addition, the research highlighted stresses the importance of developing a strong workforce that begins long before students make the transition to institutions of higher learning. It is important that early career faculty researchers, experienced researchers, as well as undergraduate and graduate students understand DHS research priority areas that can effectively support the overall mission of DHS. The collaborative research that is linked to other federal and state agencies is important in addressing complex security issues that have an impact on the general public.

DOI: 10.4018/978-1-4666-5946-9.ch012

The Department of Homeland Security will lead the unified national effort to secure America. We will prevent and deter terrorist attacks and protect against and respond to threats and hazards to the nation. We will ensure safe and secure borders, welcome lawful immigrants and visitors and promote the free-flow of commerce.

— Mission of the Department of Homeland Security

SETTING THE STAGE

The Department of Homeland Security (DHS) Science & Technology Directorate (S&T) Centers of Excellence (COE) represent a large number of research universities nation-wide that develop innovative products that support the overall mission of DHS in protecting the homeland. The chapters in this book highlight a small sample size of quality research that were a result of funding provided through the Science and Technology's Directorate through the Office of University Programs. Although a small sample size, these efforts enable researchers at minority serving institutions as well as COEs to collaborate. These research efforts provide a "snap shot" of the research priority portfolio that address short and long-term needs of the Department of Homeland Security. It also demonstrates the importance of working with federal agencies, universities, as well as business and industry to solve complex problems associated with homeland security.

These efforts serve to train the next generation of faculty and student researchers who will become the future generation of homeland security professionals. This chapter summarizes these collaborative efforts (cases) as well as why these efforts are important in addressing DHS priority research areas. In addition, a discussion on qualitative assessment of faculty and student federally funded STEM research experiences are presented.

CASE DESCRIPTION CONCLUSIONS

Case 1: The Challenges of Obtaining Credible Data for Transportation Security Modeling

The Transportation Security Administration (TSA) was created in the wake of 9/11 to strengthen the security of the nation's transportation systems while ensuring the freedom of movement for people and commerce. This case was a direct link to transportation security and focused on the National Transportation Security Center of Excellence (NTSCOE) was established to develop new approaches to defend, protect, and increase the resilience of the nation's multi-modal transportation infrastructure, and to create education and training programs for transportation security. The authors of this chapter presented a clear vision of future challenges while developing models to address critical problems associated with transportation security. The Center for Transportation Safety, Security, and Risk (CTSSR) at Rutgers University, an NTSCOE institution, developed models that address multi-modal resilience of freight and transit transportation networks. Data collection processes for each project presented significant hurdles for the research team in developing credible and accurate modeling tools. For any given data need, the potential exists for data gaps, collection and processing errors, publication and use restrictions, and the need to obtain the most timely information. These challenges must be foreseen by researchers and practitioners in order to better accommodate potential restrictions on both data collection and dissemination while still providing users with a tool that improves decision making.

Case 2: The Center for Secure and Resilient Maritime Commerce

Two goals of the Science and Technology Directorate Borders and Maritime Security Division are to: 1) Provide technical solutions to DHS operating components in order to stop dangerous things and dangerous people from entering the country; and 2) Enable the protection of the public, the environment, and U.S. economic and security interests. The authors of this case presented research data that support these two major objectives under the S & T Directorate.

This case promotes efforts from the DHS National Center of Excellence in Maritime Security's (CSR) Maritime Domain Awareness (MDA) technologies in support of layered surveillance. The layers include satellite-based wide area views; HF Radar systems providing over-the horizon situational awareness; and near-shore and harbor sensing utilizing underwater acoustic technologies. Integration of these systems accomplishes vessel detection, classification, identification, and tracking. Applications for end-users including U.S. Coast Guard (USCG) and Customs and Border Protection (CBP) have demonstrated the delivery of actionable information in operationally relevant settings. Furthermore, research in port resiliency has yielded a port disruption planning tool, the Port Mapper that assisted government leadership during the closure of the Port of NY/NJ by Hurricane Sandy. Work at the Center has been focused on delivering MDA data streams from emerging and advanced technologies into the hands of the operators in ways that are compatible with command decision support systems. Finally, this case demonstrated the importance of developing strong partnerships and collaborations in an effort to achieve the two goals previously mentioned.

Case 3: Command, Control, and Interoperability Center for Advanced Data Analysis: A Department of Homeland Security Data Sciences Center of Excellence

This case presented an overview of the educational and research programs of the Command, Control, and Interoperability Center for Advanced Data Analysis (CCICADA) in an integral way. CCICADA is based at Rutgers University and is one of the components of the Department of Homeland Security (DHS) Center of Excellence (COE) Center for Visualization and Data Analytics (CVADA). CVADA is co-led by Rutgers University and Purdue University. Purdue's Visual Analytics for Command, Control, and Interoperability Environments (VACCINE) Center and Rutgers University's CCICADA Center were established as a DHS Homeland Security Center of Excellence. Although Purdue's focus is on visualization sciences, and Rutgers' focus is on data sciences, these two CVADA components work closely on a number of research activities, projects, and programs. This case also demonstrated the importance of developing partnerships and collaborations in order to solve complex problems involving large amounts of data. Data management as well as security is important in DHS priority research efforts across all COEs.

Case 4: Detecting Electronic Initiators Using Electromagnetic Emissions

The critical infrastructure of the country is important and provides services for citizens daily. Critical infrastructure provides the energy we use in our homes, drinking water, multiple transportation systems, as well as tunnels and bridges. In addition they connect us to each other and the systems needed by citizens to communicate. The authors of this case study discussed methods for detecting and locating two different types of radio receivers. Functional stimulated emissions detectors are constructed, and their performance is analyzed. Stimulated emissions are capable of detecting super-regenerative receivers at distances of at least one hundred meters and accurately locating superheterodyne receivers at distances of at least fifty meters. These results demonstrate a novel technique for detecting potential explosive threats at stand-off detection distances that could have a devastating effect on critical infrastructures in this country.

Case 5: Maritime Security Education Programs at the Center for Secure and Resilient Maritime Commerce

Summer research programs for undergraduate and graduate students are an integral part of STEM education and research. The interdisciplinary approach to research is important in understanding complex security issues. These experiences are important in the training of the future homeland security workforce. In its efforts to respond to national workforce imperatives the Center for Secure and Resilient Maritime Commerce (CSR) led by Stevens Institute of Technology, created an intensive summer research program tailored to undergraduate and graduate-level students. The Summer Research Institute is designed to engage multidisciplinary student teams in rigorous, hands-on research in collaboration with the center's researchers and industry and government partners. The research fields include maritime security, remote sensing technologies, emergency response and management, and Marine Transportation System (MTS) resilience. The program aims to enhance the professional development of students, while increasing their interest in advanced academic study and careers in the maritime/homeland security domain.

Case 6: Frenemies: Exploring the Intergovernmental Relationships between Native American Tribes, the States, and the Federal Government in Homeland Security and Emergency Management Policy

Understanding cultural differences between ethnic groups are important in addressing the national security issues of the country. The authors of this case presented data and gave different perspectives of tribal beliefs that cultural linked the state and federal government. An understanding of emergency management policies needs to be addressed in underrepresented communities. The working relationships between Native American tribes, the states, and the federal government have been strained for centuries. These intergovernmental interactions have led to a fragmented system whose attempt to deliver public service is consistently met with opposition. One area where this has become increasingly evident is within homeland security and emergency management policy. This study used a cross sectional survey to gather information about the beliefs tribes held about the various aspects of their working relationships with states and the federal government within the context of homeland security and emergency management.

Case 7: Visual Analytics for Students and Teachers (VAST) Model at a Minority Serving Institution: A Department of Homeland Security Project for Strengthening STEM Teaching and Learning

Innovative and creative ways of teaching STEM is important to developing the next generation of homeland security experts. This training starts at the K-12 level and continues in higher education. This case demonstrated that undergraduate students and high school teachers can learn from each other. In addition, STEM teachers need to understand issues associated with homeland security and career opportunities for students. This case discusses a model for the teaching and learning of STEM by undergraduate students, teachers, and faculty at a Morgan State University that focuses on visual analytics. This project represents an interdisciplinary approach to the teaching and learning of STEM at a Minority Serving Institution funded by the Department of Homeland Security. The chapter also outlines salient strategies associated with challenges at the University. In addition, the chapter discusses partnerships developed with VACCINE, at Purdue University, a DHS Center for Excellence that supports DHS priority research in the areas of visual analytics. The authors of this case presented a unique approach to STEM education and research.

Case 8: Infrastructure Protection Higher Education Initiative

Higher Education must play a critical role in the education and training of the future homeland security workforce. Future training will involve interdisciplinary approaches to the teaching and learning of STEM. As an essential element of homeland security, critical infrastructure protection requires a professional, highly educated workforce and community of leaders at all levels of government and in the private sector. Yet there are few structured and comprehensive higher education programs in critical infrastructure protection. This case study reviewed an education initiative that partners the U.S. Department of Homeland Security with the Center for Infrastructure Protection and Homeland Security at the George Mason University School of Law in an effort to develop and distribute critical infrastructure protection courses and materials that will become part of a comprehensive, unified approach to homeland security education.

Case 9: An Examination of Challenges Faced by First Responders in the Midst of Disaster

An important feature of first responders is an understanding of challenges they face in responding to support individuals who are faced with catastrophic events whether manmade or natural. It is extremely important to understand the human and social dynamics of first responders particularly in the extensive training that is required by first responders. This case is important in examining the issues associated with first responders linked to conflict and resilience. The potential conflicts between professional and personal responsibilities that first responders face in responding to an incident can represent a distinctive feature of a catastrophic event. First responders are also impacted by disasters in a number of ways. Several research questions were answered that can have an impact on policies and procedures that are developed for first responders (police, fire, and EMS) in the midst of disasters. This project also demonstrated the importance of collaborative research among COE's, students, and faculty linked to DHS priority research.

Case 10: DHS Minority Serving Institution (MSI) Programs: Research Linked to DHS Centers of Excellence (COE)

The inclusion of faculty and students from diverse backgrounds is important to understanding the security needs of the communities where they reside. In addition, opportunities for MSIs to apply their research expertise while at the same time get training from programs linked to a COE is invaluable to students and faculty. This case highlighted seven (7) DHS programs / research that involved faculty and students at Morgan State University, a Minority Serving Institution (MSI) that were linked to a DHS Center for Excellence. The programs were developed in part from partnerships and collaborative efforts from researchers and principal investigators at Morgan State University and several DHS Centers of Excellence. Researchers from Morgan State University submitted summaries of their DHS funded programs and activities. In addition, information was gathered from DHS Websites pertaining to their collaborative work with a DHS Center of Excellence (COE). Valuable research experiences were a major outcome from these projects. This case emphasized the importance of collaborative research and programs that support the overall mission of DHS in providing opportunities for MSIs to work with COEs in DHS priority research areas.

Case 11: Homeland Security Information Technology and Engineering (ITE) Professional Development Training for Educators in Urban High Schools

K-12 Education can be viewed in some respects as a national security issue. If teachers / educators are not properly trained and do not possess the appropriate content and pedagogy needed to teach future STEM professions, the nation becomes "at risk." In terms of STEM that is linked to homeland security. This case provided much needed training of teachers in an effort to understand homeland security issues and provided much needed professional development training for STEM teachers. This case presented an information technology and engineering (ITE) professional development training project designed to increase the number of teachers in an urban school district with proficient skills, tools, and content knowledge in computer/ information technology, engineering technology, and technical certifications that will support students in science, technology, engineering and mathematics (STEM) fields. Through this process, high school teachers will use tools, resources, and training to understand homeland security issues and career opportunities for students in their schools. The overall goal of the ITE profession development training was designed to increase the technical proficiency of STEM teachers in urban high schools serving historically underserved students to support students in information technology (IT), engineering and homeland security careers, thus, nurturing a homeland security science and engineering workforce.

FEDERALLY FUNDED STEM RESEARCH PROGRAMS

Development of STEM research programs are critical for the United States' continued capacity to produce: innovative research products; advance health care; cultivate cleaner and more efficient domestic energy sources; safeguard the environment; defend national security; and strengthen the economy. In order for the US to lead the world in protecting the homeland from attacks, it is critical that the Nation maintain a highly skilled workforce in STEM research. Much improvement is needed in order to dispel evidence indicating that current educational pathways are not leading to increased numbers of a skilled STEM workforce to achieve this goal.

Thus, it is vital to the nation to enrich faculty and student engagement in STEM disciplines while inspiring and equipping institutions of higher learning with the resources for them to excel in STEM research that is linked to protecting the homeland. According to the 2013 Report from the Committee on STEM Education National Science and Technology Council, investing in STEM education is critical to the Nation and the economic future for the following reasons:

A large number of jobs in the near future will be STEM discipline careers. The demand for STEM professionals exceeds the trained and professional workforce. The integration of a STEM skilled professional is increasingly becoming a necessity within and outside STEM occupations. A recent report by the President's Council of Advisors on Science and Technology (PCAST) estimates there will be one million fewer STEM graduates over the next decade than U.S. industries will need.

Recent efforts have been made to equip more students with the tools to excel in science, technology, engineering and mathematics (STEM). The United States government has invested $3.1 billion in STEM education. A 6.7 percent increase from 2012 (see Table 1). The 2014 budget reflects investments in students to include:

Table 1. Federal STEM education program funding by agency (budget authority in millions)

Description	FY 2012	FY 2014 Budgeted	Change FY 12 – 14	
			Amount	Percent
Agriculture	86	85	-3	-3.7%
Commerce	41	36	-5	-12.7%
Defense	178	136	-42	-23.6%
Education	529	814	285	53.9%
Energy	47	33	-14	-29.9%
Health and Human Serv.	578	533	-45	-7.8%
Homeland Security	9	9	-1	-8.5%
Interior	3	3	0	-9.0%
Transportation	99	92	-8	-7.5%
Environmental Protection	26	3	-22	-86.8%

Source: Preparing a 21st Century Workforce Science, Technology, Engineering, and Mathematics (STEM) Education in the 2014 Budget

- Preparing 100,000 STEM teachers through active recruitment, support and launching a $35 million pilot program the STEM Master Teacher Corps;
- Supporting STEM-focused high schools and districts, with an investment of $150 million to create new STEM Innovation Networks to connect school districts with local, regional, and national resources;
- The Department of Education (ED) will invest $300 million to support the re-design of high schools to foster partnerships with colleges, employers, or community partners, focusing on high-demand employment sectors such as STEM fields;
- To improve undergraduate STEM education, with the National Science Foundation (NSF) by launching a $123 million program to improve retention of undergraduates in STEM fields and cultivate undergraduate teaching and learning in STEM subjects to meet the White House goal of preparing 1 million STEM graduates over the next decade; and
- Investing in breakthrough research on STEM teaching and learning, with approximately $65 million for the Advanced Research Projects Agency for Education (ARPA-ED), which would allow the Department of Education to support high-risk, high-return research on next-generation learning technologies, including for STEM education.

Table 1 shows the budgets of federal programs that have supported STEM Education funding from 2012 and also projections for 2012 through 2014 that would represent the percent change amounts. The table demonstrates the need to increase STEM Education funding. Education programs lead the way in total funds budgeted. However, because of the interdisciplinary nature of STEM education, additional funding is needed in other federal programs to enhance the teaching and learning of STEM. The trans-disciplinary nature of research requires an understanding of multiple disciplines to bridge the gaps in learning. Researchers are now being required to have content knowledge in multiple disciplines, hence STEM education programs are needed to closing large gaps in knowledge.

Undergraduate STEM Education

According to the Science, Technology, Engineering, and Mathematics (STEM) Education in the 2014 White House Office of Science and Technology budget, the 2014 undergraduate students STEM investments will include an increase in the number of prepared graduates with STEM degrees by a million over 10 years. Based on recommendations from the President's Council of Advisors on Science and Technology (PCAST), the Administration initiated a government-wide undertaking to meet this goal. This budget includes investments to:

- Enhance undergraduate teaching and learning with National Science Foundation (NSF) investments: Hence $120 million allocated for integrated programs such as Catalyzing Advances in Undergraduate STEM Education (CAUSE). Programs such as this support the goal of producing a million STEM graduates over the next ten years. The goals include: cultivating STEM learning and learning environments, increasing participation in STEM, institutional capacity, and developing a stronger STEM workforce for tomorrow.
- Increase STEM education efforts at community colleges with a proposed $64 million for National Science Foundation, Advanced Technological Education (ATE) program, with an emphasis on education of technicians for the high-technology fields and joint efforts between academic institutions and employers.

Graduate Education

The 2014 graduate students STEM investments focus on preparing highly-skilled scientists and engineers while leveraging the National Science Foundation expertise in managing fellowships. Priorities include:

- Increasing National Science Foundation graduate fellowship program through reorganization or the removing smaller fellowship programs. The plan is for $325 million dollars to be used to increase and improve NSF Graduate Research Fellowship programs by creating new National Graduate Research.
- Fellowship programs will continue to support qualified students in STEM disciplines while enabling students to gain advanced experiences in areas most deficient or of interest to an agency. With a reorganization of graduate fellowship programs, graduate education efforts can be expanded more broadly.
- Graduate training programs include $487 million for the National Institutes of Health (NIH), Ruth L. Kirschstein National Research Service Award Institutional Research Training Grants, providing funding to prepare people for careers in the biomedical, behavioral, and social sciences.

Informal STEM Education

- An additional $25 million to the Smithsonian Institution to enhance informal STEM education by improving student's classroom learning. The Smithsonian will work with other Federal Agencies and partners to utilize expertise and resources to create relevant materials, curricula and on-line resources. While improving effective delivery and dissemination methods to effectively impact more teachers and students inside and outside the classroom.
- Investigate methods to positively engage youth and adults in STEM with $48 million for NSF's Advancing Informal Science Learning program (formerly Informal Science Education). This investment will focus on research and model-building contributions of the programs to identify effective means and innovative models for engaging youth and adults in science outside of formal education environments. Select Federal agencies will partner to ensure best practices through research are disseminated and used broadly in STEM Innovation Networks and other type programs.

QUALITATIVE ASSESSMENT OF FACULTY AND UNDERGRADUATE STUDENT RESEARCH EXPERIENCES

In an effort to examine the STEM research experiences of undergraduate students at a Minority Serving Institution (MSI) several qualitative questions were provided to students that attempted to gain an understanding of key research strategies that were successful and could be implemented in DHS and research other related projects. Surveys were presented on survey monkey and further analyzed by a research evaluator. Students were given research assessment questionnaires by their research mentors and were asked to complete the survey questionnaire that was posted on survey monkey, a Web-based survey solution made it simple for faculty and students to complete on line. The pool of students and faculty consisted of primarily engineer faculty and student who had worked, contributed to and had prior knowledge of DHS research that was carried out by their mentors.

The following are assessment questions used in the survey:

Qualitative Questionnaire for Student Researchers:

1. How did your research experience help you as a STEM student?
2. What strategies did your research mentor use to assist you in your research efforts?
3. What did you like most about your STEM research experience?
4. What did you like least about your STEM research experience?
5. Specifically, how would you describe the overall impact of your research experience?
6. What technologies have you used in the processing of conducting your STEM research?
7. To what extent have these technologies improved your research?

Below represents the qualitative responses of a survey student to each question

STEM Faculty Responses

Question 1: How did your research experience help you as a STEM student?
Responses:
- Seeing how what I learned in the classroom applies in a real lab provides a better perspective on the importance of thoroughly learning subjects.
- It helped to put tangible results into perspective based on learned theory.
- Research has allowed for the realization of the bigger picture, the grand scheme. I had the opportunity to see how the theories and concepts that are learned in the classroom are applied to task in the real world.
- My research experience helped me conceptualize and apply theories taught in class.
- My research experience helped me become familiar with a new type of material.
- This opportunity has increased my knowledge base and experience in STEM related topics and issues, particularly those dealing with technology, and coding.

- It kept me engaged and motivated to finish my engineering degree.
- It helped me expand my critical thinking and opened opportunities for me to pursue graduate studies.
- Great. I learned about Arduino and C language. Moreover I increased my communication and team leadership skills.
- My research experience has helped me to have a better understanding of application developing. I am currently learning how to create programs for a specific device and it has broadened my mind.
- Helps me see my classes applied in real life. More hands on experiences.
- My research helped reinforce theory from the classroom.

Question 2: What strategies did your research mentor use to assist you in your research efforts?

Responses:

- My mentor expressed to me that my focus should impact 100 million people.
- Good explanations and demonstrations.
- Challenging questions, in depth perspective, and the ability to solve problems versus simply carrying directions.
- The use of progress reports and weekly meetings to discuss any deliverables or issues
- My research mentor always pointed towards one possible solution and had me explore different ways of accomplishing the same task.
- Weekly meetings.
- My research mentor offered me both directed research projects and opportunities, and also opened the door for me to have input on projects that I would like to work on and be a part of.
- They provided a flexible schedule to conduct research around my classes.
- He always keeps track on the progress of my research to help me stay focused on the main goals of the project. We also have discussions, often of which is a good way to help me polish my ideas.
- He assisted me with a book related to my research project and meetings and presentations were held weekly.
- My mentor helps me by providing me with useful materials and putting me in the right direction.
- Providing all the information you need. It's up to you to make proper use of it
- He gave hints that would help develop ideas instead of feeding us answers.

Question 3: What did you like most about your STEM research experience?
Responses:

- I enjoy working with groups of peers from different disciplines and backgrounds.
- How research is conducted in real life and the importance it has to the world.
- New skills and the freedom to learn.
- I liked most the hands-on experiences.
- Exposure and application of real work problems. Research and Development on futuristic hardware and software product.
- The opportunity to publish my work.
- I enjoyed the opportunity to integrate Industrial Engineering aspects with the ongoing Electrical Engineering research efforts in the lab. I am learning more about ways that Industrial Engineers can be used on the electrical side and vice versa.
- I loved most the opportunity to work on real-world problems and that the work was challenging.
- It gives freedom to expand my ideas and increase my motivation to solve challenging problems.
- It enhanced my experience in my major and helped my build a strong relationship with my professor.
- The demonstrations of applications and implementation of my work.
- The independence, I was in charge of the progress of my project. I also like the amount of responsibility I am given.
- I liked being able to collaborate on different projects to reach my desired outcome.

Question 4: What did you like least about your STEM research experience?
Responses:

- Many of our training sessions were on campus and not in other locations where it may be applied.
- N/A.
- Everything was ideal. Worked around my schedule and was always engaging.
- The shift in work type. Long period of time out the lab and in the lab.
- Having to juggle between work and research when I really need focus on research.
- The depth of reading necessary to obtain information.
- I like least that my research projects are only for a semester. I would like the opportunity to learn more, and continue to work on projects already in progress.

- That some of my fellow classmates did not take the research opportunities serious.
- It's hard to join the job market with research background.
- It can be tedious.
- Time tracking system.
- I did not like the long hours.

Question 5: Specifically, how would you describe the overall impact of your research experience?

Responses:

- Its driven me to ask more questions once I've answered my primary objective.
- Research experience has showed me a taste of the life of a scientist and graduate student. Research also is helping me do better in my physics course.
- Better understanding of theory -hands on experience versus visualization -challenged to think out of the box
- The overall impact of my research experience has been a great one. I have gained experience in the field that I am planning to make a career.
- Great impact on my personal knowledge development.
- This experience has taught me a great deal about how useful academic research can be to the US military. I have learned that pertinent and important research and data can come not only from government labs, but from Universities as well. I am very proud to be a part of this effort to assist the US Military and US Government.
- I had a great overall impact in my research experience.
- Very good.
- Positive impact.
- The overall impact my research is having on me is that it is teaching me how to manage my time effectively and how to make research to achieve set goals.
- Increase my analytic thinking and made me more independent minded. Most things you learn are outside of class.
- I believe my research experience has developed my communication and research skills.

Question 6: What technologies have you used in the processing of conducting your STEM research?

Responses:

- Java script, http, wordcloud, GeoDa, filzilla, Smarttouch tech, Android Apps

- Photo diode, photo elastic modulator, lock-in amplifier, laser, and deposition system to name a few.
- -c++ -arduino board -simulation programs
- MATLAB computer software
- Most programming tools such as C, C++, JAVA, SOARx,Delta3D, PERL, Visual Basic, OpenGL, Matlab
- Design software and various structural testing machines.
- Computers, laptops, tablets.
- I have used some top of the line hardware (The Surface), current software (Tableau, NodeXL, Visio, Flight Simulators, and more), open source applications, conferencing equipment, smart boards, projectors, laptops, computers, and more
- Arduino Xampp C/C++
- Visual Basic Microsoft SDK 2
- High end computers and compilers
- Zync Zedboard MATLAB C++

Question 7: To what extent have these technologies improved your research?

Responses:

- I had never been exposed to them until I began my research and they have all helped me to observe, collect, and sort information better than I have ever done before
- These technologies allow for the research to be done.
- better programmer versatility of equipment and testing help to better plan out methodology versus trial and error.
- This software allowed for quick production of results.
- You cannot obtain result until you use the above tools to simulate output of proposed research product/system.
- Would be able to conduct the research without them.
- Each one allows the researcher to focus in, display, and create in different ways. Combining all three is key in order to cover all bases in my research efforts.
- Without these technologies most of my research and work would never have been completed to an acceptable standard.
- Those tools are a key element of my research as they allow me to implement my algorithms.
- It was at a low cost and efficient.
- They have greatly improved my research.
- Makes the development process faster.
- They have created a way for me to complete my projects at the university.

Several (4) faculty researchers responded to ten qualitative research questions that focused on their research experiences that included research strategies, funding opportunities, mentoring of students, and success.

Qualitative Questionnaire for Faculty Researchers:

1. What research strategies have you developed to support research in STEM?
2. What skills have you acquired in the STEM proposal development process?
3. How do you learn about funding opportunities in your research area?
4. What are your keys to success in STEM research?
5. How have students benefitted from their research experience with you?
6. How would you describe the overall impact of your research experience at the university?
7. What skills did you teach your students to assist them as a researcher?
8. Describe any success stories associated with your student researchers?
9. What mentoring strategies have you employed to assist students?
10. How has your student research experience supported a career in STEM?

Question 1: What research strategies have you developed to support research in STEM?

Responses:

- In my own lab, I assign students specific research projects sometimes solo, often at the start, in teams. Students learn the techniques, at first, and then independently work to generate data. They meet with me as needed to discuss the data and the scholarly aspects of the work. In the summer, the entire lab meets weekly for long, food supported (by me) lab meetings so the students get to see what each other is working on as well. I have made some allowances in my research approaches to working with undergraduates. In particular, I have shifted towards more behavioral neuroscience (with mice) in my work since that seem to intuitively appeal to the students and is easier to them to grasp and become independent with then more molecular techniques. As Program Director (see below, #2) I have, over the years, developed many new training approaches to scaffold student research training. This includes university wide workshops, workshops specifically directed at undergraduate researchers and the implementation of interdisciplinary science writing classes. I would be happy to share more detail in person, if needed.
- All of my research is done in collaboration with faculty outside of university. Why do I do this? Because no faculty at my institution has ad-

equate funding to support the kind of research I do. The university does not provide infrastructure support.

- At my institution it is essential that ties be made to outside institutions.

Question 2: What skills have you acquired in the STEM proposal development process?

Responses:

- I have directed the same STEM research training Program (MBRS RISE) for more the 10 years and lead this grant through 4 cycles of competitive renewal. I have served on standing review panels and done ad hoc review for NIH training grants for multiple NIH institutes. I feel very comfortable with the preparation of NIH training grants. I am also currently the PI on an NSF TUES grant; I have served ad hoc on NSF review panels, predominantly for the Lewis Stokes Alliance mechanisms. I feel not as competent, but moderately comfortable with the NSF process. In terms of Research grants, until this they have been seamlessly funded by various NIH research grants since coming to my institution. I am not funded for research in my developmental neuroscience lab.
- I have been writing grants since 1973 so I have a tremendous amount of experience in this area.
- Read the instruction, contact program manager, and have colleagues review proposals prior to submission.

Question 3: How do you learn about funding opportunities in your research area?

Responses:

- By attending conferences and following program announcements on the NIH Website.
- On my own, of course. Do you think that OSPR is ever timely in announcements? Or even helpful? Sometimes, an announcement is delivered to faculty about funding opportunities but then the due-date is a week ago or next week.
- I go directly to the funding sources and search their Websites. Institutional recommendations are not of much value so far.
- Going directly to Websites for different agencies - COS Pivot - Information from my colleagues.

Question 4: What are your keys to success in STEM research?

Responses:

- Networking! It is absolutely essential to attend conferences and get you work out there in publications and presentations. Collaborations are a great way to maximize productivity.
- Outside collaborations and not depending on my institution.
- One needs outside collaborations.

    ◦   Passion for the work - Having reduced course load to focus on research - Working with students who are productive.

Question 5: How have students benefitted from their research experience with you?

Responses:

    ◦   My students co-author many of my publications. My students travel with me to professional, national and international conferences to present posters. I mentor my students through the graduate application process. Within the context of the MBRS RISE program we have numerous structures activities to augment student's research training with networking them into the professional community and helping them prepare for research (graduate careers). To date, MBRS RISE has trained close to 100 students and more than 60% are in graduate school or have completed Ph.D. and MS degrees to date.

    ◦   It is hard to say. Most are not fully engaged in laboratory research even though they are paid. UGs may be full time in the lab during summer but during the academic year, they are seldom in laboratory. It is the curriculum and culture at my institution that impairs meaningful undergraduate research.

    ◦   They are brought into the mainstream of research in our field.

    ◦   Pursue graduate studies - Marketable when they leave the institution - Exposure to new areas of research.

Question 6: How would you describe the overall impact of your research experience at the university?

Responses:

    ◦   My research Program has been a mainstay of biomedical research in the Department of Biology. I have generated approximately 4,000,000 of external funding since 1996 (not including the training grants). I have reviewed research grants for NIGMS, NIMG, NINDS and NSF. My more than 30 papers published are regularly cited in the literature. My professional standing has substantially increased visibility for biomedical research at my institution.

    ◦   Actually, very good. But those students come once every several years. I have unearthed many problems that impair our ability to do research at my institution. These include lack of appropriate fund management by the University, lack of provision of paid release time, lack of communication between restricted funds, Human Resources, Events and Planning, and others.

    ◦   Publications at national conferences

Question 7: What skills did you teach your students to assist them as a researcher?
Responses:

- In addition to obvious laboratory related skills such as how to design and carefully execute controlled experiments and statistically analyze the data, I teach them to write conference abstracts and make posters or oral PowerPoint presentations. There is also considerable "soft skills" training involved; e.g. how to conduct yourself professionally (reliability, punctuality, communication, how to dress, sometimes etc.). I introduce them to how the scientific community works and acts; I encourage them to network on their own at conferences.
- Good Laboratory Practice (GLP). Yet, they seldom display the initiative to become semi-independent. Example - they hardly read the current research literature.
- Basic neuroanatomy with emphasis on neuroendocrine control. Basic staining of brain tissue.
- How to obtain information from conference papers and journals? How to publish? How to use software?

Question 8: Describe any success stories associated with your student researchers?
Responses:

- As mentioned above, my students have co-authored many of my research papers. Working with undergraduates in the lab has allowed me to produce scholarly work that is competitive on an international level, although it slows down the process a bit. However the rewards in seeing students develop and thrive as researchers make this well worth it while.
- Continue to work in the area of research.

Question 9: What mentoring strategies have you employed to assist students?
Responses:

- I mostly employ what the literature sometimes calls a "friendship" approach to mentoring. I am not very authoritative but expect initiative, drive and independent motivation in my students.
- Critical thinking skills - at least I try to.
- I talk to students and I introduce them to others in the field when possible.
- None

Question 10: How has your student research experience supported a career in STEM?
Responses:

- As mentioned above, my students have co-authored many of my research papers. Working with undergraduates in the lab has allowed me to produce scholarly work that is competitive on an international level, although it slows down the process a bit. However the rewards in seeing students develop and thrive as researchers make this well worth it while.

- ○ See all of above.
- ○ See comments on successes.
- ○ Continue to work in the area of research.

Summary of Student Research Assessment Questionnaire

Students (n=13) were extremely candid in their responses to seven (7) questions that were presented to them on survey monkey. Individual comments made by students are included in the above section. However, several themes emerged from their responses. The following are themes that emerged from the assessment questionnaire:

- **Making Connections from Theory to Practice:** Overall, students felt research experience enabled them to conceptualize theories that they learned during class. In other words, students were able to apply practical applications. They commented on the fact that they were able to, "see the big picture."
- **Exposure and Applications to Real World Problems:** Several students commented that their research experience helped them to connect to real world problems. The mere fact that some of the research was cutting and edge and enabled them to use state of art equipment and software enhanced their learning experience.
- **Increased Critical and Analytic Thinking:** The research experience process enabled students to increase their communication and research skill while providing a framework for them to become independent and to think critically about their individual research project.
- **Utilization and Learning of New Software, Programs, and Technologies:** The research students commented on opportunities that they were exposed to where they learned new programs languages, software packages as well as instrumentation that supported their research experience. In addition, the use of state of the art equipment and technologies enhanced their learning. These four themes serve as a basis for engaging current and new students in the STEM research process. Many of the comments and suggestions can be replicated to address retention issues associated with undergraduate STEM students. The responses made by the undergraduate students are both enlightening and encouraging in advancing students into STEM careers associated with DHS and other federal agencies.

Summary of Faculty Research Assessment Questionnaire

Four faculty researchers completed the ten (10) question survey and were also candid in their remarks. Several themes emerged from their responses that include:

- Greater collaboration with outside universities,
- Utilizing agency Websites is important for funding opportunities,
- Networking is extremely import in research,
- Including students in research publications,
- Increasing the laboratory skills of students.

Although these qualitative responses were from a small pool (n=4) of faculty researchers, they can serve as basis for the need to have greater collaborations with outside universities. The comments also support the programs at the DHS namely the Office of University programs and the DHS Centers for Excellence (COE) program in which collaborative research between and among universities is encouraged. Increasing the laboratory skills of students and including students in research publications is important in the retention of students in STEM and the preparation of undergraduates for research in graduate schools.

Major challenges associated with faculty and student research in obtaining funding are real. With the recent cutbacks in federal dollars in research, there is more competition for smaller amounts of dollars. This translates into less of an opportunity for early career faculty and even experience faculty researchers to actively engage in research. This means that more collaborative funding opportunities are needed that will support not only DHS priority research, but other federal and state agencies including the military that can solve complex issues. Having students actively engage in research at the undergraduate level is paramount for their success at the graduate, doctorate, and post doctorate levels. This can translate into greater opportunities for faculty and students to help increase the workforce for competent. Academia can serve an important role in the teaching, learning, and research associated with complex national security issues facing the 21st with ever changing technology and large computing data sets.

CURRENT CHALLENGES

Current challenges associated with collaborative research include keeping a streamline of funding available for universities to compete and address areas of need associated with DHS priority research. In addition, continued training is needed by university faculty to keep pace with current security issues. "Think tanks" are needed to foresee potential threats from all areas that may be potentially at risk. These "think tanks" could come from federal and state agencies as well as university faculty from around the country.

Each COE has a clearly defined mission. However, how can COEs collaborate in such a way as to maximize efforts? The challenge also exists as to how to provide continued STEM educational training of students to support a growing national security workforce. This involves developing special programs at the university level focusing on homeland security as well as creating educational pipelines that start at the pre-college level and continue to undergraduate and graduate levels. Curriculum must be developed specifically for these types of careers. In addition, special certifications need to be developed that specialize in cybersecurity as well as other areas associated with DHS research priority areas.

Each of the chapters in this book highlighted some of the research focused on DHS priority issues. Another challenge is to examine all of the research being conducted and to see how one area interacts with another. Based on the interdisciplinary nature of research there is an increased opportunity for collaborative research. Trans-disciplinary learning involves using several disciplines to solve a problem. A challenge exists for this type of approach to be used in connection with several different areas of research from different disciplines.

Finally, a great challenge would be to compile a document that highlights all of the COE research activities. In such a document each area of DHS priority could be examined and commonalities could be explored for collaborative research efforts. This document could benefit researchers as well DHS administrators in deciding the next DHS priority research areas to explore. All of the challenges mentioned are fully within the mission of DHS and could be accomplished by developing partnerships and collaborations with all stakeholders involved in the national security of the homeland.

CONCLUSION AND RECOMMENDATIONS

Increasing the funding of programs, such as DHS's Centers for Excellences, is extremely important in fulfilling the mission of DHS. This will require even greater collaboration with universities, state, and local agencies, as well as business and industry. In order to fulfill this mission, educational programs must be developed to form a pipeline of homeland security professions who are U.S. citizens. The events of 9/11 have changed the way that we process data and information to protect our national interests. We must become more competitive in global STEM research and training. The programs highlighted in this book clearly demonstrate significant outcomes in collaborative research efforts geared to protecting the homeland. Students and faculty who participated in the various DHS-funded projects have benefitted scholarly as well as professionally from the collaborative research experiences. Without such programs students and faculty will not get the exposure to cutting edge research that is focused on the nation's security.

The Department of Homeland Security Science & Technology Directorate and the Office of University Programs (OUP) have done a tremendous job within a short period time to develop programs that are linked to DHS priority research. Unfortunately, more funding is needed to continue the DHS mission. In addition, new and creative ideas need to be developed to keep up with changing technology. Universities can play a key role in developing the innovative research and ideas to support the mission of homeland security. It is hoped that current and future administrations will recognize the importance of this agency in meeting future challenges linked to homeland security. The ability to acquire research equipment, resources, acquiring professional development for university faculty through internships has fostered new opportunities for developing partnerships and collaborations nationwide. Without DHS funded research these opportunities would not have happened.

It is hoped that these research opportunities will continue in the future through the DHS Office of University Programs (OUP), as well as the Science & Technology Directorate in supporting the research and programs presented in previous chapters of this book. It is the collaborative and continued research funding of universities through the COE program that will provide the necessary research to address critical issues in protecting the homeland. This book represents a small but significant sample size of the COE program. In tough economic times, the programs highlighted in this book clearly demonstrated how tax payer dollars are successfully being spent.

Finally, the authors of this final chapter would like to thank all of the authors who were willing to share their research and programs as a part of this collected body of work that highlights the DHS Centers for Excellence (COE) program.

REFERENCES

National Education and Technology Council. (2013). *Federal science technology, engineering, and mathematics (STEM) education, 5-year strategic plan.* Washington, DC: U.S. Government Printing Office.

White House. (2014). *Preparing a 21st century workforce science, technology, engineering, and mathematics (STEM) education in the 2014 budget White House office of science and technology policy.* Retrieved from www.whitehouse.gov/ostp

KEY TERMS AND DEFINITIONS

CCICADA: Command, Control, and Interoperability Center for Advanced Data Analysis, a DHS Center of Excellence.

CDC: Center for Disease Control.

CHIPP: Center for Health Informatics, Planning and Policy.

COE: Center for Excellence affiliated with the Department of Homeland Security.

DHS: Department of Homeland Security.

DIMACS: Discrete Mathematics and Theoretical Computer Science.

DSS: Decision Support System.

EVRL: Engineering Visualization Research Laboratory.

IDS-UAC: Institute of Discrete Sciences- University Affiliate Sciences, a DHS Center for Excellence.

iTIER: Informatics for Targeted Infusion of Education and Research in the Sciences.

MAISA: Maryland Alliance of Information Security Assurance.

MSI: Minority Serving Institution.

MSU: Morgan State University, a historical Black University and minority serving institution (MSI).

NSF: National Science Foundation.

OUP: Office of University Programs within the Department of Homeland Security.

PACER: The National Center for the Study of Preparedness and Catastrophic Event Response, a DHS Center for Excellence.

SPRETS: Special Populations Response to Emergency Health Threats Survey.

START: National Consortium for the Study of Terrorism and Responses to Terrorism.

VACCINE: Visual Analytics for Command, Control, and Interoperability Environments, a DHS Center for Excellence.

VAST MSI: Visual Analytics for Science and Technology at a Minority Serving Institution.

Glossary

AIS: Automatic Identification System.

AMSC: Area Maritime Security Committee.

ARENA: Specialized software that simulates transit operations.

CBP: Customs and Border Protection.

CDC: Center for Disease Control.

CHDS: Center for Homeland Defense and Security.

CHIPP: Center for Health Informatics, Planning and Policy.

CIP: Critical Infrastructure Protection.

Command, Control, and Interoperability Center for Advanced Data Analysis (CCICADA): A constituent of the Department of Homeland Security (DHS) Center of Excellence (COE) Center for Visualization and Data Analytics (CVADA).

Consequence Assessment: The process of identifying or evaluating the potential or actual effects of an event, incident, or occurrence.

Crowdsourcing: The observance of the behavior of large networks of people in the online or offline community as a way to solve problems. The participants are generally volunteers.

CTTSSR: Center for Transportation Safety, Security, and Risk.

Data Science: A science of analyzing, preparing, collecting, visualizing, and managing large data sets by incorporating information and study from various STEM and social science disciplines.

Data Sciences Summer Institute (DSSI): A keystone of CCICADA's education program. DSSI was initially developed at partner institution the University of Illinois – Urbana Champaign to encourage computer science students in universities with small research programs to pursue graduate studies and to expose students to the national research laboratories.

Department of Homeland Security Center of Excellence (COE): An association of many universities and businesses whose work and research is to create and produce innovative and groundbreaking high technologies and critical knowledge in homeland securities. COE is sponsored by the DHS Office of University Programs and supported by the Oak Ridge Institute for Science Education (ORISE).

DHS: Department of Homeland Security.

DIMACS: Discrete Mathematics and Theoretical Computer Science.

Discrete Science: Examines, studies, and analyzes patterns and assignments of large data sets, including schedules and arrangement. The purpose is to utilize this science to establish connections between individuals or groups and to provide better ways to identify changes in data patterns.

DOD: Department of Defense.

DSS: Decision Support System.

EMI: Emergency Management Institute.

EVRL: Engineering Visualization Research Laboratory.

Experiential Learning: The process of learning from hands-on experience.

FEMA: Federal Emergency Management Institute.

GPD: Gulfport Police Department.

High Frequency Radar: High frequency (HF) radar systems measure the speed and direction of ocean surface currents in near real time. The Rutgers University/ University of Puerto Rico–Mayaguez HF radar system is a multi-use system. The first is to measure ocean currents via Doppler effects on the radar signal due to the currents, and the second is to detect and measure position, velocity, and bearing of vessels, via Doppler shift techniques.

Homeland Security Grant Program (HSGP): Established in 2003 and consisting of three separate, yet interrelated programs: the State Homeland Security Program (SHSP), the Urban Areas Security Initiative (UASI), and Operation Stonegarden (OPSG), the HSGP provides grant funds to state and local governments to increase funding for first-responder equipment, planning, training, exercises, and the collection of intelligence about potential attacks.

Homeland Security: No definitive definition exists for this special and important entity. Its purpose is multifaceted, as one of its main purposes is to "secure" the safety and well being of all citizens of America.

IDS-UAC: Institute of Discrete Sciences- University Affiliate Sciences, a DHS Center for Excellence.

Intergovernmental Relations: The codependent and multifaceted relationships that exist between and amongst different levels of governments.

IP HEI: Infrastructure Protection Higher Education Initiative.

IPO: Individual Plan and Orientation.

IT: Information Technology.

ITE: Information Technology and Engineering.

iTIER: Informatics for Targeted Infusion of Education and Research in the Sciences.

Local Oscillator: The main high-frequency radio signal generated by a super-heterodyne receiver. This signal can radiate into the environment as unstimulated emissions.

MAISA: Maryland Alliance of Information Security Assurance.

Marine Transportation System (MTS): The Marine Transportation System, or MTS, consists of waterways, ports, and intermodal landside connections that allow the various modes of transportation to move people and goods to, from, and on the water.

Maritime Domain Awareness (MDA): The effective understanding of anything associated with the maritime domain that could impact the security, safety, economy, or environment. The maritime domain is defined as all areas and things of, on, under, relating to, adjacent to, or bordering on a sea, ocean, or other navigable waterway, including all maritime-related activities, infrastructure, people, cargo, and vessels and other conveyances.

Matched Filter: The optimal linear filter for detecting a known signal in additive white noise. Such filters are often used for detecting known electromagnetic emissions.

Modeling and Simulation: Modeling tools can be used by researchers to better understand consequences of actions or behaviors, and simulations are used to show the ultimate real effects of different conditions and courses of action or behavior. Simulation is also used when the actual system cannot be engaged, or because it may not be accessible. It may not yet be built, or it simply may not exist.

MSI: Minority Serving Institution.

MSU: Morgan State University, a historical Black University and minority serving institution (MSI).

MTSRU: Marine Transportation System Recovery Unit.

NASA: National Aeronautics and Space Administration.

National Response Framework (NRF): A guide to help governments plan and prepare for the ability to provide a unified response across jurisdictions to any manmade and natural disasters.

Native American Tribes: The term "tribe" is used interchangeably with "American Indian," "Native American," and "tribal nations." As used throughout this study, these terms refer to "any Federally-recognized governing body of an Indian or Alaska Native tribe, band, nation, pueblo, village, or community that the Secretary of Interior acknowledges to exist as an Indian tribe under the Federally Recognized Tribe List Act of 1994, 25 U.S.C 479a (FEMA, 2010)." For clarification purposes as designated by the Department of Interior, Bureau of Indian Affairs

(2013), "federally recognized tribes are recognized as possessing certain inherent rights of self-government (i.e., tribal sovereignty) and are entitled to receive certain federal benefits, services, and protections because of their special relationship with the United States."

NIPP: National Infrastructure Protection Plan.

NMIO: National Maritime Intelligence-Integration Office.

NOAA: National Oceanic and Atmospheric Administration.

NOPD: New Orleans Police Department.

NSF: National Science Foundation.

NTSCOE: National Transportation Security Center of Excellence.

NYHOPS: New York Harbor Observing and Prediction System.

OIP: Office of Infrastructure Protection.

ORNL: Oak Ridge National Laboratory.

OUP: Office of University Programs within the Department of Homeland Security.

PACER: The National Center for the Study of Preparedness and Catastrophic Event Response, a DHS Center for Excellence.

Passive Acoustics: The action of listening for sounds generated by targets of interest, often at specific frequencies or for purposes of specific analyses. These may be water or airborne vessels, or intruders, among other things.

PSL: Johns Hopkins Division of Public Safety Leadership.

Range-Doppler Processing: A method for simultaneously extracting both range and range-rate from a radar signal. The processor outputs a two-dimensional matrix with range on one axis and range-rate (doppler) on the other. For stimulated emissions, the "doppler" output is the mutual frequency drift between the transmitter and the target device.

Reconnect: Workshops that expose undergraduate teaching faculty to the interchange between the mathematical and computer sciences and the department of homeland securities by introducing the faculty to relevant research topics that can be implemented in classroom lectures, activities, and presentations.

Research Experiences for Undergraduates (REUs): REU programs provide undergraduate students with an interesting and important research experiences that will positively enhance their academic decisions and future educational and career goals.

SAROPS: Search and Rescue Optimal Planning System used by the Coast Guard.

SCIPUFF: Second-Oder Closure Integrated Puff.

SMEs: Subject Matter Experts.

Social Media: Internet, Website, and electronic means of communicating socially. Operationally defined here, social media is described in a more complex way than the term is generally expressed. It is looked at as more than being useful for socializing, but also as an Internet, networking tool for security, where humans are able to electronically and quickly communicate with each other in case of emergency or homeland threat.

Software-Defined Radio: A radio transmitter or receiver which has signal processing functions that are defined by computer software.

SPRETS: Special Populations Response to Emergency Health Threats Survey.

SSRIW: Supporting Secure and resilient Inland Waterways.

START: National Consortium for the Study of Terrorism and Responses to Terrorism.

STEM: Science, Technology, Engineering and Mathematics.

Stimulated Emissions: A method for inducing changes in a device's unintended electromagnetic emissions by using specially-crafted radio signals.

Superheterodyne Receiver: A radio receiver design used for high-quality speech or high-rate data signals. They are common in two-way radios, broadcast receivers, and cellular or cordless telephones.

Super-Regenerative Receiver: A simple radio receiver design used by many low-cost devices, such as toy cars and keyless entry systems.

Target Device: An electronic device that has stimulated emissions. Devices tested in this study include toy cars and narrow-band FM radio receivers.

Tribal Governance: Incorporates tribal culture, history, social interactions, laws, jurisdiction, and sovereignty.

Trust Responsibility: The responsibility of the federal government to honor treaties, compromises, and other bound agreements by inheriting the expectation to honor those agreements for the best interests of the tribes and its members.

TSA: Transportation Security Administration.

Unified System of Homeland Security and Emergency Preparedness: The unified approach to homeland security and emergency preparedness has included efforts to "provide a systematic, proactive approach to guide departments and agencies at all levels of government, nongovernmental organizations, and the private sector to work seamlessly to prevent, protect against, respond to, recover from, and mitigate the effects of incidents, regardless of cause, size, location, or complexity, in order to reduce the loss of life and property and harm to the environment" (FEMA, 2010). According to the Department of Homeland Security's National Response Framework (2007) , to be able to achieve an effective system of unified command, there needs to be unity of effort which must extend across multiple geographic and legal jurisdictions. FEMA made it clear that emergency management is a difficult function that must frequently cross jurisdictional boundaries (Waugh, 1994). Like the foundation for achieving a unified system of command, in order to be able to execute effective emergency management strategies, it is crucial that there be cooperation and coordination across jurisdictions. To be more specific, FEMA's agency policy warns that within the field of emergency management, the agency expresses that problems are shared and so too should responsibility. It goes on to note that the agency refrains from providing assistance to only one jurisdiction or government and consequently placing in jeopardy the interests of needs of another government (Federal Registrar, FEMA Tribal Agency Policy, 1999).

Up-Mixing Component: The high-frequency stimulated emissions of a super-heterodyne receiver. These emissions contain a nearly-perfect copy of the signal that the device is receiving.

USACE: United States Army Corp of Engineers.

USCG: United States Coast Guard.

UUVs: Unmanned Underwater Vehicles

VACCINE: Visual Analytics for Command, Control, and Interoperability Environments, a DHS Center for Excellence.

VAST MSI: Visual Analytics for Science and Technology at a Minority Serving Institution.

Compilation of References

Adams, H. (2012). Sovereignty, safety, and security: Tribal governments under the Stafford and homeland security acts. *American Indian Law Journal, 1*(1), 127–146.

Adams, T., Anderson, Turner, & Armstrong. (2011). Coping through a disaster: Lessons from Hurricane Katrina. *Journal of Homeland Security and Emergency Management, 8*(1), 19. doi:10.2202/1547-7355.1836

Adams, T., & Anderson, L. (Forthcoming). *Policing during natural disasters*. Boulder, CO. *FirstForumPress*.

Agranoff, R. (2012). *Collaborating to manage: A primer for the public sector*. Washington, DC: Georgetown University Press.

American Indian Policy Center. (2002). *Brief history of U.S. tribal relations*. Retrieved 2011 from http://www.airpi.org

Anderson, L. W., & Krathwohl, D. (Eds.). (2001). *A taxonomy for learning, teaching, and assessing: A revision of Bloom's taxonomy of educational objectives*. New York: Longman.

Annual Aspen Security Forum. (2013, July 18). *Intelligence and counterterrorism – Panel discussion*. National Counterterrorism Center. Retrieval information: CSPAN2 and http://www.aspeninstitute.org/policy-work/homeland-security

Arndt, J., Greenberg, J., Solomon, S., Pyszczynski, T., & Schimel, J. (1999). Creativity and terror management: Evidence that creative activity increases guilt and social projection following mortality salience. *Journal of Personality and Social Psychology, 77*, 19–32. doi:10.1037/0022-3514.77.1.19

Ashley, J. S., & Jarratt-Ziemski, K. (1999). Superficiality and bias: The (mis)treatment of Native Americans in U. S. government textbooks. *American Indian Quarterly, 23*(3/4), 49–62. doi:10.2307/1185828

Associated Press. (2012, January). *Ship carrying rocket parts hits Kentucky bridge*. Retrieved May 10, 2013, from, http://usatoday30.usatoday.com/news/nation/story/2012-01-27/kentucky-bridge-collapse/52813592/1

Astin, A. W. (1993). *What matters in college*. San Francisco, CA: Jossey-Bass Inc.

Aufrecht, S. E. (1999). Missing: Native American governance in American public administration literature. *American Review of Public Administration, 29*(4), 370–390. doi:10.1177/02750749922064481

Barber, J. E. (2012). Envision success: Exploring data on personal well-being could help. *Instructional Forum-The Academic Affairs Area Journal, 27*(2), 5–6.

Bard, J. D., & Ham, F. M. (1999). Time difference of arrival dilution of precision and applications. *IEEE Transactions on Signal Processing, 47*(2), 521–523. doi:10.1109/78.740135

Barkley, E. F., Cross, K. P., & Major, C. H. (2005). *Collaborative learning techniques: A handbook for college faculty. San-Francisco.* Jossey-Bass.

Bays, B. A., & Fouberg, E. H. (2002). *The tribes and the states: Geographies of intergovernmental interaction.* Rowman & Littlefield Publishers, Inc.

Beetner, D., Seguin, S., & Hubing, H. (2008). *Electromagnetic emissions stimulation and detection system.* Academic Press.

Bloom, B. S. (1956). *Taxonomy of educational objectives, handbook I: The cognitive domain.* New York: David McKay Co Inc.

Boehrer, J., & Linsky, M. (1990). Teaching with cases: Learning to question. *New Directions for Teaching and Learning*, 41–57. doi:10.1002/tl.37219904206

Bracewell, R. (1999). *The Fourier transform and its applications* (3rd ed.). New York: McGraw-Hill.

Bruno, M. (2012). Maritime domain awareness – A call for enhanced capability. *AAPA Seaports Magazine, 27*, 34.

Bruno, M., & Blumberg, A. (2004). An urban ocean observatory – Real-time assessments and forecasts of the New York harbor marine environment. *Sea Technology, 45*, 27–32.

Bruno, M., Blumberg, A., & Herrington, T. (2006). The urban ocean observatory - Coastal ocean observations and forecasting in the New York bight. *Journal of Marine Science and Environment, C4*, 1–9.

Bruno, M., Sutin, A., Chung, K., Sedunov, A., Sedunov, N., & Salloum, H. et al. (2011). Satelli.te imaging and passive acoustics in layered approach for small boat detection and classification M*arine. Technology Society Journal, 45*(3), 77–87. doi:10.4031/MTSJ.45.3.10

Bruns, A. (2009). Talent by design. *Site Selection Mag.*, 475–490.

Butts, J. (2003/2004). Victims in waiting: How the homeland security act falls short of fully protecting tribal lands. *American Indian Law Review, 28*(2), 373–392. doi:10.2307/20070712

Campo, M., Mayer, H., & Rovito, J. (2012). Supporting secure and resilient inland waterways: Decision framework for evaluating offloading capabilities at terminals during catastrophic waterway closures. *Transportation Research Record: Journal of the Transportation Research Board, 2273*(1), 10–17. doi:10.3141/2273-02

Carafano, J. J., & Weitz, R. E. (2009). Complex systems analysis: A necessary tool for home security. *Backgrounder. Heritage Foundation, 2261*, 1–7.

Caruson, K., & MacManus, S. A. (2006). Mandates and management challenges in the trenches: An intergovernmental perspective on homeland security. *Public Administration Review, 66*, 522–536. doi:10.1111/j.1540-6210.2006.00613.x

Choi, J. Y., Engle, B. A., & Farnsworth, K. (2005). Web-based GiS and spatial decision support system for watershed management. *Journal of Hydroinformatics, 7*(3), 165–174.

Compilation of References

Chuchmach, M. (2013). *Boston marathon bomb made with toy car parts?* ABC News. Retrieved from http://abcnews.go.com/Blotter/boston-marathon-bomb-made-toy-car-parts/story?id=18991380#.UXCWPde-FGoM

Chung, K., Sutin, A., & Bruno, M. (2011). Cross-correlation method for measuring ship acoustic signatures. *Proceedings, 160th Meeting Acoustical Society of America, 11*, 1-12.

Coleman, P. T., & Morton, D. (2000). *The handbook of conflict resolution: Theory and practice.* San Francisco: Jossey-Bass Publishers.

Command, C., & the Interoperability Center for Advanced Data Analysis (CCICADA). (2013). *About CCICADA.* Retrieved from http://ccicada.rutgers.edu/about.html

Committee on Prospering in the Global Economy of the 21st Century (U.S.) & Committee on Science, Engineering, and Public Policy (U.S.). (2007). *Rising above the gathering storm: Energizing and employing America for a brighter economic future.* Washington, DC: National Academies Press.

Committee on Prospering in the Global Economy of the 21st Century (U.S.) & Committee on Science, Engineering, and Public Policy (U.S.). (2010). *Rising above the gathering storm, revisited, rapidly approaching a category 5.* Washington, DC: National Academies Press.

Companion Site to the McGraw Hill Homeland Security Handbook. (2007). Retrieved 2011 from http://www.homelandsecuritybook.com/book/table-of-contents.html

Corredor, J., Amador, A., Canals, M., Rivera, S., Capella, J., & Morell, J. et al. (2011). Optimizing and validating high-frequency radar surface current measurements in the Mona passage. *Marine Technology Society Journal, 45*(3), 49–58. doi:10.4031/MTSJ.45.3.6

Cringely, R. X. (1995). *Personal interview with Steve Jobs: The lost interview.* Available on Netflix, 2012.

Dai, J., Clough, B., Ho, I.-C., Lu, X., Liu, J., & Zhang, X.-C. (2011). Recent progresses in terahertz wave air photonics. *IEEE Trans. Terahertz Science and Tech., 1*(1), 274–281. doi:10.1109/TTHZ.2011.2159550

Davey, M. (2013, April). In Midwest, drought gives way to flood. *New York Times.* Retrieved May 10, 2013, from http://www.nytimes.com/2013/04/26/us/in-midwest-drought-abruptly-gives-way-to-flood.html?_r=0

Davidson, A. J., Chellappa, Raja, S., Dattelbaum, D. M., & Yoo, C.-S. (2011). Pressure induced isostructural metastable phase transition of ammonium nitrate. *The Journal of Physical Chemistry A, 115*(42), 11889–11896. doi:10.1021/jp207754z PMID:21902257

Department of Homeland Security. (2002). *Homeland Security Act of 2002, title I.* Retrieved from http://www.dhs.gov/homeland-security-act-2002

Department of Homeland Security. (2008). *Reading by numbers.* Retrieved from http://www.dhs.gov/reading-numbers

Department of Homeland Security. (n.d.). *Centers of excellence.* Retrieved from http://www.dhs.gov/st-centers-excellence

Di Iorio, W. R. (2007). Mending fences: The fractured relationship between Native American tribes and the federal government and its negative impact on border security. *Syracuse Law Review, 57*(2), 407–428.

Donley, M. B., & Pollard, N. A. (2002). Homeland security: The difference between a vision and a wish. *Public Administration Review, 6*, 138–144. doi:10.1111/1540-6210.62.s1.23

Dourbal, P. F. (1998). Method and apparatus for detecting and locating a concealed listening device.

Eisinger, P. (2006). Imperfect federalism: The intergovernmental partnership for homeland security. *Public Administration Review, 66*, 537–545. doi:10.1111/j.1540-6210.2006.00614.x

Engle, B. A., Choi, J. Y., Harbor, J., & Pandley, S. (2003). Web-based DSS for hydrologic impact evaluation of small watershed land use changes. *Computers and Electronics in Agriculture, 39*, 241–249. doi:10.1016/S0168-1699(03)00078-4

Estellés-Arolas, E., & González-Ladrón-de-Guevara, F. (2012). Towards an integrated crowdsourcing definition. *Journal of Information Science, 38*(2), 189–200. doi:10.1177/0165551512437638

Evans, L. E. (2011). *Power from powerlessness: Tribal governments, institutional niches, and American federalism.* New York: Oxford University Press. doi:10.1093/acprof:oso/9780199742745.001.0001

Executive Order 13175. (2000). *Coordination and consultation with Indian tribal governments.* Retrieved 2010 from http://ceq.hss.doe.gov/nepa/regs/eos/eo13175.html

Federal Emergency Management Agency. (1999). Final agency policy for government-to-government relations with American Indian and Alaska native tribal governments. *Federal Register, 64*(7).

Federal Emergency Management Agency. (2013). *National exercise program.* Retrieved May 10, 2013 from, http://www.fema.gov/national-exercise-program

Federal Railroad Administration. (2013). *FRA office of safety analysis web site.* Retrieved May 10, 2013, from http://safetydata.fra.dot.gov/OfficeofSafety/default.aspx

FEMA. (2002). *About NIMS.* Retrieved 2011 from http://www.fema.gov/emergency/nims/AboutNIMS.shtm

Ferrari, P., Flammini, A., & Sisinni, E. (2009). Introducing the wireless ultra smart sensor. In *Proceedings of IEEE I2MTC* (pp. 1304–1308). IEEE.

Flintoft, I. D., Marvin, A. C., Robinson, M. P., Fischer, K., & Rowell, A. J. (2003). The re-emission spectrum of digital hardware subjected to EMI. *IEEE Transactions on Electromagnetic Compatibility, 45*(4), 576–585. doi:10.1109/TEMC.2003.819058

Flores, A. (2007). Examining disparities in mathematics education: Achievement gap or opportunity gap? *High School Journal, 91*(1), 29–42. doi:10.1353/hsj.2007.0022

Gardner, H. (1993). *Framework of mind: The theory of multiple intelligences* (Rev. ed.). New York: Basic Books.

Gardner, W. A. (1988). Signal interception: a unifying theoretical framework for feature detection. *IEEE Transactions on Communications, 36*(8), 897–906. doi:10.1109/26.3769

Gardner, W. A. (1991). Exploitation of spectral redundancy in cyclostationary signals. *IEEE Sig. Proc. Mag.*, *8*(2), 14–36. doi:10.1109/79.81007

Georgas, N., & Blumberg, A. (2009). *Establishing confidence in marine forecast systems: The design and skill assessment of the New York harbor observation and prediction system, version 3 (NYHOPS v3).* Paper presented at the Eleventh International Conference in Estuarine and Coastal Modeling (ECM11). Seattle, WA.

Giacoletto, L. J., & Landee, R. W. (Eds.). (1977). *Electronics designers' handbook* (2nd ed.). New York: McGraw-Hill.

Gleason, S., & Gebre-Egziabher, D. (2009). *GNSS applications and methods*. Artech.

Greenberg, M. R., Altiok, T., Fefferman, N., Georgopoulos, P., Lacy, C., & Lahr, M. … Roberts, F. S. (2011b). A set of blended risk-based decision support tools for protecting passenger rail-centered transit corridors against cascading impacts of terrorist attacks. In *Proceedings of the US Department of Homeland Security Science Conference–Fifth Annual University Network Summit.* Washington, DC: US Government.

Greenberg, M. R., Lioy, P., Ozbas, B., Mantell, N., Isukapalli, S., & Lahr, M. et al. (2013, June). Passenger rail security, planning, and resilience: Application of network, plume, and economic simulation models as decision support tools. *Risk Analysis*. doi:10.1111/risa.12073 PMID:23718133

Greenberg, M. R., Lowrie, K., Mayer, H., & Altiok, T. (2011a). Risk-based decision support tools: Protecting rail-centered transit corridors from cascading effects. *Risk Analysis*, *31*(12), 1849–1858. doi:10.1111/j.1539-6924.2011.01627.x PMID:21564145

Griffith, C. M. (2007). *Unmanned aerial vehicle-mounted high sensitivity RF receiver to detect improvised explosive devices.* Naval Postgraduate School.

Haddal, C. C. (2010, August 11). *Border security: The role of the US border patrol* (RL32562). Washington, DC: United States Congressional Research Service.

Hall, G. E. (2010). Technology's Achilles heel: Achieving high-quality implementation. *Journal of Research on Technology in Education*, *42*(3), 231–253. doi:10.1080/15391523.2010.10782550

Hmleo-Silver, C., Duncan, R., & Chinn, C. (2007). Scaffolding and achievement in problem-based and inquiry learning: A response to Kircshner, Sweller and Clark (2006). *Educational Psychologist*, *42*(2), 99–107. doi:10.1080/00461520701263368

Holt, T., & Pullen, J. (2007). Urban canopy modeling of the New York City metropolitan area: A comparison and validation of single-layer and multi-layer parameterizations. *Monthly Weather Review*, *135*, 1906–1930. doi:10.1175/MWR3372.1

Homeland Security Center for Dynamic Data Analysis. (2009). *DyDAn research projects.* Retrieved from http://www.dydan.rutgers.edu

Howe, J. (2006). Crowdsourcing: A definition. Crowdsourcing Blog. Retrieved from http://crowdsourcing.typepad.com/cs/2006/06/crowdsourcing_a.html

International Telecommunication Union (ITU). (2010). [*ICT facts and figures*. Retrieved from www.itu.int/ict]. *WORLD (Oakland, Calif.)*, *2010*.

Jackson, K., & Wilson, J. (2012). Supporting African American students' learning of mathematics: A problem of practice. *Urban Education*, *47*(2), 354–398. doi:10.1177/0042085911429083

Jacobs, A. (2009, July 1). The pathologies of big data. *ACMQueue*. Retrieved from http://queue.acm.org/detail.cfm?id=1563874

Jankiraman, M. (2007). *Design of multifrequency CW radars*. SciTech Publishing.

Jha, M. K., Udenta, F., & Kang, M. W. (2011). *A dynamic capacitated arc routing problem for optimal evacuation strategies in disasters: Formulation and solution algorithm presentation*. Retrieved from http://ccicada.rutgers.edu/Workshops/ResearchRetreat2011/Jha.pdf

Jobs for the Future. (2007). *The STEM workforce challenge, the role of the public workforce system in a national solution for a competitive science, technology, engineering, and mathematics (STEM) workforce*. Washington, DC: U.S. Department of Labor, Employment and Training Administration.

Keefe, B. (2010). *The perception of STEM: Analysis, issues, and future directions. Survey*. Entertainment and Media Communication Institute.

Kessel, R., & Pullen, J. (2011). Summary of the 2nd international waterside security conference. *Marine Technology Society Journal*, *45*(3), 12–13. doi:10.4031/MTSJ.45.3.14

Kettl, D. F. (2007). *System under stress: Homeland security and American politics* (2nd ed.). Congressional Quarterly Press.

Koebler, J. (2012, November 16). *Phones become the 'frontline' of human sex-trafficking*. U.S. News and World Report. Retrieved from http://www.usnews.com/news/articles/2012/11/16/report-phones-become-the-frontline-of-human-sex-trafficking

Kuh, G. D., Kinzie, J., Schuh, J. H., & Whitt, E. J. (2005a). *Assessing conditions to enhance educational effectiveness: The inventory for student engagement and success*. San Francisco, CA: Jossey-Bass.

Kumar, T., et al. (2012). *2012–2013 factbook* (Tech. Rep.). Missouri S&T. Retrieved from http://ira.mst.edu/factbook/1213/

Lee, J.-Y., & Scholtz, R. A. (2002). Ranging in a dense multipath environment using an UWB radio link. *IEEE Journal on Selected Areas in Communications*, *20*(9), 1677–1683. doi:10.1109/JSAC.2002.805060

Lenhart, A. (2010, April 20). *Teens, cell phones, and texting*. Pew Internet and American Life Project. Retrieved from www.pewresearch.org

Lester, W., & Krejci, D. (2007). Business not as usual: The national incident management system, federalism, and leadership. *Public Administration Review*, *67*, 84–93. doi:10.1111/j.1540-6210.2007.00817.x

Levanon, N., & Mozeson, E. (2004). *Radar signals*. Wiley. doi:10.1002/0471663085

Leventhal, H., & Niles, P. (1965). Persistence of influence for varying durations of exposure to threat stimuli. *Psychological Reports*, *16*, 223–233. doi:10.2466/pr0.1965.16.1.223 PMID:14283967

Compilation of References

Leventhal, H., & Watts, J. C. (1966). Sources of resistance to fear-arousing communications on smoking and lung cancer. *Journal of Personality*, *34*, 155–175. doi:10.1111/j.1467-6494.1966.tb01706.x PMID:5939211

Levin, A. (2012, December). *NJ transit had $400 million in Hurricane Sandy damage*. Retrieved May 10, 2013, from,http://www.bloomberg.com/news/2012-12-06/nj-transit-had-400-million-in-hurricane-sandy-damage.html

Mansouri, M., Nilchiani, R., & Mostashari, A. (2010). A decision analysis framework for resilience strategies in maritime systems. *IEEE Systems Journal*, 484 - 489.

Maryland High School Assessments. Test Support. (2009). *Practice test*. Retrieved from http://hsaexam.org/support/practice.html

Maryland State Department of Education. (2001). *Keys to math success a report from the Maryland mathematics commission*. Retrieved from http://www.msde.state.md.us/Special_ReportsandData/keys.pdf

Mason, D. W. (1998). Tribes and states: A new era in intergovernmental affairs. *Publius: The Journal of Federalism*, *28*(1), 111–130. doi:10.1093/oxfordjournals.pubjof.a029943

Maton, K. (2004). Increasing the number of African American PhDs in the sciences and engineering: A strengths-based approach. *The American Psychologist*, *59*(6), 547–556. doi:10.1037/0003-066X.59.6.547 PMID:15367090

McCombs, B. L., & Lauer, P. A. (1997). Development and validation of the learner-centered battery: Self-assessment tools for teacher reflection and professional development. *Professional Educator*, *20*(1), 1–21.

McCool, D. (1993). Intergovernmental conflict and Indian water rights: An assessment of negotiated settlements. *Publius: The Journal of Federalism*, *23*, 85–101.

McDonald, D. (2012, June). *Federal industry logistics standardization: Supporting a federal navigation information framework and integration*. Paper presented at Diagnosing the Marine Transportation System: Measuring Performance and Targeting Improvement. Washington, DC.

McGuire, T. R. (1990). Federal Indian policy: A framework for evaluation. *Human Organization*, *49*(3), 206–216.

Meir, T., Orton, P., Pullen, J., Holt, T., Thompson, W., & Arend, M. (2013). Forecasting the New York City urban heat island and sea breeze during extreme heat events. *Weather and Forecasting*, *28*(6), 1460–1477. doi:10.1175/WAF-D-13-00012.1

Menzel, D. C. (2006). The Katrina aftermath: A failure of federalism or leadership? *Public Administration Review*, *66*, 808–812. doi:10.1111/j.1540-6210.2006.00649.x

Mirabbasi, S., & Martin, K. (2000). Classical and modern receiver architectures. *IEEE Communications Magazine*, *38*(11), 132–139. doi:10.1109/35.883502

Moseley, F. (1955). The automatic radio direction finder. *IRE Trans. Aeronautical and Navigational Electronics*, (4), 4–11.

Moseley, C., & Utley, J. (2006). The effect of an integrated science and mathematics content-based course on science and mathematics teaching efficacy of pre-service elementary teachers. *Journal of Elementary Science Education*, *18*(2), 123–132. doi:10.1007/BF03174684

Moynihan, D. P. (2005). Homeland security and the U.S. public management policy agenda. *Governance: An International Journal of Policy, Administration and Institutions, 18,* 171–196. doi:10.1111/j.1468-0491.2005.00272.x

Myers, D. G. (2010). *Social psychology* (11th ed.). New York: McGraw-Hill Publishers.

Nambayah, M., & Quickenden, T. I. (2004). A quantitative assessment of chemical techniques for detecting traces of explosives at counter-terrorist portals. *Talanta, 63*(2), 461–467. doi:10.1016/j.talanta.2003.11.018 PMID:18969454

National Association of Colleges and Employers. (2012). *Job outlook report.* Bethlehem, PA: Author.

National Association of Mathematicians. (2013). *NAM.* Retrieved from www.nam-math.org

National Congress of American Indians. (2011). *An introduction to Indian nations in the United States.* Retrieved 2011 from http://www.ncai.org/fileadmin/initiatives/NCAI_Indian_Nations_In_The_US.pdf

National Congress of American Indians. (2011). *NCAI commends FEMA support for direct authority of tribal governments to apply for presidential disaster declaration.* Retrieved 2013 from http://www.ncai.org/policy-issues/tribal-governance/emergency-management

National Congress of American Indians. (2013). *Homeland security.* Retrieved 2013 from http://www.ncai.org/policy-issues/tribal-governance/homeland-security

National Education and Technology Council. (2013). *Federal science technology, engineering, and mathematics (STEM) education, 5-year strategic plan.* Washington, DC: U.S. Government Printing Office.

National Research Council. (2011). *Successful K-12 STEM education.* Washington, DC: The National Academies Press.

National Resource Council. (2010). *National resource council report: The national research council's assessment of research-doctoral programs.* Retrieved from http://www.gsas.harvard.edu/faculty/national_research_council_report_2010.php

Noble, D. E. (1962). The history of land-mobile radio communications. *Proc. IRE, 50*(5), 1405–1414.

Norris, F. H., Stevens, S. P., Pfefferbaum, B., Wyche, K. F., & Pfefferbaum, R. L. (2008). Community resilience as a metaphor, theory, set of capacities, and strategy for disaster readiness. *American Journal of Community Psychology, 41*(1-2), 127–150. doi:10.1007/s10464-007-9156-6 PMID:18157631

Nylés, L. (1996). Disaster prevention and management. *Bradford, 5*(5), 23-25.

Oak Ridge Institute for Science Education (ORISE). (2003). *ORISE supports research for solutions to homeland security needs.* Retrieved from http://orise.orau.gov/scientific-peer-review/difference/homeland-security.aspx

Oppenheim, A. V., Schafer, R. W., & Buck, J. R. (1999). *Discrete-time signal processing* (2nd ed.). Pearson.

Orfanidis, S. J. (1988). *Optimum signal processing: An introduction* (2nd ed.). New York: McGraw-Hill.

Compilation of References

Organick, A. G., & Kowalski, T. (2009). From conflict to cooperation: State and tribal court relations in the era of self-determination. *Court Review*, *45*, 48.

Ortiz, J. (2002). Tribal governance and public administration. *Administration & Society*, *35*(5), 59–481.

Orton, P., Georgas, N., Blumberg, A., & Pullen, J. (2012). Detailed modeling of recent severe storm tides in estuaries of the New York City region. *Journal of Geophysical Research-Oceans*, *117*, C09030. doi:10.1029/2012JC008220

Pacheco-Londoño, L., Ortiz-Rivera, W., Primera-Pedrozo, O., & Hernández-Rivera, S. (2009). Vibrational spectroscopy standoff detection of explosives. *Analytical and Bioanalytical Chemistry*, *395*(2), 323–335. doi:10.1007/s00216-009-2954-y PMID:19633965

Pascarella, E., & Terenzini, P. (2005). *How college effects student: A third decade of research* (Vol. 2). San Francisco: Jossey-Bass Higher & Adult Education.

Pata, J. (2013). *The state of Indian country: Global tribes?* National Public Radio. Retrieved 22 February 2013 from http://www.npr.org/2013/02/15/172102688/the-state-of-indian-country-global-tribes

Patwari, N., Hero, A. O. III, Perkins, M., Correal, N. S., & O'dea, R. J. (2003). Relative location estimation in wireless sensor networks. *IEEE Transactions on Signal Processing*, *51*(8), 2137–2148. doi:10.1109/TSP.2003.814469

Pink, D. (2005). *A whole new mind: Moving from the information age to the conceptual age*. New York: Riverhead Books.

Pinsky, M. A. (2002). Introduction to Fourier analysis and wavelets. In *Graduate studies in mathematics* (Vol. 102, pp. 131–133). American Mathematical Soc.

Posner, P. L. (2002). *Combating terrorism: Intergovernmental partnership in a national strategy to enhance state and local preparedness (GAO-02-547T)*. Washington, DC: General Accounting Office.

Powers, S. E., & DeWaters, J. (2004). Creating project-based learning experiences university-K-12 partnerships. In *Proceedings of the American Society for Engineering Education Frontiers in Education Conference*. Savannah, GA: ASEE.

Prager, F., Beeler, Asay G., Lee, B., & von Winterfeldt, D. (2011). Exploring reductions in London underground passenger journeys following the July 2005 bombings. *Risk Analysis*, *31*(5), 773–786. doi:10.1111/j.1539-6924.2010.01555.x PMID:21231940

Pullen, J., & Bruno, M. (2013). The center for secure and resilient maritime commerce: A DHS national center of excellence in maritime security. In *Cases on research and knowledge discovery: Homeland security centers of excellence*. Hershey, PA: IGI Global.

Pullen, J., Chang, J., & Hanna, S. (2013). Air/sea transport, dispersion and fate modeling for the Fukushima nuclear power plant crisis. *Bulletin of the American Meteorological Society*, *93*(13), 31–39. doi:10.1175/BAMS-D-11-00158.1

Pullen, J., Ching, J., Sailor, D., Thompson, W., Bornstein, R., & Koracin, D. (2008). Progress toward meeting the challenges of our coastal urban future. *Bulletin of the American Meteorological Society*, *89*(11), 1727–1731. doi:10.1175/2008BAMS2560.1

Pullen, J., Holt, T., Blumberg, A., & Bornstein, R. (2007). Atmospheric response to local upwelling in the vicinity of New York/ New Jersey harbor. *Journal of Applied Meteorology and Climatology*, 46, 1031–1052. doi:10.1175/JAM2511.1

Pyszczynski, T., Greenberg, J., & Solomon, S. (1999). A dual-process model of defense against conscious and unconscious death-related thoughts: An extension of terror management theory. *Psychological Review*, 106, 835–845. doi:10.1037/0033-295X.106.4.835 PMID:10560330

Report, C. I. P. (2002). George Mason University school of law's national center for technology and law in conjunction with James Madison University, launches critical infrastructure protection project. *The CIP Report*, 1(1), 2.

Report, C. I. P. (2010). Joint George Mason University and department of homeland security initiative on critical infrastructure higher education programs. *The CIP Report*, 9(2), 12.

Report, C. I. P. (2012). 2012 critical infrastructure symposium. *The CIP Report*, 10(12), 2.

Roarty, H., Lemus, E., Handel, E., Glenn, S., Barrick, D., & Isaacson, J. (2011). Performance evaluation of SeaSonde high-frequency radar for vessel detection. *Marine Technology Society Journal*, 45(3), 14–24. doi:10.4031/MTSJ.45.3.2

Roberts, F. S. (2004). Why bioMath? Why now? In F. Roberts, & M. Cozzens (Eds.), *BioMath in the schools* (pp. 3–34). Providence, RI: DIMACS – American Mathematical Society.

Ronquillo, J. C. (2011). American Indian tribal governance and management: Public administration promise or pretense? *Public Administration Review*, 71, 285–292. doi:10.1111/j.1540-6210.2011.02340.x

Sanders, M. (2009). Integrative STEM education primer. *Technology Teacher*, 68(4), 20–26.

School Improvement in Maryland. (2010). *HSA test performance status*. Retrieved from http://mdk12.org/data/HSA/TestPerformanceStatus.aspx?Nav=1.5:5.1:10.99:15.10#bargraph-all

Schwartz, J. (2012, November). After drought, reducing water flow could hurt Mississippi River transport. *New York Times*. Retrieved May 10, 2013, from http://www.nytimes.com/2012/11/27/us/hit-by-drought-mississippi-river-may-face-more-challenges.html

Sekiguchi, H., & Seto, S. (2008). Proposal of an information signal measurement method in display image contained in electromagnetic noise emanated from a personal computer. In *Proceedings of IEEE Instrum., & Measure. Tech. Conf.* (pp. 1859–1863). IEEE.

Shaik, A., Weng, H., Dong, X., Hubing, T. H., & Beetner, D. G. (2006). Matched filter detection and identification of electronic circuits based on their unintentional radiated emissions. In *Proceedings of IEEE ISEMC* (Vol. 3). IEEE.

Shaw, A. (2004). *University research centers of excellence for homeland security: A summary of a workshop*. Washington, DC: National Research Council, National Academies Press.

Skolnik, M. I. (1960). Theoretical accuracy of radar measurements. *IRE Trans. Aeronautical and Navigational Electronics*, (4), 123–129.

Compilation of References

Smith, I., & Coderre, M. (2008). The continuing war against IEDs. *WSTIAC Quarterly*, *8*(2), 3–6.

Southworth, F., Peterson, B., & Lambert, B. (2007). Development of a regional routing model for strategic waterway analysis. *Transportation Research Record: Journal of the Transportation Research Board, 1993*, 109–116. doi:10.3141/1993-15

Spencer, Q., Rice, M., Jeffs, B., & Jensen, M. (1997). Indoor wideband time/angle of arrival multipath propagation results. In *Proceedings of IEEE Vehicular Tech. Conf.* (Vol. 3, pp. 1410–1414). IEEE.

Staelin, D. H. (1969). Fast folding algorithm for detection of periodic pulse trains. *Proceedings of the IEEE, 57*(4), 724–725. doi:10.1109/PROC.1969.7051

Stagner, C., Conrad, A., Osterwise, C., Beetner, D. G., & Grant, S. (2011). A practical superheterodyne-receiver detector using stimulated emissions. *IEEE Transactions on Instrumentation and Measurement, 60*(4), 1461–1468. doi:10.1109/TIM.2010.2101330

Stagner, C., Halligan, M., Osterwise, C., Beetner, D. G., & Grant, S. L. (2013). Locating noncooperative radio receivers using wideband stimulated emissions. *IEEE Transactions on Instrumentation and Measurement, 62*(3), 667–674. doi:10.1109/TIM.2012.2219141

Stanton, J.M. (2012, May 20). *Introduction to data science*. Syracuse, NY: Syracuse University School of Information Studies.

START. (2005). *START hosts DHS faculty/student research teams*. Retrieved from http://www.start.umd.edu/start/announcements/announcement.asp?id=3

Steinman, E. (2004). American federalism and intergovernmental innovation in state-tribal relations. *Publius: The Journal of Federalism, 34*(2), 95–114. doi:10.1093/oxfordjournals.pubjof.a005031

Stone, M., & Petrick. (2013). The educational benefits of travel experiences a literature review. *Journal of Travel Research, 52*(6), 731–744. doi:10.1177/0047287513500588

Stove, A. G. (1992). Linear FMCW radar techniques. In Proceedings of Inst. Elect. Eng.—Radar and Signal Process. F (Vol. 139, pp. 343–350). Academic Press.

Swinyard, W. O. (1962). The development of the art of radio receiving from the early 1920's to the present. *Proc. IRE, 50*(5), 793–798.

Talavera, V. (2013). *The national center for border security and immigration*. El Paso, TX: University of Texas El Paso, Homeland Security Summer Scholars Academy, Program Summary.

Thotla, V., Ghasr, M. T. A., Zawodniok, M., Jagannathan, S., & Agarwal, S. (2012). Detection and localization of multiple R/C electronic devices using array detectors. In *Proceedings of the IEEE Int'l. Instrum. Meas. Tech. Conf.* (pp. 1687–1691). IEEE.

Tinto, V. (1993). *Leaving college: Rethinking the causes and cures of student attrition* (2nd ed.). Chicago, IL: University of Chicago Press.

Transportation Security Administration. (2012). *Mass transit*. Retrieved May 10, 2013 from, http://www.tsa.gov/stakeholders/mass-transit

Turin, G. (1960). An introduction to matched filters. *I.R.E. Transactions on Information Theory, 6*(3), 311–329. doi:10.1109/TIT.1960.1057571

U.S. Department of Homeland Security. (2006). *National infrastructure protection plan.* Washington, DC: Author.

U.S. Department of Homeland Security. (2008). *National infrastructure protection plan: Education and training assessment report and implementation plan.* Washington, DC: Author.

Ulversoy, T. (2010). Software defined radio: Challenges and opportunities. *IEEE Comm. Surveys & Tutorials, 12*(4), 531–550. doi:10.1109/SURV.2010.032910.00019

United States Army Corps of Engineers. (2012). *Civil works navigation.* Retrieved May 10, 2013, from, http://www.usace.army.mil/Missions/CivilWorks/Navigation.aspx

United States Coast Guard. (2008). *Commandant instruction 16000.28.2008.* Retrieved May 10, 2013, from http://www.uscg.mil/directives/ci/16000-16999/CI_16000_28.pdf

United States Constitution. (1787). *Article 1, section 8: Commerce clause.*

United States Department of Homeland Security. (2012). *USCG missions: Maritime security.* Retrieved May 10, 2013, from http://www.uscg.mil/top/missions/MaritimeSecurity.asp

United States Government Accountability Office. (2012, September 11). *Maritime security: Progress and challenges 10 years after the maritime transportation security act, statement of Stephen L. Caldwell, director homeland security and justice* (Report GAO-12-1009T). Retrieved May 10, 2013 from, http://www.gao.gov/assets/650/647999.pdf

Van Trees, H. L. (2001). Detection, estimation, and modulation theory. Wiley.

Wenger, D. E. Quarantelli, & Dynes. (1989). Disaster analysis: Local emergency management offices and arrangements. Newark, DE: University of Delaware, Disaster Research Center.

White House. (2014). *Preparing a 21st century workforce science, technology, engineering, and mathematics (STEM) education in the 2014 budget White House office of science and technology policy.* Retrieved from www.whitehouse.gov/ostp

Wild, B., & Ramchandran, K. (2005). Detecting primary receivers for cognitive radio applications. In *Proceedings of the IEEE Int'l Symp. DySPAN* (pp. 124–130). IEEE.

Wilkins, D. E. (1993). Breaking into the intergovernmental matrix: The Lumbee tribe's efforts to secure federal acknowledgement. *Publius, 23*(4), 123–142.

Wilson, C. (2006). *Improvised explosive devices (IEDs) in Iraq: Effects and countermeasures* (Congressional Research Service Report No. RS22330). Washington, DC: Library of Congress.

Wilson, P. I. (2002). Tribes, states, and the management of lake resources: Lakes Coeur d'Alene and Flathead. *Publius: The Journal of Federalism, 32*(3), 115–131. doi:10.1093/oxfordjournals.pubjof.a004951

Winstead, A., Williams, R., Zhang, Y., McLean, S., & Oyaghire, S. (2010). Application of microwave assisted organic synthesis to the development of near-IR cyanine dye probes. *The Journal of Microwave Power and Electromagnetic Energy, 44*(4), 207–212. PMID:21721469

Wise, C. R. (2002). Organizing for homeland security. *Public Administration Review, 62*(2), 131–144. doi:10.1111/0033-3352.00164

Compilation of References

Wise, C., & Nader, R. (2002). Organizing the federal system for homeland security: problems, issues, and dilemmas. *Public Administration Review, 62*(Special Issue), 44–57. doi:10.1111/1540-6210.62.s1.8

Wise, C., & Nader, R. (2008). Developing a national homeland security system: An urgent and complex task in intergovernmental relations. In T. Conlan, & P. Posner (Eds.), *Intergovernmental management for the 21st century* (pp. 77–101). Washington, DC: The Brookings Institution.

Wojtkiewicz, A., Misiurewicz, J., Nałecz, M., Jedrzejewski, K., & Kulpa, K. (1997). Two-dimensional signal processing in FMCW radars. In *Proceedings of XX KKTOiUE* (pp. 475–480). KKTOiUE.

Wollendeck, J. M., Gray, B., & Bryan, T. (2003). Us versus them: How identities and characterizations influence conflict. *Environmental Practice, 5*(3), 207–213.

Yang, J., Adamic, L., & Ackerman, M. (2008). Crowdsourcing and knowledge sharing: Strategic user behavior on taskcn. In *Proceedings of the 9th ACM Conference on Electronic Commerce*. ACM.

Yin, R. (2000). *Case study research: Design and methods*. Thousand Oaks, CA: Sage Publications.

Zeidler, D. L. (2002). Dancing with maggots and saints: Visions for subject matter knowledge, pedagogical knowledge, and pedagogical content knowledge in science teacher education reform. *Journal of Science Teacher Education, 13*, 27–42. doi:10.1023/A:1015129825891

Zheng, L., & Tse, D. N. C. (2003). Diversity and multiplexing: A fundamental tradeoff in multiple-antenna channels. *IEEE Transactions on Information Theory, 49*(5), 1073–1096. doi:10.1109/TIT.2003.810646

Zimmerman, T. G. (1999). Wireless networked digital devices: A new paradigm for computing and communication. *IBM Systems Journal, 38*(4), 566–574. doi:10.1147/sj.384.0566

Zucker, M., Sedunov, A., Zhdanov, V., & Sutin, A. (2009). Passive acoustic classification of vessels in the Hudson River. *The Journal of the Acoustical Society of America.* doi:10.1121/1.3249261

About the Contributors

Cecelia Wright Brown is an Assistant Professor in the School of Science, Information Arts and Technology at the University of Baltimore. Dr. Wright Brown has over twenty-five years of experience in engineering and education. She has facilitated workshops on the use of instructional technology for teachers in public schools systems, applied mathematical applications in homeland security critical infrastructure, facilitated panels of technical professionals on homeland security/terrorism, and has presented before government officials on the topic "Enterprise Resource Planning & Development Role in Decentralization and Civil Reform Programs" in Expo, 2006, Port au Prince, Haiti. In addition, she has mentored, conducted STEM workshops for students in grades 6-12, implemented training sessions for teachers, created University-Business partnerships, and coordinated University programs in Homeland Security and STEM.

Kevin A. Peters is a career STEM educator and researcher with over thirty years of experience in teaching, educational research, and developing and facilitating programs for STEM faculty, teachers, and students. His work has included programs that operate at the K-12, community college, and university levels. Dr. Peters earned the Ph.D. in Higher Education from Morgan State University in 2007. The topic of his dissertation research was "The Academic Success of Students at an HBCU in Maryland," He earned the B.S. and M.S. degrees in Science Education from Morgan State University in 1978 and 1985, respectively. He is currently the Director of the Center for Excellence in Mathematics and Science Education (CEMSE). His expertise includes developing partnerships with schools and school systems, grant writing, teaching in the physical and natural sciences, and public speaking related to the retention and persistence of African American students.

Kofi Nyarko is an Associate Professor in the Department of Electrical and Computer Engineering at Morgan State University (MSU). He also serves as Director of the Engineering Visualization Research Laboratory (EVRL). He has conducted research for MSU since 2005, consecutively under the titles of Research Engineer,

Director, and finally Associate Professor. As a Research Engineer, Dr. Nyarko worked under the Chesapeake Information Based Aeronautics consortium (CIBAC) with engineers at NASA Langley on various projects involving aviation safety. Under his direction, the Engineering Visualization Research Laboratory has acquired and conducted research, in excess of $10M, funded from the Department of Defense, Department of Energy, Army Research Laboratory, NASA, and Department of Homeland Security, along with other funding from Purdue University's Visual Analytics for Command, Control, and Interoperability Environments (VACCINE), a DHS Center of Excellence.

* * *

Terri Adams, Ph.D., is an Associate Professor of Criminology in Howard University's Department of Sociology and Anthropology. Dr. Adams's research takes a multidisciplinary approach to examining issues that have both theoretical and practical implications. Her specific research interests include emergency management, policing, violence against women, and the impact of trauma and disasters on individuals and organizations. Her most recent work centers on the decision-making processes of both individuals and organizations in the face of crisis events. She is currently the principle investigator for the "Examination of Resilience and Role Conflict Among First Responders" project supported by the National Center for the Study of Preparedness and Catastrophic Event Response. She also serves as the lead investigator for the Social, Behavioral, and Economic component of the NOAA Center for Atmospheric Sciences at Howard University. In addition to her academic work, Dr. Adams has served as a research consultant for a number of agencies and non-profit organizations, including the Williams Institute, the Metropolitan Police Department of Washington DC, the Johns Hopkins Public Safety Leadership Program, the National Organization of Black Law Enforcement Executives, the Prince George's Center for Youth and Family Research, and the Urban Institute.

Timothy A. Akers is the Assistant Vice President for Research Innovation and Advocacy, in the Division of Research and Economic Development, Professor of Public Health, and Director of the Center for Health Informatics, Planning and Policy (CHIPP), Morgan State University. Dr. Akers is also serving as the Principal Investigator to the U.S. Department of Homeland Security (DHS) Visual Analytics for Science and Technology at a Minority Serving Institution (VAST-MSI). Additionally, Dr. Akers has also held other positions as Senior Behavioral Scientist with the U.S. Centers for Disease Control and Prevention (CDC) and as a Senior Research Scientist at Michigan State University's College of Human Medicine. Professionally, he has worked in law enforcement and as a former U.S. Air Force

Security Police, specializing in nuclear weapons security and counter-terrorism. He has degrees in criminology, criminalistics, criminal justice, urban studies, and environmental science.

Leigh R. Anderson, Ph.D., was born and raised in St. Louis, Missouri. She has a Masters of Public Administration-Inspector General Degree from John Jay College of Criminal Justice and two B.A.s in Administration of Justice and Spanish from Howard University. Dr. Anderson received her Doctorate in Public Policy and Management from the John School of Public Affairs at The Ohio State University. She is a Department of Homeland Security (DHS) Science and Technology fellow as well as a graduate affiliate of the Criminal Justice Research Center. Dr. Anderson also works as a research analyst with the DHS Research Team Program for Minority-Serving Institutions in conjunction with Howard University and the National Center for the Study of Preparedness and Catastrophic Event Response (PACER) at Johns Hopkins University. Dr. Anderson's current research is twofold and surrounds intergovernmental relations with a particular focus on the interactions between the Tribal and U.S. systems of governance as well as assessing the policy and practice implications of first responders that are personally impacted while responding to a crisis. She presently works with the Washington D.C. Homeland Security and Emergency Management Agency.

Beth Austin-DeFares is the Director of Education for the Center for Secure and Resilient Maritime Commerce (CSR), a DHS Center of Excellence in Maritime and Port Security, led by Stevens Institute of Technology. Ms. DeFares is responsible for the coordination and delivery of the CSR's Summer Research Institute and is the primary coordinator for the university's DHS-funded Maritime Systems Fellowship program. Ms. DeFares has more than 18 years of experience in academic administration, student recruitment, advisement, and outreach. Prior to her position with CSR, she served as the Director of Communications and Outreach for Stevens's School of Systems and Enterprises. Ms. DeFares holds a master's degree in Urban Policy Analysis and Management from the New School for Social Research and a bachelor's degree in Sociology from Western New England University.

Janet E. Barber is a social science educator, writer, researcher, leadership institute member, and educational consultant with over 25 years of teaching and administrative experience in higher education. Her most recent research studies the connection between well-being and coping strategies of college students through a positive psychological theoretical frame. Dr. Barber has worked as lead behavioral modification teacher, and her present research studies and writing are in behavioral and coping strategies in the face of stressful situations and post-traumatic stress. Her past research is on the historical and contemporary literature and study of dissociative identity disorder (multiple personalities). Dr. Barber holds a doctorate degree in higher education leadership from Morgan State University, an M.A. in sociology from the University of Wisconsin, and a B.A. degree in psychology with graduate work in community and counseling psychology from North Carolina Central and Duke Universities. She has a career background in federal government administration and is a former campus dean. Dr. Barber teaches sociology, psychology, and educational leadership at the college and university level: Prince George's Community College (Maryland) and Central Michigan University.

Daryl G. Beetner is a Professor of Electrical and Computer Engineering at the Missouri University of Science and Technology, Rolla. He received his B.S. degree in Electrical Engineering from Southern Illinois University at Edwardsville in 1990. He received an M.S. and D.Sc. degree in Electrical Engineering from Washington University in St Louis in 1994 and 1997, respectively. He also conducts research with the Electromagnetic Compatibility (EMC) Laboratory at Missouri S&T on a wide variety of topics, including EMC at the chip and system level and detection and neutralization of explosive devices.

Michael S. Bruno is Dean of the School of Engineering and Science, and Professor of Ocean Engineering at Stevens Institute of Technology. He is the Principal Investigator and founder of CSR. His research and teaching interests include ocean observation systems, maritime security, and coastal ocean dynamics. He is the author of more than 100 publications. Bruno is a Member of the Ocean Research Advisory Panel, Member of the Naval Research Advisory Committee, and serves as the Editor-in-Chief of the Journal of Marine Environmental Engineering. From 2006 to 2012, he was a Member of the National Academy's Marine Board, the last two years as Chair. Bruno holds a B.S. degree in Civil Engineering from the New Jersey Institute of Technology, an M.S. degree in Civil Engineering from the University of California at Berkeley, and a PhD degree in Civil and Ocean Engineering from the Massachusetts Institute of Technology and the Woods Hole Oceanographic Institution.

Barry Bunin is the Chief Architect for the Stevens Maritime Security Laboratory (MSL), and a Research Professor in the Civil, Environmental, and Ocean Engineering Department, specializing in Maritime Security. As MSL architect, he has directed maritime security experiments in multimodal intruder detection involving acoustics, infrared, visible light video, and environmental sensing technologies. He is Co-Director of the Maritime Systems graduate program and is the Faculty Advisor for the Stevens Department of Homeland Security (DHS) Fellowship Program and the

Maritime Security Certificate Program. Prior to this, he has held senior executive positions in Research and Development at Bell Laboratories and in International Operations for AT&T.

Matt Campo is a Senior Research Associate for the Environmental Analysis and Communication Group at the Edward J. Bloustein School of Planning and Public Policy at Rutgers University. He earned a Masters in City and Regional Planning from Rutgers University after spending several years in corporate consulting. His fields of expertise include freight transportation and infrastructure planning, land use planning, and transportation security.

Steven L. Grant received his B.S.E.E from Missouri S&T in 1979, M.S.E.E from the California Institute of Technology in 1981, and Ph.D. from Rutgers in 1994. In 1980, he joined Bell Labs, worked at International Telephone and Telegraph Corporation–Defense Communications Division from 1982–1984, and then returned to Bell Labs where, in 2001, he became manager of the Acoustics Research group. From 2002 to 2004, he worked at Massachusetts Institute of Technology Lincoln Laboratory. He is now the Wilkens Missouri Telecommunications Professor at Missouri S&T. Dr. Grant has twice served as chair of the International Workshop on Acoustic Echo and Noise Control, has edited and/or authored three books, and has served as an associate editor of IEEE Signal Processing Letters and Transactions on Signal Processing.

Michael Greenberg, Ph.D., studies environmental health and risk analysis. He is distinguished professor and associate dean of the faculty of the Edward J. Bloustein School of Planning and Public Policy, Rutgers University. He has written 30 books and more than 300 articles. Currently, Professor Greenberg is writing *Protecting Seniors Against Environmental Disasters: From Hazards and Vulnerability to Prevention and Resilience*. He has been a member of National Research Council Committees that focus on the destruction of the U.S. chemical weapons stockpile and nuclear weapons, chemical waste management, and the degradation of the U.S. government physical infrastructure. Dr. Greenberg served as area editor for social sciences and then editor-in-chief of *Risk Analysis: An International Journal* during the period 2002–2103, and continues as associate editor for environmental health for the *American Journal of Public Health.*

Douglas F. Gwynn is the Director of The Office of Residence Life & Housing at Morgan State University. Mr. Gwynn has nearly 20 years of experience in Student Affairs Administration. Additionally, he has 10 years of professional experience in corporate management, training, and development. Mr. Gwynn earned his B.A. of

318

Letters, Arts, and Sciences with a minor in Diversified Resource Management from The Pennsylvania State University; he also holds a Master of Arts in Urban Student Affairs Administration from Morgan State University. Currently, Mr. Gwynn is a doctoral student in Higher Education at Morgan State University. Mr. Gwynn's research is focused in student engagement, student academic support, and merging technology with student academic advancement. As the Director for the Office of Residence Life & Housing, he has responsibility for an auxiliary enterprise consisting of six operational areas inclusive of Student Life, Assignments, Conferences & Marketing, Housekeeping, Maintenance, Facilities, and the Academic Enrichment program.

Willie David Larkin is Chief of Staff in the Office of the President at Morgan State University, Baltimore, Maryland. He brings more than 39 years of senior level experience in higher education administration to his leadership portfolio. Dr. Larkin is a trained scholar, educator, and higher education executive having received his Bachelor of Science in Agricultural Education and Master of Education degrees in 1973 and 1974, respectively, from Tuskegee University. He earned his Ph.D. in Agricultural Education-Extension with a specialization in Four-H and Youth Development from The Ohio State University in 1980 at the age of 29. Dr. Larkin devotes much of his professional energies toward senior leadership and organizational effectiveness research, speaking, mentorship, training, and educational and administrative consulting. Scholastically and scientifically, Dr. Larkin is the author of numerous scholarly publications comprising journal articles, manuals, handbooks, reports, and audio training tapes.

Karen Lowrie, Ph.D., is Associate Director of the Environmental Analysis and Communication Group at the Edward J. Bloustein School of Planning and Public Policy at Rutgers University. She earned a doctorate in urban planning from Rutgers University and a Masters in Public Administration from Syracuse University. Her fields of expertise include land use planning, urban redevelopment, environmental health, risk communication, and transportation security. She has led numerous projects and authored peer-reviewed articles and book chapters on these topics over the past two decades.

Henry Mayer, Ph.D., is Executive Director of the Environmental Analysis & Communications Group (EAC) and the Center for Transportation Safety, Security, and Risk (CTSSR) at the E.J. Bloustein School of Planning & Public Policy, Rutgers University, and Director of the PORTS Program, a joint initiative of the Center for Advanced Infrastructure and Transportation (CAIT) at the School of Engineering and the Bloustein School. He has extensive experience in the corporate, academic,

319

and government arenas, with a focus over the past fifteen years on the large and complex environmental, infrastructure, and land use issues associated with the redevelopment of many of the country's older cities and towns.

Asamoah Nkwanta is the interim chairman of the Department of Mathematics at Morgan State University in Baltimore, Maryland. He received his Ph.D. in mathematics from Howard University and has many years of teaching experience. In addition to his academic experience, he also has over eight years of industry experience as a member of the technical staff at the Jet Propulsion Laboratory and Logicon Incorporated. His professional mathematical interest is algebraic and enumerative combinatorics. In particular, he is interested in relations among topics from combinatorics, linear and abstract algebra, classical number theory, discrete mathematical biology, and special functions. He has numerous publications in the areas of enumerative combinatorics and discrete mathematical biology. Other topics of interest are experimental mathematics, fuzzy partially ordered sets, random matrix theory, applied topology, the history of mathematics, and mathematics education. Dr. Nkwanta has worked and provided leadership on many higher education and K-12 initiatives and partnerships.

Julie Pullen is the Director of CSR. She is a Research Associate Professor in ocean engineering at Stevens Institute of Technology and also an adjunct research scientist and past Marie Tharp visiting fellow at Columbia University's Earth Institute. She was previously a science fellow at Stanford's Center for International Security and Cooperation and a research scientist at the Naval Research Laboratory. In Dr. Pullen's research projects, she employs ultra high-resolution coupled ocean-atmosphere models in order to understand and forecast the dynamics of coastal urban regions throughout the world, with a particular emphasis on predicting chemical, biological, and radiological (CBR) dispersion in coastal cities in the event of a terrorist or accidental release. Her Ph.D. is in physical oceanography, with a postdoctoral appointment in meteorology. She also holds a master's degree in applied mathematics and was the first undergraduate intern at the Santa Fe Institute.

Sarah A. Seguin received the Ph.D. degree in electrical engineering from the Missouri University of Science and Technology, Rolla, in 2009. She is currently an Assistant Professor with the Department of Electrical Engineering and Computer Science, The University of Kansas, Lawrence. Her main research activities, carried out at the Radar and Remote Sensing Laboratory, focus on electromagnetic compatibility, electromagnetic interference, spectrum engineering, and antenna design.

Kendal Smith is the Education Program Manager at the Center for Infrastructure Protection and Homeland Security (CIP/HS) at George Mason University, where she leads the Infrastructure Protection Higher Education Initiative and is the editor of *The CIP Report*. She received her J.D. with a concentration in Homeland and National Security Law from the George Mason University School of Law and is a member of the Virginia Bar. She also holds a graduate degree from Baylor University and a B.A. in Philosophy from the University of North Texas.

Colin B. Stagner is a radar systems engineer for a federal contractor in Huntsville, Alabama. He received a B.S. degree in computer science from the Missouri University of Science and Technology in 2008 and a Ph.D. in electrical engineering in 2013 from the same. He specializes in software-defined radio systems, communications, and radar signal processing, and has developed new methods for detecting electronic devices using their electromagnetic emissions.

Nira C. Taru is currently an Associate Professor in the Department of Teacher Education at Morgan State University. She has been employed at Maryland State Department of Education (MSDE) as the Race to the Top Elementary STEM Specialist. She holds a Philosophy Degree from Syracuse University in the area of Teaching and Curriculum. Dr. Taru has established a wealth of knowledge as a curriculum specialist in the area of elementary education. Dr. Taru was also employed by Syracuse University as the Site Director for "Say Yes to Education" and has several years of teaching and research experiences from various colleges and universities. She has served as an elementary curriculum director; school administrator at the Central New York Charter School for Math and Science in Syracuse, NY; faculty member at Virginia State University, Virginia Commonwealth University, and Syracuse University; and has over thirty years of working experience in urban and suburban school districts.

Index